Comparative Media History

In memory of Liz Farkas and Valerie-Lee Chapman

Comparative Media History

An Introduction: 1789 to the Present

JANE CHAPMAN

polity

First published in 2005 by Polity Press
Reprinted 2006, 2008 (twice), 2010

Polity Press
65 Bridge Street
Cambridge CB2 1UR, UK

Polity Press
350 Main Street
Malden, MA 02148, USA

ISBN 10: 0-7456-3242-4
ISBN 10: 0-7456-3243-2 (pb)
ISBN 13: 978-0-7456-3242-1
ISBN 13: 978- 0-7456-3243-8 (pb)

A catalogue record for this book is available from the British
Library and has been applied for from the Library of
Congress.

Typeset in 9.5 on 12pt Utopia
by Servis Filmsetting Ltd, Longsight, Manchester
Printed and bound in Great Britain by the MPG Books Group

For further information on Polity, visit our website:
www.politybooks.com

Contents

Detailed Contents

List of Illustrations

Acknowledgements

The idea for this book grew organically out of the undergraduate curriculum for journalism theory at the London College of Communication (previously the London College of Printing) that I devised and taught, so I have the students to thank for their positive reactions and intellectual curiosity, as well as the research office led by Janice Hart and Angus Carlyle for their financial support. My PhD students Dessy Pontikos and Kate Allison contributed research and many other colleagues in the School of Media kindly contributed information, gave opinions and booklists and read sections, including Tony Delano, Alan Sekers, Sue Dawson, Martina McLaughlin, Helen Phillips, John Gibbs, Jason Copley, Photini Papatheodorou, Julian Rodriguez and Paul Charman, in addition to visiting tutors Carol Tongue and Gavin Weightman. In the United States, Carol Kasworm and the Department of Adult and Community College Education at North Carolina State University extended hospitality to me as a Visiting Scholar via our mutual friend Valerie-Lee Chapman, who tragically lost her battle against cancer while I was writing this book. In the NCSU department, Pooneh Lari and Kathy Miller worked hard with research. Meanwhile in California, just a few months earlier my aunt Liz Farkas, who had donated the essential tool of a laptop for this book, also passed away. Other friends on the West Coast, such as Mary Wilk and John Montgomery, gave their help during this difficult time. At Polity Press, I am grateful for the vision that John B. Thompson showed from the early days, to Andrea Drugan for constant clear thinking, enthusiasm and efficiency, and to Caroline Richmond, Jane Taylor, Neil de Cort and the rest of the team for dedication. Thanks to the staff of the British Library of Political and Economic Science (LSE) and the library at LCC. Finally, I am grateful to Martin Clarke and to my sons Miles and Toby for continuing to be supportive, and to Peter Sanderson for sharing ideas.

I am grateful to the following for permission to reproduce photographs: akg-images Ltd, fig. 2 (Musée Royaux des Beaux-Arts, Brussels); Corbis, figs 9 (Hulton) and 12 (Bettman Archive); Getty Images, figs 1 (National Museum of American History), 10 (photo Reg Speller), 11 (photo Cunningham), 14 (photo Susana Gonzalez) and 15 (photo Alberto Pizzoli); The Kobal Collection, fig. 8; *The Lady*, fig. 4; Marconi Corporation plc, fig. 7; Mary Evans Picture Library, figs 5 and 6; Punch Cartoon Library, fig. 3; Ronald Grant Archive, fig. 13.

Long live books!

Introduction

The media make the world even as the world makes the media.

Aims

This book aims to give a greater insight into the modern history of the media by considering influences on developments within a framework that uses a comparative approach to weigh up continuity versus change. This is a study of a selected number of countries and media industries, not cultural or social theory applied to history. As such, the aim is to encourage a broader understanding of cause and effect using the comparative method.

Rather than providing a continuous narrative of media development in each country and industry, the study looks at the basic concepts behind the origins of various trends that reveal aspects both of previous developments and of new ones that start to emerge. To this extent it is influenced by the history of political thought, political economy, and economic and social history, as well as communication studies and some media theory. While it is difficult to do justice to all of these disciplines, the reader can borrow from them in order to gain greater insights into the thinking behind major developments, an appreciation of the issues of the past, and the extent to which they remain with us today.

What is the comparative approach?

If the voyage of discovery involves travel through the environments of continuity and change, this begs the question 'which environments?' Other industries, or economy, politics, technology, society and culture? Other countries, or other periods of history? Modern communications are dependent on all of these. To weigh up the relative importance of each element, we need to make comparisons. Only then can the past as it relates to individual industries and countries be seen in perspective. Therefore the comparative approach is an essential first step to a better understanding of industry and national media histories.

The comparative nature of this enquiry is what makes this study unique: comparisons between countries, between industries and between periods of time, the past and the present. With over two hundred years, five countries – Britain, France, the United States, Japan and Germany – and seven media industries – newspapers, radio, music, film, television, advertising and the Internet – there is scope for some creativity of approach. Some controversial individuals emerge, as well as movements: people such as E. W. Scripps, Julius Reuter, Émile de Girardin, W. T. Stead and John Stuart Mill, for instance. Not all media historians will agree with the choice of people as influences. Others may see different points of comparison.

Of course, it is possible to carry comparisons too far, and in the process either to become obsessed with them or to be overselective: both pitfalls should be avoided. The risk arises also that comparative statements can become too simplistic, tenuous or generalized – that is, open to intellectual challenge as being inaccurate or misguided. Therefore the comparative approach is not without its difficulties and should be taken with enthusiastic caution. Yet we should not be deterred by these caveats: after all, the course of history never did run smoothly. There are continuities and discontinuities, and these are flagged in each chapter. Despite postmodernist thinking, this book deals with the notion that the present has developed from the past, but without any inevitability. As one historian puts it: 'we do not think of history as some blithe spirit and easy glide towards the future. We acknowledge that disruptions – even revolutions – happen, and that in culture, almost nothing gets transmitted unproblematically. But we believe transmission happens anyway' (de la Motte and Przyblyski 1999: 352–3).

How to use this book

As the scope covered by the book is wide, it is likely that readers will dip in and out, according to specific aspects of enquiry. For this reason, the chapter breakdowns and index are crucial. In addition, each chapter has an introduction and a summary, together with a conclusion. The division of chapters is chronological and also thematic. The thematic summary page at the beginning provides an 'at a glance' comparison by decade, as featured in the main text. Boxes are used for case studies and national examples, and in some places two-column presentations are used for dual comparisons.

Further research

Parallels and differences between different countries with media as the focus lead on to a logical next step that involves uncovering the varying political, cultural and economic structures of those countries. This book is a starting point for such investigations, but further study could take a number of different routes, via social and cultural theory, different countries during different epochs, or in greater depth on aspects dealt with in this study. For the last, the bibliography listing the more detailed monographs, scholarly articles and primary sources used to compile this book can be used for further research.

In creative projects, boundaries and word limits have to be constructed and adhered to! As the needs of the present and perceptions of the future continue to influence our approach to the past, definitions will always be questioned. For instance, the course of modernization in the Middle East and the role of the media in this controversial process form a fascinating area of scholarship which is not within the scope of this study (Thompson 1995: 188–92; Lerner 1958; Schramm 1964; Sreberny-Mohammadi and Mohammadi 1994). In some cases there are brief references in the following pages that merit an entire study: the fact that India now leads the world in total film production means that its roots constitute a subject worth following up, for instance (Armes 1987; Ramachandran 1985; Hill and Gibson 2000). Therefore, armed with the concepts, arguments and methodology of this book, the reader has a springboard. This is precisely the purpose of the 'study questions' based on individual, and sometimes across, chapters: they can prompt further research and discussion.

Similarly, the reader should be aware of the limitations of historical periodization that occur in most research. For example, what John Thompson has called the 'mediazation of culture' – the development of media organizations as a result of cultural transformation – can be dated to the fifteenth century (1995: 46). Here we are dealing only with how the modern media began to emerge during a period when the industrial and political revolutions fused into what we now regard as the modern world. This formidable dialectical process revealed that the relationships between technology, culture, industry, business and the state are fluid and constantly changing, while always retaining contradictions and dilemmas.

Arguments

The main argument in this book involves the importance of continuity in international media history. This breaks down into three main aspects.

The importance of the nineteenth century

The implication of the fact that this is a thematic comparative study examining the ideas that underpin media development is that this book emphasizes the importance of the nineteenth century for the roots of the media and for their continuation into the twentieth century and beyond. Arguably all the characteristics of the present-day media – including American hegemony in certain areas – had already begun to emerge by the end of the First World War, although extensive cross-media ownership and convergence became more obvious from the 1920s. Technology became more comprehensive and all-pervasive as new platforms were launched, but the issues that media personnel and people dealing with them had to face remained the same.

Contemporary nineteenth-century literature demonstrated that the different parts of the world were being drawn together by early modern technologies, so that the globe was increasingly becoming a smaller place. By the advent of the twentieth century, railways, telegraphs, rotary presses, telephones, typewriters and linotype machines had all combined to influence both the extent and the speed at which information was transmitted globally, as well as the nature and presentation of content involved.

Theories and themes have early roots

It would be too simplistic to argue that the path to present-day media globalization was set in the nineteenth century, yet the foundations do appear there – for example, film emerging from the roots of nineteenth-century visual culture. The beginnings of radio and of media industry internationalism both date from before 1914. For instance, the seeds of public-service broadcasting were sown in Britain in 1904, when the Post Office first took responsibility for early wireless communications – seen as an extension of the telegraph system. Radio's 'golden age' and the growth of television were still a long way away. Simultaneously, in 1912 the United States was experiencing a 'free for all'. Attempted transmissions after the *Titanic* disaster had demonstrated the significance of wireless; hence national values were quick to show their influence, and differing patterns of development in Britain and the United States were apparent at an early stage.

The process by which globalization emerged is more debatable because of its complexity. Certainly, the nineteenth-century origins of internationalism prepared the foundations for modern globalization. There were three aspects to this process. Firstly, some media industries started off as international – for example, radio, film and music. Secondly, some grew regionally and nationally and became international only via the development of modern business practices, aided by new technology – for instance, newspapers. Thirdly, within some industries, international thinking started very early: for example, Julius Reuter used pigeons to carry business 'intelligence' across national boundaries before the telegraph emerged. Monsieur Havas began by translating documents from other countries for the French government. When technology intervened, the commodification of news via worldwide communication networks became possible, although to many this form of commercialism appeared undesirable.

Such developments are often labelled as part of the process of 'modernity'. There is disagreement among historians as to whether or not the process of globalization began before modernity, therefore meaning that modernity merely changed the nature of globalization, or whether globalization was a consequence of modernity. There are many pre-modernity examples, such as imperialism and pre-capitalist trade networks, but this study makes a distinction between three different stages of development: origins, take-off and acceleration of intensity. The dialectics of the picture are not simple, which is why continuities and discontinuities, diversities and complexities, are emphasized throughout.

Continuity of issues

One way of looking at history is to examine continuity and change and the way in which they interact. Very often change ends up being analysed more thoroughly, because it is attention-grabbing and more dramatic. In contrast, the existence of continuity may be assumed, but can be left unmentioned. This book emphasizes continuity, arguing that there are certain ongoing strands, although the level of their significance varies according to circumstances and period.

Continuity does not mean a continuous narrative revealing constant improvement until the present, which then becomes a 'Panglossian' (as in Voltaire's *Candide*), best-possible state of progress in media evolution. Equally it does not entail a simple narrative of gradual American hegemony (Starr 2004). Roots come from elsewhere, and this study finds influences not just in Europe's heritage, but also in that of Japan.

The decisive factors for the evolution of media developments in different countries and in the different industries have remained constant until recently: they are the social use of technology, the character of the institutions in which technology is applied and the political organization of the specific countries involved. But, in the future, concentration

An example of continuity: ongoing struggles for freedom of expression

One writer has characterized press freedom in Western capitalist societies as following four main stages (Williams 1969: 6–9). First early political society is characterized by censorship and licensing, but, as the public appetite for news increases, so does the demand for free expression of opinion. This is illustrated by the experiences of eighteenth-century France and Britain, where censorship was defied and newspapers were started, suppressed and restarted as part of a 'guerrilla war' between the press and the authorities. As the ranks of the 'freedom fighters' increase, the second stage emerges. Now governments find themselves obliged to concede to demands for a free press, and so censorship and licence are abandoned in favour of more complex but less obtrusive controls on the nature of expression, exemplified by laws of libel, sedition and contempt. At the same time development is restricted by financial penalties such as newspaper taxes. These two stages characterize the experiences of France, Germany and Britain featured in chapter 1. America emerged from these first two stages at an earlier date than Europe, although the American Civil War provided a challenge to press freedom.

By stage three, newspapers have achieved an independent self-sufficiency via advertising and sales revenue, and often 'predominant individuals' emerge as strong journalistic personalities. However, the evolution of the franchise and political and constitutional issues (a protracted process in Europe and also not complete elsewhere until women finally received the vote, mostly in the twentieth century) led to a fluidity between stages two and three. Stage four represents the age of the press as business, a twentieth-century phenomenon of monopoly which continues through to the present.

of media ownership (originally a form of cultural imperialism) and homogeneity of communication products, empowered by neo-liberal deregulation, are likely to prove more powerful forces. However, predictions are not the order of the day for historians. The reader must look elsewhere for the crystal ball approach. The bibliography contains specialist studies that analyse the present and its more immediate background.

It is possible to argue that the rise and fall of communications empires from a political and a business perspective was, and still is, a transcontinental capitalistic phenomenon (Picard 1996). Yet this does not reduce our need to appreciate national context, if only to understand power and difference. For example, common technologies have been adopted in different countries in differing ways, necessitating an understanding of some background history of individual countries. Furthermore, the speed and range of technological developments are influenced by social, economic, political and cultural factors.

The approach of this study can be appreciated more fully in the context of the editorial choices which are necessitated by such a broad canvas.

Choice of starting point

The French Revolution which erupted in 1789 was a turning point in history. The idea that people can overthrow government set a precedent within history for change. The way that France achieved the change from 'old' to 'new' has defined our understanding of 'revolution' ever since. It has also influenced our modern perceptions of the democratic process, human rights and political discourse. Four modern movements that came to dominate the thinking behind public affairs – nationalism, liberalism, democracy and socialism – received inspiration from 1789, so this date gives us access to the all-important nineteenth century and to the pivotal influence of European heritage on media development. In comparison, chapter 1 discusses the influence of the American Revolution (or American War of Independence, as the British call it).

Choice of countries

Media history in the West is often dominated by the volume of Anglo-American scholarship, but comparisons need to go beyond Britain and the USA for the arguments above to be properly explored. In the context of the Enlightenment, the world of ideas, both political and cultural, was heavily influenced by the French and their language. Yet France now has a lower profile. Economically, the British empire dominated the world. Britain's lead in world trade was later overtaken by the United States, Germany and Japan. Therefore it is not possible to give equal weight throughout to each country. Individually they feature only when they are influential for origins, cause and effect, comparison, continuity and change. There is never all of one country all of the time: for that, the reader must refer to a national history.

Nevertheless, there is very little point in disputing who did what, particularly if we simply descend into national chauvinism – a frequent tactic of popular newspapers in the nineteenth and early twentieth centuries. But the selection here of Germany and Japan does merit some explanation. The economic importance of these two countries today, with their important media multinational conglomerates, is one reason; the way that politics, ideology and media interacted in the twentieth century, both before and after the Second World War, is another. Japan's pioneering contribution to the institutionalization of the media has been grossly underrated; furthermore, the way in which the Japanese have reacted to 'detraditionalization' via media usage and the creative process brings an important non-Western dimension to what Giddens (1991) has called 'late modernity' and the process of 'reflexive modernization' (Beck 1992).

During the nineteenth century, issues of press freedom surfaced in different ways, as did examples of media business organization and its relationship with politics. Interesting examples of public-service broadcasting emerged in both countries during the post-war period, accompanied by a remarkably strong newspaper industry in Japan. One of the conclusions of this book is that pluralism remains an essential prerequisite in communications: the study of Germany and Japan helps us to reflect on diversity, form, method and choice.

Choice of industries

Print was the dominant form of media communication right through the nineteenth century, and newspapers were the principal medium for several hundred years. Before the arrival of radio there were not many ways in which people could acquire political information: they could attend rallies or political speeches, they could talk to friends, or they could read a newspaper – hence the importance of the press within the democratic process, which constitutes a main theme in chapters 1 and 2. In their role as the fourth estate, newspapers acted as a watchdog on government and formed a crucial element in the process of shaping public opinion. 'News' represented the reformulation of 'information' as a commodity gathered and distributed for the three purposes of political communication, trade and pleasure, and directed in its generic form by technology (for example, the telegraph), scientism (for example, the belief in the value of 'facts') and the development of mass media markets (Boyd-Barrett and Rantanen 1998: 1).

By the twentieth century, cinema was becoming a new form of entertainment that was to challenge print, just as radio presented a threat to written communication. From the press–radio wars of the twentieth century, it is clear that interaction between industries is important.

Newspapers faced another dilemma: coverage of 'new' media developments sold newspapers by giving a window to the phenomenon. Yet ultimately that very phenomenon challenged the strength of the print industry. The popularity of film offered similar contradictions. Both these examples also serve to justify the case for inter-industry comparisons. A better appreciation of the modern history of advertising, for instance, helps our understanding of the commercial development of newspapers.

Hitherto, the history of the music industry has been studied by and large without comparison – a reason in itself to break the mould. The way that structures have emerged presents important messages for the future. In this case, capitalism created sophisticated production and distribution machinery for the consumption of music, but the economic contradictions within that system meant that it did not reflect creative potential to the full. Yet the democratization of musical expression through technological breakthroughs continues to challenge traditional structures. The struggles of the past which are reflected in the pages that follow prompt us to wonder whether creativity will continue to challenge dominant trends. This book cannot provide all the answers, but it can provoke thought and further investigation.

PART I

ANTECEDENTS, CONTINUITIES AND DISCONTINUITIES

> Notre siècle vit encore sur la lancée du XIXème siècle.
> (Our century is still living on the nineteenth century's momentum.)
>
> Kristeva 1974: 618

1 Newspapers: Radicalism, Repression and Economic Change, 1789–1847

In a constitutional government, freedom of discussion and assembly is the people's most important right. Without freedom of expression there can be no constitutional government. Freedom of expression brings constitutional government to perfection . . . . We must demand this freedom. A study of the history of the world's presses reveals clearly that people do not win freedom overnight.   (Masaichi 1930: 1)

Summary

The *objective* of this chapter is to launch the main argument of this study – the importance of continuity within comparative media history – and to introduce three major themes within this heritage: the right to freedom of expression, the difficult relationship between media and politicians, and the impact of industrialization and technology.

The first two themes are illustrated mainly by the impact on newspaper development of the French Revolution. The third is exemplified by the social and political influence on media development of the world's first industrial revolution, pioneered in Great Britain.

As industrialization spread and progressed, newspapers also moved from a craft base towards integration within a new market economy. Indeed the demand for mass circulation has its roots in this period, when the mechanical and organizational basis was being laid for the popular newspaper that later emerged, exemplified by the approach of Girardin in France and the success of New York's penny press. Other experiments, such as Britain's radical press, which was inspired by the French Revolution, also catered for new readerships. Whereas journalism had first emerged in France as a profession during 1789, in Britain and America it was older, hence elements of continuity in these two countries were more prevalent in this case. By the nineteenth century the characteristic profile of journalists differed from country to country, but the same process of specialization was emerging at varying paces. In Japan the process of modernization which was to introduce newspapers had not yet begun.

Introduction

From the French revolutionary period onwards the potential of newspapers for the transmission of knowledge and ideas was explored with particular enthusiasm by readers and writers alike; for it was the relationship between the first media industry – printed publications – and politics that allowed newspapers to emerge as a force within modern society. The simultaneous revolution in communications from 1789 to 1792 provides a case study of how the press can influence public debate (Wilke 1989; Reynolds 1971). Unbridled freedom of expression in France during this period was short-lived but influential, exemplified by the fact that the first ever modern revolutionary papers inspired a political press elsewhere and set trends over the longer term in political communication and participation within the democratic process (Chapman 2005).

Although America had been the first country to establish legalized press freedom, by the mid-nineteenth century Japan and most of the continent of Europe were experiencing domestic censorship, and in Britain the main constraints were fiscal. At a time when the state acted as the enemy of free expression, people in the commercial world as well as political activists used the newspaper as a vehicle towards the achievement of greater liberty. Nineteenth-century press freedom has been referred to as the 'great question of the century' (de Rémusat 1958: 3.193); during this period the issue emerges and re-emerges in all its complexities with constant contemporary resonances. Of course, the whole concept was not new: struggles for freedom of expression have always appeared in history. The idea that newspapers can act as a force for change was highlighted during the English Civil War and the American War of Independence. But during the nineteenth century these struggles for the first time became intertwined with emerging modern democracy and the development of industrial capitalism. The convergence of these two seminal trends at this point in history serves to emphasize the importance of the period, but it also makes the comparative picture more complex.

In essence, newspaper reading was a form of participation in politics. Throughout the nineteenth century the role of the media in the process of democracy was being continually tried and tested. The extension of political power to a wider number of people required the means to give them knowledge of politics: in the nineteenth century, of necessity this entailed newspapers free from government control as public argument became an instrument of social transformation (Brown 1992: 191–202).

In countries where democracy was more established, the liberal ideal of a press as an independent institution could take hold more easily, as it did in America and later in Britain. But in other parts of Europe, for the moment, progress seemed to conform to the definition set by Lenin in the twentieth-century revolutionary context: 'one step forward, two steps back'. In Germany, for instance, press development was retarded because of its association with the forces of liberalism and incipient nationalism. Even in Britain, where many features of press development first appeared, and where constitutional and political fluctuations were less dramatic, the growth of newspapers was restrained by what would now be viewed as an attitudinal problem on the part of much of the established order. Contemporaries thought that the lower orders were not to be trusted and that newspapers should be kept from them, for the working class should remain in 'god fearing' ignorance in the interests of national stability and order (Wadsworth 1955). Equally, the Tokugawa government of this same period in Japan desired the people to 'be stupid, be stupid', believing that the ruling class should provide its subjects only with as much information as was necessary to maintain rule. For instance, laws were only displayed as bill posters and not published, in case this might assist potential offenders or stimulate debate or discussion (Huffman 1997: 13).

Nevertheless, some key words were beginning to emerge in early nineteenth-century conversation: 'conspicuous consumption', 'technology', and (first used by the French) the phrase 'industrial revolution' (Briggs and Burke 2002: 110). Their significance was already becoming apparent.

The influence of the American Revolution

There were two crucial aspects to media development that emerged out of the War of Independence from Britain: legalized press freedom and the growth in the political influence of publications. America was the first country in the world to take the step which is necessary for media growth of detaching its press from the official machinery of government. Before war broke out, radical propaganda was particularly influential in helping hitherto undecided readers to commit to revolution in the run up to the event, although historians are sceptical about the influence of the press during the revolution itself. By that time many minds had already been made up. Journalism was important not simply for the reporting of events in the change from colonial to republican rule, but also because it involved the people, speaking for and to them: 'Journalists as radical propagandists were able to articulate a particular moment in the aspirations of people to be involved in politics' (Conboy 2002: 37).

The First Amendment of the American constitution specifically identifies the press, freedom of speech and worship which cannot be legislated against: 'that Congress shall pass no act that will abridge the freedom of speech.' This established the idea of 'media immunities', that is, the concept of the media as a vehicle for public communication, making that industry different to any other and therefore worthy of singling out for special treatment in the eyes of the law. However, as the course of media history proves, press freedom is a relative concept. Other legislation can and does get passed which challenges the absolute principle in areas such as libel (to defame or accuse falsely and maliciously), official secrets, obscenity and economic competition.

Despite the fact that the Americans overturned colonial rule, the power of the propertied classes was not challenged as it was in France, where the

The influence of the democrat Thomas Paine

Of the contemporary writers who managed to strike a chord at precisely the right time, the radical journalist Thomas Paine was the most famous. Paine moved to America after meeting Benjamin Franklin in London in 1774, and fought against his native Britain in the war. These words of his that appeared in the *Pennsylvania Journal* on 19 December 1776

Fig. 1 Benjamin Franklin's printing press

could well have been written for France thirteen years later: 'Tyranny, like hell, is not easily conquered; yet we have this consolation with us, that the harder the conflict, the more glorious the triumph.' More importantly, his pamphlet *Common Sense* (1776) was an instant bestseller, prompting hesitant and moderate patriots to join the revolutionary side. The text did not project a charismatic leader but rather a 'republican charisma' and a new rhetoric which articulated the emerging egalitarian ethos (Hogan and Williams 2000). Every literate American household knew of Paine's doctrines, which were mirrored in the Declaration of Independence within a mere six months.

His next major work, *The Rights of Man*, sold 200,000 copies in three years and inspired working people more than any other radical publication up to the appearance of the *Communist Manifesto* in 1848. By 1809 *The Rights of Man* had sold one and a half million copies all over Europe; it had enjoyed huge sales in Ireland, despite a ban being immediately imposed in Britain. Paine made it known that he sought no profit at all from the work, so anyone who wanted to reproduce it could do so. It seemed as if every village in Britain had a copy, along with the Bible and John Bunyan's *The Pilgrim's Progress*. The importance of Paine's influence lies in the ideological basis that he provided for radical journalism during the nineteenth century.

change in political authority was both radical and fundamental. Issues of press freedom re-emerged in America later during debates on the abolition of slavery, when, for example, in 1829–31 two abolitionists were sued for criminal libel for condemning a shipowner and captain for transporting slaves (Reynolds 2001). Yet, although America had introduced the principle of a free press, it was Europe that grappled with the implications of the concept within developing democratic systems throughout the nineteenth century. One reason that this process was so tortuous was because political parties on both sides of the Atlantic were underdeveloped: they needed to become more focused in their power, philosophy and organization. Politicians were in the process of discovering the scope of the press as a vehicle for persuading their electors.

The impact of French revolutionary newspapers ▨▨▨▨▨

These days a revolution in communications would require a worldwide impact to warrant the term 'revolution', but the French went it alone. One historian has commented that 1789 and the years that followed cannot be understood without an examination of the role played by newspapers, for they had 'the vocation of measuring the new era and defining its rhythm' (Rétat 1985: 142). From the perspective of the nineteenth century, the impact was political rather than technical: the dramatic change that took place was in the power of the media to influence events as they were happening by being part of them, something that had not happened before in history to the same extent. This new role was a powerful but delicately balanced one, prompting a description of the press as not only the 'child' but also the 'father' of the revolution (Gilchrist and Murray 1971; Popkin 1990). This relationship between the press and political control is a crucial starting point for many ongoing themes: the interaction between politics and the media, the concept of the fourth estate, the influence of the media on democracy, and the impact of technology (or lack of it) on development.

The scale of newspaper influence mushroomed temporarily to such an extent, and was so widespread, that for the first time the press was taken seriously as a force within society. Here, in serious measure, was the beginning of the idea of the media as a fourth estate (that is, an additional centre of power together with the existing three: monarchy, church and aristocracy), although the phrase was not yet used by contemporaries.

The influence of press freedom on newspaper style and operations

Liberty of expression existed during these years in France, but thereafter it was gradually taken away. There are examples of press freedom being suddenly removed in America, with the Alien and Sedition Acts in 1798, and to a certain extent also in Britain during this period. The difference with France is that the political effects of the process of both implementation of press freedom and ensuring its demise were much more dramatic and protracted, lasting right through to 1881.

Before the revolution there had been only one official daily paper, the mainly cultural rather than political *Journal de Paris*, with the result that the printed word became a huge underground industry, largely produced abroad. Inside France, the king had presided over a harsh environment of censorship and restrictions whereby licences had been granted only to supporters and to preferred, tame publishers, who had been organized into guilds with special privileges. Outside of France, the king had secretly manipulated the foreign press and restricted their access. Despite this apparent control, research into the influence of the press has revealed that newspapers still assisted in the general loss of faith in the monarchy before 1789 (Censer 1994: 213–14).

Camille Desmoulins, the most eloquent of revolutionary journalists

Camille Desmoulins was one journalist who rose to fame in 1789. In the second edition of his newspaper *Révolutions de France et de Brabant*, he summed up the excitement of the moment: 'Here I am a journalist, and it is a rather fine role. No longer is it a wretched and mercenary profession, enslaved by the government. Today in France it is the journalist who holds the tablets, the album of the censor, and who inspects the senate, the consuls and the dictator himself.'

Although the storming of the Bastille on 14 July 1789 was not caused by political journalists, the latter were preparing for a new role before the event. When the first two revolutionary periodicals appeared in mid-1789, they unilaterally grasped press freedom. The new age of liberty was formally recognized on 24 August 1789 in the Declaration of the Rights of Man, when one of the revolution's politicians, Robespierre, ensured that written into this seminal document was the right of every individual to 'speak, write and print freely, on his own responsibility for the abuse of this liberty in cases determined by law'. What followed was a flood of publications: 184 new periodicals were launched in Paris in 1789 and 335 in 1790. In all, 2000 titles appeared between 1789 and 1799. This significant new opportunity permitted the journalist who was 'brought in from the cold' of the Ancien Régime to make an entry into political life in a big way, opening up careers both locally and nationally to men who might otherwise have remained relatively unknown (Gough 1998: 229–36). Thus journalism became one of several recruiting grounds for the new political elite.

The press gave legitimacy to the new law-making process by publicizing it for those who could not be there. 'Publicity is the people's safeguard', stated Bailly, mayor of Paris. Since the collapse of the old regime, secrecy was considered counter-revolutionary, so the French insisted that, to be legitimate, all politics had to be carried out in public. From 1789 through to 1799, when Napoleon made himself dictator, law-making was conducted in public assemblies open to the people. The aim of newspaper writers was to re-create the drama of debate in the assembly, as if the reader was there. The editor of the *Bulletin national* said in July 1789 that a reader would 'follow the progress of opinions, discuss them himself and believe himself to be actually participating.' Every editor wanted to influence both the assembly and the people, but their political opinions as stated in their journals differed. Hence press freedom in France became a double-edged sword as this educative role was overtaken by a less restrained war of ideas. Perhaps this was inevitable once the people were in charge.

In France, the thinking about where power lay was different to that in other countries. Even in America, the seminal writings that made up the *Federalist Papers* did not go as far in their concept of popular sovereignty as those of the editor Loustallot, when he wrote in the newspaper *Révolutions de Paris*: 'Our representatives are not, as in England, the sovereign of the nation. IT IS THE NATION THAT IS SOVEREIGN' (19–25 September 1789). For a country the size of France, with a population of 26 million, freedom of the press was essential to make this 'sovereignty of the nation' work. Thus newspapers helped to influence the events that they recorded – as they were happening. Detailed historical research, for instance, on the march of the market women from Paris to Versailles to fetch the royal family back to Paris, concludes that the press 'not only prepared the disturbances and made them possible, but also gave them their shape and purpose' (Rudé 1958: 22; Mathiez 1998: 41–3).

One of the remarkable features of the French Revolution was the speed of events and the scope of change that was necessary in order to demolish the old regime which had been burdened by the arbitrary baggage of history. For instance, the new legislators were faced with a haphazard administrative system with a profusion of boundaries for differing functions, such as weights and measures, customs areas and taxation zones. Support for a new system was not possible without the press. As a consequence culture and communication now became a central feature of public affairs, unifying the diverse parts of the country into a new political order. This involved a fresh revolutionary vocabulary: a Declaration of the Rights of Man and a constitution, new administrative systems, measures to reduce the power of the church, a different currency, map and calendar, new weights and measures, and even new forms of address.

The press freedom that existed between 1789 and 1792 was unrivalled in history. During this short period, editors had fewer constraints than exist today: no accountability to boards of directors, shareholders or advertisers and less organizational bureaucracy. They were freed up to concentrate on their literary efforts to influence events, making a genuine impression on all levels of society. Influence was not achieved by today's methods of mass circulation. In 1789 there was a high level of illiteracy everywhere by modern standards, and a circulation of 10,000 copies for a revolutionary paper was considered a success. To understand how publications made an impact by other means, it is necessary not only to examine the relationship between politics and the printed word, but also to note habits in newspaper usage and political discussion.

During this era of active street culture newspapers were often pasted up as bills in public places, then pasted over with rival newspapers. Ideas were disseminated via handbills and posters, via reading aloud and through fierce discussion in the streets, in clubs and in other public places. The coffee house had long been the common eighteenth-century venue in America and Europe for newspaper reading and political discussion. In France, as in Britain and Japan at a later date, reading rooms were also popular, and the bigger ones would subscribe to thirty-five or more different papers.[1] The Manchester Exchange had 1800 subscribers and took 130 newspapers a day, making multiple purchases of popular ones. In 1870s Japan, a newspaper would take about ten days to be passed around a village, and in Europe during this earlier period it was not uncommon for good journals to have a high second-hand value as they were passed around; a single edition of *The Times* of London, for instance, commanded an established used price of 5*d.* to 1*d.* as it aged. As one edition could reach as many as twenty different people, real readership figures were actually about five times that of the sales figure. Expensive original sales prices perpetuated this phenomenon: a year's subscription to a revolutionary journal cost the equivalent of several weeks' wages. The revolutionary period saw the introduction in France of street vendors at a time when the public were eager to keep up with fast-changing events, for fresh news was regularly needed. The phenomenon posed a noise and numbers problem for municipal authorities. It seems that passion for reading goes in waves: the craving for printed matter reached America between 1820 and 1830, but the country was still dependent on overseas publishers for books, with 70 per cent imported from Europe.

The journals of the revolutionary period are remembered for their diversity of writing and scope in the generation of ideas, not for their technological breakthroughs, which were virtually non-existent. One writer has commented that the inventory of equipment used and its nature were as suitable for the fifteenth century as for the early nineteenth (Lambrichs 1976: 12). Publishing was an uphill struggle. Most newspapers were first written by hand, often by candlelight. Under the old regime, guild restrictions had restricted night work, but the free-for-all of the revolution meant that night work became increasingly common. To produce 10,000 copies, a publisher would have to set the copy several times, often using five to ten presses and about sixty employees, consisting of compositors, pressmen, clerks and women to fold the papers, and an additional army of 200 or so street vendors would then disseminate them. As publishing took off, new entrepreneurs started up, and workers were able to move around for more money. Business boomed for anything printed: iconography or revolutionary visual emblems became an important form of communication because of the high levels of illiteracy. Revolutionary logos and motifs managed to find their way on to posters as well as pictures, song sheets, stationery, board games, playing cards, ration cards, money and almanacs.

Everywhere at this time journals remained traditional in production style, to the extent that these days they would be hardly recognizable as newspapers. At first they were small, and therefore did not require any new equipment. Their size made them easy to bind into collections for libraries, particularly because newspapers often started as pamphlets, prompted by one special event or one person's urge to communicate. For example, Louis Proudhomme's *Révolutions de Paris*, one of the most successful papers of the time, had been launched to describe the events surrounding the storming of the Bastille. What was later to become the prime production tool of the sub-editor – the technical ability to position items on the page with varying size and lay-out according to their relative importance – did not yet exist. In addition, there was no advertising in French newspapers. Content lacked consistency, with articles of great literary merit appearing next to very shoddily constructed columns, and both production style and frequency often changed during the short life of a newspaper.

None of these shortcomings, as we would view them from a present-day perspective, were unique to France. Newspapers in all countries sold at a high price, and frequently suffered from a short lifespan and a poor lay-out due to technical constraints. American newspapers carried advertising and adopted a more commercial perspective from the earlier time of the New England traders (Emery et al. 2000: 20), but *The Times* of London led the world in 'modern' business organization, journalistic quality and reach.

The reality of the fourth estate

If the organizational form of the media did not vary much between countries, the content certainly did. Once free, French newspapers vented grievances and expressed public emotions with a vehemence that was unparalleled hitherto within the history of printed political rhetoric. For the first time, and not the last, the press could make or break. Because the French recognized the importance of communication in the public sphere, they were the first to experience the implications of this dilemma.

Writings from this epoch allow us to enter the mind of revolutionary France, offering 'the background of fire and violence that gives meaning to the cold print of the government's impersonal decrees' (Gilchrist and Murray 1971: 1). During this period there was no distinction between 'comment' and the factual reporting of events, so the latter could easily become self-indulgent slander or support for a faction. Among the many volumes of printed word, a trend emerges. While the writings of the early years of the revolution reflected the reforming zeal that emphasized progress and the universal rights of man, gradually the lively contrast of opinions and didactic enthusiasm became ominously sullied by two closely entwined threats: the monarchy and the possibility of foreign invasion.

As Louis XVI and his queen, Marie Antoinette, secretly conspired to gain the support of Europe's monarchies against France, events evolved in a way that eliminated gradual change as an option. The dilemmas and very real dangers to the newly born and still unconsolidated French republic were the subject of enormous debate both within the assembly and in the press, articulated with remarkable foresight in many cases. Major decisions such as the execution of the king and the war undertaken as defence of the country against Prussian invasion were not taken impetuously, but only after extensive and painfully detailed debate in the assembly and in the pages of the press. The king's plotting and the flight of the royal family to Varennes represented far more than a desperate attempt to escape in order to raise support from Austria and other royal families.

Marat, the vitriolic bestseller

One of the most highly charged pens was that of Jean Paul Marat, in his newspaper *L'Ami du peuple*: on 22 June 1791 he predicted the future. His commentaries on the assembly were aimed at exposing certain deputies' treasonous intentions, and also at mobilizing citizens against them. To him, the issue for the revolution was now 'Dictatorship or Defeat': 'this perjurer of a king, without faith, without shame, without remorse, this monarch unworthy of a throne, has been restrained only by the fear of being shown up as an infamous beast. The thirst for absolute power that consumes his soul will soon turn him into a ferocious murderer; soon he will be swimming in the blood of his fellow citizens who will refuse to submit to his tyrannous yoke. Meanwhile he is laughing at the folly of the Parisians who stupidly took him at his word.'

Marat's newspaper was supposed to be a weekly, but when he felt inspired by anger at events or people he would rush out an edition that would be selling on the streets in a few hours. He took to the quill frantically, obsessively and continuously, sometimes only sleeping two hours a night. Ironically his popularity among the people increased as the danger to the republic worsened. Marat's calls for violence were uncompromising, yet his paper's circulation was sometimes up to 15,000. He was regularly threatened with arrest, often led a fugitive existence and at one time was forced into exile. The end that he met – murder in the bath (frequent bathing was necessary to ease his skin disease) – poignantly depicted by the painter David and now displayed in the Louvre and in Brussels, happened while he was preparing his newspaper.

Hébert, the 'Homer of Filth'

The first ever tabloid writer was Jacques René Hébert, with his satirical journal *Père Duchesne*. He was originally against the execution of the king, but eventually called for the 'monster's blood' in his publication, expressing frustration that it was such a long and complicated business to 'knock off a tyrant's head: yes, damn it! The traitor Louis, shut up like an owl in the Temple tower, would not be so complacent there, if he did not have a strong following in Paris. Already, damn it, they have tried more than one surprise attack to release him. . . . It must not happen that the greatest scoundrel that has ever been should remain unpunished. It is good that the sovereign people become used to judging kings' (Hatin 1866: 6.518).

History has judged Hébert's crude writing harshly, but his aim was to speak the language of the people and, in doing so, to articulate working-class anger and class consciousness for the first time ever. He believed that 'you must swear with those who swear . . . anyone who appreciates frankness and probity will not blush at the "*foutres*" and "*bougres*" that I insert here and there with my joys and my angers.' The style had instant appeal to 'sans-culottes' readers because it was well suited to reading aloud for those who were illiterate. The *Père Duchesne*, which took its name from a mythical foul-mouthed and familiar fairground character, spawned up to six rival imitations, all claiming to be the 'real' *Père Duchesne*, for there were no laws to protect copyright or intellectual property rights.[2] During the Terror it became fashionable to purchase the paper 'pour sans-culottiser' (to appear like the common people). It also helped to avoid one's name being on a list of suspects for imprisonment and the guillotine. Hébert himself was eventually guillotined: his paper ran to 368 issues.

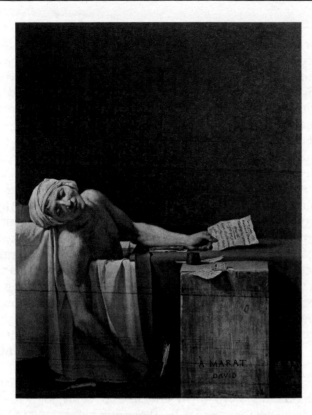

Fig. 2 *The Death of Marat*, by David; Marat's assassin was paid 25 sous (cents)

Meanwhile, French journalists such as Marat and Desmoulins had become famous through their newspapers; some were also leading politicians, such as Robespierre and Hébert.

The king was executed in January 1793. He had provided a focus for anti-Jacobin writing which was as didactic as any work produced by the republican side and even more destabilizing. Indeed the counter-revolutionary press had a number of the most talented journalists in addition to substantial financial backing and, in some cases, subsidy from the king's civil list (Murray 1986). Royalist papers such as *L'Ami du roi* portrayed the assembly as divided and disorderly, while the satirical *Actes des apôtres* thought it mad.

Unlike in America and Britain, constitutional initiatives in France had not created any formal space for dissent, although revolutionary leaders tried to make one. The knock-on effect for journalism was that, as power invested in the sovereignty of the people was largely ideological, the responsibility for its definition lay with writers. Thus, late in 1793, Desmoulins made a brave attempt to launch an eloquent new journal with the express purpose of questioning the direction of the revolution. When the *Vieux cordelier* argued for a general relaxation of the Terror, it created a sensation. The third edition provoked crowds to gather around the Convention demanding the release of suspects from prison. Then people queued to buy the fourth edition, and those who could not obtain a copy tried to outbid one another for second-hand copies. But the paper had provoked the wrath of the Jacobins. Despite Robespierre's defence of him, Desmoulins went to the guillotine at the age of twenty-eight. He was the only famous revolutionary writer to work exclusively as a journalist. Robespierre eventually followed him to the guillotine. A sixth of all those journalists writing during the Terror met a similar fate.

Unfortunately, unconstrained press freedom has never in history survived during wartime, and France in this instance was no exception to the rule. The revolutionary wars destroyed many of the earlier progressive measures passed by the assembly and imposed an unbearable pressure on the new republic. Across the political spectrum in France, nationalism induced by war tended to clash with the intrinsic universalism and egalitarianism of the revolution. The enormity of the problem helps to explain the decline of democracy: by the spring of 1793 France was faced with the combined forces of Austria, Prussia, Britain, Holland, Spain, Naples, Rome, Venice and Sardinia. The range of coverage ensured that there was no shortage of criticism from both the extreme right and the extreme left of legislative debates, highlighting the dichotomy of the press as expressed by François Furet: 'It strove for power, yet denounced the corruption power inevitably entailed' (1981: 49).

If the price of democracy is eternal vigilance, then the price of newspaper freedom was inevitably a critical and damaging press. The continual slander of the newspapers, the venting of grievances and the publicity in support of various factions all had the disconcerting effect of keeping France, and especially Paris, in a state of permanent unrest and incipient revolt (Popkin 1990).

Reaction and repression

For every action there is a reaction, and between 1789 and 1815 it was momentous. The impact on newspapers of the forces of conservatism also needs to be considered, first in Britain, then in France. Regressive measures to control newspapers in Britain failed to stem debate, whereas in France Napoleon's control was temporarily far more effective.

Newspapers and political discourse in Britain, 1789–1815

Events in France rapidly became the big news story in Britain, having a more immediate impact there than in any other European country and provoking an upsurge of not only radicalism but also conservatism. After the traumatic experience of 1789, growth of the newspaper industry in Britain and Europe was tempered by hostility and mistrust of its power, temporarily unleashed during the French Revolution. The prime minister, Robert Walpole, spent £50,000 on secret handouts against France in the last ten years of his administration. The precedent had been set in

The father of conservatism, Edmund Burke, versus the father of nineteenth-century radicalism, Tom Paine

The most elaborate of all critiques emanated from the pen of Edmund Burke in his *Reflections on the Revolution in France*, which provided the propertied class, who were frightened by events across the English Channel, with a new bible. Burke argued for a natural order that placed the constitution firmly in the hands of traditional inherited monarchy, rendering such matters beyond the reach of ordinary people. His point was that Britain had achieved constitutional change in 1688 by continuity, preserving what was best of the custom and practice of government. By contrast, France had thrown all caution to the wind, a fact that inspired great hope among radicals and liberals in Britain. The writings of Burke boosted a wave of conservatism, in stark contrast to the idealistic radicalism of Tom Paine. In his *The Rights of Man*, Paine criticized Burke's 'government by precedent' as one of the vilest systems possible. All governments, he wrote, except the revolutionary regimes of France and America, were based on conquest and superstition: 'Political Popery'.

1785, when *The Times* had been launched as a government-subsidized sheet; nevertheless, one writer comments on the 'limited return' from this investment given the appeal of radicalism (Conboy 2004: 90).

It is a feature of both eighteenth- and nineteenth-century European history that the aspirations of people for change, and their communication of such desires, came long before their achievement of these aims. In Great Britain the struggle for press freedom and for basic democratic rights only narrowly preceded the business roots of international media development. Responses to the French Revolution generated some seminal writings which impacted on attitudes towards press development.

A 'class of 1789' emerged from supporters of the French Revolution, not unlike the 'class of 1968', full of the optimism articulated in this case by Wordsworth, in 'The French Revolution as it Appeared to Enthusiasts at its Commencement' (1804):

> France standing at the top of golden hours
> And human nature seeming born again.
>
> . . .
>
> Bliss it was in that dawn to be alive,
> But to be young was very heaven!

Very soon, both sides organized themselves to respond to France's new order. The British middle classes formed a dining society in support called the Society for Constitutional Information. The working class set up the London Corresponding Society as a vehicle and school for writers of radical pamphlets inspired by Paine, although it was suppressed within a few years. The latter society called for universal suffrage and for annual parliaments, acknowledging that political liberation lay with constitutional change.

As the revolution evolved into the threat of revolutionary war and Burke's predictions of violence came true, France dominated the news agenda. The public's thirst for news meant increased sales and more papers, as events came thick and fast. For the first time in the history of British journalism, the timing of coverage became an issue. This presented a new challenge and opportunity: how to report on and explain the rapidly changing situation. Newspapers boasted about the speed and accuracy of their coverage of the proceedings of the debates of the legislative assembly and successive bodies, on which they all simultaneously relied for their source of information. If diversity of news-gathering was lacking, so too was the modern style of objective coverage. The British press tended to see events in France in British terms, and this ethnocentric approach was made worse by the lack of professional foreign correspondents, meaning that editors were dependent on the unpaid contributions of amateurs.

Nevertheless, from the national debates sparked by Burke and Paine, a new language of the politics of class had begun to develop. The historian Alfred Cobban described the pamphlet debate that followed Burke's *Reflections on the Revolution in France* as 'perhaps the last real discussion of fundamentals of politics in this country [Britain]. . . . Issues as great have been raised in our day, but it cannot be pretended that they have evoked a political discussion on the intellectual level of that inspired by the French Revolution' (Butler 1984: 1). Indeed, the British response to the French Revolution has been the subject of much debate among historians, because, according to another writer, this was the first major opportunity for 'popular, democratic reform of the British social and political order' (Philp 1991).

Under the influence of Burke, the political elite laid stress on continuity, precedent, privilege, law and nationhood, while pro-government papers used the war with France, which lasted more than twenty years, as an excuse to accuse the opposition of disloyalty, to the extent that any ideas connected with progress were attacked. Meanwhile, two government-sponsored newspapers were founded in order to increase the amount of conservative propaganda. Given the political climate, *The Times* made a brave move in 1803 when it turned away from government handouts – an early form of press release – and began to develop its own news-gathering, an example of increasing journalistic maturity.

The government strategy for dealing with dissent was threefold: taxes on newspapers, a tightening of laws relating to seditious and criminal libel, and legislation to ban the association of workers. One historian of the press has referred to this attitude as a 'fault-line' in British public culture, a discontinuity in political and social positioning (Black 2001: 143). Unacceptable reform was now typecast as class based; the government differentiated between the 'people', who were respectable, and the 'mob', who were protesters.

Meanwhile radicals had indeed reacted passionately to Burke's literary references to 'the swinish multitude', that is the working class, who he believed should not be allowed to meddle in constitutional matters. This incendiary insult provoked a number of retaliatory new titles such as *Hog's Wash, Pig's Meat* and *Mast and Acorn. Hog's Wash* was published by a bookseller who by 1812 had been prosecuted seven times and served three years in jail for his printing activities. In truth, from the period of the revolutionary wars onwards, in Britain movements for social and political reform and their press became associated with a critique of government and society. The fact that debate evolved into official campaigning at a time when Britain was also at war with France led to government fears over treason, security and a possible uprising by the 'lower orders'.

The collapse of press freedom in France, 1794–1815

The problem in retrospect seemed to be that Europe had not yet embraced the modern-day concept of plurality of expression in democracy. In the eyes of contemporaries, stability was associated with unity, which was threatened by dissent. Dissent therefore had to be eliminated because it divided society into hostile factions. In defence of the revolutionary leaders, it can be said that they were struggling against the odds to establish a new society: '[essentially] practical men, but blinded by enthusiasm for a new ideal to the value of tradition and forced by events to forgo gradual change' (Gilchrist and Murray 1971: 1).

By the time that the Directory took control, gone were the golden days of competing partisan publications uninhibited in their challenge of political institutions. Politicians now argued that the press no longer acted responsibly, therefore should not benefit from constitutional guarantees of free expression. Some journalists were arrested and their papers banned several months before Napoleon took power on 18th Brumaire in year 8 of the revolutionary calendar (9 November 1799). Censorship was reinstated in 1805, and not long afterwards newspapers were only allowed to report news that had appeared in the government's official organ, *Le Moniteur*.

A skilled propagandist, Napoleon created his own newspapers to publicize his early successes in the Italian campaigns. By 1810 entry to the print trade was once more controlled, and by the following year the number of newspapers was limited to four for Paris and one for each department. The system was now rationalized and under Napoleon's control.

In 1814, before Napoleon's brief return to power during the Hundred Days, Louis XVIII granted a charter that later acted as a certain safeguard for journalists during the harsh years of the Restoration after 1815. One historian argues that the political mentality which had developed among the public during the revolution also survived, nourished by the remnants of the political press (Rader 1973: 258). Although one scholar has described the revolutionary press as 'an ephemeral product of that equally ephemeral phenomenon, the French Revolution itself' (Popkin 1990:179–80), this view overlooks the fact that lasting principles were established, such as the right within democracy to use political discourse as a means of mobilizing public support. Furthermore, as Claude Labrosse and Pierre Rétat conclude in their study of newspapers in 1789 (1989), a better understanding of the profusion of journalism that erupted in that year may help us to negotiate our way through the maze of today's surfeit of information, which can leave us feeling powerless and overwhelmed.

The worldwide development of local newspapers, 1815–1847

In this period the ground rules for newspaper success were still being established. Newspapers were on the threshold of take-off, but patterns of development were uneven. Although journalism was still a craft with individual characteristics rather than an industry with uniform definitions, it interacted with a number of international trends. The first industrial revolution in Britain was paving the way for the rise of the nation-state and further colonialism, and this was made possible by the ability to communicate. Westerners began to settle in larger numbers than ever before in all parts of the world and imperialism spread English-language papers worldwide. As many settlers were literate and affluent, demand for such newspapers increased, bringing with it a call for imported newspapers from England and also the establishment of local English-language journals. In 1824 *The Australian* was launched in Sydney and six years later stamp tax was abolished in that country; in 1833 the *Daily Advertiser* was founded in Montreal. As new countries, Australia and Canada tended to follow the American model of newspaper development, but elsewhere in the world the British influence was predominant. In 1838 the *Times of India* was established. The year 1845 saw the first publication of both the Malaysia *Straits Times* and the Hong Kong *China Mail*. The first modern newspapers in China were weeklies and monthlies established by British missionaries, such as the *Eastern Western Monthly Magazine*. Later on local newspapers were started in the vernacular around the world, though often the prerequisite for commercial success was not present, since the wealthier and educated clientele usually spoke English. Indeed, local – as opposed to national – newspapers did not really take off in Europe either until the second half of the nineteenth century.

America

In the early nineteenth century papers tended to survive on a shoe-string as either personal or political organs in a way similar to those in France during the revolution. However, America showed the healthiest business prospects for regionalized communication, partly because of greater political stability than in Europe, and partly because the vast size of the country and lack of fast travel and communications meant that local newspapers of necessity had an important role to play.

The American local newspaper scene, by a contemporary

The most common newspaper was the country weekly, about which Alexis de Tocqueville wrote during 1831–2 in his classic *Democracy in America* (1835). While he disliked its provincialism, de Tocqueville was impressed by its virility. He also discovered that journalists were 'generally in a very humble position, with a scanty education and a vulgar turn of mind', but he noticed a close relationship between the press and the public because of the active participation of readers in the local justice effort. According to de Tocqueville, the American public respected the fourth estate, illustrated by the freedom given to it.

In America some regional newspapers had circulations of 40,000 when Britain had no daily press outside of London. The fragmented, dispersed, and essentially agricultural nature of life was represented in many of the smaller journals, and this continued in some parts well into the twentieth century, alongside developments in chain ownership. At the same time, the distance to be covered for newspaper distribution in America militated against the establishment of a national press. Equally the size of the United States allowed small community papers to survive, such as foreign-language journals (especially German) for the growing immigrant community. Yet the state of the newspaper industry in mainland Germany was very different.

Germany

Germany's place in newspaper history had, in the past, been a distinguished one, yet by the early nineteenth century press development was at a low level compared to elsewhere. Within this context, an analysis of the problems demonstrates the central influence of political climate and lack of industrialization.

Historians have frequently bemoaned the extreme provincialism of German life and the commensurate quality of its local press. Although every town expected to have its own newspaper and other periodicals, there was a proliferation of what one historian has called 'insipid' journals (O'Boyle 1967–8). The fact was that, before the 1848 revolutions erupted in Europe over most of the continent, newspapers were compelled either to give domestic politics a wide berth or simply to reproduce government propaganda. Germany as a nation did not exist during this period; in 1848, the Austrian Chancellor Metternich (in charge of most of the territory) famously complained: 'I have spent my life propping up a mouldering edifice.'

This 'edifice' consisted of a confederation of mainly absolutist states, in which formally constituted political parties were prohibited. Political information emanated from the top, but this power base was fragile. Furthermore, the ideas of the French Revolution had led to an unease among monarchs and the nobility that resulted in liberal opposition to press censorship being associated with incipient nationalism and the movement for German unification. The concept of a unified

The German newspaper heritage

After *The Times* of London, Johann Cotta's *Augsburger Allgemeine Zeitung* was probably the greatest paper in Europe during this period. The *Frankfurter Journal*, the first genuine newspaper in the world, had been offering the commercial and educated classes of Germany a regular weekly service of serious news for more than two hundred years. The *Frankfurter Postzeitung* and the *Magdeburgische Zeitung*, which survived until 1955, were almost as old. The first daily newspaper in the world, the *Leipziger Zeitung*, dated back to 1659–60.

state was reinforced by the growth of an increasingly economically important but still disenfranchised middle class. This divisive climate inhibited the press because newspapers could be blamed for encouraging the formation of party politics. Censorship, embodied in the repressive policies of the Karlsbad decrees, became a thorny issue.

Liberals discerned that governments were on the defensive and urged them to submit to the inevitable, arguing that only freedom of expression would bring about the moral and intellectual unity of the German people. The problem in the context of the nineteenth-century relationship between the media and political change was that, under the German absolutist system, the concept of public opinion and its authority over government had not yet emerged. Slow industrial development made things worse.

France

In 1830 France experienced another revolution. This time shorter and less fundamental, it began significantly from the offices of the newspaper *Le National*. The Bourbon monarchy, which had been reinstated after the fall of Napoleon, was replaced by the Orléanist dynasty under Louis Philippe. Research into the influence of the political press in the run-up to the debut of what became known as the July Monarchy has revealed that, despite the introduction of a harsh press law in 1828, a political press survived and was able to influence events (Rader 1973: 256–9).

By the 1830s, two sorts of newspapers co-existed in France: the new, more commercially orientated press (see p. 35) and the old-style political newspapers, who were the true descendants of the revolutionary press. French provincial newspapers, with their precarious existence, were the real victims of government interference. It had become obvious to both government and journalists that the law of libel and controls over the financial organization of newspapers acted as the most effective constraints on political debate, so their scope was widened to everyday newspaper work. This happened at a time when in Britain, after the first Reform Act of 1832, prosecutions for seditious libel were becoming more rare.

Costly legal obligations could have a devastating effect on the survival prospects of newspapers that were undercapitalized and

Provincial newspapers create 'imagined communities'

Research by Jeremy Popkin (2002: 263–70) into the oppositional press in Lyons from 1830 to 1835 touches on the core role of political newspapers in nineteenth-century Europe's evolving class system and democracy. He has revealed that newspapers were used as a vehicle to help define the emerging public identities of workers, women and middle-class groups. This provided a new 'pluralism' which is an essential ingredient of liberal society. Using Pierre Bourdieu's idea that the process of journalism creates a 'field', that is, a means of framing the public presentation of images and ideas, Popkin examines the emergence of new 'imagined communities' (Anderson 1991) and periodicals claiming to speak for them at a local level. These, he claims, had the effect of multiplying conflicts and tensions within society, manifested by the discourse between rival newspapers reacting to each other's arguments. Thus, through a dialectical process evocative of the 1789–92 period, social classes realized their very existence via competing newspaper presentations.

not financially independent. Yet politicians still tried hard to create a provincial press. In her correspondence, the novelist George Sand recounts her uphill struggles to find a local editor and a printer for the paper *L'Éclaireur de l'Indre*, which she founded in her area in order to spread her socialist ideas (Sand 1883–92: 2.212). Successive laws at the time demanded that political journals paid a deposit, or caution money, yet very many newspapers faced prosecution for evasion of the payment. In addition, all of the press was burdened by stamp duty and postage costs as, unlike their counterparts in Britain, most journals in the 1830s were still distributed by subscription (despite the advent of street hawkers during the revolution).

What is remarkable is not only that so many newspapers actually survived these apparent government attacks on contrary opinion, but that some circulations, such as that in Paris, remained relatively high (Zeldin 1980: 2.192).[3] Significantly, in the run-up to 1848, France's political press was more in touch with public opinion than many politicians who did not realize that another revolution was imminent.

Britain

In comparison, British newspapers had already proved their profitability; a well-run regional paper selling 1000 copies a day could make its owner between £1500 and £3000 profit a year. The *Manchester Guardian* made nearly £7000 a year (Smith 1979: 144; Cranfield 1978; Barker 2000). Britain's active political culture demanded a constant flow of information and, as regional news developed, with it the status of local newspaper offices increased. They became central to other forms of politics such as the receipt of petitions and the organization of campaigns – all of which helped sales. In order to survive, newspapers were now reflecting the political views of readers by appealing to the localized nature of public opinion, which meant that the political stance of the editor was crucial.

But it was not until after 1855 and the complete abolition of the Stamp Acts that local papers really took off. Earlier in the nineteenth century, often the front and back pages of a local paper were printed first, leaving the middle for late news, so both old and new news appeared together in a jumble, with only limited use of headlines. In Britain as elsewhere at this time, local news could be days old, especially in the provinces, so newer intelligence had to be rushed to print in order to beat the arrival of the London papers by the coach and horses postal service. The arrival of the railways changed this way of working dramatically, and more generally trains had a momentous effect on society.

Industrialization and improved distribution

Not only did the Industrial Revolution create a new urban population or 'proletariat', as Karl Marx called them, it also brought inventions that helped media development. Marx also correctly flagged the invention of the steam engine as the great breakthrough in human history, 'separating past from present and opening up a revolutionary future' (Briggs and Burke 2002: 110). In pre-industrial eighteenth-century Britain, the newspaper production trade had been a low-status industry, employing women at every level of distribution and production, but by the time the Industrial Revolution had taken effect in the nineteenth century it was becoming more respectable, better paid and ready for the modernization that the new steam technology offered. But the impact on newspapers worldwide was relatively slow, as at first very few of them could afford to invest.

In America, as the craft of printing became separated from both publishing and editing, the capital costs of investment in print production were becoming increasingly important (Rorabaugh 1986: 77). The replacement of flatbed presses by the cylinder press enabled a greater

The Times of London as pioneer of newspaper technology

The Times invested first in the Stanhope iron press, which appeared in 1800 and facilitated clearer print impressions but did not increase the speed of printing. Then in 1814 it made use of the highly priced Koenig steam-driven printing machine. This invention increased printing speed four times, to 1000 copies an hour, enabling later production and therefore more up-to-date news. Other British papers were slow at first to follow the lead of The Times in investing. The Manchester Guardian invested in steam technology only in 1828, although by the 1830s such machines were commonplace. The Times was also the only British newspaper with sales and advertising revenue great enough to warrant technical innovations such as improved feeding for the paper. The arrival of the rotary press, invented for The Times in its own works by Ambrose Applegarth, quintupled speed and enabled the entire newspaper to be printed from a single machine. By the 1840s the newspaper dominated the field as the voice of basic ruling-class interests, commanding daily sales of 40,000. However, in general high newspaper sales prices kept circulation down in Britain, retarding investment until the abolition of the Stamp Acts.

speed and volume of printing. During the 1830s newspapers bought the Napier double cylinder press, but its 4000 copies per hour were out-performed in the 1840s by the American Richard Hoe's revolving press, which produced 20,000 copies an hour. In 1846 Hoe brought out the first version of the rotary press and sold it to the Paris newspaper *La Patrie*, and more cylinders were added later. However, in the earlier nineteenth century it was *The Times* which led the way in new production technology.

Railways

Distribution of the press in 1840s Britain received its biggest boost from the invention of railways: now the London newspapers could be circulated to most parts of the country on their day of publication. This meant that they were able to compete with the provincial press, and an increasing number of nationals published simultaneously in London and also in Manchester or Glasgow.

The opening in 1830 of the Liverpool to Manchester railway line as a debut to the arrival of the train is an underrated landmark in railway history. Everywhere communication and trade was opened up, accelerating the distribution of newspapers and enabling more up-to-date news to be produced. In Britain, the creation of a stronger national press, centralized in Fleet Street, was now on the agenda; circulation was further facilitated by the arrival of news vendors and newsagents. W. H. Smith established a monopoly over the dispatch of newspapers to agents, and set up shops selling newspapers and cheap books at the new railway stations.

In effect, the construction of railways launched modern-day tourism by eventually offering worldwide travel to passengers at a hitherto unknown speed. Moreover, it provoked a huge demand for coal and iron, lowered business costs, spearheaded new markets, stimulated employment in many industries and created new communities as well as sometimes damaging older ones. Dickens's novel *Dombey and Son* uses the metaphor of death to tackle the impact on communities and other human issues created by the debut of industrial capitalism in London.

The mail

Newspapers were distributed by the mail, which was carried not only by the new railways but also by ships and coach and horses; 80 per cent of American newspapers were distributed by the Post Office, and this remained the main way in which rural populations received information about the wider world outside of their communities well into the twentieth century. The first postage stamps in the world were introduced in the United Kingdom by Roland Hill in 1840; since the UK was the only country to do this at the time, it was not considered necessary to print its name on the stamps – the historical reason why British stamps still do not carry the country's name. As this service preceded the development of the education system, people often employed intermediaries to read and write their letters. British radicals such as Richard Cobden welcomed the introduction of the stamp as a boost to tackle illiteracy and as a help to their campaign for free trade.

Strategies for new readerships on both sides of the Atlantic

Two main early nineteenth-century themes, political communication and experiments with commercialism, can be compared during the 1830s in America, Britain and France. Commercial developments in America were followed by similar attempts in France, then Britain, where a largely illegal political press fought to educate new readerships in a different way.

The American penny press

Very soon after the American War of Independence, the press started to become a branch of the commercial community, for the revolution was the last time that mass readerships were attracted to genuinely radical politics not linked to economic self-acquisition (Conboy 2002: 43–6). Earlier nineteenth-century newspapers were aimed mainly at the economic and political elite, supporting a particular party or dealing with business, finance and shipping (Gorman and McLean 2003: 12), but gradually they became part of the economic and industrial growth of the 1830s in a society where the old social structures were changing.

Business orientation has a heritage on this side of the Atlantic dating back to Benjamin Franklin's *Pennsylvania Gazette*, which was probably the first modern newspaper to be commercially viable. In the 1720s, the Franklin brothers were also the first to produce newspapers successfully without specific authority from the British colonial government, but it wasn't until 1833 that the first viable penny paper reached the 'common people'.

As the penny press was developed to reach all classes, literary standards gradually improved, and within ten years respectable newspapers

Sensationalism: a never-ending story?

According to the American press historians Michael Emery, Edwin Emery and Nancy L. Roberts (2000), whenever the needs of the masses are ignored by the established organs of communication this need is eventually met by 'sensationalism'. In support of this argument they quote some of the key media history dates: 1620, when the first 'corantos' news sheets, reporting on the important events of the Thirty Years' War, were produced by Dutch printers for the English market;[4] 1833, when the penny press was introduced; the 1890s, the decade of 'New Journalism'; and finally 1920, the year in which the first American radio stations to seek a regular public audience were launched.

joined the trend, offering 'significant information and leadership' (Emery et al. 2000: 97). In America 'quality' newspapers co-existed with the popular from an early date, but the arrival of the new penny press in 1833 represents the beginning of the integration of journalism into a capitalist framework. According to Ralph Nerone (1987), this is the key change in American press history, for journalism henceforth developed along commercial lines. Some historians say that the penny press represented a new democratic world where notions of public and private were being redefined; others argue for the continuity of traditions inherited from the popular broadsheets and ballads. The two are not incompatible. Readerships were undoubtedly hungry for papers with egalitarian ideas for politics, economics and social life. What was new was its combination with commercialism and technology. J. L. Crouthamel (1989) points out that the emergence of a press aimed at a wider audience, selling at a lower price, is due to the development of technology: mass circulation could be produced more quickly and cheaply. Michael Schudson emphasizes the 'democratic market society' that was emerging: the writers of the penny press 'were spokesmen for egalitarianism ideals in politics, economic life, and social life through their organization of sales, their solicitation of advertising, their emphasis on news, their catering to large audiences, and their decreasing concern with the editorial' (1978: 60).

Benjamin H. Day's *New York Sun*, with its motto 'It Shines for All', was written in a language for ordinary people. Readers were seen as involved and informed. Unlike the readers of Britain's radical press at this time, they were also perceived as happy with the socio-economic system. The paper had lots of adverts, including a new 'wanted' section, but no information for the financial classes other than a small amount of shipping news. Day copied the idea of crime reporting from the successful reporting of Bow Street Police Station in London. The appeal was non-partisan, although one study has drawn attention to the wide coverage given to the women's rights movement. During the Jacksonian 'antebellum' era, politics for the 'labouring classes' was beginning to win recognition as white male workers had the right to vote and the public sphere was being extended to the lower middle classes (Hoffert 1993).

Day had watched similar attempts to introduce a penny press and thought it would work if financed on a pre-issue basis with sales using street vendors: the so-called London Plan. Previously, subscriptions had been $6 to $10 a year, which was more than a weekly wage for a skilled worker. Subscription sales only suited stable, financially secure, professional middle-class workers, while encouraging only a small circulation and conservatism in the press. However, industrialization and urbanization were leading to a change in previous notions of class and status as popular culture began to reflect life in the expanding cities. Newspapers influenced the newly emerging social groups. The price cut meant new immigrants to cities could afford to buy a paper for the first time; and the street vendors meant that a community of readers who would identify themselves with the newspapers' views had to be encouraged, with slogans and different catchy news every day.

The new penny press combined serious journalism with entertainment, but sometimes the truth was sacrificed as standards were lowered in a quest for circulation. The prime example was the 'moon hoax', purporting to describe life on the moon and written by a reporter who, although he was a descendant of the philosopher John Locke, appeared to have inherited none of the latter's moral probity. The defence of *The Sun* to criticism about this coverage as one of the first and most bizarre newspaper frauds in America was telling. The paper claimed it was offering a diversion from the more serious issue of the abolition of slavery which was achieved in Britain by legislation passed in that year (Thornton 2000). The tendency to use entertainment as a distraction from more important public issues is still a prime feature of the popular press. One early example of a precursor of today's tabloids and television was America's *National Police Gazette*, which, despite (or maybe because of) its title, dealt with sex, sport, violence and racial provocation (Gorn 1992).

However, James Gordon Bennett's *New York Herald*, which was launched two years later, displayed a greater sense of social responsibility when it widened its coverage of a sensational 1836 court drama, the Robinson–Jewett case, from a regular crime report to a debate on the morals of society. The approach, with more extensive use of interview technique than ever before, plus background details, reports from friends and acquaintances, and speculation on multiple theories about the murder, was an example of how gossip could be used as a feature. Again, the appeal was to those outside the social and financial elite, for Robinson (the accused) was a society mover, whereas the victim, Jewett, who gained public sympathy, was a prostitute. Such was the interest in the case that it spawned eleven 'chap-books' (single chapter publications) – an indication of both demand and cross-over between publishing formats.

Unlike the British radical press, the *New York Herald* did not encourage resentment about inequalities of wealth in a left-wing way. Issues were diffused in an unpolitical fashion, illustrated by a scepticism about economic and political leadership that was not altogether unjustified: for the political system at this time often displayed mediocrity in government, 'bossism' and the 'spoils system' in business (Emery et al. 2000: 100). Indeed, Bennett's conservatism was clear from the jingoism and patriotic chauvinism that emerged fifty years before that shown by Britain's *Daily Mail*, William Randolph Hearst and Joseph Pulitzer. He clearly supported the contemporary 'manifest destiny' concept of Anglo-Saxon supremacy:

> The Anglo Saxon race is intended by an overruling Providence to carry the principles of liberty, the refinements of civilization, and the advantages of the mechanic arts through every land, even those now

barbarous. The prostrate savage and the benighted heathen shall yet be imbued with Anglo Saxon intelligence and culture, and be blessed with the institutions, both civil and religious, which are now our inheritance. Mexico, too, must submit to the o'erpowering influence of the Anglo Saxon. (Crouthamel 1989: 57)

In a 'popular' statement for the first edition, Bennett used the vernacular of his readers: 'well I have got a paper of my own which will tell me all about what's doing in the world – I'm busy now – but I'll put it in my pocket and read it at my leisure.' The *New York Herald* was the first paper to develop society reporting, the precursor of today's celebrity news; the first to employ a full-time sports reporter and to feature racing; the first to use the wood-cut tradition, in a whole-page illustration of President Jackson's funeral procession in 1845; and the first successfully to monopolize a large market. Notwithstanding,

Girardin, 'creator of the modern press'

Up to 1836 in France, two categories of newspapers existed – the political press, which had to rely on partisan subsidy because circulations were too low to attract advertisers, and the 'petit journal', the small paper that was exempt from stamp tax and caution money because it excluded politics, specializing instead in vitriolic gossip. The result was that the 'petits journaux' of the 1830s relied precariously on financial bribery for 'puffs' and protection money donated by the powerful and famous in order to avoid bad reviews and scandal.[5] It became clear to the pioneer newspaper entrepreneur Émile de Girardin that only advertising and increased sales income would enable the press to be independent of political groups and forsake blackmail, so he advocated an information-based, politically neutral press.

Girardin's paper *La Presse* aimed to reach a wider audience by replacing the standard protracted political debates with fashion, gossip, journalistic stunts and, last but not least, a remarkably successful innovation – the serial story. He also cut the sales price dramatically, from the usual 80F a year to 40F (de la Motte and Przyblyski 1999: 149, 153–5). Girardin wanted to abolish the financial constraints on newspapers and to emulate the British press. However, his motivation in founding a newspaper to attract a wider public was to increase his own wealth and power in order to force his way into society, which he believed despised him.

There is a debate among historians as to how far the introduction of a commercialized press in France during 1838 represents a complete break with the past. Current thinking stresses the existence of paid advertisements from 1827 and Girardin's limited success in making advertising a source of revenue, as well as the revelation that the high circulation of *feuilletons* (tabloids) could not be achieved by cheaper sales prices alone. For instance, the journal *Débats* refused to lower its price, but became the most popular newspaper in Paris, according to contemporaries, on the strength of its serialization of the great classics *Les Mystères de Paris* by Eugène Sue and *Le Comte de Monte Cristo* by Alexandre Dumas. This idea of using literary product consciously to boost sales, in a format where marketing clearly determined narrative structure, heralded a boom period for the *roman-feuilleton* (serial story) in Britain as well.[6] The old French newspapers fought against Girardin's innovations and, although they eventually had to make some concessions on price and the introduction of the serial story, most retained the essence of their existence, the high level of political discussion.

the French can also lay claim to a pioneer in popular commercial journalism.

Britain's radical press

The British tradition of radical pamphleteers is a long one, dating back to *corantos* and ballads in 1620. In addition, the influence of the French Revolution, political repression in the face of industrialization and the accompanying social and economic hardship, plus lack of press freedom illustrated by the financial imposition of the Stamp Acts, all helped to contribute to the remarkable phenomenon of the radical press in the first half of the nineteenth century. Over 700 people were imprisoned for publishing, writing in or selling illegal unstamped newspapers, of which there were hundreds. Some journals paid the stamp tax but still faced prosecution, usually for seditious libel, that is, incitement to revolt against constitutional authority, referred to earlier in British history as a 'malleable offence' (Conboy 2004: 13).

The radical press, inspired by Cobbett, soon became a small shop industry employing editors, local agents, booksellers and hawkers, even if their work was interrupted by sporadic jail sentences. Britain's Six Acts, 'the high water mark of legislation restricting the press' (Williams 1969: 12), further tightened criminal libel and imposed a new

William Cobbett: champion of the rural poor and pioneer 'documentary' journalist

In the early nineteenth century the most influential popular journalist was a self-educated former farm labourer called William Cobbett. His weekly journal the *Political Register* was first published in 1802 in support of the government and opposing the French Revolution, but two years later Cobbett was convicted of libel for criticizing the government's conduct of the war. His personal experience of repression gradually turned him into a radical. Cobbett became a passionate champion of the poor and underprivileged, concentrating on rural life. As he wrote in 1816: 'Whatever the pride of rank, of riches or of scholarship may have induced some men to believe, the real strength and resources of a country ever have sprung and ever must spring from the labour of its people.' In the 1820s he travelled throughout the English countryside campaigning against enclosures of land and defending traditional agrarian ways that were dying; his descriptions of these journeys were published in *Rural Rides*, a pioneer book of journalistic 'documentary' writing. Despite the fact that the legally stamped *Political Register* sold at the necessarily high price of 7½d., in 1821 it reached a circulation of 60,000 – more than any other newspaper in Britain. In his writings Cobbett blamed 'misgovernment' for economic distress and attacked the 'old corruption', by which he meant the patronage system and control of parliament by the landed aristocracy and gentry. Predictably, Cobbett was one of the first to campaign for parliamentary reform, although he was forced to flee temporarily to America when habeas corpus (literally, the body of a person, meaning a writ to produce a person before a judge or court) was suspended and the Gagging Acts were introduced, banning meetings of more than fifty people. That same year Shropshire magistrates had men flogged for selling Cobbett's works.

tax on newspapers that sold for less than 6*d.*, such as Cobbett's second edition of the *Political Register*.

An episode in 1819 illustrates the relationship between newspapers and political unrest with an economic base. Between 60,000 and 100,000 working people attended a rally in St Peter's Fields, Manchester (one of the main centres of industrialization), in favour of parliamentary reform. The event became known as Peterloo, named after the battle of Waterloo. As the main speaker, 'Orator' Hunt, rose to his feet, troops with sabres charged on the crowd and within ten minutes eleven people were dead and 400 injured. Watching was a radical journalist called Richard Carlile, who immediately took the mail coach to London and wrote up the story. When Hunt arrived in London for his trial, 300,000 turned out to welcome him. The (stamped, therefore legal) *Manchester Guardian* newspaper, probably Britain's foremost regional daily and later to become national as *The Guardian*, was founded that same year in the wake of Peterloo.

Carlile was not the only defiant journalist. Some editors avoided stamp duty by not using paper: the *Political Handkerchief* was printed on calico and the *Political Touchwood* was produced on plywood. The unstamped *Police Gazette* was hidden in coffins for dispatch, but still sold 40,000 copies in 1836. The ruse was discovered only when a

Carlile: a media record for prison sentences

Radical press activists such as Carlile survived countless prosecutions for seditious libel and challenged a tax system designed to control the supply of newspapers and hence communication within the public sphere. At the time of Peterloo, he already had eight indictments against him and was awaiting trial for serializing the entire works of Paine, which were banned. The story of Carlile's tenacious battle for freedom to publish, which inspired John Stuart Mill to write his classic essay *On Liberty*, is a salutary reminder of the price that has been paid in the past for media freedom. During his trial that same year – 1819 – Carlile succeeded in reading the whole of Paine's *The Age of Reason* into the court record. He was found guilty of blasphemy and the entire contents of his shop in Fleet Street, named the 'Temple of Reason' as another reference to Paine, were confiscated to pay the fine. While Carlile was in prison his wife continued the business, publishing the proceedings of the trial and all of the hitherto unpublished works of Paine, until the whole family found themselves in jail. By this time Carlile had his own fund-raising organization to counter that of the religious and anti-radical groups who were prosecuting him. Donations flooded into the Temple of Reason at the rate of £500 a week, as well as new (seditious) writings by Shelley, Byron, Southey and Bentham. Very soon 'General Carlile's Corps' consisted of 150 volunteer shop men and vendors in 'branches' all over Britain, each of them provided with a written defence to read out in court. They spent a combined 200 years in jail. Carlile himself served nine and a half years. Although one of the prosecuting societies, having spent over £30,000, went bankrupt, business continued as usual at the Temple of Reason, where a conveyor belt operated with money in the slot and titles of publications arranged around a dial: this self-service Heath Robinson-style machine supplied the publications via a chute to preserve anonymity and avoid prosecution. In 1825 Carlile emerged from jail unconditionally discharged with all his fines remitted.

concerned neighbour, who had seen a delivery of coffins, suspected an epidemic and contacted the authorities (Harrison 1974: 94). Henry Hetherington, when not in prison, travelled in disguise as he moved about Britain founding new branches of the National Union of the Working Classes and establishing agencies for the *Poor Man's Guardian*, which one contemporary claimed was the 'first messenger of popular and political intelligence which reached the working classes' (ibid.: 92). This newspaper expressed a generally held view that British society was unjust because workers were simultaneously robbed of the right to vote and the products of their labour. The issue of class was at its height in the 1830s and 1840s in Britain when Marx was writing the *Communist Manifesto* and Engels was describing factory conditions in *The Condition of the Working Classes in England*. According to two leading social historians, 'The opposition between the middle class (the word capitalist was rarely used) and the working class was more universally taken to be the key to current history than it has ever been before or since' (Cole and Postgate 1938: 261).

The campaign for the extension of the franchise (or vote), best exemplified by the Chartist movement, was generally viewed by reformers as the main means of furthering working-class interests. Chartism was a political protest movement which achieved huge support (2 million signatories on a petition and mass rallies). One contemporary recalled that, 'on the day the [Chartist] newspaper, the *Northern Star*, was due, the people used to line the roadside waiting for its arrival, which was paramount to everything else for the time being' (Curran and Seaton 2003: 14). Over a fifteen-year period it was the most influential of many Chartist journals, reaching a circulation of 48,000 despite the stamp tax that it paid. The scope for comment by the radical press was not restricted to parliamentary reform, for its overall aim was to describe and expose the dynamics of power and inequality in the belief that knowledge equalled power. Other issues included the 'social questions', such as factory conditions and rural poverty, political organization, clubs and trades unions, corruption and repression, humour, and crime, as well as anti-clerical newspapers such as the euphemistically entitled *Slap at the Church*.

Although both Chartism and the radical press were the last movements to draw inspiration from the French Revolution, they also constituted the first significant attack upon the social order to emerge from the growth of capitalist industry (Tawney 1920: x). Chartism may have destabilized the social system by encouraging class-conscious protest such as strikes, but the movement also initiated a form of inclusiveness which was necessary to the future development of the newspaper industry.[7] The circulation in Britain of the illegal (unstamped) press was actually larger than that of legal newspapers in 1836, proving the demand for cheap newspapers – a potential market that Sunday and weekly publications successfully exploited.

The true popular descendants of the radical press and early news sheets in Britain were the Sunday newspapers, with weekly sales of

270,000 by the end of the 1840s, despite the fact that it was technically illegal to sell anything other than milk or mackerel on the Sabbath; by 1812 there were eighteen in London. *Lloyd's Weekly News* and *Reynold's News* supported radical and libertarian causes and were especially popular with working-class readers, for Sunday was the only day that they had the opportunity and time to read a newspaper. *Lloyd's Weekly News* sold 100,000 copies even during the era of the stamp taxes. Although the Sunday papers in Britain were organized along commercial lines with no party politics, the very radically minded *News of the World*, started in 1843, delighted the authorities by putting much illegal, unstamped journalism out of business by soon selling more than 100,000 copies a week. This follows a trend analysed by Richard Terdiman (in relation to France), whereby commercial journalism co-opts 'counter discursive irritants' (de la Motte and Przyblyski 1999: 2, 351–6).[8] The content of the press on the Sabbath comprised more fiction than news. The readership was increasingly the newly literate who could not afford six papers a week. New readerships meant new jobs for journalists as the industry expanded.

The emergence of the profession of journalism

In this period, written communication was accompanied by a sense of mission, sadly lacking in the twenty-first century. It was summed up by the editor of America's *Springfield Republican*, who saw his role as 'the high priest of history, the vitalizer of society, the world's great informer, the earth's high censor, the medium of public opinion and the circulating life blood of the whole human mind' (Williams 1969: 44). Indeed opinion and commentary were considered the essence of contemporary journalism – except for parliamentary coverage, where accuracy was all-important.

Development of the industry came not so much in terms of new technology as in the increase in the numbers of staff and gradual job specialization as news-gathering began to change. In the first half of the nineteenth century, specialization varied according to the culture of different countries. For instance, in France the profession of journalism first emerged from the 1789 revolution, when the influence and esteem attributed to belles-lettres and the eighteenth-century *philosophes* passed to journalism, which caused Balzac to comment in 1840: 'Public opinion is manufactured in Paris; it is made with ink and paper' (Girardin 1859: 55, 76). The path via journalism to politics that created a new political elite continued in France throughout the nineteenth century, exemplified by the careers of Guizot and Thiers. Alexis de Tocqueville considered the desire for office to be 'the great, chronic ailment of the whole nation' (1970: 31–2). Yet the English contemporary commentator Walter Bagehot, writing in 1852, was envious: 'Here a man who begins his life by writing in the newspapers has an appreciable chance of coming to be Minister of Foreign Affairs. The class of public writers is the class from which the equivalent of Lord Aberdeen, Lord Palmerston or Lord Grenville will most likely be chosen' (1915: 1.126).

By comparison, in Britain journalism was able to develop as a profession in its own right independent of politics, even if it did lack prestige. The novelist William Makepeace Thackeray felt obliged to adopt a pseudonym when he wrote as a journalist. The long-established tradition of open political debate and the development of industry, which provided a plentiful supply of openings in business and the professions, and of a more commercial press, led by *The Times*, all meant that the potential journalist was less tempted by political office. To some contemporary observers such as John Stuart Mill, the emergence of the commercial press and the professional journalist represented a loss rather than a gain:

> You know in how low a state the newspaper press of this country is. In France the best thinkers and writers of the nation, write in the journals and direct public opinion; but our daily and weekly writers are the lowest hacks of literature, which when it is a trade, is the vilest and most degrading of all trades, because more of affectation and hypocrisy, and more subservience to the baser feelings of others, are necessary for carrying it on, than for any other trade, from that of a brothel keeper upwards. (Mill 1963)

Even as a pseudo-brothel-keeper, the editor was sovereign, and small business ruled, with ownership tending to be by individuals or families, especially in provincial locations. In Japan too, when newspapers started in the late 1860s and the 1870s, the moral high ground was attached to editors and newspaper political essayists. News-gatherers were closer to Mill's analogy, for they tended to be poorly educated and underpaid menials who went into the streets, to brothels and to government offices to listen to gossip, then reported it verbally or in note form to cheap fiction writers who would turn it into 'news'. By contrast, editors saw themselves as members of the same society-shaping elite as the government officials, sharing a role synonymous with that of their patrons. Although the early Meiji editors were also all-powerful and wholly dedicated to politics, their emphasis was on obligation, loyalty and harmony, a well-refined argument and an ability to write political analysis rather than readability.

Everywhere where newspapers functioned, there was often no formal distinction between ownership, management, editing and reporting: the majority of owners were also active editors. Although most news from abroad tended to come from foreign newspapers, the job of the reporter was on the increase. All of these trends were to become more significant later with improved technology and communications.

In Germany, with its lack of unification and representative government and slow industrial growth, professional journalism was struggling, but for different reasons. The profusion of books and other publications meant that many small journals would publish anything as long as they didn't have to pay for it. Part of the reason that the literary field in Germany was so oversubscribed was because there were a large number of intellectuals who formed a kind of intellectual proletariat, which was deemed to be a problem even by contemporaries. This was partly on account of the cheapness and hence easy availability of higher education, unusual for the period, and partly because a large number of professional people existed within society as a by-product of higher education. Since most available jobs were associated with the government, there were limited career opportunities in the professions for those who did not make it into the civil service, resulting in too many poorly paid writers supplying indifferent publications. In Germany the journalist was therefore likely to be a jack of all (up-market) trades: 'man of letters, at once artist, professor and political thinker' (O'Boyle 1967–8: 312). Openings did not exist on the scale that was offered in France. Media development still had a long way to go in a climate where politics and economy were the decisive influences.

Conclusions

Elements of both continuity and change emerged during this period, often forced by events and circumstances into an uncomfortable, unresolved coexistence. The French, for instance, were grappling with questions of sovereignty, government and institutions in an ongoing attempt to resolve where ultimate authority lay – with the monarch, the chambers, the people via a republic, or a combination of the three. Conflict was omnipresent as newspapers continued to be the vehicle for persuasion and expression.

The positive contribution of the early revolutionary period to the evolution of the relationship between media and democracy was the introduction of the idea that people now had the power to change society via political campaigns and rival claims to representation and the winning of votes. In the twenty-first century this appears as a self-evident feature of the party political democratic process, but to people in the late eighteenth century it was new. The way that political campaigns are influenced by media communication is of seminal importance today, with its own growth industry of advisors and specialists and a reach beyond all the expectations of early pioneers.

The revolutionary press has provided a continuing inspiration since this period: even today there are resonances in the 'alternative media' (Chapman 2005). Struggles by journalists such as Carlile have parallels in other countries and other periods of history. In 2002, at least 1420 journalists were beaten, abducted, charged by the police, harassed or threatened with being killed. Around 400 news media were censored (Reporters sans frontières 2003).

The rise of an industrial working class posed an issue for newspaper communication, with three sorts of reaction. First was opposition to the extension of a press providing information that was considered dangerous. The second option was for workers to ignore restrictions and publish journals anyway, as a means of political self-expression. The third option was commercial popularization, along the lines championed by Girardin, America's penny press and Britain's Sunday newspapers. Although the idea of commercialization was by no means new, the growth in support for this concept facilitated its emergence as a competitor to political publishing.

Although the role of technology in newspaper development has since become pivotal, in these earlier days a content-led communications revolution could be achieved without any new production breakthroughs (although these did come later). The expression of ideas with passion and to provoke emotion in consumers has always been a specific feature of media communication. It is an element of continuity in this study.

Study questions

How did the issue of pluralism and dissent differ in the various countries featured here?

Should we analyse the concept of pluralism and dissent historically without applying modern-day criteria of assessment, and is this possible?

Is there already evidence that American media history was beginning to take a different route? Do you believe that this was the case, or are there similarities at this stage with the European experience?

2 The Focusing of Political Communications and the Newspaper Business, 1848–1881

[The telegraph and the printing press together] have converted
Britain into a vast agora, or assembly of the whole community, in
which the discussion of the affairs of State is carried on from day to
day in the hearing of the whole people.   W. T. Stead

During the last century the amount and the accuracy of information
. . . increased enormously; moreover the time elapsing between an
event and the general knowledge of an event has dwindled to a small
fraction of what it used to be.   Sydney Chapman, 1904

Summary

The *objective* of this chapter is to examine why it was that, under very
different circumstances to those outlined in chapter 1, during the
period 1848–81 the three main themes that the last chapter identified –
freedom of expression, the relationships between politics and the
media, and industrialization – all remained dominant. The way in
which these subjects continued to provide a backdrop in the various
countries differed, but the bigger issues still provided continuity.

Events and changes arrived thick and fast: for instance, the invention
of a consumer product – the phonograph – inadvertently sowed the seeds
of a music business. Meanwhile other improvements and inventions
within the field of communications such as the telegraph opened the way
for the international business of news agencies. It was in this period that
communication networks were organized on a global scale, linked to
economic, political and military considerations (Thompson 1995: 152).

The continuation of government interference in newspaper freedom illustrated by events in 1848, the attack in Britain on the power of
The Times and further press curbs in France (before eventual legalized
press freedom) served to demonstrate that politicians still feared the
media.

In Japan newspapers made their debut under heavy government
influence. In Germany, too, Bismarck waged war successfully against
newspapers in an effort to dominate them. Conflicts such as the
Crimean War, with its pioneer war reporting, and the American Civil
War had the effect of focusing the politics–media relationship while
simultaneously acting as a catalyst for change.

As the 'workshop of the world', Britain continued to dominate internationally during the heyday of its huge empire, while improved communications, including the new telegraph, proved a convenient tool for imperialism. Newspaper production adopted further industrial manufacturing techniques as technology continued to make an impact.

Introduction

Before the development of technology and distribution people were often restricted to oral communication and local commerce, but the nineteenth century was characterized by profound change. Economic development, urban growth and technological breakthroughs from the 1830s onwards all helped to create a more favourable environment in which the business of communication could grow and political democracy be extended.

While an industry was just developing in Japan, in America, Britain and continental Europe experimentation in style, content and the format of newspapers was already taking place. News, or 'intelligence' as it was often called, was in greater demand than ever before throughout the Western world, manifested by the increase in both newspaper sales and the number of new publications. The three prerequisites for newspaper development were now evident: better systems of communications, improvements in production, and demand, stimulated by the growth of a reading public.

Thanks to industrialization, millions of new consumers were being brought inside a manufacturing economy. In 1803 a local paper in Britain was already describing their era as the birth of the consumer society. In fact scholarship has established that England became a consumer society earlier in the eighteenth century when traditional views of luxury were overturned by a revolution in economic thought. Most of the major industries during early industrialization were involved in consumer goods, and a wave of 'fashion' in clothing, books, clocks and crockery spread from the aristocracy to the middle class, with various members of Europe's royal families endorsing 'medical' products in advertising (McKendrick et al. 1982; Williams 1980).

Linked to the new consumerism was a fresh attitude towards 'intelligence', highlighted by the arrival of news agencies: it became a commodity for trading, both internally and internationally. For the speeding up of this distribution process we also have the railways, mail, and steamships to thank: 'Among [the] transformations few had results as dazzling as the network of communication and transportation that arose to link Europe with the rest of the world' (Headrick 1981: 129–30).

Industrialization, improved education, population and urban growth all contributed to the creation of a reading public. For politicians these people were often a disenfranchised, or only partially franchised, constituency. While recognizing newspapers as a potential vehicle for influence, elitism prevailed in many quarters, still accompanied by a fear of newspapers and a continuing desire to control them. Control could take a number of different forms, and ruling politicians in most countries adopted a range of tactics, both subtle and heavy handed. The permutations of the relationship between the press and the authorities provide a continuity that was both complex and central to any media history of the period, despite the potential of growing commercialism to create some distance between government and press.

According to contemporary 'classic' economic liberalism, both industry and press institutions should be private, for laissez-faire thinking and free enterprise went hand in hand with individual freedom of expression. Although there should be only a minimum role for government intervention via legislation, the nation-state was still sovereign and its leaders accountable to citizens, while industry had freedom of action. In reality, theory and practice were not always consistent: politicians had difficulty in distancing themselves from the press, especially when newspapers proved truculent during turbulent times, such as 1848.

Press freedom

The year 1848 was a unique moment in history – a year of abortive revolutions throughout most of the continent of Europe, with a domino effect. The uprisings were aided by clandestine communication via the exiled radical press. In fact, the press took an important role during the events, underlining once more its relationship to contemporary politics. As temporary successes by liberals were gained, press freedom was granted, only to be removed again when they were eventually lost.

Most of Europe's nineteenth-century nationalist movements were born not out of armed struggle but through newspapers established to 'express a certain set of expectations of the nature of new civic life' (Smith 1979: 116–220). The revolutions that broke out in 1848 were an expression of the desire for unity articulated as a form of nationalism and led to press freedom, often for the first time. For example, the constitution of the short-lived Frankfurt parliament, convened to achieve German unification, also contained an article which represented the liberal argument that a free press was the key to a progressive society. As in France, liberty proved to be ephemeral. When the parliament collapsed because the major states could not agree on the achievement of its aims, the reformed confederation of states reintroduced press controls. However, the statement had been made. The whirlwind experiences of France in these three years demonstrate the complexities of the potential relationship between politics and newspapers, and the many permutations that are available across the scale that extends from total freedom of expression to full control of the press.

During the nineteenth century, liberal opinion genuinely believed that press freedom would lead to a flowering of political discussion on a variety of ideas. The journalist James Mill, writing in the *Edinburgh Review* in 1811, considered that, had a free press existed in France

The 1848 revolution in France, led by a newspaper

In February 1848, after two days of initial chaos, Émile de Girardin decided it was time for Louis Philippe to go. He rushed into the Tuileries and told the king so. Only after news of the abdication had passed around the barricaded city did the newspaper Le National intervene to call a meeting. The list of ministers for a provisional government which was drawn up in its offices, and in those of the newspaper La Réforme, contained the names of two chief editors of leading republican newspapers – clear evidence of the central role of journalism in politics. One of them, Armand Marrast, later brought in so many friends and colleagues to posts that a visiting Englishman was prompted to comment that France was 'absolutely governed by the National' (Phipps 1857: 2.17).

Both stamp duty and caution money were suspended, although it is worth noting that the latter was not officially abolished, staying intact from 1814 right through to 1881. Nevertheless, the initial euphoria for press communication had the air of a celebration: within two months 450 journals sprang up in Paris. The poorly typed brave rhetoric and the titles themselves, La Guillotine, Robespierre, Père Duchesne, Le Tocsin and Vieux Cordelier were clearly reminiscent of the Jacobin period. A variety of different colours were used for papers, including white with yellow stripes and green; appropriately, red ink on white paper was chosen for La Guillotine. Copies were sold on the streets by armies of hawkers wearing fancy headgear (Collins 1959: 102).

As universal suffrage had been introduced, newspapers purveyed politics to readers who had never previously had the vote, and such was the enthusiasm that journals were either given away or sold at ludicrously low prices. Many editorial staff worked for nothing and, as some papers lasted only a few weeks, collectors competed to obtain the shorter-lived publications while publishers made a profit on reprints.

However, the first flurry of freedom became tinged with fear, for conservative and propertied elements were disturbed by the 45 per cent rise in direct taxes, the violent attitudes of the more radical papers and the political agitation within the national workshops – a scheme for the unemployed. In June there were riots, and a small number of newspapers began to appear exploiting both conservative elements and working-class discontent because of poverty. They championed an outsider as future leader – Louis-Napoleon Bonaparte. In August some press offences were reintroduced and caution money was demanded once more: unfortunately not all editors had the clout of the popular anarchist Pierre Joseph Proudhon ('property is theft'), who managed to raise his caution money for Le Peuple by public subscription.

Hence elections took place amid an atmosphere of growing hostility between government and press. Papers all lined up behind one of the candidates, but the victor, Louis-Napoleon, did not have majority press support despite the fact that Bonapartists spent a lot of their limited funds on press propaganda and were strong believers in the power of the press. After his election, President Louis-Napoleon clamped down on the press. By 1850 the government had very few supporters in the press, especially in the provinces. So Louis-Napoleon appointed a loyal journalist – Granier de Cassagnac – to win over the newspaper Le Constitutionnel and then to prepare the ground for a coup d'état to extend the president's length of office.

After the coup, ministers were drawn into the Bonapartist cause and prefects were given arbitrary powers to prevent newspapers from criticizing the coup. Many papers were either suspended or closed down. In 1852 the coup was endorsed by a plebiscite and Louis-Napoleon declared himself emperor. A new press law was introduced which stayed in force for the sixteen years of his rule as Napoleon III: no journal or periodical could now be published without government permission.

National Assembly debates could only be published in official bulletins. Officials could punish journalists for activities that could not be described as offences under the law but which the government happened to dislike, and the emperor could suppress any journal without previous warning. Once again France had moved from complete press freedom to a complete lack of it – this time in an even shorter space of time than previously.

before 1789, the revolution would never have taken place. His son John Stuart Mill expanded on the need for public discourse in *On Liberty*. His essay remains one of the classic defences of freedom in the English language, along with John Milton's *Areopagitica* of 1644.

J. S. Mill was concerned that society should encourage a tolerant public opinion in order to ensure the survival of minority views. To achieve this he put the emphasis not on constitutional change but on political communication: the 'protection of the magistrate is not enough'; freedom of speech needs political rights to protect it, not merely legal ones. A liberal society must be behind a liberal government, for the biggest threat to liberty is likely to be an intolerant majority. The solution to this problem is debate, with genuinely tolerant political discourse. Ideas develop via argument and in the process there is an obligation to ensure that others, who may have an alternative view, are heard.

Mill also emphasized the obligation held by people with powerful voices and in powerful positions to exercise responsibility over their right to speak. There are two preconditions here: firstly, competing voices should be independent of each other; secondly, voices should reflect varying economic conditions and circumstances. As Seaton (1998) points out, in the context of the press, this should be interpreted as diversity of style, content and ownership, which modern society has not always guaranteed (see also Whedbee 1998). It was in the context of lack of media diversity that the most technically advanced, businesslike and influential newspaper in the world during this period – *The Times* of London – became the focus of government complaints that heralded a debate on press power and freedom.

Similar government concern over what was construed as the inordinate power of a small number of 'great press barons' existed in France during the period. Whereas the British government's attack on the independent power of *The Times* was a financial one, in France legislation directly controlled newspaper existence at source. Only a few of the political journals were allowed to continue, with the result that the few opposition newspapers that survived increased their circulation hugely and, with sales of 50,000 or more, could speak with authority.

The 'grands seigneurs' were *Le Siècle*, *La Presse*, *Le Constitutionnel* and *La Patrie*. By 1859 the circulation of *Le Siècle* was up to 50,000, so the following year the government decided to weaken all of them by creating 'petits seigneurs' (Paris, Archives Nationales: F18, 295), and, in the ensuing three years, thirty-one new papers were founded. Yet the government action backfired as the old journals kept their level of subscriptions

The British government's attack on the monopoly of 'The Thunderer'

By the mid-nineteenth century, *The Times* had more than proved itself as the main establishment voice, to the extent that some commentators have seen its history and that of the British press during the early years as synonymous: 'for almost forty years the history of the press in Britain is for all practical purposes the history of this one newspaper' (Williams 1969: 15). *The Times* had long been very profitable: in 1845 it made £30,000. In 1850, a period described as the 'age of *The Times*', it sold four times more copies than its main rivals put together, accounting for 80 per cent of circulation in Britain – a result of editorial policy with flair and of astute commercial management. The paper was in a 'position of authority never before or since equalled by any other newspaper' (Williams 1998: 51).

The paper originated truly independent daily newspaper journalism, spearheaded by editors Thomas Barnes then J. T. Delane. It was the latter who defined the paper's role as: 'to obtain the earliest and most correct intelligence of the events of the time and instantly, by disclosing them, to make them the common property of mankind.' This was accompanied by the potential to formulate public opinion, although the talent of Barnes was rather to discover and express it.[1] However, the 'mankind' to which Delane referred was an influential middle-class one, a factor involved in the British government's attack on the newspaper. *The Times* considered its duty was 'to teach, urge and thunder' its message to the public – hence its nickname 'The Thunderer'.

Serious concerns existed within governing circles over the concept of monopoly. *The Times* itself was careful to define the difference between the role of the newspaper and that of the statesman, arguing that the former should not have any alliances with political power if independence and freedom of expression were to be maintained. In an article examining the impact on public opinion published on 7 February 1852, Robert Lowe wrote that the press gives argument and discussion on topics to the public, but if the press was not free, no discussion would occur. If the newspaper does not 'represent the opinion of the country, we are nothing.' The prime minister, Lord Russell, saw the issue differently. To him, the newspaper was doing its job too well, and becoming excessively powerful. He wrote to Queen Victoria: 'the degree of information possessed by *The Times* with regard to the most secret affairs of State is mortifying, humiliating and incomprehensible.' In Britain's oligarchic, hierarchical society, where democratic party politics had not yet come to replace the self-interest of a governing minority, it was tempting for a politician to settle a score or go for retribution by talking to a newspaper such as *The Times*, whose pages would be read by this same circle of the great and the good. Thus *The Times* had the confidence to challenge statesmen while also having access to the secrets of state, which also prompted Queen Victoria to refer to 'the reckless exercise' of its 'anomalous power'.

The resulting shot at *The Times* was direct: under new legislation, newspapers that used the mail were required to pay a surcharge if they exceeded 4 ounces in weight, and only *The Times*, with its twelve to sixteen pages per day and its regular advertising supplements, fitted this category. So the newspaper was forced to choose between reducing its size or increasing its sales price; it opted for the latter, deliberately shunning a circulation war in order to maintain its character.

and the new ones recruited fresh readers; thus the opposition increased. Some provincial newspapers that were the only permitted opposition journals gained not only circulation but also nationwide recognition, ending up richer than the government newspapers – an impressive achievement as the circulation lead of government newspapers from 1861 onwards was created artificially through large amounts of subsidy to their supporters (ibid.: F18, 294).

On a day-to-day level, government interference in the workings of the press could be burdensome for those involved. French officials were constantly writing reports on the state of the press. Nevertheless, an industry did evolve, and by the mid-1820s more newspapers were sold in Paris than in London. Parisian figures are staggering: 235,000 dailies by 1858, 1 million by 1870 and 2 million by 1880 (Zeldin 1980: 2.192). The main nineteenth-century French newspapers were well-capitalized businesses with advertising, news and polemic. When the cheap mass press arrived after 1860, it was entertainment-based and sensational.

After Napoleon III stood down as a result of France's defeat in the Franco-Prussian War and the Third Republic was proclaimed on 4 September 1870, the struggle for press freedom was virtually over. Yet politics was still confused and not yet stabilized. The episode of the Paris Commune intervened,[2] and elections that returned conservative politicians interrupted the flow of the movement towards liberty. It took sixty-seven years for French newspapers to obtain the rights promised to them in 1814, but the eventual 1881 Act was a great example of liberal legislation.

Government–media relations

By now the relationship between politics and the media in Great Britain, America and continental Europe was changing. As the press became dependent for its profits upon commercial advertising rather than political subvention or a high cover price, this influenced the presentation of politics and the relationship of editors and proprietors to politicians and parties. By the 1860s in Britain parties had moved to the centre of the political stage. In the case of the new newspapers launched after the abolition of the Stamp Acts, the editors were party men. But although these papers usually supported one party or the other, they were ready to criticize these organizations and denounce them when their political consciences called for it, for they had a concept of journalistic independence learned from *The Times* which has remained with most of the Western press through to modern times. Indeed, this concept of political independence became evident on the continent of Europe with the establishment of the *Frankfurter Zeitung* in 1856, *Le Temps* in 1861 and Milan's *Corriere della Sera* in 1870. All these papers followed the model of serious independent journalism of information and opinion.

Although the general trend was clearly towards greater newspaper independence from government, this trend is always challenged during wartime when the relationship between the two comes under intense pressure. Hence the American Civil War and the Crimean War both highlighted important aspects of media history.

The Crimean War and the American Civil War: challenges and constraints

The Crimean War in 1853–6 was the first big international news story to highlight changing communication needs and usage. News-gathering required agents at strategic locations, although styles of coverage varied: many of the preoccupations of the reporter on the ground were to do with survival and with how to get news out from behind the lines. The most famous and effective reporter was W. H. Russell of *The Times*, who is considered to be the father of war correspondents. His revelations about the army's shoddy performance helped to bring down the Aberdeen government in Britain and influenced the creation of the post of secretary of state for war as well as the involvement of the pioneer nurses Florence Nightingale and Mary Seacole. Russell initiated a tradition of factual, eye-witness, truthful reporting that has remained to the present. His dispatches were so powerful that he fell foul of the censors, the first occasion in modern times that the constant and ongoing dilemma of the war correspondent was highlighted: how to remain loyal to the side in order to maintain access and trust, but not be influenced by military and government propaganda. Russell did not criticize the institution of war itself, but neither did others: as Philip Knightley has pointed out, war was regarded at this time as 'a big factor in the joy of living' (1989: 46).

Unsurprisingly, therefore, the American Civil War soon became the main story internationally as the public on both sides of the Atlantic craved news about the events. Not only was the conflict bloody and exciting, but there was also a moral issue, with black slavery, and a huge economic problem for one of Britain's greatest international industries – the Lancashire cotton trade – which was decimated on account of the 'cotton famine'. Within America, previously the Mexican War and now for four years (1861–5) the Civil War provided an impetus for more systematic news-gathering, which was facilitated by improved communications.

From the government's perspective, the American Civil War brought into focus the dilemma of how to influence opinion, given the now well-established tradition of a free press. In the past, presidents such as Andrew Jackson had openly influenced government printing contracts and the political press. But by the 1860s the number and range of newspapers had expanded, and therefore Abraham Lincoln did not patronize any one newspaper, for he wanted to reach the widest possible public in the North. Nevertheless, access to the mails was restricted in the case of papers that were too strongly against the federal policy; this presented a particular problem in New York, where many papers opposed Lincoln. Journals in the confederate area also faced pressure from both the government and the mob. So the hapless war reporter at the sharp end found himself under pressure from editors, armies and government censors alike. W. H. Russell experienced similar difficulties.

German and Japanese government control of the press:
similarities and differences

Germany and Japan were allies during the Second World War, but there are also comparisons that can be made from an earlier period. Despite the obvious contrast in culture and political background and Germany's very long newspaper heritage in contrast to Japan's short one, the two respective government approaches towards newspapers from the 1860s through to 1874–5 shared some common features. These were the years when both countries introduced a repressive law to curb press freedom. Both countries also experienced a change of regime beforehand, albeit under very different circumstances.

Mention should first be made of Bismarck's manipulation of the German press. Within individual states, the introduction of constitutions led gradually to the emergence of political parties and, simultaneously, the development of the newspaper industry. The relationship between the media and political change in nineteenth-century Germany is a direct one, especially during the 1860s, when the question of constitutional reform and the unification of Germany under Prussia came to a head. Yet the debate about it was conducted in a relatively low-circulation press which was read mainly by the politically active. These were the people that the conservative-minded Bismarck needed to influence, together with opinion in other European states, in order to oppose pro-Austrian sympathies.

In Japan, the creators of the pioneering press also catered for an elite readership and considered themselves to be part of the restricted circle of government. Newspapers emerged as part of the early political struggles linked to the country's evolution as a modern nation. Although Japan is a traditional society, it is a relative newcomer to newspaper communication, with developments in most Western countries pre-dating Japan by at least a century. The circumstances of early newspaper development present a celebration of difference that has modern-day relevance.

Japan's newspaper history has always been heavily influenced by its feudal tradition. Under the Tokugawa regime, which lasted until 1868, every aspect of life was regulated, including communication; yet the latter still flourished, but within a makeshift, idiosyncratic oral tradition of street ballads, joke books, manuscript books and nationwide lending libraries. Indeed, one scholar has argued that Japan has indigenous traditions of argumentation and debate which pre-date Western contact (Branham 1994). Nevertheless, the country's first sustained news publication, which lasted just two months in 1860, was a collection of articles from the foreign news columns of the Dutch *Javasche Courant*, published on the island of Java. The first real newspapers were English-language papers, starting in 1861 with the *Japan Herald*, previously called the *Nagasaki Shipping List and Advertiser*, produced by the Englishman A. W. Hansard. This was followed by a dozen more during the decade, mainly translations from leading English, Dutch and French newspapers, produced by the shogunate 'Office for Reviewing Barbarian Papers', which meant that the items were frequently out of date and resembled official announcements rather than written modern news, a concept which had not yet been established. In 1865 the Japanese-language *Kaigai Shimbun* was launched. In 1868, when the emperor seized power from the shogunate, the 'Meiji Restoration' (as the new regime was called) opened up the country to Westernization and modernization following more than two centuries of relative isolation.

From the beginning the Japanese press was a tool of a paternalistic establishment who wanted to use it as a civilizing influence and to increase national consciousness, for, as the French had found in 1789, newspapers were the only method by which the authorities could reach people apart from government institutions. Therefore officials gave newspapers financial and editorial support, which served to fuel the growth of the press. Measures included the encouragement of newspaper reading meetings and the government purchase of 225 copies, which could amount to up to a quarter of total circulation (Lee 1985: 13).

Undoubtedly the Meiji press was an establishment institution. Early press leaders were ambitious, politically orientated intellectuals with elitist values: at least three of them eventually became prime ministers, and they produced small, erudite papers with long columns of political discussion. As with *The Times*, editors believed in their role as educators: 'it was this role that so many of the early Meiji editors had in mind when they wrote editorials encouraging "civilized" people to eat meat and abstain from public nudity so as to "prevent ridicule by prudish aliens"' (Huffman 1997: 5, 65). Papers also stated that 'civilized' people drank beer and coffee, ate Western-style sweets and onions with beef, took new medicines and read Samuel Smiles and John Bunyan.

Very soon after the new regime took over, ten newspapers sprang up; these papers undertook a war of words to argue for their version of how to save the country from the recent usurpers of imperial authority. They talked, for the first time ever, of extending the circle of discussion to a wider public, although their conception of the 'people' was constrained by traditional Confucian elitism, and their loyalty to Japan still came before any thoughts of press freedom or even profit. The war of words was framed within traditional cultural values of the subordination of the individual to the group, the importance of the nation and the acceptance of authority, manifesting itself not so much in rebellion as in an expression of nineteenth-century nationalism.

In Germany, the war of words was different. The press was seen as a weapon with which the opposition could attack the government, even under the new conservative, autocratic system established in 1871. Constitutionally, and in terms of the relationship between the growth of democracy and the media, the problem in Germany was that the new 'unification' separated the government's running of the country from party politics and did not allow the people self-rule. Therefore, despite the election of the Reichstag by universal male suffrage, newspapers were not an integral and essential part of real democracy, which did not yet exist. History and constitutional framework differed considerably between Germany and Japan, but the end result in terms of the inability of the press freely to articulate all strands of opinion in society was the same.

In Japan, soon after the Restoration divisions began to appear within Meiji governing circles and, because they were under political control, the newspapers too were implicated and began to reflect the in-fighting. This dissent caused the authorities to suppress the temporary and limited experiment with a relatively free press. In 1871 a Newspaper Ordinance was introduced: it decreed that the contents of a newspaper should always be 'in the interest of governing the nation', a principle with which Bismarck would have sympathized, but one that was by now anathema to most European and American publishers. In the same year the country's first Japanese-language daily, the *Yokohama Mainichi*, was launched. According to Richard Halloran (1970: 160), 'The press in Japan started as an independent force but was quickly brought under control by the nation's rulers and has remained so ever since. It has not developed a tradition of independence but has been subject to domination by the authorities or to their indirect influence.'

The Meiji leaders never intended full liberty of the press as part of the people's enlightenment. Both editors and patrons received protection from the 'all-knowing, all-powerful government that was stimulating the growth of industry and production and pushing forward civilization and enlightenment' (Huffman 1997: 61). To that end, several hundred Western advisers were taken on board as part of a deliberate strategy that was to underwrite media history well into the twentieth century: 'To avoid ending up as one of their colonies, Japan chose to emulate Western powers, and became a colonial power itself. In its by now notorious eclectic way, and in a breathtaking tempo, Japan began to copy from the West concepts, institutions, and methods to a degree no other non-Western country had done before' (de Lange 1998: 33).

The attitude of Germany's 'Iron Chancellor' was that, because the press was politically dangerous due to its ability to influence the public, a totally free press was out of the question. Such liberty would only give a platform to opposition within the new state, which was an especially sensitive problem during the formative years. Although he held the press in disdain, Bismarck managed the news astutely and made the control of the press part of government policy. He achieved unification by the incorporation of some Austrian-owned German-speaking territories, so he battled against Austria within the confederation state. He also opposed France within Europe and fought internally against liberals within Prussia, so manipulation of the press became an essential strategy. In practice, he used the power of the state to restrict opposition newspapers via court proceedings, suspension or economic sanctions imposed by the Post Office, which managed the telegraph and news agencies (Ward 1989: 12).

From 1871 government finances put the main news agency under government control. From Bismarck's point of view it was an investment to ensure government management and exploitation of news in Germany and, by means of the external arrangements, favourable coverage throughout the world. In addition, Bismarck was not averse to using payments to journalists and editors to win support, funded by money confiscated from the king of Hanover.

In Japan, the ruling class soon realized the potential of the press. Henceforth the growth of newspapers everywhere was encouraged, since the government could use them to inform local populations of the measures it was taking and of the laws and policies that it was enacting. By 1873 Japan had a 'national' press in the sense that leading Tokyo and Yokohama papers were sent to every prefecture, where they influenced political debate. Within a two-year period after the introduction of a very repressive new press law in 1875, approximately 300 journalists were imprisoned for infringements (Lee 1985: 14).[3] The law specified that 'The Home Minister [might] prohibit the sale or distribution of newspapers or if necessary seize them when it is deemed that articles disturbing to the peace and order or injurious to morale' were featured.

In Germany, a press law, introduced in 1874, gave newspapers legal status and removed many of the previous controls that had existed in individual German states. However, the government could, and did, use an emergency clause to censor both the Catholic press during the so-called *Kulturkampf*, when Bismarck was battling over independent rights within the state, and the socialist press throughout his whole period in office. He also used the clause against other organizations which, from time to time, he considered to be a threat.

Nevertheless, as in the rest of the Western world, German political parties developed during this period and Bismarck recognized the role of the party press in mobilizing support in between elections. In Japan, perceptions of what constituted the 'people' gradually evolved. From about 1874 the press in Japan started to change from being 'official' to more popular, but it was still restricted to the well educated, even if the influence was wider. A changing class system and demographics – namely the emergence of an urban population who had migrated from the countryside – started to make an impression, prompting the argument that

> from the very first it was the non-governing groups whose voice the press pioneers wanted to amplify . . . by the seventh year of Meiji, most dailies were in the hands of vocal proponents of 'representative' government who lambasted the government for dallying in the creation of a popular assembly. And as the era progressed, it was newspaper essays that ignited and heralded nearly every popular movement and rebellion. (Huffman 1997: 7)

Consumers, media industrialization and imperialism ▓▓▓

Education, consumption and mass literacy

The Prussians had led the way in the eighteenth century by initiating public education. Britain's first Education Act did not arrive until 1870, although literacy was already increasing before that date; school attendance became compulsory in 1880. In France education became fully secularized in 1882. Contemporaries talked of the ideal of an informed public, a principle which was later challenged by the concept of the written word as just another business. In America, education developed as individual consumption and part of an economically self-interested market in entertainment. Industrialization had increased wealth and leisure, with numerous lending libraries and the cheaper publication of novels extending consumer democracy. Through its dependency on advertising, the press had an interest in supporting this process.

Meanwhile, in the forty years from 1850, the hours worked in many industries fell from sixty a week to fifty-four, and during the second half of the century wages increased by an estimated 84 per cent (Curran and Seaton 2003: 34). People therefore had more time and money to spend on leisure pursuits and reading, which was also boosted by the invention of the kerosene lamp. In Britain the first 'Bank Holiday Act' in 1871 established some compulsory national public holidays for all, whereas previously holidays had often consisted only of local religious or seasonal festivals.

In the long term, broader public access to education and mass literacy was required. The decision to make government responsible for mass literacy was already providing a huge market for the printed media. All of the countries featured here exceeded the general levels of literacy and urbanization that are considered to be necessary for newspaper take-off – 20 per cent and 10 per cent respectively (Huffman 1997: 60). Indeed, there was already a demand for reading matter for the less well educated. As early as 1858 the novelist William Wilkie Collins had written an anonymous article in *Household Words* entitled 'The Unknown Public'. In the 1860s America alone experienced the establishment of 5429 new journals, and by 1881 it was estimated that there were between 5 and 6 million penny publications, weeklies and monthly magazines in circulation in London. At the time this was called a 'remarkable phenomenon of modern times' (Briggs and Burke 2002: 198).

International comparisons tend to involve complex cultural and economic factors. For example, lack of literacy acted as a definite brake on the development of Italy's press. In 1875, when mass-circulation newspapers were being founded across Britain and the United States, two out of three Italians still could not read, and, with the exception of *Il Corriere della Serra*, Italian newspapers have never had a reputation for quality (Dunnett 1988: 157–8). It is said that Italians have an oral rather than a written tradition. In Japan the oral tradition for discussing news was also strong, yet, despite low levels of literacy during the nineteenth century, the Japanese newspaper industry eventually evolved into the largest in the world in terms of employment and circulation.

In Japan literacy was one of the main contributory factors towards the development of the modern newspaper, impinging on circulation and sales income, which was required if advertising revenue was to be used to finance the modernization of newspaper production techniques. Japan had a long way to go, even by the admissions of contemporaries: 'what could be done with this country of ours, when there were so many people as ignorant as this! . . . People themselves invited oppression', bemoaned Fuzukawa (Huffman 1997: 46–7). The fact was that most people not only could not read or write, they also had no awareness of politics outside of their village or of their role as citizens within the merging nation. The press could be one of the main tools for fighting this ignorance, as the government recognized by encouraging the creation of newspapers that would 'foster people's knowledge'. In 1871 compulsory education and a national school system were established.

Newspaper growth

Worldwide newspapers – national, regional and local – were thriving. In Britain it was within the provinces that newspaper growth was most rapid after abolition of the taxes by 1855; within fifteen years, seventy-eight new provincial dailies had been established, thirteen of which were evening papers. Indeed, the phenomenon of the evening paper was a noticeable trend at the time: by 1880 there were slightly more evening papers than morning ones within the British regional press. In Japan regions developed their own newspapers more slowly, as the Tokyo–Osaka press continued to dominate, to set the news agenda, to compete for readers in the areas of the locals, and to swallow up the latter.

Conversely, in the vast geographic expanse of the United States, urban centres were obliged to generate newspapers at an early stage in press development. As America was unconfined by stamp tax or social hierarchy, diversity flourished. For instance, one of the features of nineteenth-century newspaper development was the growth of an ethnic press as the size of urban black communities increased. In total, before the Civil War, there were 387 dailies in America and a press of ten times that number throughout the country. In 1864 the American News Company set up rapid delivery systems which meant that the metropolitan dailies could arrive in rural areas early enough to compete with local country dailies.

By the mid-nineteenth century, New York clearly enjoyed a greater variety of daily newspapers than London, where *The Times* still dominated. Outside of Washington and New York many famous names, such as the *Baltimore Sun*, the *Boston Herald* and the *Boston Times*, the *Chicago Tribune* and the *Chicago Times*, the *Detroit Free Press* and the

Philadelphia Public Ledger, all prospered. Subscription newspapers in a focused market for politics and business, paying up to $10 a week for six issues, also survived. In 1851 Henry Raymond's *New York Daily Times*, which achieved a circulation of 40,000 within six years, proved that success was dependent less on scandal and sensationalism than on identification of a new market – in this case one similar to that of *The Times* of London, the aspiring commercial classes who wanted objective facts to inform their lifestyle and business.

Up to about the late 1860s *The Times* led the world in pioneering international coverage and use of technology and as an articulate mouthpiece of British imperialism; this position was to change. Previously a copy of *The Times* would remain in circulation for some days, but now many more of the public bought their own copies of other newspapers for reading on the day of publication, and at a cheaper price. Furthermore, the reading was easier: definitive daily parliamentary coverage in *The Times* had been known to carry in excess of 33 columns – over 61,000 words – while an important court case often stretched to 8 columns or 15,000 words (Engel 1996: 24, 32, 34; Cranfield 1978). The challenge was led by the significantly named *Daily Telegraph*, followed by *The Standard* and the *Morning Star*; this represented a trend towards a major redistribution of readers as penny dailies now appeared. In addition, there were now a whole range of London evening papers: the *Pall Mall Gazette*, the *St James' Gazette* and *The Globe*. By 1861 the *Daily Telegraph*, with its emphasis on what it called the 'human note' rather than just politics and current affairs, was selling over twice the number of copies of *The Times*.

Production technology

The changes in the nature of newspaper production technology are a reflection of the wider developments in the economic organization of society: in nineteenth-century Japan, as in France during the revolutionary period, a newspaper could be launched very cheaply because the production techniques that were used were primitive, but in Meiji Japan circulations were tiny compared to those in Europe and America.

In contrast, after the abolition in Britain of the Stamp Acts, advances in print technology became essential to meet escalating demand. Newspapers experienced rapid industrialization during the second half of the nineteenth century. The introduction of the rotary press made possible larger print runs. Although the typewriter, the telegraph and the telephone all revolutionized newspaper offices and news-gathering after the 1860s, and the linotype machine transformed typesetting and improvements in page composition with the use of keyboards, nevertheless some other areas of production still advanced slowly. Composing remained unmechanized and therefore labour intensive until the late nineteenth century.

By 1860 newspapers were being produced from rolls of paper instead of single stamped sheets. This formed a significant part of the great economies of scale that helped to bring prices down to 1 penny, 1 cent or 1 sou. During this period first esparto grass then wood pulp replaced rags as the raw material of paper. Consequently by 1880 the price of paper in America had dropped to 5 cents per pound and newspaper production costs were helped tremendously, to such an extent that, in England, the halfpenny paper was just round the corner.

The invention of the phonograph: the roots of the music industry

Unlike the telegraph, which was an invention that offered a clear and obvious business application, the phonograph did not appear to lend itself to rapid commercial exploitation. According to Allen Koenigsberg (1990), all the component parts were already familiar to amateur scientists and mechanics, so there is no reason why this pioneer instrument for mechanical sound reproduction and playback could not have been introduced much earlier. However, the combination wasn't obvious: 'The idea of a contraption that could talk could be found in fanciful literature for centuries, but any attempt to build such a machine became impossibly complex. . . . No one contemplated going into the record business, and the word phonograph referred only to a system of stenography invented by Isaac Pitman years before' (ibid.).

Admittedly there had been precedents in experimentation dating back to 1806, when the British physician and naturalist Thomas Young had first registered the tiny vibrations of a tuning fork on a rotating drum covered with wax. Two Frenchmen also developed prototypes, but nobody thought about reproducing the recordings until 1877. In that year Edison produced a successful model, and patented it, but nobody knew what to do with it. Suggestions for talking dolls, clocks and paid exhibitions were all eclipsed by the public's new enthusiasm for the arrival of the telephone – until in 1880 Alexander Graham Bell used some prize money for inventing the telephone to finance research on improvements to recording and reproducing sound. Both he and Edison shared a fascination with sound because of their own intimacy with deafness, but rivalry over commercial exploitation of the phonograph came later. For the moment people continued to enjoy music in the opera house or music hall, with marching bands or by playing the ubiquitous piano at home. Nobody yet realized that the invention of the phonograph was the first step in the development of a recorded music industry.

The telegraph and other communications systems

Just as the pioneering steps towards the phonograph were not confined to one country, so too the gradual introduction of steamships and the linking of oceans with canals such as Panama and Suez acted as an encouragement to intercontinental relations. This was a concept that was supported by businessmen of the period. Thomas Cook, for instance, attended the opening of the Suez Canal, designed by the Frenchman Ferdinand de Lesseps, who in turn was inspired by the influential 'utopian' socialist philosopher Claude Henri Saint-Simon, believing that industry and commerce could transform history (Briggs and Burke 2002: 129). In the case of ships, sails co-existed with steam for some time, and 1864 was a peak year for the construction of sailing boats, but improvements in ocean steam transportation proved indispensable for the technology of intercontinental telegraph construction.

National and international markets were linked not only by steamships, railways and canals, but most importantly from the 1840s onwards by the first great electrical breakthrough. The telegraph was the first medium of communication to benefit from the potential of electricity. 'Of all our modern wonders the most wonderful', said Dickens of the telegraph, which was to begin the process of reshaping what we now call 'the media'. This new invention benefited all sorts of business by speeding up the transmission of communications information. Both public and private information were transmitted by the new telegraphs: they were used, for instance, by commodity markets such as cotton and corn for information on prices, by stock exchanges for the same purpose, and by governments for imperial and local administrations, as well as by newspapers for the transmission and collection of news.

At first the usage was national rather than international, for the engineering challenges of the marathon technical operations involved in large-scale underwater cable-laying were considerable. Hence news of the outbreak of the 1848 revolution in France reached Manchester by telegraph from the late editions of the London newspapers. Such information could not travel directly across the English Channel until the London–Paris telegraph was constructed in 1851. By 1854, 120 provincial newspapers within Britain, then at the height of their influence, were receiving columns of parliamentary news by telegraph, which assisted the growth of the local press by enabling it to gather news for itself, thereby reducing dependency on the London press. Although the famous war reporter W. H. Russell only ever sent one telegram during the entire course of the Crimean War (for his dispatches were intended to give not the latest news, but rather descriptive analysis of military shortcomings and strategy), by the time of the American Civil War, 15,000 miles of telegraph line were in use, with more than 1000 operators working the system. In 1857–8 an unsuccessful attempt had been made to cross the Atlantic by underwater telegraph cables. The project was realized in 1866, a year after Britain was first linked to India by cable, again after an initially unsuccessful attempt.

This was the first time in history that the transmission of information and messages was separated from the physical act of delivery, which

Rail: regulation in the public interest – a new concept

By the 1870s, railways had changed the maps of Britain and the United States with new towns that were created because of the train, such as Derby, Crewe and Swindon. The scale of railway construction linking communities and creating new ones became continental, yet no great change comes without opposition. In America, a massive protest movement called 'the Grange' was launched in the late 1860s and the 1870s by midwestern farmers – the 'Patrons of Husbandry'. Lawsuits led to a supreme court ruling in 1877 that state legislature had the authority to regulate businesses 'clothed with a public interest'. This new concept was to be significant for media history in the twentieth century.

in itself had been slow – it took between five and eight months to reach India from Britain. A reply could take two years, with monsoons in the Indian Ocean (Headrick 1981: 130). In 1868 the management of the telegraph system in Britain was transferred by the government of the Conservative prime minister Benjamin Disraeli from private companies to the Post Office. Three years earlier the International Telegraph Union had been established by twenty European states to set up international standards and to deal with technical problems, and it was later to take on a role of international management of the electromagnetic spectrum. Today, policy-makers worldwide argue more strongly than ever for international media regulation, a concept with formalized nineteenth-century origins.

By the 1870s, the telegraph had replaced the 'newsletter' as the preferred medium for hard news reporting, and European postal services were later either required by government or took the initiative to determine national policies on what became known as 'telecommunications': railways, telegraphs and telephones.

The American Post Office was staffed through patronage, and never assumed the same strategic authority. Nevertheless, in terms of the relationship between the growth of postal services and the distribution of information, a positive step was taken in America in 1852 when a new law allowed postage to be pre-paid on newspapers, at 1 cent within the state. This had a notable effect of helping newspaper distribution. Similarly in Japan, during the early development of newspapers fostered by the Meiji Restoration, the postal service was given special treatment, although this encouragement was soon withdrawn when newspapers became critical of the government. Although, worldwide, post offices were multiplying, stamps did not make their debut in America until the year that the New York to Chicago rail link was completed – 1853.

The birth of news agencies and the worldwide growth of Reuters

The influence of the telegraph on the growth of news agencies, which were established to bring information across frontiers, was ground breaking. Although American agencies remained internal until late in the century, with the advent of news agencies the world became a smaller place and, arguably, the seeds of globalization were sown. Indeed, much of the impact of nineteenth-century new technologies manifested itself by means of international agency networks marketing news as a commodity. The pioneer business that was first to organize news by collecting it and then selling it on was Havas in Paris. The company started in 1832 as a lithographic news service, collecting and translating items from the foreign press, then in 1835 it became known as Agence Havas and began to provide an extended service to govern-ment ministers, departmental prefects, bankers and newspapers. The next step was to sell news to subscribers in other countries.

One of the employees of Havas for a brief period was a man called Julius Reuter, a businessman who built on the pioneering work of others in telegraphy and journalism, but before he became famous he had to change his name, his religion and his country. Reuter had previously been an unsuccessful publisher of radical pamphlets in Paris (Read 1999: 9),[4] and after leaving Havas he set up his own news and feature subscription service in the city. However, when creditors seized his assets in 1849, he returned to Germany to start again. The timing was important: the Frankfurt parliament had encouraged greater freedom of the press, and this was the year that the telegraph line between Berlin and Aachen was opened. Reuter operated a three-way service for busi-nessmen and newspapers, to Berlin, Vienna and Paris, using telegraph lines, railways and postal services. His first newspaper subscribers were probably the *Kölnische Zeitung* and *L'Indépendance Belge* of Brussels. Others, including Havas, Rothschilds and the *Kölnische Zeitung*, used pigeons to bridge the gaps in the patchy telegraph communications network. Reuter did the same, but his genius was to see, as a Belgian journalist put it, 'that a telegraph wire could be a source of great wealth, provided one puts a journalist at either end.'

The growth of news agencies was a product of the new telegraphic technology. Although the same journalist had also stated 'I can think of no other fortune amassed so quickly and so cheaply' (Read 1999: 10), in fact a more detailed examination of the path to Reuter's success reveals that he had a rocky ride. Walter Siemens, the telegraph pioneer who supervised the construction of many German telegraph lines, later told the story of how, while building the line from Aachen to Verviers in Belgium in 1850, he met a Mr Reuter, 'owner of a pigeon post between Cologne and Brussels, whose lucrative business was being relentlessly destroyed by installation of the electric telegraph.' When Mrs Reuter complained about the destruction of their business, Siemens advised the pair to go to London and start a cable agency there (Storey 1951: 2). It was good advice: Paris, New York and Berlin had agencies, but there were none in London, despite the fact that the city was the financial centre of the world. In fact the need for information from around the world was enormous, but interested financiers and newspapers were too much in competition with each other to start their own service.

Reuter's London business opened in 1851, providing a service of market information and general news as well as expertise in operating the telegraph network, for there were as yet no agreed procedures internationally. Although Reuter had newspapers refuse to take his 'intelligence' at first, in 1853 he did manage to make a temporary breakthrough via the local press in Manchester, the world centre for the cotton trade, and also in its all-important port, Liverpool. *The Times*, with the biggest newspaper circulation in the world at the time, did not want to collaborate with its rivals, but Reuter gradually began to service them. He made three attempts to procure their business and in 1858 was finally successful, securing in addition the subscriptions of seven other London morning dailies – a foothold that was to challenge the predominance of 'The Thunderer'. *The Times* preferred its own journalism, but recognized the need for increased world coverage as Britain was the only world power at the time.

Reuter's aim in every country was to gain recognition for his agency as the preferred outlet for circulating official announcements to the foreign press; however, some contemporaries were quick to seize upon the significance of this new operation: 'Mr Reuter's office . . . the first centre of that organisation which has since gathered up into the hands of one man for all general and public purposes the scattered electric wires of the world' (Storey 1951: 2). The ergonomics involved in the collection of news at this time were considerable. During the Crimean War, for instance, the military telegraph across the Black Sea to Varna was used only for official accounts from the Anglo-French lines, but Havas and Reuter both had agents in St Petersburg, Vienna and Constantinople to collect news and rumours from the Russian side and for reports of diplomatic manoeuvres.

In the early days, Reuter's business was dogged by the technical failure of cables and also by initial mistrust within Britain: a Foreign Office

American agency cartels

The successful New York penny press spawned imitations in other American cities, prompting a change in the style of news presentation, aided by the telegraph and other means of communication. For instance, the speed of news source transmission facilitated the rationalization of foreign news-gathering. By establishing the New York Associated Press in 1848, the six main New York newspapers reached an agreement to obtain European news by means of a monopoly agreement with news agencies from the 'old continent' and one telegraphic transmission via a Boston agent, who received the information through steamships arriving at the Eastern seaboard. Then in 1855 the monopoly of this New York cartel was further reinforced by an agreement that secured an exclusive franchise for regional and local papers to use the Western Union Telegraph Company. The establishment of Associated Press as a confederation of local and regional news-gathering organizations with access to the new telegraph had meant that smaller subscribing papers could afford a greater range of reports than previously, but business deals such as the 1855 agreement deprived the special interest press of a source of foreign news.

official asked the editor of *The Times*, J. T. Delane, 'why do you still give credence to Mr. Reuter's telegrams? He is an imposter.' Karl Marx referred to him in a letter to Engels as 'this grammatically illiterate Jew Reuter' and accused Reuter's right-hand man, Sigmund Englander, of being a spy in the pay of both France and Russia, who was 'at present editing European world history in Reuter's name' (Read 1999: 21–9). The point about the name is important: Reuter insisted that all newspapers which printed his telegrams had to agree to carry his name at the end of each published message. This served the dual purpose of making him famous and providing transparency, so that the public knew who was responsible for the information in the message. Reuter was the first person to stand by the research that he was making public in news dispatches. Readers did not complain that identical Reuter telegrams appeared in a number of different newspapers, but they did care about the reliability of what this unknown Mr Reuter was reporting. There had been criticism of errors and falsehood in the news telegram business, so Reuter had to work hard to establish a reputation for accuracy, speed and impartial distribution to all equivalent subscribers.

During the American Civil War, Reuter was accused of being pro-South, although American historians have found no evidence of this. His agency was supplied by the Associated Press of New York, but much

The assassination of Lincoln as breaking transatlantic news in record time

Reuter's big success, for which he was accused of profiting from early knowledge, was the assassination in 1865 of Lincoln, when the president was tragically shot through the head by John Wilkes Booth in Ford's Theatre, Washington. Reuter's American agent performed the extraordinary feat of hiring a tug, catching up with the steamboat (as yet there were no transatlantic cables) as it was leaving New York harbour, and throwing aboard a canister containing his report. The agency had the news in London two hours before any other source. To speed up the final leg of the journey, agencies and newspapers would send smaller boats out to collect news canisters, which were dropped into the sea near the coast of Ireland, from where they were taken to the nearest telegraph station and cabled to London. At night, the canisters would be lit by phosphorus, and fished out of the often rough and dangerous water by Reuter's staff using poles. Staff would busily sort through the messages while the boat returned to the harbour. Thus four to five hours of breaking transatlantic news time could be gained (Read 1999: 40). But newspapers looking for an exclusive would also resort to the same practice, such was the competition for hot (or rather damp and cold!) American news. On this occasion Reuters distributed the item simultaneously to their business clients. Thus it was a client bank who broke the story, but many believed that it was a hoax started by stock market speculators – until it was confirmed by a dispatch received nearly two hours later. Reuter was eventually winning the game of trust, which led *Punch* magazine on 22 May 1869 to muse 'On the Eminent Telegraphist':

> England believes his telegrams
> Whether they please or fright her;
> Other electric sparks are right,
> But he is always right-er.

Fig. 3 *Britannia Sympathizes with Columbia*: on the death of Lincoln, 1865

of the output consisted of lengthy quotes from local American newspapers. Pro-southern bias was a general accusation against the English press; *The Standard* was raising circulation by 20,000 copies a day thanks to the passionately pro-southern 'Manhattan letters' of its editor, Captain Hamber. For some period Reuter's telegrams were boycotted by considerable sections of the European continental press. Conversely, the American press often had a pro-North bias, and the standard of war reporting was frequently low (Knightley 1989).

Global agency deals

Agencies viewed their business as a form of commodity trading: this was the power of news, enhanced by the large increase in the number of newspapers, the wider market for general news, and hence larger profits. Although news and press business formed a significant part of Reuters' activity, most of its revenue came from the supply of commercial intelligence and private telegrams. For 150 years the company has supplied one of the strongest international financial news services. The profits from this could be used to finance new ventures on the journalistic side, which provided the basis of Reuter's personal prestige and reputation and for which he had the ambitious strategy to make the agency global, although the word used at the time was 'worldwide'. This necessitated agreements with the two main agencies of continental Europe – Havas in France and Wolff in Germany.

The German agency was under pressure. After its establishment by Bernhard Wolff in 1849, it had rapidly expanded into Central Europe and obtained reciprocal agreements for the exchange of market prices with Havas and Reuter, which were extended to political news in 1859. Reuter had been attempting an expansion by concluding separate telegraph agreements with individual German states. The threat to Wolff's business increased when in 1865 Havas made an offer to buy him out, and this in turn stimulated the Prussian government to act. Wolff solicited their support by arguing that very soon the transmission of news by telegraph would be in foreign hands. The Continental Telegraph Company (CTC) was established to fund Wolff's business, and, as Havas and Reuter continued their hostile moves, a secret agreement between the CTC and the Prussian government gave Wolff's political dispatches precedence over private telegrams, offered loans to WTB (Wolffsches Telegraphenbureau) and in exchange took news direct from the company. This agreement effectively gave Wolff a monopoly in the German empire after 1871 and was followed by a number of 'agency treaties' between Havas, Reuter and WTB carving out 'spheres of interest' for the collection and transmission of world news outside the United States. According to this nineteenth-century version of a global trade agreement, Havas reported from the French empire and South America, Reuter had the exclusivity of the British empire and the right to develop in the Far East, while Wolff covered the territories of Central Europe, Scandinavia and Russia.

The cartel arrangement has been described by one scholar as a control of the news market by an 'oligopolistic and hierarchical structure', by which the triumvirate of Reuter, Havas and Wolff supplied world news to national news agencies in exchange for national news and the payment of a subscription fee by the national agencies, which in turn had the right to distribute cartel news exclusively within their territory, while the cartel had exclusive rights to the national agency news service (Boyd-Barrett and Rantanen 1998: 26–7). This arrangement remained the principal feature of the world's news market until the first third of the twentieth century.

Developments in the regulation of the telegraph industry demonstrate that new technologies in communications, as in other industries, destabilize long-established markets, forcing adjustments. This process, with its nineteenth-century roots, tends to concentrate power in the hands of a few dominant companies, a process which is influenced by both economic and social forces and has been called the 'scenario of centralization' – reoccurring at various points in twentieth-century media history and beyond (Du Boff 1984).

The effect of news agencies on newspaper style, content and jobs

News agencies inevitably became pre-selectors and pre-processors of news, and, because they supplied a range of different customers, the emphasis had to be on hard facts rather than comment, which gradually led the profession to distinguish between the two. Cost also dictated brevity: at $1 per word for the telegraph from Europe to America, editors were constantly urging conciseness! Coverage became so short that one observer commented, 'we see the world through a glass darkly' (Hardman 1909: 140–1). Now the business of news dictated a relentless requirement for newspapers to cover the events of the day, every day – which created an onus to meet deadlines with accuracy and reliability.

Press historians have assumed that there was a relationship between the changes in the news-gathering process, brought about by the telegraph and news agencies, and the trend towards 'objectivity', exemplified by the gradual use across the board of the 'inverted pyramid' style of writing, with clear, verifiable facts up-front. However, one researcher's detailed examination of both agency stories and non-agency local news in America reveals little difference over the years 1865 to 1874 in objectivity (Stensaas 1986–7). Whether or not objectivity can be directly attributed to the influence of news agencies, or whether it was a general trend merely sparked off by the advent of agencies, there is nevertheless little doubt that it was accompanied by uniformity and conformity – a feature which in the longer term influenced how society received political messages and transmitted information.

At the same time the increase in the volume of foreign coverage provided by telegraphic news agencies helped to encourage a cheap daily press, so to this extent they were also great 'levellers-up' of the standard in foreign correspondence. Client newspapers could now obtain access to an extensive system of reporting without having to spend on their own foreign staff. The telegraph enabled news to be delivered quickly to local audiences, so city-based papers offered more local stories. In the United States these were often portrayed in a sensationalist and personalized style.

This increase in local stories was one reason why, despite its status as the capital of news-gathering and news transmission, New York was unable to supply an American national daily press: distribution from the city could not always keep up with other more distant centres using the telegraph for local news (Ward 1989: 28). In Britain, too, the telegraph helped the development of regional papers by enabling them to gather local news and therefore reducing their dependency on the London press. However, rail communications in this smaller country meant that the London press could be dispatched to most parts and still arrive the same day, which allowed dailies from the capital to compete with the provincial press.

The gradual challenge to the pre-eminence of *The Times* in overseas coverage, and hence circulation by Reuters and the numerous newspapers supplied by it, hit that paper more than any other (Times 1947: 787; Catterall et al. 2000: 149–68). Although it still employed the largest number of in-house foreign correspondents, *The Times* found that explanation, distinctive commentary and perspective were the answer.

The telegraph and empire

Reuters had always seen itself as an empire company, and the telegraph formed the basis not only for the rise of the agency but also for a genuinely new form of imperialism. Britain either owned or had an interest in 80 per cent of all submarine cables. For the first time in history, colonial capitals such as London were able to communicate instantly with their outposts, with far-reaching results. In 1825 information by mail had taken four months to travel from Calcutta to Falmouth, but by 1906 this time had been reduced to thirty-five minutes. It meant not only that British newspapers could carry detailed reports faster to the public; in addition it facilitated the rapid implementation of an imperial grand strategy, both military and naval. It also opened up public administration more directly to the scrutiny of the government's Colonial and Foreign Office or, in the case of the 'Jewel in the crown', the India Office, for, as one historian has observed, the British empire was sustained as much by cheap pulp paper as by the gunboat (Innis 1972).

Of all the cable projects that the establishment of such a network entailed, the Indian cable constructed between 1858 and 1865 was the most spectacular, and it also brought in big profits: £100,000 a year at nineteenth-century rates! Similarly, in Canada, Sandford Fleming's work in developing technologies with the Pacific cable was important to institutional politics and imperial telecommunications as well as to late nineteenth-century Canadian nation-building and British empire-building. Equally, the dispatch by Reuters of the key corporate player Henry Collins to Australia in 1878, six years after the opening of that country's international telegraph link, represented the consolidation of its domination of the commercial communication business throughout the British empire (Thompson 1990; Livingston 1993). For Australia, the telegraph was more important than the railway (Briggs and Burke 2002: 134).

For the first time, 'world politics' became possible, and in this Britain led the way, a role in leadership that was facilitated by what was later to become known as the 'All Red Route' of telegraphic cable communications that connected up all British territories with London. The result of such ambitious investment was that there was a greater volume and variety of information upon empire than had ever existed before. The demand was there, backed by public belief in the civilizing internationalism of British colonialism, epitomized by the impact of Queen Victoria's diamond jubilee speech and by the fascination of a mass market of newspaper consumers in a world that was increasingly influenced by European imperialism and commercial domination.

Conclusions

Throughout most of the nineteenth century, contemporaries believed that the role of the press was to disseminate information that would encourage the political education of the public. This thinking underpinned the importance of the relationship between media, government and democracy and helps to explain the continued pre-eminence of the last theme.

In Europe and the United States, population increase and the emergence of new urban masses were to make political education all the more urgent, which in turn highlighted a major strand in parts I and II of this book: the relationship between commercialism, the exploitation of technology and the extension of the newspaper market.

Although it was the late nineteenth century that was to become the great era for technical innovation in media, earlier technical changes were enabling entrepreneurs to enter and exploit the newspaper market. Technology, the bedrock of the first Industrial Revolution, was now entering the domain of journalism history in a more significant fashion.

Press freedom remained an unresolved issue because the parent theme of popular sovereignty was still unresolved in most of the world. As constitutions and democracy continued to evolve, political newspapers remained essential and crucial to the functioning of civil society.

Education increased the demand for all sorts of printed information and entertainment, including political discourse. Thus, although events and technical developments were fast moving, everywhere contextual themes displayed elements of continuity.

Study questions

What are the links between consumers, communications and imperialism?

How did different countries respond to the issue of the extension of education and why was it so crucial to newspaper industry development?

Was freedom of expression finally resolved by 1881? If not, why not?

Is there any evidence during this period that the applications of technology are socially determined?

PART II

POPULARIZATION, INDUSTRIALIZATION AND THE TRIUMPH OF TECHNOLOGY, 1881–1918

> . . . to make instruments to make other instruments, to make still other instruments ad infinitum.

> Bertrand Russell on the effect of the Industrial Revolution

3 Commercialization, Consumerism and Technology

Commercialism is at present the greatest menace to the freedom of the press.
Hamilton Holt, 1909

The newspaper is a private enterprise. Its object is to make money for its owner.
Speaker to the Social Science Association, 1881

There is probably no industry in modern times in which the part played by labor is so large, and the share in the profits received by labor so small.
The Nation, 1873

Summary

The *objective* of this chapter is to explore how content creation and technology were used to develop business. The resultant connection between commerce and ideology revealed the tensions of continuity and change during this period. Change prevailed.

This was an era of technological inventiveness, exemplified by break-throughs in music reproduction, combined with commercial opportunity throughout industry, as the ubiquitous and ever-encroaching machine continued to replace hand labour. Increased urbanization and literacy created a new mass market for the media, pioneered by newspapers. For this reason, the changes in the newspaper industry are important. The main features of today's press – mass-circulation popular and quality newspapers with chain ownership – had emerged by the beginning of the new century. Hence newspapers paved the way for other later media organizations to become global commercial concerns.

In this respect branches of the media, such as music recording, mass-circulation newspapers serviced by international news agencies, and the early film industry (featured in the next chapter), were aided by forces of modernism, facilitating a scale and volume of operation that allowed for globalization. This trend was to accelerate in the twentieth century. Within modernity, different forms of globalization are influenced by the development of the nation-state, industrialization, urbanization, technology and democratization, as Giddens (1990) has pointed out. The convergence of these influences is dealt with in this chapter and the next.

There were three types of changes up to the end of the First World War: in the economic structure of the industry, in lay-out, design and typography, and in content, which still presented a lot of scope for pioneering change, such as stories which emphasized the human interest element. The drive for mass circulation necessitated investment in technology, which in turn led to a greater dependence on advertising as a source of income. This latter industry developed from a small enterprise, supplying persuasive announcements to a few marginal users, into a major player within capitalist industry and its new forms of business organization.

Introduction

The late nineteenth century was a period of industrial expansion for America and much of continental Europe. Britain had already experienced the phenomenon much earlier, and Japan was to continue the process at a faster rate in the twentieth century. In the Western world, the twentieth century's age of consumption had clearly arrived in the form of popular fashions promoted by department stores and a wealth of other new consumer goods, from the bicycle through to the typewriter and gramophone records that were already capable of hitting a million in sales.

During the last decade of the nineteenth century and the first ten years of the twentieth, the United States transformed itself into primarily an urban society. After the Civil War its agricultural production really took off, it became the largest oil producer in the world and its energy consumption came to equal that of Britain, Germany, France, Russia and Austria-Hungary combined, although as an industrial power it still lagged behind trading partners such as Britain, France and Germany, to whom in the early twentieth century it owed hundreds of millions of dollars (Kennedy 1987: 242, 244). According to government figures, the population increased from almost 40 million in 1870 to 76 million by 1900. Industry moved into the city centres and the middle classes moved out to suburbs; their place was taken by migrants from the countryside and new immigrants, frequently from Eastern and Southern Europe. These people, often with very little English, were to form the new mass market for newspapers and, later, cinema. Between 1890 and 1914, 18 million immigrants moved to the United States.

Newspapers during this period paved the way for what Kellner has described as 'one of the main trends of contemporary capitalist societies . . . the synthesis of advertising, culture, information, politics and manipulation' (1989: 132). Hence, from the circumstances that created the new newspaper forms of this period, the roots of late twentieth-century changes are discernible: evidence of continuity. In general, technical change has always tended to reach newspapers later than other industries, so the twentieth century added only speed and quantity to their production process – until the 1970s.

During the earlier period dealt with here, urbanization and increased literacy continued to produce a growth in demand for newspapers. Speed of process and precise timing varies from country to country. In Germany, for instance, the epoch after unification in 1870 witnessed a mushrooming of industry and urbanization which was accompanied by a similarly huge increase in the size of the industry. In Britain the growing influence of commercialism and the changing nature of the press reflected political needs, together with the economic and social changes in society.

The transformations in editorial practice of the late nineteenth century were a product of the drive to reach new audiences, which itself arose not just from the emergence of working-class markets, but also from the imperative for mass circulation that investment in technology necessitated. This in turn led to an increasing dependence on revenue from advertising as part of a bigger innovation in systems of business organization; these by definition required a continuous process of further industrial growth and organizational adaptation. The rise in the importance of advertising, nurtured by the press and chain ownership, created a climate where powerful proprietors could consolidate their influence with economies of scale and further concentration of owner-ship. Such was the capitalistic cycle that now prevailed: journalism had become a product of the new corporatism, which sought less to supply the market than to organize it into a large-scale and increasingly integrated economy.

Some contemporaries were sceptical: 'You left journalism a profes-sion, we have made it a branch of commerce', an employee of Lord Northcliffe, Kennedy Jones, told John Morley, the veteran editor of London's influential *Pall Mall Gazette* (Briggs and Burke 2002: 207). Yet many saw this as a golden age for communication, from which 'New Journalism' was born. This view is evidenced in terms of quantity by the increase in all forms of newspapers in America: from 9810 titles in 1880, to 16,948 in 1890, to 21,272 in 1900 (Holt 1909: 6–7).

As Britain had discovered from the second half of the eighteenth century onwards, there was a human cost to mechanization. In general, the old institutions of classical liberalism were being challenged by corporate reorganization to find new solutions to the social effects of production and distribution. For the press, ever-rising start-up costs, increased rationalization and cost-cutting meant that news workers did not labour under ideal conditions. Meanwhile a twentieth-century irony emerged: newspaper and periodical readership expanded and public opinion became increasingly important, yet, after a period of expansion, the number and variety of newspapers began to contract in the face of the rising concentration of ownership.

The capitalist model of newspaper development that America was spearheading formed part of this economic growth: the number of daily newspapers almost quadrupled during the same period, but the trends that emerged were not exclusively American – they were experi-enced on both sides of the Atlantic. All over the world, new forms of printed publications were created, and by about 1890 numerous tech-nological changes both within and outside the newspaper industry had influenced the content, production, distribution and marketing of the product. The opportunity to expand both the reach and the appeal of existing media was accompanied by the biggest milestone in the consolidation of the capitalist development of the Western media: the change to shareholding as a form of ownership. Investment enabled mechanization, which also led to new structures of work within production processes. In short, this whole process meant changes in the content, business practices and work routines of newspapers, dealt with in more detail later in this chapter.

Illustration, photography and new print technology

By the end of the century photography was thriving and its usage had actually become a branch of the journalism industry. This development was facilitated by a number of technical breakthroughs. Rotogravure illustration – etching on the cylinder – for instance, started in Britain in 1895, but was featured regularly in the American press only after the Great War (1914–18). A key year was 1838, when Louis Daguerre displayed the first precise photographic images, which he called daguerreotypes, and William Henry Fox Talbot, using a different process with silver nitrate, made 'negatives' on paper. An improved method for etching on metal plates was introduced in France in 1859 by Firmin Gillot. In 1872 his son invented zincography, which combined etching with photography so that the picture could be sized up or down as required, but the technique was limited to black and white. *The Times* had bravely used it for weather maps. In 1880 Britain's *Daily Graphic* introduced a way of making intermediate tones directly from a photographic plate which eliminated the process of drawing. This was the real breakthrough. The revolutionary system of half-tones, which used dots of differing sizes to represent lighter and darker areas, was perfected by various other photographers, including the American Frederick Ives.

Photography's ability to change perceptions as part of the process of the creation of modernity has been much debated among cultural theorists. Photos allowed for the simultaneous placement on a page of contrasting images unconnected in time and space, in order to grab attention. This, along with the presentation of news 'items' which appeared to be systematically decontextualized, allowed the increasingly passive reader to forget whatever had preceded the current 'commodity' or 'fad', losing connections with the past. Girardin first referred to the ability of the press to conjure up oblivion (Morienval 1934: 86; Postman 1985: 66), a process to which the telegraph, railways, cinema, radio and television all contributed.

A late nineteenth-century wave of industrialization produced technical changes which enabled news stories to be produced more quickly with easier production in bigger volume. Even in Japan, where the industry had a lot of catching up to do, the first Marinoni press was imported in 1890, and this made mass production possible. By 1910, there were 250 thriving newspapers. Generally, the newspaper product also became more attractive as print production achieved a number of improvements, including better typefaces, the linotype machine, photoengraving and colour printing. Within the world of magazines, the adoption of colour plates became the key to success; the three-penny journal *Weldon's Ladies Journal* in Britain, for instance, used them for fashion and survived until 1963. When the American *New York World* introduced colour presses, Sunday comics soon became a feature of the paper.

Faster presses could run off 48,000 twelve-page papers in an hour, using stereotyped plates and webs which allowed the breaking of column rules for illustrations, headlines and advertisements. (This had not been possible with type revolving presses.) In fact by the turn of the century, when electricity had replaced steam everywhere for energy, American newspapers were able to use electrotyping and to produce editions of well over a hundred pages. Unit-type presses were introduced whereby a number of machines with duplicate stereotypes were linked for large circulations, while smaller local newspapers used just one or two units – an innovation that was particularly efficacious for owners with a chain of titles to produce.

Illustrators and photographers became much in demand for sports news. Some newspapers, such as Britain's Sunday paper *The Observer*, developed as pioneers of pictorial journalism, although the latter also built its early reputation on gratuitous crime reports.

Over the years, improved machinery and a diversifying market of readers have led to several 'New Journalisms'. The first 'New Journalism' was characterized by visual as well as content and business developments.

New Journalism across continents: individuals and institutions

The original 'New Journalism' laid the roots of the twentieth century's popular newspapers with the use of new technologies to produce more eye-catching lay-outs, complemented by a writing style that was popular and emotive. In Britain the visual change extended to front pages, where in some papers the old style of densely crammed advertisements gave way to an attractive design of content. The main development in content at this time was a move from editorial towards more news, in an attempt to offer access to more and different types of information. Therefore definitions of what constituted news and how it could be presented were also undergoing a fundamental shift. 'New Journalism' tended to have a levelling effect, representing a further move towards mass appeal, exemplified by entertainment and sensationalism and also by high profile campaigns and investigations. As W. T. Stead said, 'Society . . . outwardly, indeed, appears white and glistening, but within is full of dead men's bones and rottenness.' However, there are episodes in the development of New Journalism in Britain, and within its extension 'Yellow Journalism' in the United States, that illustrate the power both of the media and of the individual journalist, raising ethical questions about modus operandi that are still crucial today.

W. T. Stead: the father of modern journalism at its best and worst

W. T. Stead was the nineteenth century's most sensational journalist. When he was appointed editor of the provincial *Northern Echo* at the age of twenty-two, he wrote, 'what a glorious opportunity for attacking the devil', which he proceeded to do with a quasi-messianic fervour, for, as he later explained, 'I felt the sacredness of the power in my hands, to be used on behalf of the poor, the outcast and the oppressed.' Stead's emotive, popular journalism was at its most successful on the social front. His graphic stories of slum squalor, based on a nonconformist pamphlet, 'The Bitter Outcry of Outcast London', led to a royal commission recommendation in Britain that the government should clear the slums and encourage low-cost housing in their place. Yet Stead disapproved of giving the vote to the poor, for fear of their ignorance.

In 1883 he was appointed editor of the genteel but dull evening newspaper the *Pall Mall Gazette* and proceeded to transform it into a controversial, visually arresting political journal that became required reading within Victorian society. Greatly influenced by practices in America, Stead introduced the cross-head, which made long stories accessible to readers who were not used to scrutinizing them in full. His use of heavy black headlines, illustrations, the gossip column and the personal interview were also new to the English press. Most of the examples of the last were written by Stead himself from his phenomenally accurate memory after meeting interviewees (Lloyd 1999: 50).

Contemporaries were divided over Stead. While one prime minister – Lord Grey – considered that the journalist was 'a sincere patriot, with a fervent desire to make things better and a keen sense, too, of the value of the Empire', another – Gladstone – considered that 'That man has done more harm to journalism than any other individual ever known.' The 'G. O. M.' ('grand old man' of British politics) had probably been thinking of the episode in the Sudan, when, as he

hesitated to defend the country against the Mahdi and Islamic nationalists, Stead agitated for the defence of Western religion by urging the dispatch of a Christian general to Khartoum. This popular clamour resulted in the death of General Gordon and the defeat of the Gladstone administration.

However, another of Stead's campaigns had helped the Liberal Party leader: the prime minister had been able to relaunch his political career on the basis of the public indignation that Stead had encouraged over the massacre of 12,000 Bulgarians by the Turks during the rebellion of 1876. Equally Stead's 'Truth about the Navy' campaign was unscrupulous and largely an invention: with the help of a young navy officer, he argued that British naval superiority (close to the hearts of most Victorians) was threatened by underfunding. The campaign resulted in a £3.5 million improvement programme that the country could ill afford.

But it was Stead's exposure of white female slavery, entitled the 'Maiden Tribute to Modern Babylon', that provoked the most criticism – in essence that he was putting attention to circulation before his desire to improve society. The taboo social issue of child prostitution was drawn to his attention by the women's rights advocate Josephine Butler and by the Salvation Army. Stead's revelations in the *Pall Mall Gazette* were reviled and condemned, although it was clearly true that children could be purchased for a few pounds for the sex trade in London or exported like cattle to Europe. In his campaign he described all the details, including the brothels where the upper classes could 'enjoy to the full the exclusive luxury of revelling in the cries of an immature child' (Stead 2003).

Stead was outraged that the government appeared to be turning a blind eye in order to protect the trade's wealthy clientele, so he set about proving how easy it was by doing it himself. However, he became the victim of his own exposé, for, by faking the purchase and 'ruin' of a girl, he was breaking the law.

Crowds besieged the offices of the *Pall Mall Gazette*, some in outrage at the damage done to the upper classes, others clamouring for a copy of the issue, which was selling at premium second-hand prices.

Although Stead believed in socially responsible, campaigning investigations, the sensational way these were presented, with bold subheadings such as 'Violation of Virgins' and 'How Girls are Bought and Ruined', backed up by extensive personal testimonials and use of on-the-scene 'live' interviews, incurred the wrath of advertisers. The *Pall Mall Gazette* lost revenue but increased circulation.

George Bernard Shaw telegraphed Stead and sarcastically offered to act as a paper boy by selling a thousand copies at street corners (Hattersley 2003). Stead became a victim of the very offence that he sought to expose: he was arrested and sentenced to three months in jail. Despite the outcry over the 'Maiden Tribute', or perhaps because of it, Stead had successfully exposed corruption. The age of consent was raised from thirteen to sixteen, and the first step was taken to protect children from sexual exploitation. But faking had raised ethical questions about the integrity of journalistic method.

Although the contemporary novelist Matthew Arnold believed in journalism's power to change society, nevertheless he complained to a colleague: 'Under your friend Stead, the *Pall Mall Gazette* . . . is fast ceasing to be literature' (Stead 2003). He considered the new approach was 'featherbrained' and dubbed it 'New Journalism'. In an 1887 essay entitled 'Up to Easter', he described features that could well be applied to today's tabloid style: 'It throws out assertions at a venture because it wishes them to be true; does not correct either them or itself, if they are false; and to get at the state of things as they truly are seems to feel no concern whatever.' The huge moral responsibility of the press within the public sphere was further illustrated when the careers of two politicians, the Irish Home Rule movement leader Charles Stewart Parnell and the member of parliament Charles Wentworth Dilke, were ruined by the exposure of their divorce cases, which were viewed by contemporaries as sexual irregularities. For these too, Stead, along with other journalists, must carry some blame.

Stead outlined his modus operandi in an 1886 essay in the *Contemporary Review* entitled 'The Future of Journalism'. He argued that 'the first duty of every true man, if he believes public opinion is mistaken, is to change it.' But if you want to change public opinion, you must first find out what it is. Finding out what the man on the street is thinking directed Stead's views on how a newspaper should be run: he focused on the importance of the journalist as an individual ('impersonal journalism is effete') rather than merely arguing for changes in journalism as an institution. He emphasized that principles such as independence, the right to question and criticize, the exposure of injustice and the articulation of the voice of the voiceless all have a place within the media. However, he also recognized that an established system would be needed for the principles of New Journalism to be fully implemented.

Later, Stead took another outspoken stand when he bitterly opposed the Boer War, and he was nominated for the first Nobel Peace Prize in

1901, but his career never fully recovered from the controversy of the 'Maiden Tribute to Modern Babylon'. He died dramatically on the *Titanic* in 1912. As A. G. Gardiner said, 'There has never been in English journalism a more versatile or bewildering figure, or one that challenged the judgement of his fellows in so many ways. . . . He did not belong to our narrow ways and our timid routines. The wide waters of the Atlantic are a fitting grave for his bones' (Stead 2003).

Although the newspapers of the New Journalism were trying to widen their market to a new readership by extending the range and types of information that could appeal, they were held responsible for the debasement of cultural standards because of an emphasis on entertainment instead of instruction. Stead had demonstrated a finely tuned balance between a campaigning morality and the needs of circulation, but others who were influenced by him tipped the scales in favour of the latter.

Newspapers could now target a whole new generation of potential readers who were not greatly educated but were nevertheless curious for information. The question was not whether they should be catered for, but how. It was the evening papers in Britain which pushed the morning press to introduce content suitable for the masses. The Jack the Ripper serial murder of women case, sometimes described as Britain's first real tabloid crime story, exemplified the new trends. The editor of the *Daily Star*, the radical journalist T. P. O'Connor, was influenced by Stead, as the headline on 1 October 1888 illustrated: 'THE MURDER MANIAC SACRIFICES MORE WOMEN TO HIS THIRST FOR BLOOD'. The style of coverage is closer to that of the modern tabloid than that of the Robinson–Jewett case in Bennett's *New York Herald* of 1836.

Other modern-day comparisons can also be made: 110 years later, during the Clinton–Lewinsky scandal, the press struggled to publish a monumental story without pushing the envelope of 'tasteful reporting' too far. The Victorian press was obliged to adopt sanitary euphemisms for the acts committed by the Ripper, while CNN and the American press had the same sort of difficulty in directly reporting the accusations in the Clinton–Lewinsky case.

The distinguishing aspects of American New Journalism were the lively style of writing and the energetic mission that journalists were given to be constantly out and about, scouring the city for news, with their own 'beats' and 'exclusives' to supplement material gathered by the cooperative news agencies. The time was ripe for such an approach. Almost half the American population were now town dwellers, and city life was a fertile hunting ground for the poetry of life's vicissitudes, as Dickens, Hogarth and others had already discovered. Two-thirds of the newspapers started during this period were evening editions, capitalizing on the telegraph, time-zone changes and new city lifestyles. As urban energy gained pace rapidly, editors of the great city newspapers competed to be the first to seek, gather and present stories. For Joseph Pulitzer, editor of the *New York World*, as with Stead, campaigning

Pulitzer, 'one of the creators of America's consumer culture'

A Hungarian immigrant who had entered journalism via the German ethnic press, Pulitzer had campaigned for street repairs, cleaning and against financial corruption in St Louis. He continued the last when he took over the *New York World*, calling for controls against the big monopolies and corruption, and for the defence of income tax, death duties and the right to unionize. Pulitzer recognized that ordinary folk were beginning to emerge as a mass market (Steele 1990). The *New York World* was to be 'not only large but truly democratic – dedicated to the cause of the people rather than to that of the purse potentates – devoted more to the news of the New World than that of the Old World – that will expose all fraud and sham, fight all public evils and abuses – that will battle for the people with earnest sincerity.' In 1885 he launched a 'people's cause' in line with this statement of principle: a campaign to raise money in nickels and dimes from the readers for a pedestal for the Statue of Liberty, which had been donated by the people of France. Very soon the combined circulation of his daily and Sunday editions was greater than that of any two other New York papers.

Pulitzer's definition of news as that which is 'apt to be talked about' – in other words,

gossip – was consistent with his pioneering of the 'stunt' as a circulation-building piece of news created by the newspaper itself. Regular stunts and crusades, such as the battles waged against the Standard Oil Trust and other monopolies, ensured that the *New York World* was continually in the public eye, but Pulitzer's style caused much offence to both politicians and 'responsible' journalists.

Other newspapers observed the cocktail of sensationalism and idealism, but the emphasis on crime and scandal was emulated the most. As for the readers, once they were hooked, they stayed with their paper as consumers and front-row spectators of a rich tapestry of emotions, rather than as active citizens. To this end, Pulitzer's greatest journalistic skill was the banner headline designed to attract the attention of street passers-by, such as 'A Brother on the War Path – He Attacks his Sister's Dentist Then Kills Him'. News was presented as a prodigious series of earth-shattering and disconnected autonomous dramas, with each staccato episode generating a kind of hypertension. Pulitzer also endowed the Columbia School of Journalism with $2 million and wrote about his views on the training of the profession (Pulitzer 1904).

journalism was essential, for it provided a means of creating solidarity with the paper's readers. Later on in Japan, Kuroiwa viewed the challenge in the same way, influenced by these earlier pioneers.

The longer term trend that was emerging was important: the 'intellectual quest of journalism', as Anthony Smith calls it (1979: 159), was changing from the great liberal causes such as press freedom, free trade and the extension of the vote to crusades and stunts. Probably the best-known stunt is 'Dr Livingstone, I presume?' – the words of H. M. Stanley of the *New York Herald*, spoken on his trip to Africa in 1871–2 to find the missing Dr Livingstone; another famous one was the challenge of the journalist Nelly Bly to the fictional record of Phileas Fogg in travelling around the world. On 1 January 1900, Pulitzer invited Northcliffe to edit the *New York World* for one day. The British press baron produced a twelve-page, four-column tabloid half the size of the regular paper, with no story of more than 250 words. 'I ask America for an impartial verdict for this twentieth-century newspaper', he appealed, and the response

Japan's campaigning journalism after 1895

Up to 1920, two-thirds of the Japanese population still lived in the countryside and smaller communities, but early twentieth-century urban dwellers had the kind of problems that made them interested in the news of their world – presented via simple, lively reading materials. There were 150 industrial disputes in the decade after 1895, despite the fact that labour was still not officially organized. By the turn of the century, the focus on political discussion had been overtaken by a news orientation. Front pages were frequently filled with natural disasters and the vagaries of Japanese weather, but politics could still find prominence if it involved scandal, assassination, corruption or intrigue!

The top circulation in Tokyo went to *Yoruzo*, which was considered the most representative daily of the era, for its simple four-page format appealed to all classes, as did its cheap price and attacks on the establishment. The editor Kuroiwa bravely took on anybody who stood in the way of social justice at a time when urban growth and the beginnings of modernization were creating a class division in Japan. Like Pulitzer, Kuroiwa became more reflective on his profession and respectable when he had achieved success, writing a seven-part series of articles which attacked the unrestrained

capitalism of contemporary newspaper owners. He also initiated literary prizes, published his own translations of European novels and introduced a popular English-language column. But his pioneering of campaign journalism on behalf of the poor and powerless is probably his biggest contribution in setting the pace for the country's era of 'campaign journalism' after the Sino-Japanese War.

The exposure of facts on corruption and seaminess among the rich and powerful was replacing editorial as a vehicle for persuasion. Sustained treatments of the rising labour movement, of poverty among the labouring classes, of pollution disasters, even journalistic diatribes against alcohol abuse and the sex lives of famous men, were all issues that reflected the preoccupations of early twentieth-century Japanese society in the process of modernization but still lacking the constitutional means to make itself felt. Many social taboos were discussed openly for the first time, but, as with Stead's approach in Britain, the sensational method of presentation led critics to question whether it was circulation or journalistic commitment that came first. However, during this period, radical protest against bureaucratic abuses and injustice in Japan extended beyond Kuroiwa.

was a sell-out, with reprints needed – a clever stunt, according to William Randolph Hearst.

During the 1890s in Britain a number of halfpenny newspapers were launched, prompted by the *Daily Mail*. Obviously, a halfpenny purchase price required a huge volume of sales, the purpose of which was to attract advertising revenue, as financial staying power was needed if profits were to be realized. The paper's success was also due in no small part to first-class distribution using newspaper trains and careful organization by the owner, Lord Northcliffe (previously Alfred Harmsworth), making it what his most recent biographer, J. Lee Thompson, has called Britain's 'first truly national newspaper'.

The impression is sometimes wrongly given that Northcliffe invented mass circulation in Britain. In fact, the *News of the World* and *Reynold's News* both achieved very high circulations among working-class readers long before mass circulation became the norm. The impression is also

Britain's *Daily Mail*

Although the *Daily Mail* was the product of a series of journalistic developments dating back to Stead (Smith 1979: 157), the paper's lay-out was unadventurous, except for coverage of emotional events such as the Boer War and the death of Queen Victoria, when it hyped national pride. Content was short and simple and carefully directed towards its lower-middle-class market, for whom no one had yet provided an appealing, cheap daily. A pamphlet of Northcliffe's claimed that, before the *Daily Mail*, 'journalism was only a few aspects of life. What we did was to extend its purview to life as a whole', although it is worth remembering that all newspaper 'realities' are a construct influenced by news values and rules of presentation (Catterall et al. 2000: 10, 12). The paper was the first British daily to become a public company, yet it was also the only national daily to remain in the same family ownership for the entire twentieth century.[1]

wrongly given sometimes that mass circulation is totally dependent on the strength of advertising: such a connection is not always automatic. In France some of the press hit a million very early, with four 'grands journaux' sharing a combined circulation of 4.5 million before the First World War, although modern French newspapers were traditionally less reliant on advertising than those in other countries.

In 1909 the *News of the World* in Britain sold 1.5 million copies. Like *Reynold's News* and *Lloyd's Weekly News*, it was originally a radical publication. In contrast, the newspapers of Bennett, Pulitzer, Northcliffe and Hearst developed a tendency towards more traditionally conservative appeals to nationalistic chauvinism to manipulate the minds and feelings of the masses (see chapter 4). It was becoming clear that this powerful tactic was not confined to advertising.

Advertising and its relationship to the growth of newspapers

By the early twentieth century the growth of the press had become so phenomenal – in America, for instance, the number of English-language dailies had grown from around 850 in 1880 to 1970 in 1900 and the number of weekly papers had trebled – that newspaper production was now a major industry in its own right. Generally, this new industry contributed to the economy and helped to shape other new forms of social and economic activity that depended on it for survival, such as advertising, which also emerged as a modern industry and was sustained in the process by a cheap, popular press.

The combination of the timing of the Jack the Ripper case with the installation of the first American Hoe rotary printing press in Britain enabled *Lloyd's Weekly News* in 1896 to become the first newspaper in the world to sell a million copies. Aided and abetted by newspapers and periodicals, advertising grew from a limited strategy for transmitting local, specific information and attention to an institutionalized system of commercial information and persuasion. This continuing thread of

Table 3.1 *Estimated/actual newspaper start-up costs*

	Britain (£ sterling)	America ($)
1840–1	20,000	1000–10,000
1846–50	100,000	100,000
1894–6	500,000	1,000,000

Sources: Hardt and Brennen 1995; Briggs and Burke 2002; Barker 2000

change needs to be connected to society, the economy and also the context of changing organizations and intentions, both nationally and internationally (Williams 1980: 170).

With the advance of technology, newspapers were becoming more complex businesses, consequently increased capitalization costs required a heavy financial commitment. As start-up costs also rocketed, commercial concerns became more important in the launching of a newspaper. Costs were higher in Britain earlier in the century, probably because of its advanced lead generally in industrialization and also because of the dominance of the national press. Elsewhere in Europe a decentralized press kept entry costs lower, but by the end of the century they were equally high on both sides of the Atlantic. For instance, a London paper such as Charles Dickens's *Daily News* had needed £100,000 for its launch in 1846, but the *Daily Mail* demanded £500,000 in start-up costs by 1896 (see table 3.1).

In 1894 the American editor Charles Dana estimated that a daily would need $1 million to start up. He resisted buying a linotype and wished that newspapers did not need advertising (Steele 1990). Considerable ongoing marketing costs were required to ensure the continuing survival of a paper, as Charles Dickens discovered. Yet the expense of buying a newspaper had come down as a result of the income from advertising, which was necessary for financial stability. And as potential consumption moved down the economic pyramid, advertisers also exerted pressure for cheap sales prices.

Meanwhile newspapers responded to pressure to develop techniques in advertising drawn from the poster. In 1897, contemporaries noted that even *The Times* was allowing 'advertisements in type which three years ago would have been considered fit only for street hoardings' (Williams 1980: 176). But the publication of reliable sales records was a problem.

As newspapers vied for business from advertisers in a buyer's market, the latter needed proof of readership in the form of information on circulation, which was not readily available until such newspaper entrepreneurs as Britain's Alfred Harmsworth created systems to make statistics available. In 1904 he certified numbers and fixed advertising rates according to the number of readers. By publishing sales figures and challenging his rivals to do the same, Northcliffe in effect 'created the modern structure of the Press as an industry, in close relation to the new advertising' (Williams 1980: 179). In 1914 the Audit Bureau of Circulations was established in America to deal with the same problem, and in Britain the Association of British Advertising Agencies was founded in 1917, although the basic structure was not complete until 1931 when the Audit Bureau of Circulations was set up to publish audited net sales.

By 1907 advertising expenditure was £20 million in the United Kingdom, and in America it rose from $40 million in 1881, to over $140 million in 1904, to $1 billion in 1916 (Briggs and Burke 2002: 207). There was a fivefold increase in the volume of Japanese newspaper advertising in the 1880s. Newspapers competed to keep the top-circulation *Asahi* out of their market, and during the next decade they struggled just as bitterly to outdo each other, resorting to snatching rival papers from the newspaper racks and hiding them; sometimes there were even physical fights between deliverymen. The problem with competition from the point of view of both advertisers and investors is that it entailed uncertainty, and a loss of readers could mean a loss in advertising, whereas monopoly meant safety with a guaranteed service. Hence advertising revenue tended to gravitate towards the most successful organs, which meant that big ownership chains became even bigger. The trick was to retain and increase the number of readers.

New consumerism and the advertising industry

All over the world, dependence on advertising led the press to adapt its content to the needs of commerce. The approach was to popularize articles, by generalizing any criticism and thus offending the least number of people. The influence was visual as well: quarter-, half- and full-page advertisements now dictated the whole shape, design and layout of a paper. In business terms, publishers had to offset substantial investment in new production methods, leading some people to argue that newspapers simply exchanged one set of masters for another – from politicians to businessmen. In the case of Japan, 'Newspapers . . . became a paying business', as Hanazono Kanesada comments, but not independent as the control was 'of investor or advertisers' instead of censors (Kanesada 1924: 47).

The rise of advertising is explained not just by the repeal of taxes, as in Britain for instance, but also as part of a new 'promotional' culture. Mechanization had led to an increase in the production of consumer goods as a by-product of industrialization. However, capitalist mass production also involved periods of economic depression when overproduction created surpluses. Manufacturers, who defined this as underconsumption, had to bring their products to the attention of the public in order to even out fluctuations in demand. Hence the concept of advertising represented an attempt to control the market. Commodities became standardized and easier to use and were consumed in increasingly public ways.

The emerging urban department stores exemplified the new consumer culture in the way that they revolutionized the market with low-cost mass-buying methods and advertising campaigns, in an attempt to propagate the new concept of 'fashion'. This fledgling industry promoted its concept to females who read the new women's journalism, but it needed to attract customers to the city centres en masse. In America the pioneers for retail store advertising were John Wanamaker of Philadelphia, Marshall Field of Chicago and A. T. Stewart of New York. After 1870, and also during the 'golden age' between the wars, the 'grands magasins' of Paris were influential in Britain (Lancaster 1995). A press with increasing circulation presented the ideal outlet for advertising: readers with spending power.

The attractive proposition of consumers with purchasing power extended beyond the new fashion industry: any section of society could be classified as consumers. By far the most successful newspaper in Japan for generating advertising income was *Jiji*, which aggressively promoted itself by highlighting the fact that it attracted the most affluent business community from Tokyo, plus wealthy farmers and landowners from elsewhere, with its informational content on the stock markets, the rice exchanges and the state of the silk thread trade. Accordingly its adverts and its sale price were the most expensive, but its growth was impressive: from 20,000 to 86,279 daily readers within ten years of the end of the Sino-Japanese War (1895).

The idea of promotion via newspapers wasn't new. The press had always drawn a proportion of its income from this source. Adverts had appeared in the first newspapers, notably Nathan Tyler's *The Intelligencer* in England in 1647. By 1725 the practice was firmly established in Europe and the American colonies as the primary medium for advertising by local business concerns. The use of promotional techniques was not new either, although newspaper adverts in the earlier period had tended to announce information rather than persuade. What changed was that, from the beginning of the twentieth century, newspapers began to view their readers as groups of consumers: marketing techniques had become more intricate and were adopted in greater quantity as advertising took on a greater importance. For example, the *Encyclopedia Britannica* ran highly successful international sales campaigns that involved the timing of newspaper promotions to coincide with launches of the series.

Advertising had an image problem in the early days – even Alfred Harmsworth believed that to 'display type' for advertising in Britain's *Daily Mail* was 'vulgar': words made images, although, as Briggs and Burke point out, he was prepared to advertise his paper on poster hoardings and in the sky (2002: 207). Indeed, display adverts originally appeared only in outdoor form such as on cabs and billboards. Advertising lacked respectability because of its earlier association with

Patent medicines – still an issue

The most widespread use of advertising historically was for patent medicines, which seems to have developed independently in Europe, America and Japan. Each continent had its fair share of deception: in 1888 in Japan the first adverts for soap claimed that it would cure cholera, while one of the country's pre-eminent manufacturers today, Kao, first marketed its soap on the medical grounds that the pack of five different coloured bars would produce a 'whiter and more beautiful skin', as well as being effective against skin diseases. In the United States, some of the patent medicine makers marketed aptly named products such as 'Lydia Pinkham's Female Compound', 'Scott's Emulsion' and 'Castoria', which were not only useless and fraudulent, but sometimes contained deadly poisons (Marz 1977). Manufacturers of pharmaceuticals, initially 'medical' products such as stomach cures and eye drops, became the major advertisers in Japan soon after the beginning of the twentieth century. In America, Congress did not move towards regulation until the period of the First World War, and it wasn't until 1935 that the Federal Communications Commission regulator undertook its first public interest programming campaign aimed at the removal of fraudulent medical radio advertising. Even today, despite attempts at government intervention, useless and sometimes harmful over-the-counter drugs are still promoted via the media, especially television (Smith 1994). In Britain, Acts of 1939 and 1941 and a Code of Standards in 1950 banned misleading advertising such as the claim of cures for specific diseases.

circuses and quacks, but it was still accepted by newspapers because of the huge amounts of money involved. Thus, by the 1880s even *The Times* in Britain had introduced display ads.

An early example of how advertising can be severely affected by legislation took place in 1904 when the Japanese government merged all tobacco companies into a single government-controlled monopoly, in an attempt to solve the country's financial problems caused by the Russo-Japanese War. Tobacco had been one of the new industries that took up advertising on such a scale that total expenditure had exceeded that spent by the food and drinks industry and rivalled that of cosmetics. At a stroke newspaper advertising columns were instantly cut or stopped altogether. Tobacco's role in advertising provides an ongoing thread within advertising history (see chapter 5), including a place in the rapid expansion of export advertising in Britain. In 1901 an advertising campaign of record size was undertaken by the newly merged Imperial Tobacco Company as a reaction to American competition. *The Star* newspaper refused the huge sum on offer for an eight-page special, but allowed four pages, which was still billed as a 'world's record', to print 'the most costly, colossal and convincing advertisement ever used in an evening newspaper the wide world o'er'. The American companies responded with even bigger advertisements of their own in what turned out to be the first major, heavy and prolonged advertising battle (Williams 1980: 178).

Although the volume and content of adverts, as well as the use of additional media for promotion such as electric signs, billboards and balloons, varied from country to country according to the respective state of industrial development, there were many similar trends. Nevertheless, British history demonstrates that industrialization does not necessarily entail advertising as an automatic economic corollary. As Raymond Williams points out, 'The strange fact is, looking back, that the great bulk of products of the factory system had been sold without extensive advertising, which had grown up mainly in relation to fringe products and novelties.' In the 1850s the advertising pages of news-papers ranging from *The Times* to the *News of the World* were basically the same as they had been a hundred years earlier. Although there was a general increase in advertising as a result of the increase in trade during the mid-century golden years of Britain's economic growth, stimulated by the abolition in the early 1850s of advertisement tax and stamp duty, it was in the 1880s and 1890s that the real signs of change became evident. For Williams, 'The formation of modern advertising has to be traced, essentially, to certain characteristics of the new "monopoly" [corporate] capitalism, first clearly evident in this same period of the end of the 19th century and beginning of the 20th century.'

The corporate trend expressed itself in a growing desire to organize and control the market. Advertising on a new scale and applied to a wider range of products was a way of achieving this. 'Modern adver-tising . . . belongs to the system of market control which, at its full development, includes the growth of tariffs and privileged areas, cartel-quotas, trade campaigns, price-fixing by manufacturers, and that form of economic imperialism which assured certain markets overseas by political control of their territories' (Williams 1980: 172–9). Although

Big international spenders

In America, the big spenders of the 1880s were also soap (Ivory: 'It Floats'), food and drink (Royal Baking Powder and Coca Cola) and, surprisingly after the diffidence following its invention, the phonograph (His Master's Voice and Victor). In the 1890s these were followed by Eastman Kodak, Wrigley's chewing gum and Kellogg's cereals. Similarly, in Britain, Pear's soap became a leading advertiser (the famous 'Bubbles' poster dates back to 1887), typifying the pioneer attempts by manufacturers to establish standardized national brand identity in order to distinguish between competitor products that were actually quite similar. The first branding dates back to 1688, when Holman's Ink Powder was patented in Britain. In Japan, brand advertising gave a newspaper status.

Such qualities are still considered important today.

While Bovril, Nestlé, Hovis, Fry, Cadbury and Kellogg became household names, some products, such as typewriters, bikes and sewing machines, as well as the phonograph, were new inventions. This allowed the nascent industry to overcome the lack of respectability as it grew, but in many ways the kind of products advertised has not changed substantially over a century: fashion, cosmetics, personal transport and home utensils are still with us. However, the increase in their promotion between 1890 and 1914 was accompanied by the origination of the modern-day apparatus of agencies, copywriters, designers and campaigns, and also the development of the concept of brands.

modern economic growth came later in Japan, corporate development became a way of catching up with the West, illustrated by the fact that its advertising industry was directly influenced by patterns in America and elsewhere.

The rise of agencies

Advertising rate-cut wars, the emergence of national brands and the profusion of potential newspaper outlets all added complexity to the business of newspaper promotion, which created an opening for middlemen as links between advertisers and the press. In the eighteenth century certain shops had sold advertising space on behalf of newspapers, then in the nineteenth century this system was extended as agents bought space and sold it on to advertisers, and this became a form of space brokerage as agencies became more important as intermediaries for the press.

The first agency in the United States was founded by Volney B. Palmer in 1841. Relationships were symbiotic. Manufacturers needed agencies; advertisers needed the press; and newspaper proprietors needed advertisers: the middlemen placed the business by doing price deals and charged a percentage. Finding reputable agencies could be a problem, but in America the system became standardized via the American Newspaper Publishers Association (ANPA), which acted as the employers' voice and also issued a list of recognized agencies. Contemporary reports stress that the ANPA was founded primarily because of the strength of trades unions in print production (*The Journalist*, 1892). They set the trade discount at an agreed 15 per cent. Meanwhile leading agencies worldwide started to publish their own advertising and media data as a means of presenting a more socially acceptable image.

In Japan three different models of agency development emerged with implications for future corporate development, such as the understandable concept of a newspaper agency as an offshoot of the paper itself. Mannensha was nicknamed 'Mr Mainichi' because of the close connection with the Osaka *Mainichi* newspaper, but the founder of this 'house agency' decided to move its focus from newspapers to clients after a study trip to Europe in 1910. Whereas Mannensha's success was related to the medium in which it placed its clients' adverts, another successful agency, Hakuhodo, established a second model, consisting of an intellectual reputation which it has retained to this day, because of the content of its advertising on behalf of major publishers. A third model with implications for a history of the globalized media is provided by Dentsu, which grew through a combination of advertising placements and wire services as the business relayed information one way and advertised it the other. The agency provided correspondents throughout Japan and also in Korea and China, and in 1918 concluded a news deal with America's United Press that was to provide the first ever competition for Reuters in Japan. The business concept of 'total communications' rather than merely 'advertising' is one adopted these days by most agencies.

In Britain and America, agency activity extended to the supply of serial fiction to publications. Top popular authors such as Conan Doyle, Kipling and Jack London were signed up by McClure's, a service complemented by Edward Bok's (*Ladies' Home Journal*) supply of women's reading material to American papers, while in Britain the Tillotsons of the *Bolton Evening News* provided a similar service. Gradually agencies extended their role from simply selling newspaper space to also serving and advising manufacturers on specific campaigns.

As agencies grew, both the proportion of newspaper income derived from advertising as opposed to circulation, and the ratio of space devoted to promotions as compared to editorial coverage, continued to rise. In 1892, one American commented that 'the most important part of the newspaper . . . is the writing of advertisements. . . . The advertising department of a newspaper offers more rich rewards than any other' (*The Journalist*, 13 February 1892: 2–3). The ratio of space devoted to promotions as opposed to editorial had reached 50:50 in the United States by the First World War, but the amount of income that newspapers derived from advertising was challenged by the rising popularity of magazines during this same period.

Magazines

The demand for advertising during this period was further stimulated by the growth in magazines as an entertainment medium, especially women's publications and weekly journals, which provided competition for revenue with newspapers. They too offered a cheap sales price combined with popular content in digestible snippets for a niche market, such as fiction and illustrations, although magazines also developed innovations such as the new photo-journalism and in-depth personality profiles. Between 1880 and 1900 in Britain, forty-eight new magazine titles were launched: the ones for women studiously avoided the subject of women's rights, specializing in domestic activities such as needlework, plus fiction and fashion (Gough-Yates 2003). More discerning publishers were beginning to identify sub-groups within the female population rather than trying to appeal to all women: *The Lady*, Britain's oldest privately owned magazine, was launched in 1885 for 'women of education'. Magazines for the younger woman were to follow.

In America *Munsey's* led the monthlies, with a circulation of 65,000, closely followed by *McClure's* and *Cosmopolitan*; in the field of women's magazines *Ladies Home Journal* was in the forefront; 5 cent weeklies such as the *Saturday Evening Post* and *Collier's* outstripped the monthlies in circulation, while the more up-market *Harper's*, *Century* and *Scribner's* still had influence. The reaction of the newspaper industry in the United States, as Michael Emery and his colleagues point out (2000: 188), was to fight back by organizing a structure for promoting their

Fig. 4 *The Lady* magazine – one of the pioneer women's periodicals

medium to the advertisers. Various associations, both regional and national, were established, and in 1913 the ANPA sponsored the founding of the Bureau of Advertising. The result was successful: whereas magazines had accounted for 60 per cent of national advertising revenue, by the First World War the split was 50:50; taking into account local advertising as well, newspapers held their own with a share of 70 per cent of the cake.

In Britain, cross-ownership was a feature: it was periodicals that established the new owners of mass newspapers in business. Magazines such as Alfred Harmsworth's *Tit Bits* and C. A. Pearson's *Pearson's Weekly* reached circulations of close to half a million. These helped to finance the more demanding newspaper ventures, but the main problem was that such ventures were now beyond the resources of a small family business, which was still the usual form of ownership for most British newspapers.

Changes in the structure and working practices of the newspaper industry

Of course, the transfer of our newspapers from personal to corporate ownership and control was not a matter of preference, but a practical necessity. The expense of modernizing the mechanical equipment alone imposed a burden which few newspaper proprietors were able

> to carry unaided. . . . Partnership relations involve so many risks, and
> are so hard to shift in an emergency, that resort was had to the form of
> a corporation, which afforded the advantage of a limited liability, and
> enabled the share holder to dispose of his interest if he tired of the
> game. (Frances Leupp 1910; cited in Hardt and Brennen 1995: 51)

As one analyst has observed: 'The impact of trading newspaper securities on the stock market has meant that news companies must
constantly expand in size and rate of profit in order to maintain their
position on stock exchanges' (Bagdikian 1979: 24).

To contemporaries, the implications of this were all too evident: one
observer noted: 'the newspaper business is essentially a moneymaking
scheme, dependent on one hand upon its popularity with the public,
on the other hand, upon the money market. It takes money to run it and
it is run to make money' (Rogers 1909: 197).

In America commercial newspapers had been moving away from
an editor–publisher model to one of publisher–financier since the
mid-nineteenth century. Whereas de Tocqueville had observed in the
early 1830s that 'the facility with which newspapers can be established
produces a multitude of them' (1945: 194), by 1909 the number of
dailies had peaked at 2452 and thereafter continued to decrease. As
this trend started well before broadcasting began to compete, the
reasons lie more obviously with the cost of starting and running
a newspaper, which necessitated the change to joint-stock ownership.
By the outbreak of the First World War, this system had become the
norm. Now the newspaper was an institution rather than a personal
vehicle for expression. The corporate structure of ownership and
management ensured that those who survived became bigger and
more profitable.

One way in which small and medium-sized newspaper businesses
rationalized for survival in the post-Civil War competitive climate in
America was to buy written material from syndicates, for the 1870
copyright laws ensured that written work could no longer be 'stolen'
from elsewhere. During this period Kellogg consolidated his intellectual influence beyond the cereal packet first by distributing partially
complete newspapers to editors, who could then add a page of their
own news. Next he sent out thin stereotype plates ready for printing,
and then he offered his clientele a variety pack of specialist services,
ranging from agricultural services to serial fiction.

The operation of chain newspapers offered additional potential for
rationalization. The pioneers in America of the 1870s and 1880s were the
Scripps brothers, William Randolph Hearst and Frank Monsey. In the
period from the late 1880s to 1910 the chain became standard business
practice in America; by 1900 the Edward W. Scripps newspaper empire
had the largest chain, and by 1914, in partnership with Milton Macrae,
Scripps had established a 'league' of twenty-three newspapers. The
league's approach was to buy an interest in a newspaper, invest in it,
but pull out if expansion was not forthcoming. Scripps dealt with

competition from publishers such as Hearst and Pulitzer by forming cooperative and anti-competitive joint ventures, such as uniform advertising and subscription rates to create and continue profits (Adams 1996). Even before 1914 this new climate influenced all levels of the industry, as other people copied Scripps's methods but not necessarily his radical outlook, which favoured serving the local community 'to make it harder for the rich to grow rich and easier for the poor to keep from growing poorer' (Williams 1969: 89). Scripps's newspapers were radical and pro-labour, in contrast to the 'yellow journalism' of the Hearst group, although recent scholarship has cast a critical light on the Scripps chain's lack of commitment to localism, pointing out that this, plus a heavy dependence on syndicated material, contributed to the subordinate market position of most of the newspapers (Adams and Baldasty 2001). The corporate split in the Scripps newspaper empire was the first in a US newspaper company (Adams 2001).

William Randolph Hearst was in the process of acquiring an even larger business empire through his chain: soon after the end of the First World War it extended to thirty-one newspapers, six magazines, a number of film interests and some wire services (Smith 1979: 165). Media empire-building was also prevalent in 1890s Britain. In addition to newspapers such as the *Evening News*, the *Daily Mail*, and the *Weekly Dispatch*, Northcliffe was launching a new magazine every six months, transporting both the ideas and profit from periodicals into the world of newspapers. The so-called Northcliffe revolution turned the press into a business branch of consumer industry, and at his zenith Northcliffe was in charge of a larger share of Britain's newspaper circulation than was Rupert Murdoch in the 1990s.

Yet the actual Northcliffe 'revolution' amounted largely to an implementation in organizational terms of strategies that recognized the reality of newspaper dependency on advertising linked to the size and nature of the readership. Northcliffe did not invent popular journalism – many developments in style and content were influenced by the United States and change would have come anyway, given contemporary economic and social forces (Ward 1989: 40; Catterall et al. 2000: 10–12). He took advantage of them by making the commercial potential of journalism into a reality. The precedent had been set for future mass media to be cheap, entertaining and free from party political influence. 'Incontrovertibly, Northcliffe bolstered capitalism by encouraging acquisitive, materialist and individualist values' (ibid.: 23). In the process he made a fortune, and in 1908 he proceeded to purchase *The Times* as a symbol of his own political kudos.

Northcliffe ran his empire jointly with his brother Harold (Lord Rothermere) and another brother; it became Associated Newspapers Ltd in 1905. Already by 1910 Northcliffe, Cadbury and Pearson controlled 80 per cent of all evening sales and a third of the morning circulation in Britain (Smith 1979: 163). Similarly, Northcliffe and three other British publishers controlled 80 per cent of all newspaper sales on a Sunday.

The reduction in the number of newspaper proprietors because of concentration of ownership had become so prevalent in Britain before the First World War that a monopoly was emerging. Before the Great War many British newspaper editors, who were considered to be 'gentlemen', feared both for their social status and for the future of the more intellectual papers in the face of this business onslaught. A large number of liberal-orientated regional penny dailies gradually became the victims of the Northcliffe revolution as mass-circulation London papers advanced into the provinces. These journals had made a living on circulations of 40,000 or fewer by providing a valuable service in the reporting of local political discourse. Although Harmsworth went lower down the social scale for readers, he did not reach the bottom of Britain's hierarchical society: 'The most startling social fact about the Northcliffe revolution, indeed, is that despite, or perhaps because of it, British popular daily journalism avoided right up to the 1930s the kind of mass appeal that gave American popular journalism its strength' (Williams 1969: 78).

The trends outlined above were not confined to the United States and Britain. In Germany, the number of newspapers almost tripled by 1914, to over 4200 titles; nearly half of the new titles were 'non-political' newspapers, called 'General Anzeiger', dependent on advertising with a low subscription rate, similar to America's penny press. But circulations were generally not large, with only a very small number of newspapers selling more than 15,000 copies, despite some popular *Boulevardblatt* tabloid newspapers, with eye-catching sensational headlines, simple news and plenty of pictures, all designed to draw the readers via street sales.

One exception was Ullstein's *Berliner Morgenpost*, which sold nearly 400,000 copies by 1914 (Williams 1969: 48). Large publishing companies invested heavily in the technology required to meet demand. Entrepreneurs such as Rudolf Mosse bought up and founded new papers in the Berlin area (in addition to his traditional style but successful *Berliner Tageblatt*), but the phenomenon of the popular, liberal-orientated, large-circulation daily was able to thrive only in a large city environment.

The move from editorial to news was an international phenomenon, initiated by the growth of news agencies. This had led to an increase in the number of journalists, necessitated by the emphasis on news-gathering, accompanied by an enlargement in the size of newspapers as a business operation. As the production process became more and more rationalized, so the division of labour in the newsroom also increased.

However, in the United States, although the number of editors and journalists tripled during the last thirty years of the century, a drive to keep operating costs down was well established by the 1880s. This required a form of control which was provided by the creation of a hierarchical division of newsroom work, still in existence today, and facilitated by technological invention.

By the 1880s, the telephone and the typewriter were exerting a dramatic influence both on the way that newspaper reporters operated and on the public's expectations of their output. Time and speed were now of the essence. The telephone also made work more specialized, leading to a further subdivision in the profession.

The age of the reporter: changing role of editors

Not unlike in the Japanese system, in the West 'legmen' or reporters went out and about, collecting news and telephoning it in. The first new story to be telephoned in to a newsroom was, symbolically, about a lecture held in Alexander Graham Bell's laboratory, published in the *Boston Globe* on 13 February 1877 with the by-line 'Sent by telephone' (Hardt and Brennen 1995: 50). They became entirely responsible for the gathering and initial drafting of news; 'rewrite men' stayed in the office and fine-tuned this output to the house style. Copyreaders then wrote the headlines. There were also now female reporters for the women's news (and occasionally mainstream reporting).

Although there were more job opportunities for reporters, with an increase in both the quantity and the range of positions as reporting became a specialized task within the industry, job security and holiday and sick pay were non-existent, salaries were relatively low, hours tended to be long and unsocial, and work conditions were poor. A contemporary survey in America stated that the annual salary of 'news editors, copy readers and space-writers' was $1800 and that of reporters an average of $1200, about the same as a junior lieutenant in the navy (King 1895).

From the Civil War onwards, the reporter had developed a public image as a folk hero, 'unabashed by authority, undeterred by threats, committed only to the public right to know' (Williams 1969: 52), but the reality of the work conditions left much to be desired. Yet *Collier's* magazine, in its edition of 21 January 1911, dubbed the era 'the age of the reporter. In even its simplest form news is the nerves of the modern world.' Although trades unions became well established in print production, in America they struggled to achieve recognition on the editorial side of production. Motivation to continue lay within the jour-nalist's unique sense of social altruism and intellectual calling – a feature already identified in France and Germany fifty years earlier. What had changed was the more focused business ethic on the part of proprietors: 'Unlike other business ventures, the newspaper could claim a public service mandate that allowed publishers to submerge their profit motive within an appeal to their newsworkers' sense of public duty' (Solomon, in Hardt and Brennen 1995: 119). Solomon claims that the older ones were driven out of a job and that all journal-ists consequently faced the choice of 'quitting, accepting the oppres-sive conditions of newsroom work or organizing.' Establishing their own paper was no longer an option because of the prohibitive start-up cost (ibid.: 126).

Change had permeated all levels of the industry. As the newspaper became less of a personal organ and more of an institution, distinctive and unique editor–publishers who wrote with energy from conviction, principle and purpose became a dying breed. In sharp contrast to pioneer propagandists such as Desmoulins and Carlile, editors were now autocrats within a corporate structure that was one of the fastest growing industries of the time in the United States. Although the earliest editors of America's penny press had tended to support working-class interests, ironically the success of their ventures tended to orientate future editors away from such sympathies. This can be explained by the huge increase in newspaper start-up costs and the subsequent commercialization of the industry that led to rationalization, subdivisions within news work and consequently the employment of 'management-style' editors less likely to be from a working-class background. Such people either encouraged anti-trades union coverage or ignored industrial relations altogether (Saxton 1984; Hardt and Brennen 1995: 113).

In France, the period up to the First World War is considered to be the epoch when the profession finally came of age, a time when today's definitions of the job of journalist became clearly defined (Delporte 1999; Ferenczi 1993). The picture was less brutal, although not without its contemporary critics. In *fin de siècle* continental Europe, with its intellectual blossoming, people bemoaned the decline of literary influence on newspapers and the moral decadence of journalists (due mainly to work for hire: Chapman 2005). People also discussed the impact of new technology, competition and the interference of financiers in the freedom of the press. But news workers had not yet experienced the full impact of modern capitalist management, although in Britain the Northcliffe revolution was evidence that it was fast approaching the agenda. The demands of war influenced the volume and cost of publishing, and many French newspapers were forced out of business by the difficult choices that the First World War forced on them.

In the United States lower start-up costs in the earlier period had enabled an artisan approach and outlook, but now prospective candidates were likely to have less sympathy with working-class interests because they themselves came from a higher social level (Foner 1947: 460; Zinn 1980). The positions of managing editor and city editor appeared, then night editor, and lower down the scale the lower-status job of copyeditor or, at first, copyreader. The copyeditor polished and trimmed the reporter's writing and also decided on the number of words that were to be submitted – a somewhat invidious and thankless task under the 'space and time' system of payment per word to which reporters were subject in America up to the First World War. The artisan approach was also being challenged in the new music industry.

Newspaper modernism: a repeatable treadmill

By gradually redefining itself, the newspaper industry had put itself on a treadmill of selling a repeatable experience. In the context of 1870s Japan, a contemporary memoir describes a conversation with a merchant who had purchased his first ever newspaper: asked whether he would subscribe annually, he replied, 'Why? I've got it. What more do I want?' 'Yes, you have one day's issue; and it comes out every day.' 'So I understand', the merchant replied, 'but having it already, why should I take it every day?' Only after a lengthy explanation was he convinced that each day's newspaper contained 'something new' (Huffman 1997: 58). Hegel once called the daily reading of a newspaper modernism's answer to the daily prayer (Anderson 1991: 35).

However, within the debate on the nature of modernism and its relationship to globalization, one scholar has pointed to the occidental bias of most interpretations. Part of the spatial as well as the temporal effect of modernity should be to analyse non-Western examples found in countries such as Japan, which, according to Featherstone, both Giddens and Habermas fail to do (Featherstone 1995: 145ff.). However, while acknowledging the idiosyncrasies of individual national cultures, we should also recognize that the concept of modernity, with its European roots, has a universal application (Tomlinson 1999: 66).

If the mass daily had already managed to induce the expectation that a central part of day-to-day existence involved reading the news, in technological terms, the repeatable experience was self-propagating. 'Each step taken towards capturing, recording, and making replayable another aspect of experience opened the way and created a demand for still another improvement and still newer techniques' (Boorstin 1973: 379). The treadmill of modernism's repeatable experiences was part of the relentless logic of capitalist development first identified by Marx: it also applied to the nascent music industry.

The early recording industry

'The question of profits does not seem to be of importance, but like stock gamblers, they are happy to do business forever – or as long as they can – at a loss. Some mysterious fascination seizes those who are initiated into that fanatical circle of activity called the talking machine business.' This was a contemporary assessment (1908) by the business pioneer Eldridge Johnson, the partner of Emile Berliner in the Victor Talking Machine Company (Koenigsberg 1990).

The crucial development that made the music industry 'modern', fast moving, profit motivated and multinational was the growth of mechanical recording. Within this process, the introduction of Emile Berliner's 'gramophone' in Philadelphia in 1888 and Thomas Edison's 'phonograph' in London in 1890 were milestones. The potential use of the phonograph for the reproduction of music was not initially obvious on account of the limited quality of the sound, a problem shared by the early telephone. During the 1880s both Edison's company, with his 'talking tin foil', and Bell's Columbia Phonograph Company tried to introduce the phonograph and graphophone to the market as dictation equipment, but when this failed as a business proposition they turned

Fig. 5 The HMV dog and gramophone on a gramophone needle box

to the idea of coin-operated entertainment, which had not yet acquired the name 'jukebox'.

Bell improved the standard with his 1887 phonograph, but the period 1888–94 saw a recession and economic panic; in addition the price of records needed to drop to $40 before popularity could be assured. Although there were by now three versions of the machine, what really held the phonograph back was the fact that use of a cylinder rather than discs meant that there was no bulk replication, for every recording was original. 'In short, in its original form the invention that promised the repeatable recording but not its replication was able to capture the imagination of a potential market but not to satisfy it' (Chanan 1995: 5).

The introduction of the celluloid single-sided disc – at first 7 inch diameter – made mass production possible, although the inventor, Emile Berliner, was not taken seriously until 1901, when he founded the Victor Talking Machine Company with Eldridge Johnson. The previous year Berliner astutely made that now famous dog called Nipper, listening to 'His Master's Voice', a trademark. It first appeared in England and has since become the most famous of advertising icons.

Double-sided discs initially appeared in Europe and reached the United States in 1904. Clearly, the record industry, like film, was destined to be an international one from the outset, for a record could be produced anywhere, then sent elsewhere for reproduction. By 1910 the new industry had bases in many countries worldwide, with two big multinational companies from the beginning: the Gramophone Company, established in Hayes, Middlesex, and Victor of Camden,

Opera becomes top of the pops

In 1904 Enrico Caruso made history as the first performer to sell a million with a disc recorded in Milan. It achieved high sales among the Italian communities internationally, for whom opera was a form of popular culture. Brian Winston (1998: 63) has pointed out that it was no accident that the earliest hit recordings were of singers: 'The non-electric technology produced a limited acoustic response which favoured the strong human voice.' The idea for the 'Red Seal' label had germinated three years earlier in Russia. A gramophone dealer persuaded one of Berliner's European subsidiaries – Deutsche Grammophon – and the head office in England that, if they paid an exorbitant fee to four of the tsar's favourite singers, they could still make a profit by charging five times as much for the record if the label was made red, since this would create a prestige series which the aristocracy would be prepared to buy. It worked; what is more, the artists received a novel royalty system of payment.

New Jersey, half of which was owned by the former company (Gronouw, cited by Martin 1995: 56).

Music, theories of modernity and creative trends, including African-American music

Whereas the previous integrity of musical performance rested in the specificity of location and moment, modern communication technologies compress perceptions of time and space. The steamship, the railway and the telegraph were all developments of modern capitalism with the same effect. Performance was transformed into a tangible material object for trade: in *Civilization and its Discontents*, Freud describes both photography and the disc as 'materializations of the power of recollection, of memory' (1969: 25, 27–8). In the past, fashions could lead to the elimination of certain styles, with only sheet music to preserve the essence. Now culture could be opened up and captured for posterity. Henceforth, music could travel worldwide and, for the first time ever, performance was separated from listening, as the recording process created a distance between the artist and the audience. In the longer term this had the effect of redefining both audience and ways of listening to and using music, which influenced musicians as well. Technology had given them the opportunity to create an international language, whereas previously musical entertainment had been culturally specific, confined to a particular social group or community with its own vernacular. As Marx famously said: 'All that is solid melts into air.'

Marx was not exaggerating, if one accepts the interpretation of Anthony Giddens: 'The modern world is born out of discontinuity with what went before rather than continuity with it' (1984: 239). Although definitions of modernity are diverse and sometimes ambiguous, the concept does seem to involve a different form of social formation linked to a period of history when new values, beliefs and cultural imagination emerged, encapsulating ideas of novelty and the importance of contemporaneity (Tomlinson 1999: 34). But if modernity represents a discontinuity, isn't that at variance with the thrust of this study, which argues for continuity within media history? The short answer is that both exist within a longer time span.

Social theorists recognize that aspects of modernity emerged in various countries at different dates (Hall et al. 1992: 9). While attempting to avoid historical periodization, they still attribute the origins of modernity to seventeenth-century Europe. It could therefore be argued that the period covered in this study forms part of a longer term movement. Furthermore, even Giddens recognizes that continuities exist between the pre-modern and the modern, such as the survival of world religions (1990: 4–5).

The various modernization theories that were developed in the 1950s and 1960s all pointed to a decline in tradition as part of this process, although John Thompson has questioned the argument (1995: 179). The general metamorphosis of tradition in the light of media growth is well illustrated elsewhere in this study by examples of Japan's reactions. Suffice it here to say that part of modernity's definition in relation to media history relates to the effect on individual consumers, who were able to appreciate different worlds as a result of the development of communications. This experience could involve education and/or entertainment, for the brave new worlds were both imaginary and real. The different dimensions of time and space are illustrated by the arrival of 'wireless' and film, dealt with in the next chapter.

The nascent music industry also brought a longer term impact for global appreciation. Recording was able to capture some musical aspects, such as improvisation, that had previously been unrepeatable, which presented huge implications for later cultural influence and taste. This 'enabled Afro-American music to replace European art and folk music at the heart of Western popular culture' (Lull 1987: 72). Scholars dealing with the sociology of music have struggled to account for the development of the music business in the United States in the form that emerged during this period.

Rapid industrialization is traditionally pointed to, but this does not account for the forms that popular music took, which did not occur during the growth of industrialization, urbanization and nationalism in Britain and Germany. American black music traditions are crucial, but here too 'the nature of the music that emerged can be understood only as the unpredictable outcome of a field of contrasting and often conflicting forces' (Martin 1995: 242). A further ingredient in the mix was the influence of the influx of immigrants from Europe, especially the Jewish entrepreneurs and songsmiths who created the roots of the present-day business, based on the thriving Tin Pan Alley.

Technology and the business of music

As a technological product of the process of modernization, the phonograph and discs also had economic effects. Both musicians and film actors soon found that other people made more money out of their job than they did, but there was also a whole new wave of job creation. Early record producers scouted for fresh discoveries: in India just before the First World War, the Gramophone Company set up 'training centres' to turn out popular recording artists. Musicians were engaged to teach new talent and to set poems to music for them to sing, which resulted in 2000 to 3000 – albeit formulaic – new songs a year (Chanan 1995: 15).

Already by 1918 the music industry's emphasis on style and rapid change seemed to epitomize modernity: indeed the commodification of music was an effect of modernization, but it also contributed to the creation of the condition of modernity, and as such is another example, like the press, of how the media is 'implicated as both symptoms and agents of the whole process' (Chanan 1995: 21). The privatization and personalization of the musical experience which the recording industry offered is often considered a feature of twentieth-century culture, as is the choice of music to purchase, which gave people a new freedom for their leisure entertainment that had not existed before.

By today's standards, the market was small, and in business terms it was cheap to start up, with the result that there was a proliferation of small record labels, reminiscent of the early nineteenth-century mushrooming of newspapers. By 1914 there were almost eighty record companies in Britain alone, and many more in the United States. Yet the priorities of the business were not the same as today's. Technical equipment for the production of records was a first priority, followed by ornate furniture to house the gramophone – an approach followed later by the manufacturers of the wireless, who supplied an attractive if bulky artefact for the living room. Records came a poor third (Chanan 1995: 55).

The industry was dividing into 'majors' and 'minors', and the activities of the former involved complicated cross-licensing and mergers in order to acquire patents which gave access to new technology – a process with which the film and early radio industries were also familiar. Technological innovations connected to music were to come thick and fast, usually having the effect of increasing consumer choice at the expense of the existing industry's ability to control the market, which was generally expanding. The new gramophones and phonographs had challenged piano makers and retailers, music hall, vaudeville and the sheet music business.

Now that recording and playback were separated, research also became fragmented, leaving a vacuum to fill when it came to the development of electrical recording. This gap was filled not by record companies but by radio developers after the First World War. Developments in the reproduction of music had a controversial effect: 'mechanical reproduction not only removed the performer from the presence of the listener, robbed the listener of the act of participation in the act of performance, and deprived the performer of the listener's encouragement. It also made recording into an exclusively commercial business' (Chanan 1994: 250). In future, the impact of technological innovations on the record industry's market was to maintain a business dynamic while also creating the circumstances for the process of its institutionalization. The pattern had been similar in newspapers.

Conclusions

There are a number of features that emerged during this period as the forces of technological and business change prevailed over forces of continuity.

- Technological breakthroughs went hand in hand with industrialization, which was structured to maximize profit through the exploitation of mass markets of consumers, aided by advertising. This process was pioneered in print journalism.
- The overall impact of the business development of newspapers had the effect of connecting commerce to ideology, which was used to legitimize marketplace practices.
- The new music industry was already manifesting some of the tensions between content creation on the one hand and technological, business trends on the other that the print industry had long experienced.
- New forms of business organization, especially the introduction of share ownership, had a strong influence on other trends, such as economies of scale, industry structures and drives for high sales with low cover prices – achieved through dependence (some say overdependence) on advertising revenue. Greater mass appeal was achieved by moves towards 'objectivity' of content within the framework of a new organizational base. 'The dominant institutional factors [have] pressed for a decontextualized, depoliticized and conservative journalism' (McChesney 1997: 14, 17). This is dealt with in the next chapter.

Study questions

Using the nineteenth-century example of Stead, the illegal campaigns of the radical press in Britain and other political newspaper activists in chapters 1 and 2, and the response of the authorities to dissent, would you say that, in terms of media ethics, the end justifies the means?

What were the advantages, disadvantages and social implications of new business practices in newspaper management?

How new was 'new' consumerism and advertising?

How does the early music industry help us define 'modernism'?

4 Politics, New Forms of Communication and the Globalizing Process

A political party without a newspaper is like an army without weapons. With what else could we hope to topple our rival parties or exert our influence throughout society?

Jiyu Shimbun, 24 June 1882

Printers . . . like the clergy, live by the zeal they can kindle, and the schisms they can create. Thomas Jefferson, 1801

Every two months the entire population of the globe was exceeded in number by the total of all who visited the world's silent movies.

James Card, curator of George Eastman House

Summary

The *objective* of this chapter is to examine how a major thread of continuity – the relationship between communication and the political process – was transformed and also challenged by the emergence of new media, which formed part of the ongoing influence of modernity from 1881 to the watershed date of 1918. The argument is that the cultural and social impact of new inventions resulted in the eventual emergence of a common mass culture, aided by the longer-standing print medium which itself was having to change. This process continued into the inter-war period, dealt with in part III of this study.

Throughout the entire nineteenth and twentieth centuries there was one main motivation for media communication which was shared by every country, and that was to use it to influence the political process in the public sphere. As previous chapters have argued, newspapers were already under challenge. Now further challenges appeared: film and radio and a strengthening of commercialism that was changing the nature of the content transmitted to the public. Furthermore, the public itself was also changing – in composition and in its taste. All these factors were to converge by the end of the nineteenth century to such a fundamental extent that their combined dialectics produced a new synthesis.

Although many people argue that the ideological platform of modern mainstream journalism in the Western world has emerged from the marriage of commercialism and political independence, throughout the nineteenth century newspapers continued to appear that provided the function of organizer of opinion among groups in the public sphere.

It was during the period 1881 through to the First World War that the origins of these two conflicting approaches came into sharpest focus. Despite the extension of the vote, which was accompanied by an increased demand for political information, mass daily newspapers did not live up to expectations in this area because of the tendency for the entertainment function to overshadow civic debate.

The First World War provided a landmark because communication needs and media technological progress in Europe were diverted to the military effort while regular commercial competition was halted. In comparison with other countries this gave the United States a clear run for economic self-sufficiency during a crucial three-year period of normal development. America entered the arena of conflict in 1917.

Finally, the strands of media development that emerged up to 1918 are assessed in the light of theories of modernity and globalization, first touched on in chapters 2 and 3.

Introduction

Throughout the nineteenth century, the gradual lifting of property restrictions on the right to vote and their elimination in many countries had the effect of increasing demand for political information. Accordingly, those who argued for press freedom earlier in the nine-teenth century had genuinely believed that newspapers would become a forum for educated citizenship through political debate. Even in tsarist Russia, where there was debate despite the autocratic form of government, a clandestine press existed that was heavily implicated in politics. Yet over the longer term hopes for the press as a vehicle for plurality of political discourse were to be disappointed. The mass daily created the conditions for its dissident competitors, but the latter were forced to survive on unequal terms, for publications do not enter the market on the same terms just because they share a sales shelf (de la Motte and Przyblyski 1999: 357).

The diversity of opinion that John Stuart Mill (chapter 2) and others sought to cherish often gave way to intolerant chauvinism and an atten-tion-seeking lowest common denominator of agreement and ubiquity. The newspaper was beginning to create a concept of the 'mass' that was fostered via the presentation of society to a public of consumers 'in a form that was least capable of offence to the largest number' (Ward 1989: 25). Daily entertainment tended to eclipse civic enlightenment. Nevertheless the press contributed towards the foundation of a common modern identity which was largely urban and 'up to the minute, . . . the process by which individuals were typed into the social order by their public construction in grey print and black and white images' (de la Motte and Przyblyski 1999: 3). Part of this new image involved support for inventions such as film and radio, which, although they underlined modern life, were eventually to challenge print as the dominant genre for both communication and entertainment.

The news in papers tends to be out of date by the time the journal is purchased, a situation that the technology of live radio helped to rectify. The arrival of radio and film forms part of the end-of-century changes in information and consumption, and as such both have cultural roots which were also influencing the newspaper industry. Unlike radio, which focused on local and national content, and newspapers, which became mass circulation contiguously with cinema's debut, movies were international from the very beginning. Their geographic appeal always stretched beyond national boundaries: 'Far more people today are reached by the moving picture than by the daily press, and while we read the newspaper only in parts, the moving picture we see complete', a reporter remarked in 1908 (Ross 1998: 5).

The invention of film was also highly dependent on science and machinery, but its origins as an industry cannot simply be explained by a straight process of theory leading to its application, which in turn led to its exploitation: there are also social and cultural influences. The appeal of films always defied class and distance. The first twenty years of film consists of a story of unprecedented expansion, starting as a novelty in a few big cities – New York, London, Berlin and Paris – then stretching rapidly across the whole world, with ever larger audiences everywhere it appeared, displacing other forms of entertainment. Venues became bigger and better and films became longer, expanding from a mere twenty seconds' duration to feature length. At the beginning, French influence was the most important but, as the most significant centres of supply gradually changed in the 1910s from the cities mentioned above to Los Angeles, US development proved to be the most crucial.

It would be a mistake to see the early years of film merely as a precursor to Hollywood: the foundations of a global film industry centring on the United States were laid from the 1890s through to the period of the Great War, yet this achievement was by no means inevitable. The United States emerged as the largest single market for films; by protecting this, and pursuing a vigorous export policy, the Americans achieved a dominant position in the world market. While Europe literally suffered the devastation of the Great War, cinema in the United States continued to develop, pioneering new techniques as well as consolidating industrial control.

America also gained a breathing space to develop radio domestically in three crucial years before its entry into the First World War, at a time when wireless technology in Europe had been requisitioned for the military effort. Previously, a venerable history of invention had also been characterized by a battle between wireless telegraphy and wireless telephony, without any real concept of mass broadcasting as we know it today. During 1914–18, technological breakthroughs were achieved.

Newspapers: political influence versus political independence

There have been stages in the development of modern democracy when the function of the newspaper has clearly been one of opinion-forming as part of competition within the public arena for the attention of voters and interest groups, for example 1789 in France and 1881 in Japan (see below). This priority has presented itself at differing times in various countries, depending on the stage of constitutional development and the culture. Many associations between party politics and the press had already emerged: 'The growth of competing political parties in nineteenth-century Europe was widely paralleled by the rise of newspapers supporting them – in Britain, France, Germany, Russia, and Scandinavia, for example ... the press in widely varying types of political system is given a role explicitly or implicitly that connects it to party . . . [and] the functions of parties are highly compatible with the capabilities of newspapers' (Seymour-Ure 1974: 157–9).

This experience goes to the heart of the relationship between the media and political change, raising the issue of how far newspapers should be aligned to a political party or how far they should retain their independence. An independent press is a comparatively recent phenomenon, as is highlighted by David Weaver's work (1990) on the press baron Roy W. Howard in the United States and the relationship between newspapers and politicians. Indeed, the issue transcends both country and historical era. 'Throughout the [nineteenth and twentieth] centuries, the main intellectual tension among newspapers has been between the ethic that demands "independence" and an older ethic, surviving in many places, by which the newspaper is supposed to belong to one of several contending ideologies', as Anthony Smith puts it (1979: 166–7). Ironically, at the very time when the vote was extending democratic national political life in most countries, and when consequently the voice of larger groups in society needed to be heard more than ever, many newspapers were turning their backs on the requirement to service public life. Large-circulation newspapers certainly offered the potential for communication with the views of organized sections of society, but, as the economic function of newspapers grew, the imperative for revenue that advertising provided made the newspaper indispensable to consumers of goods rather than to citizens.

It would be a mistake to think that consumerism does not have implications for the political process. Some scholars challenge the 'objectivity' that commercial newspapers came to espouse. The argument is that 'independence', 'objectivity' and 'social responsibility' emerged as ideological corollaries of commercial strategies which were adopted to stabilize marketplace crises and class conflict within journalism (Kaul 1986). According to McChesney, America's adoption of an objective 'professionalism' in journalism throughout the twentieth century has adversely affected democracy:

> It was hardly neutral. On one hand, the commercial requirements for media content to satisfy media owners and advertisers were built implicitly into the professional ideology. . . . On the other hand, corporate activities and the affairs of the wealthy were not subject to the same degree of scrutiny as government practices; the professional codes deemed the affairs of powerful economic actors vastly less newsworthy than the activities of politicians. In this manner 'objective' journalism effectively internalized corporate capitalism as the natural order for a democracy. (McChesney 1997: 14, 17)

It can also be argued that the media are equally compromised by their dependence on advertising and the requirement to satisfy shareholders, patrons and owners (see previous chapter).

Once newspapers began to supply large quantities of non-political information, then their political views as expressed through editorial columns were unlikely to be the main reason that people bought them, and one of the influences of New Journalism had been to offer a wider range of subject matter. As Hippolyte de Villesmessant, the founder and editor of *Le Figaro* in Paris, explained in his memoirs, 'Like a well stocked store a newspaper should offer in its different departments,

News agencies, national interest and the importance of state subsidy

Although Reuters, Havas and Wolff/Continental, the leading news agencies of the nineteenth century, were independent companies (a newer model of agency ownership was emerging in the United States with the cooperative Associated Press), it is generally acknowledged that these news services reflected their respective national interests. Agency income tended then, as now, to come from the sale of information services principally to their home markets, for use by financial or economic institutions, governments (to whom they were indirectly linked) and other media. Oliver Boyd-Barrett has looked at the relative contributions of political subsidy, financial services, income and media sales to the main agencies, and concluded that, in the case of Reuters, financial services have always been the most important but that, in the case of Havas and Wolff, the political category possibly rivalled the media as a source of revenue, and that,

in the first half of the twentieth century, the importance of the political probably increased as states supported news agencies during the First and Second World Wars (Boyd-Barrett and Rantanen 1998: 23, 30). Without such help during times of national crisis agencies would not otherwise have been able to continue reporting overseas, especially in areas that were important to government but normally poor sources of income.

Yet political subvention generally goes against the tendency of Western news values to assume that impartiality is an essential prerequisite for news providers and that this is based on independence from political and government control. However, the idea that commercial media should be guarantors of the public sphere, as Boyd-Barrett points out, 'privileges concerns about formal political processes over concerns about economic and financial processes.'

known in the profession as columns, everything that its clientele could need. . . . I expand my columns in order that everyone can find ample supply of what he needs' (Williams 1969: 81). Politics had to compete for space alongside an increasingly varied and diverse menu of information, so traditional debate and coverage of speeches suffered.

However, some newspapers managed to retain their political priorities but also espouse modern production and writing style together with the popularism needed for mass readership. In addition, it is worth remembering that contemporaries were often more concerned about the institution of journalism as a generally corrupting influence, irrespective of a newspaper's politics. In France, the metaphor of prostitution was used regularly in discussions about the press. Richard Terdiman points out that commodification produced a mass press whose 'overt crassness was bitterly deplored by the partisans of an elite or politically or socially engaged press' (de la Motte and Przyblyski 1999: 355).

In Japan, the relationship between politics and newspapers and the status of the latter was illustrated by two movements, for constitutional government and for universal suffrage. In 1881, the year that press freedom finally arrived in France, Japan went through a wave of newspaper development that was tied like an umbilical cord to debate about the development of a modern political system, a phase reminiscent of the boom in oppositional press politics of the French Revolution. Although political influence and patronage were a feature of the Japanese press from its beginnings, historians are all agreed that 1881 was a landmark year in press history, for it heralded the 'era of political party organs' in which most papers were turned into mouthpieces of outside parties. This proved to be short-lived as the 'era of campaign journalism' and the commercial route gained ascendancy. In the ensuing journalistic battle between editorialists and essayists versus reporters and feature writers, the latter gained the upper hand; but the lack of democratic rights and poverty that ordinary people experienced ensured that this trend in the development of the written word had a political punch to it.

The Japanese government's response to newspaper development was one of carrot and stick. Historians differ in their interpretations concerning the degree of pro-government newspaper compliance. Conservatives point to the oppositional nature of the press as an apologist for the left, whereas many other writers give evidence of establishment pressure on newspapers and of the press giving way. What is clear is that the role of government was crucial, in both censorship and economic encouragement, which was extended to nearly every prefecture to set up one or more newspapers by the 1880s. However, change was slower in the provinces: 70 per cent of Japan's prefectures had only one subscription per hundred residents, compared to one per 5.6 citizens in Osaka and Tokyo in 1898. The average circulation of the 152 newspapers outside of these two main cities was only 3237 copies, so

Japan's 1880s political crises and press development

On the constitutional front, there were two issues that contributed to the early 1880s crisis in public affairs in Japan, one economic and one political. The first, 'Hokkaido', was a scandal over the sale of government lands in the country's least advanced area, together with the fruits of a protracted, huge development project and its profit: all of this was handed over, interest free, as an insider 'sweetheart deal'. Press coverage represented Japan's first big exercise in 'campaign' journalism. The second equally controversial crisis was precipitated by the recommendations of Japan's influential finance minister, who broke ranks by calling for a rapid transition to liberal democracy in the drawing-up of the first ever constitution. This called into question the speed at which the country should democratize and touched on popular impatience for change, prompting passionate debate and protest about the sort of government model that would integrate some of the existing power of the emperor with party politics into a British-style constitutional monarchy – a political system that was admired by advocates of reform.

For the first time an institutionalized political opposition in the form of political parties was formed in 1881–2, and all the participants recognized the importance of communication even at local level. One contemporary journalist and political activist called Yano recollects: 'We engaged in war through the medium of print. When we would take control of some prefectural paper, the government would respond by creating a publishing company on its own or attaching itself to an allied newspaper. Never in my recollection has there been another era of such brilliant editorial confrontation' (Huffman 1997: 123).

The government retaliated with jail sentences, but newspapers managed to institutionalize the fight for press freedom by creating a post for which there was no shortage of volunteers: a member of staff whose sole job it was to go to prison while the real editor proceeded with the serious business of muckraking (Williams 1969: 82).

regional papers were reluctant to break connections with political organizations to whom they owed their origins and their continuing existence.

Out of a list of fifty-three leading newspapers which was published in summer 1883, all followed the party model. Anti-government papers attracted a lot more readers. The year 1883 saw a further tightening of the press law. During the 1880s more independent newspapers were also started, including the Osaka *Asahi Shimbun* and *Mainichi Shimbun* – two of the world's three largest circulating newspapers one hundred years later. The world's largest in 1986 was also Japanese – *Yomiuri Shimbun*, established in 1874 as a literary paper (Dunnett 1988: 173).

The period after the Sino-Japanese War (1894–5) is referred to as one of 'profit' because the main newspapers espoused this cause, and in this new 'commercial' era declared that they were politically impartial. In Japan a dual category of newspapers evolved, similar to the French one of the 1830s. The serious 'big' papers, such as the Tokyo *Nichi Nichi* and the Yokohama *Mainichi*, staffed and read by intellectuals and former samurai aristocracy, were also subsidized by political interests,

Table 4.1 *The two sides of the coin for newspapers in general*

	Pros	Cons
Party	Definite financial support	If party slumps, paper slumps
	Clear editorial line	No editorial independence
	Content focus	If party splits or folds, paper also vulnerable
Non-party	Broader appeal	Possible uniformity of content
	Advertising revenue	Trivialization of content to cater for wider readership
	Potential for bigger market	Pressure to please advertisers
		Depoliticizing influence
		Less emphasis on democratic citizenship
		Constant need for promotional sales

and focused on the 'hard' political news of their sponsors, which was written in a heavy style. Profit was the distinguishing characteristic of the 'little' ('eiri') newspapers or tabloids, such as *Asahi* and *Yomiuri*, that were staffed and read by small businessmen and people in the entertainment world. They were written in a more accessible style, steering clear of politics and relying on 'soft' news such as gossip, crime and accidents. They also tried to maintain political and financial independence. *Asahi* reached a daily circulation of 6.5 million in the second half of the twentieth century.

Outside of North America and Australia during the last decades of the nineteenth century, there were very few newspapers that spoke directly for or to the masses, but there was now almost everywhere an increasing recognition of the needs of this new public. Examples of this trend, such as the hugely popular postcard correspondence columns in Japan, tend to reflect individual cultures. This invitation to ordinary people to send in their written thoughts was the most successful press initiative, but others, such as the organization by newspapers of community discussion groups on political issues, also demonstrated a readiness to capitalize on public desire for discourse.

Japanese newspapers also promoted huge labour rallies in a strikingly successful effort to win a working-class readership – in sharp contrast to the anti-trades union coverage of America's popular press during the same period. Similarly, the press clashed seriously with the government over the 'rice riots' of 1918 because they were banned from coverage. After the successful inauguration of Japan's first ever party cabinet, they turned their attention to the next stage in the struggle for democracy: the cause of universal suffrage, achieved in 1925, but only for men over twenty-five years of age (Lee 1985: 36–8).

American yellow journalism and national chauvinism elsewhere

During this period imperialism and expansion provided a continuing backdrop to press development in all of the countries featured. In Japan, for instance, there were two ongoing themes up to 1945: democracy and expansion, with a series of conflicts culminating in the Pacific arena during the Second World War. Both Japan and America had remained isolated from world affairs for most of the nineteenth century.

America's emergence coincided with an economic depression from 1893 through to the early twentieth century which led to intense competition for working-class readers not only between newspaper owners, but also from magazines that were feeling the pinch. The combined effect of national chauvinism and cut-throat circulation battles was significant. Developments in content and presentation, which were actually an extension of techniques evolved over the previous ten years, were labelled 'yellow journalism'. The name derives from a comic strip called Hogan about a New York 'alley kid' who suddenly appears in yellow (Nasaw 2000). Luckily the worst excesses of this notorious phase in press history, which was heavily criticized for its ethics, did not endure for much more than a decade.

As competition for readers increased, so did the size of the headlines: huge, page-dominating, emotional 'scare heads', backed by sensational stories with fake interviews and an abundance of artists' illustrations for crusades and campaigns. After 1897 the use of half-tone photographs enabled further stylistic adaptations, augmented in Sunday supplements and comics. The newspaper magnate William Randolph Hearst exploited such visual opportunities, accompanied by the concept of pace and action in coverage. He also popularized sport – the boxer John Sullivan became America's first sporting personality via newspapers. Yet it is Hearst's personal style that still provokes the greatest discussion. He was not the first or the last owner to use newspapers as fodder for megalomania – Northcliffe and Beaverbrook also gave this a good run.

When the Japanese newspaper *Yomiuri* heard about Hearst's original achievements at the *San Francisco Examiner*, the paper adopted his methods so successfully that other dailies with ambitions for large circulation all created a 'black third page' with scandal about politicians and businessmen. Meanwhile, in the United States, Hearst decided that a real war required American intervention, and fictitious atrocity stories were a good way to achieve support for this. Hearst managed to promote national hysteria 'by telling lies with ever increasing emphasis in ever larger print' (Williams 1969: 60–1). First his *New York Morning Journal* latched on to three Cuban girls who had been searched for incriminating documents by the Spanish. But when the girls protested that they had not been treated badly at all, the *Journal* switched attention to a dentist who had joined the rebel cause, then committed suicide. The paper called for an immediate declaration

William Randolph Hearst: 'Citizen Kane'

In 1887 the former silver-mine prospector George Hearst donated a newspaper that he had purchased – the *San Francisco Examiner* – to his son William, an act of parental generosity that facilitated one of the most notorious careers in journalism history (and the inspiration for Orson Welles's classic film *Citizen Kane*). Hearst Senior had originally purchased the journal to further his own career in Californian politics, but Hearst Junior had ambitions in the newspaper business. Having observed Pulitzer's success in New York he was determined to emulate it. After increasing his newspaper's circulation and advertising, in 1895 he moved to New York armed with $7.5 million from his mother's sale of a mine to Rothschilds, bought up the ailing *New York Morning Journal* and launched headlong into a circulation war with Pulitzer.

Hearst claimed that his journalists were more successful at their detective work assignments than the city police: 'What is frequently forgotten in journalism is that if news is wanted it has to be sent for ... the public is even more fond of entertainment than it is of information.' Although he campaigned bravely against the power of the Southern Pacific Railroad in Californian politics, it seemed that what really excited Hearst was the news he could make up or make into something different. Reporter missions on the *Examiner* tended towards the bizarre: to catch a grizzly bear and bring it back in order to prove that they still existed; to jump off a ferryboat to see if the crew knew what to do about a man overboard; to become committed as insane to an asylum; to infiltrate a brothel – although the female reporter was not required to take up the profession herself (Williams 1969: 57).

Hearst's biggest challenge was a self-imposed one: to start an international war. Undaunted by the American policy of 'splendid isolation', Hearst famously employed an illustrator to capture blood and tyranny in the Spanish colony of Cuba, where an obscure group of guerrillas had begun to agitate for independence. 'Everything is quiet. There is no trouble here. There will be no war. I wish to return', the artist cabled Hearst. 'Please remain. You furnish the pictures and I'll furnish the war', was the reply. And he did: an ignoble episode which demonstrates the extent to which, during this era of the powerful proprietor, the exploitation of newspapers as instruments of personal whim could lead to extreme excesses. One scholar claims that this exchange probably never took place (Campbell 2000). Either way, Hearst certainly carried his exploration of the extent, and limitations, of press power to the limits.

of war in defence of American citizens who were being murdered by the Spanish.

When this did not work, the *Journal* managed to find an eighteen-year-old Cuban girl who was awaiting trial in the relative comfort of a Havana jail for involvement in an attack on a Spanish military commander. She had invited him back home, where he was set on and beaten by a group of rebels who were lying in waiting for him. Evangelina Cisneros became the *Journal*'s 'Cuban Joan of Arc', and 'The Flower of Cuba' who had defended her chastity against the brutal advances of a Spanish officer, despite the fact that the American consul called the campaign 'tommyrot', stating that she had admitted being implicated in the insurrection, but would have been pardoned long ago had it not been for the drama created by the newspapers. 'At least nine tenths of the statements about Miss Cisneros printed in this country seem to have been sheer falsehood', commented the *New York Commercial Advertiser*. The Spanish authorities were preparing to release her, yet petitions circulated wildly; in England Lady Rothschild collected 200,000 signatures. When interest began to wane, Hearst ordered one of his correspondents in Havana to kidnap Cisneros from jail. She was then brought triumphantly to New York, installed in a plush hotel suite, bought a trousseau in Fifth Avenue, banqueted and acclaimed amid brass bands and fireworks. But, as yet, there was still no war.

In Spain, a new, more liberal government had already decided to cede independence, thus ending centuries of colonial presence. Hearst was beginning to lose interest in Cuba, given the public ingratitude as he saw it. But just after he had instructed the intrepid reporter Decker to turn his attentions instead to freeing Captain Dreyfus from the French penal colony of Devil's Island in order to launch a new campaign,[1] the American battleship *Maine* blew up in Havana harbour. It appears to have been an accident, for the captain reported that the Spanish authorities were offering every possible assistance and sympathy in their readiness to recognize American interests. 'Public opinion should be suspended until further report', he recommended, but the *Journal*'s front page carried a seven-column drawing of the Spanish attaching a mine to the boat. By now the *Journal*'s combined morning and evening circulation was often reaching 1,500,000. Two months later, Congress voted for war.

'How Do you Like The Journal's War?' asked the front page, offering a $1000 prize for the best suggestion on how to get it off to a good start. Many newspapers across the country carried wire stories that repeated the reports of the pro-war New York press. Fabrication of events was not confined to the newspaper medium. Although no motion-picture films were made of the fighting in Cuba, in 1898 the Edison company presented a reconstructed execution by firing squad in *Shooting Captured Insurgents, Spanish-American War*. Sham combat was also shot in New Jersey, and naval battles using miniature models were filmed. The war gave a boost at a critical time to the nascent film industry in America as audiences cheered such moving pictures in the vaudeville theatres (Sklar 2002: 28). However, the press carried the main responsibility, encouraged also by Pulitzer's *New York World* in competition with Hearst. 'Nothing so disgraceful as the behaviour of these two newspapers has been known in the history of American journalism', wrote the editor of the *New York Post*, E. L. Godkin (Williams 1969: 64) – but, at a time when both the *Journal* and the *World* reached over a million, his newspaper never exceeded 35,000 in circulation. Later Pulitzer stood aside, revamping his newspaper into a more respectable image nearer to his own conception of popular journalism. Although the war had offered certain advantages – it was conveniently close, short and relatively undemanding – the real end for Hearst had been to beat the sales of the *World*, whatever the means.

The '*Journal*'s war' had been the newspaper tycoon's biggest adventure, but the cost of the bloody New York circulation war had been considerable. Other weaker newspapers had folded, although many elsewhere had adopted the 'yellow' format. On a comparative note between both epochs and countries, another writer has observed that some popular '19th century American newspapers were cheap, ferociously competitive, rude, sensationalist, scurrilous and insulting – much like the British popular press today' (Engel 1996: 32; see also Neuzil 1996). The implication that the *Journal* had been responsible for encouraging the assassination of President McKinley contributed to the decline of 'yellow journalism'.

Before the First World War and during the later part of the nineteenth century, there were plenty of conflicts to make news: many of them, such as the Afghan Wars, the Indian Mutiny, the revolt in Sudan, the Boxer Rebellion, the Zulu War and the Boer War, were linked to the defence and international expansion of the British empire; others, such as the Franco-Prussian War, the Eastern question and the Balkan Wars, the Russo-Japanese War and the Spanish-American War, were influenced by the rise of incipient nationalism. Demand for news was huge; the circulation of Britain's *Daily News* trebled during the Franco-Prussian War. The role of press coverage in the Boer War became so important that it was dubbed 'the first media war', not only because of more extensive coverage than during any war previously, but also because the press helped to whip up pro-war feeling beforehand and was used for propaganda during the conflict.

From the public's point of view, in Britain and possibly also in the United States, as long as the conflict wasn't on home soil there was no real danger, therefore the coverage provided an entertaining narrative of gallant, bloodthirsty adventure. In retrospect it can be said that nineteenth-century war correspondents pandered to the morbid tastes of their age, displaying more enthusiasm for the thrill of battle and for the challenge of being the first to get a report back than they did for recognizing context or turning points in history, which are rarely appreciated at the time. In their favour was the fact that, with the notable exception of the Russo-Japanese War, organized censorship was slow to be introduced during what has been called the 'golden age' of the war correspondent, 1865–1914. During this heyday of nineteenth-century imperialism, foreign reporters became not only 'professional observers at the peep show of misery' (Knightley 1989: 43–6) but also heroes with a free hand to write under their own names. In Milan, news vendors shouted out 'article by Barzini' rather than the headline of the story. 'The reporter and his notebook (occasionally even her notebook) bore something of the magic of the new television teams of the 1960s, moving from riot to battlefield, demonstration to sit-in, while being widely accused of causing scenes which they recorded and reproduced' (Williams 1998: 54).

The responsibility of papers such as Britain's *Daily Mail* for encouraging national chauvinism and scaremongering in the run-up to the

Fig. 6 Lord Northcliffe caricatured as *The Napoleon of Slander*: the German view of his propaganda during the Great War

Great War has been much debated among historians in a similar way to Hearst's chauvinism. During the conflict government enlisted the press barons to help. Lord Beaverbrook, as minister of information, had a strong influence on war strategy, as did Lords Rothermere and Northcliffe: by 1918 the latter was in charge of propaganda in enemy territory on aspects such as recruitment, censorship, air power, munitions and the terms of peace (Thompson 2000a, 2000b).

Like Hearst, Northcliffe created a precedent for the press baron to set his own agenda. Ignoring the wartime censorship that was put in place by the government, he exposed problems within the British army such as the lack of explosive shells. However, when he lost readers over this unpopular campaign, he backed down: sales, as ever, took precedence over political ambition. Yet this guiding principle did not deter press barons Rothermere and Beaverbrook from influencing the removal of the prime minister, Herbert Asquith, in 1916 after he was blamed for a badly organized war, or from having a part in the success of his replacement, David Lloyd George.

Muckraking, public relations, power and popularism

The system of public-affairs communication in the United States, like the 'lobby' in Britain, dictated that the increasing number of accredited journalists had to be able to form relationships with politicians across the board, from all parties and groupings. The Japanese were not alone in devising a method of communication between government and journalists (see p. 115). The common issue in terms of the presentation of information is how far the 'realities' of society should be packaged by intermediaries, making it increasingly difficult for journalists to sift and write up information directly themselves.

During this period a vast industry arose around the management of news: public relations. This originated as an attempt to sell people rather than simply products – an extension of the new organizational growth of advertising, particularly in the field of entertainment, with film actors. Newspapers carried 'personality' items presented as ordinary news or gossip, but usually paid for in a system that, according to Raymond Williams, 'makes straightforward advertising, by comparison, look respectable.' In 1910 Congress employed a press agent to send handouts to Washington newspapers, and it escalated from there. Politicians no longer instructed journalists directly, with the consequence that the journalist became the 'piggy in the middle'. In a society where selling was becoming a primary ethic, the extension of public relations to apparently independent reporting appeared almost natural (Williams 1980: 184).

American presidents since the time of Andrew Jackson had always paid special attention to the press. Whereas Jackson had relied upon the support of close political friends who owned helpful newspapers, it was Woodrow Wilson who invented the presidential press conference. By Theodore Roosevelt's presidency, promotional image was carefully cultivated in a more organized fashion. 'Teddy' was the first to provide a continuous 'moral drama of American values' (Smith 1979: 157) by supplying daily human-interest news as a consequence of activities such as his nightly rambles through the streets – a throwback to his days as police commissioner of New York. The United States had already experienced a transition from party to non-party newspapers, which meant that the way politics was packaged and the relationship between newspapers and politicians had also changed. Yet, because the press had always been closer to ordinary people, there was not a sharp break between the old and new journalism as in Europe and Japan.

During this period newspapers in the United States became larger and their owners became richer, although this was not always the case elsewhere. There was a bigger increase in the number of newspapers because growth was more rapid than in other countries. However, the size and diversity of the United States had led to a complex relationship between mainstream society and subcultures, still articulated by political newspapers such as the *Appeal to Reason* – the most successful and powerful of the early twentieth-century socialist press (Hume 2003). For commercial papers, it was a question of 'shaping the news to please advertisers', with devices such as the 'puff' promotionally sponsored story (Solomon and McChesney 1993: 113), favourable

Japanese press clubs: coverage of politics is institutionalized

Gradually Japanese press communications became institutionalized within the unique 'press club' system. Legend has it that during the early Meiji period a group of reporters would meet together under a big tree in the Marunouchi section of Tokyo to share the information they had gathered (Lee 1985: 64). The first press club was established in the imperial Diet in 1890, and this led to the establishment of many others in different government ministries, with the aim of using collective efforts to overcome government secrecy. However, instead of being a means whereby journalists would together exert pressure on the government, this soon became a system whereby, if they were to retain the privileged membership of the club, they were obliged to receive and publish, without changes, information as presented by the authorities. One critic sums up the effect:

> it [also] induced an exclusionist attitude. . . . As a consequence, the actions of many a journalist became inspired by a strong sense of allegiance to the institution to which they were attached. Soon this unwholesome form of loyalty would not only threaten to undermine the reporter's sense of independence; but also, and more disturbingly, his commitment

to accurate reporting. (de Lange 1998: 87–8)

Conversely, as newspapers shed their political allegiances and became more independent, the politicians found press clubs increasingly useful as a means of influencing public opinion. Rules were devised for the modus operandi of individual clubs and, because of internal pressure for consensus, even 'confidential news' was fed equally to all the reporters in membership. As the information was reproduced verbatim, a high degree of uniformity of articles emerged, although uniformity was considered a problem elsewhere as well: examples included branded goods in chain stores and, in the United States, on account of the widespread influence of news agencies and syndicated features, the coverage of local papers (Williams 1969: 91). Over the years, Japanese press clubs have spread from government agencies to political parties, large economic and industrial organizations, the courts and the police. In 2001, one writer estimated that 75 per cent of all stories emanated from press clubs (Herbert 2001: 81–2). Despite the fact that these days some clubs allow foreign journalists to join, it is still argued that the system militates against the free flow of information for those who are left out in the cold.

mention of their products or organizations in stories, and sympathetic profiles of business people. Impartiality also became a justification for excluding certain sorts of coverage which may appear to be partisan. By not giving serious coverage, the commercial press helped to marginalize social reform movements 'by asserting implicitly that to ignore or trivialize them was an eminently fair and reasonable act, because they were beyond the political pale' (Hardt and Brennen 1995: 115).

American newspapers which aimed to reach working people found that their social and economic investigations often brought them up against deprivation that was a direct result of laissez-faire policies. In Britain, Stead had the same experience. However, the exposing of scandals and campaigns conducted on behalf of the working man presented a good example of social principles also making sound business. The prime example was the most famous political crusade of the time, when the *New York Times* exposed and smashed 'Boss' Tweed, the corrupt head of Tammany Hall, who offered the editor George Jones $5 million to withdraw the investigation – probably the biggest bribe ever extended and refused by a journalist (Williams 1969: 53).

It was certainly possible in a country the size of America for a newspaper to build up a commercial profile based on 'local muckraking' and politically independent local crusades that exposed the corruption of city officials. This was another form of stuntsmanship whereby readers were shocked by revelations of political huckstering into buying more newspapers. The tone of such journalism has been described as 'a kind of non-partisan crusading cynicism' (Smith 1979: 157). Nevertheless, there were some highly successful proponents, such as Victor Lawson's *Chicago Daily News* and William Rockhill Nelson's *Kansas City Star*. The latter is credited with encouraging a civic morality and doing much to help civilize the Midwest at a time when mobster rule and corruption were rampant.

Although, according to the historian of Britain's political press Stephen Koss, nineteenth-century newspapers were the 'gears which kept the party machinery in motion' (1984: 1.4), they were now less political than newspapers in continental Europe and also in Japan. Relationships between editors, publishers and politicians were changing; so too was the presentation of politics and the prominence given to it, influenced in part by developments in America. Even during the height of the late Victorian newspaper's political influence, ownership tended to be by rich individuals or groups of party sympathizers rather than by the parties themselves, but proprietors rarely made money; and the concept of newspapers as an objective forum for debate within the public sphere ran along parallel lines, a strand which has continued with today's broadsheets.

The popular press brought mass circulation, but also depoliticization and greater independence. In these respects Northcliffe's influence set a trend for the twentieth century by detaching the financial control of the daily newspapers from the party system while at the same time increasing readership. Although British advertisers became increasingly reluctant to buy space in political newspapers such as the *Pall Mall Gazette* and *The Standard*, many people in the newspaper industry disagreed with Northcliffe's view that to be politically independent a newspaper should be free of any political subsidies. They believed that newspapers could still be independent even if political organs funded them.

The way politics was written about also changed. The agency-style shortened use of the third person, individual interviews and human-interest devices all became commonplace. Many editors still supported a party, but were also individualist. For instance, C. P. Scott, the veteran editor of *The Guardian*, became outspoken against official Liberal Party policy on the Boer War, and took a lead in propagating the rights of both women's suffrage and the Irish to home rule in advance of his party's conversion to these great causes. Indeed, he is credited not only with building the status of his Manchester paper to world class, but also with having considerable influence on Prime Minister Gladstone for these and later Liberal Party initiatives, such as the introduction of state benefit for old-age pensions.

Furthermore, with the advent of mass circulation, owners of newspaper chains such as Northcliffe were able to claim popular authority based on their own huge constituency of readers. This new form of political power was both independent of and a challenge to parliament and political parties, as well as being unaccountable apart from an arbitrary responsiveness to the market, prompting one scholar to conclude: 'Taken together, these possibilities constituted a destabilising force in the organisation of British politics. . . . the daily press played a smaller part than it might have done in sustaining mass based political parties' (Smith 1979: 157). This view is supported by a former editor of the *Daily Mirror*, Hugh Cudlipp, who describes 'Northoleon' (as he was called in Fleet Street) as 'a man corrupted by power and wealth, who desecrated journalistic standards and became dominated by the pursuit of political power, unguided by political prescience' (Thompson 2000a: xii).

Conversely, the polemical role of the press in Germany increased as political parties began to form out of factions in the new constitutional structure that Bismarck had spearheaded. Yet the 'Iron Chancellor' continued to dominate the press until 1890. While the autocratic state remained, the press inevitably served as a weapon with which opposition groups could attack the government. So interpretative reporting persisted, either as a vehicle for polemicists or as an upholder of the status quo, but coexisting alongside a small city-based section of the press, whose lively style also reflected the concept of the paper as an objective observer, independent of dominant economic or political allegiance. But the German backdrop was local, not national, as the regional differences which still existed despite unification meant that newspapers were also decentralized. However, during the First World War, government exerted a centralized effort on the media (including film), though admitting that their propaganda measures were too little and too late compared to the British influence on enemy and neutral territories.

In France, the combination of previous repressive censorship, the industrialization of the press and political disillusionment had created a permanent division between high and low cultures. Yet Paris newspapers such as *Le Figaro* and *Le Petit Journal* were ahead of Britain in achieving high circulations and catering for lightweight public taste. Indeed Harmsworth met Marioni, the founder and editor of the latter paper, before starting up the *Daily Mail* and was much impressed that the menu of gossip, lively news and political attack was selling 650,000 copies a day and making a profit of £150,000 a year (Williams 1969: 81; Bellanger et al. 1969: 327–8). But such newspapers were not typical of the continental European press at the time, which tended to remain closer in style to *The Times* of London.

Recent scholarship has emphasized the diversity of France's press; for instance, nearly every political faction had its own satirical paper and feminist journalism emerged in the form of the daily *La Fronde*, dubbed '*Le Temps* in skirts' because it was staffed and produced entirely by women (de la Motte and Przyblyski 1999: 302–50).[2] Another historian has attributed the weaknesses of the press over the years to its reluctance to encourage commercial advertising, leading to a consequential dependency on hidden subsidies, often political (Martin 1993).

However, different perspectives do not deflect from the fact that, by the fin de siècle, increased literacy, technological inventions and the liberating effect of legalized press freedom all contributed to a golden age for French newspapers. The Parisian mass press almost tripled its circulation between 1880 and 1914. However, throughout the period up to the end of the First World War, French newspapers always reflected the dichotomy of newspapers as the 'dominant discourse of the age': while they encouraged instability and subversiveness as agents of the changing nature of political discussion, they were also under constant pressure to elaborate the 'cult of objectivity' (de la Motte and Przyblyski 1999: 2, 7).

The First World War also provided a turning point for early wireless, although even this milestone is open to interpretation by historians.

Wireless before broadcasting

There is disagreement about the date that 'wireless' was invented, and the nature of its origins depends on definitions. Many histories of radio start in 1920 and, in doing so, tend to deprive radio of its earlier heritage and give the impression, supported by contemporary press euphoria (see <www.earlyradiohistory.us/>), that it suddenly appeared from nowhere. But this is to ignore the existence of twenty-five years of technical improvements, economic and organizational change, and unanticipated applications which amounted to a form of cultural experimentation. The historian Susan J. Douglas argues that there was a social construction of radio, but earlier than previously assumed (1987: xv–xvii). The term 'radio' did not come into usage until the 1910s and did not take over until the 1920s. At first it was known as wireless telegraphy; when the human voice and music were transmitted, it became important as wireless telephony.

For most of the nineteenth century the world of communications was dominated by the telegraph, the 'Victorian internet', which had been in place since the 1870s with cables crossing the oceans: all the main centres of administration of the British empire formed part of the network. The development of the telephone from 1876 did not have any impact on this global communication network as technological limitations restricted the transmission of speech to only a few miles, whereas the Morse telegraph could travel thousands.

When, in 1894, Marconi first conceived the idea of sending Morse code signals, with dots and dashes, by means of a wireless transmitter and receiver using the recently discovered electromagnetic or Hertzian waves, he was aware that there was one remaining gap in the Victorian 'internet' – communication between ships at sea with each other and land stations. Cable could not do this. Wireless might also be useful when a cable went down between an offshore island and the mainland, but to have any function at all a huge technical problem had to be overcome. Scientists believed that electromagnetic waves would behave like light waves. They travelled at the same speed, and would doubtless head off in straight lines. As the earth is spherical, the curvature of the surface would mean that wireless waves would be restricted in range to a mile or two. Guglielmo Marconi, who described himself to a journalist in 1897 as an 'enthusiastic amateur of electricity', proved the scientists wrong.

The phonograph, film and many other inventions evolved through a process whereby their ultimate application differed from their intended purpose. Innovations are influenced by the needs and effects of the age (Aikat 2001). Such was the case with radio. Wireless technology was often seen as an upgrade of the telegraph, not as something that would revolutionize how we listened to the world. At a time when electricity was not yet in households, the concept of invisible airways was viewed by some as an audio illusion, whereas telegraphy was more easily understood because the wires along which the information flowed could be seen.

After Marconi linked the liner *Philadelphia* with Cornwall as it steamed from Southampton to New York, he soon became a media celebrity and won worldwide renown for his shipboard 'Marconiogram' network. Very rapidly, all the big liners were fitted with wireless and their lonely isolation at sea was ended. His greatest triumph, the saving of 700 passengers on the *Titanic*, would have been impossible without on-board Marconi operators. This proved the power of his invention: 'everyone seems so grateful to wireless, I can't go about New York without being mobbed and cheered', he wrote to his wife (Douglas 1999: 49).

Once Marconi had shown that there was no limit to the distance wireless messages could be sent, he faced fierce competition. The technology was crude and easily replicated. Amateur enthusiasts in America were making their own sets from 1902 and listening in to transmissions from ships, but the real interest was not domestic – it was commercial and military. At a time of growing international tension the potential of radio waves for long-distance communication implied a new means of maintaining links across Britain's many colonial territories. The navies of the other major powers also took a close interest. Rivals appeared in the USA, France and Germany, where Telefunken was set up as a company with full government support specifically to challenge Marconi worldwide.

Yet Marconi managed to stay in the lead until the First World War with his Wireless Telephone and Signal Company, supplying merchant

Fig. 7 Marconi and Father Neptune, 1912: a reference to the *Titanic*

fleets. According to the American scholar Hugh Aitken, Marconi corporate ambitions were 'suspect' because they threatened to extend and perpetuate the 'hegemony' that Britain had achieved in the age of worldwide submarine cables, which by 1914 were mainly British owned (1985: 252). This was backed up not only by British possession of the cable companies, but also by their control of the raw materials used for production – a situation not dissimilar to America's domination of the film industry later in the century. Marconi did not market to individuals. He had no concept of broadcasting. In fact he tried desperately to develop 'tuning' so that signals could not be intercepted. Early pioneers saw radio not as a mass medium but as a means of one-to-one communication: wireless was telegraph without the wires for transmitting messages from point A to point B.

The early history of radio was partly a battle between two technologies – wireless telegraphy and telephony – for application and acceptance, and of their adoption by different commercial, military and political interests (Barnard 2000: 9). Yet because wireless telegraphy was one of the greatest inventions of the age, if not the greatest, it was not regarded by contemporaries as primitive or limited in any way, and in his own terms Marconi was spectacularly successful. By 1914, wireless telegraphy was a well-established international business. It had been used for the first time in a major conflict in the Russo-Japanese War of 1904, with disastrous consequences for the Russians.[3]

In Britain wireless was put under government control from the early days. The Post Office, which had been a self-financing branch of the state under nominal royal patronage since 1876, controlled the telegraph because the latter was seen as an extension of the postal service.

Since the telephone message was then viewed as an expansion of the telegraphic principle, there was a certain logic to the decision that the same body should control wireless communication as well as these other forms of communication. In 1904 the first licences were issued and the Post Office was also called upon to operate two government transmission stations on an experimental basis. Here lie the seeds of the concept of public-service broadcasting, demonstrating a recognition of future strategic potential (Macdonald 1988: 5–6). In the USA, there was a free-for-all until after the *Titanic* disaster of 1912, when amateurs were accused of spreading false rumours about the ship. This comparison provides an example of how differing national values shaped radio broadcasting, implicating politics, cultural identity and consumerism, all of which are emphasized by more recent scholarship.

In 1907 a Canadian, Reginald Fessenden, who wanted to compete with the landline telephone by developing continuous wave transmission, had transmitted the first ever 'programme' on the air to a fleet of ships and a few amateurs who had the necessary receiving equipment. Although transmission of speech and music was now technically possible, it was made much more viable just before the First World War by the development of the wireless valve. In the USA, Lee de Forest, a bitter rival of Marconi, invented the prototype of the three-electrode vacuum tube to amplify voice transmissions, which he called the 'audion'. De Forest was aided considerably by radio 'amateurs' ('hackers of the early twentieth century', later called 'hams') who took up radio as a hobby, listening in to military messages as well as transmitting their own (Douglas 1999: 51). He interested the United States navy in his work, and in 1908 they installed radio-telephone equipment on North Atlantic fleet vessels, but they were not impressed when they discovered that ships were picking up ear-splitting renditions of Rossini instead of vital information about manoeuvres! The early attempts of the 'father of radio' (a title de Forest took for himself in an autobiography) to transmit music included a broadcast of phonograph records from the Eiffel Tower in Paris and a live broadcast from the Metropolitan Opera, New York. American amateurs also used radio telephony to play records

The 'town crier' – early telephone programming

Already in the 1870s, telephone was being developed as a quasi-broadcasting tool, using one central point to communicate with a multiplicity of reception points. Public demonstrations of the telephone stressed how music and lectures could be received down the wire from distant places. The most celebrated experiment using the telephone was Telefon Hirmondo, in Budapest. From 1893 subscribers were offered news and concerts – here there was a concept of broadcasting, together with a studio, newsroom and programming schedule. "Hirmondo' is Magyar for 'town crier', and, for around twenty-five years, up to 6000 citizens could pick up a telephone in cafes, hotels or at home to hear this profit-making station, but the requisite technology and capital investment for popularization was lacking.

to each other over the air, sometimes provided by the record companies in exchange for advertising (de Forest 1950).

Significantly, the US telephone giant AT&T began to invest in wireless telephony, buying up patents from inventors such as Lee de Forest. The US navy, which had been unconvinced by Marconi's system, preferring at first to retain the use of homing pigeons (Weightman 2003: 208), now became interested. It was during the First World War, in 1915, that the first transmission of speech was made across the Atlantic from Arlington, Virginia (a US navy base), to the Eiffel Tower, using the AT&T equipment. For three critical years, from 1914 until it entered the war in 1917, the USA was free to develop 'peaceful' uses for wireless. Although the American David Sarnoff apparently defined a vision of broadcasting in a memo: 'I have a plan of development which would make radio a household utility like the piano or electricity . . . . the idea is to bring music into the house by wireless' (Curran and Seaton 1997: 111), the memo has never been found. Scholarship has challenged the validity of the 'radio music box memo' (Benjamin 1993).

The fact is that, before 1914, the thinking on radio was still not quite what we would expect today, as Brian Winston explains:

> Getting beyond the idea of point to point communication was the real inhibitor suppressing the potential of wireless communication until after the First World War. Radio, broadcast radio, essentially involved not knowing in advance where signals would be received. In other words, further exploitation depended on seeing that a major perceived fault of the technology, that anybody could listen, was actually its raison d'être. One did not have to be in danger of sinking or in the midst of a revolution or a war to make use of this possibility; yet that possibility did not quite add up to a supervening social necessity. (1998: 75–6)

Meanwhile, in Britain and elsewhere in Europe, the 1914–18 war 'harnessed the new powers of wireless to the needs of separate armies, navies and intelligence services', which in itself created a large wireless manufacturing industry to meet the needs of the war (Briggs 1961: 36). Marconi's men and equipment had been commandeered for the war effort. As the British had cut cable connections with Germany, the Germans were obliged to use the airways for communications: 'the air crackled with occult codes; everywhere the recording and studying of coded material went on day and night' (Barnouw 1966: 50). While the British maintained radio silence, they listened and decoded. After America entered the war, the study of captured German technological artefacts became part of the effort: a Marconi employee in New Jersey was given the job of studying a German trench transmitter and producing a similar one for American troops. 'It was a peculiar thing, though, to handle this thing with blood all over it', he later remarked (ibid.: 51).

At the end of the war and of trench communications, the era of wireless telegraphy was over: broadcasting was now taking off among the amateurs in North America. Although these early enthusiasts were receiving and transmitting by themselves, as Chanan points out, 'what happened to radio was the same thing that had happened with the gramophone: reception was separated from transmission in the same way as playback from recording' (1994: 253).

The early film industry

Movies formed the first mass medium of the twentieth century and were the most popular for a full fifty years. Certain technical preconditions were necessary for motion pictures, such as improvements in photographic equipment, the invention of celluloid as a substance strong enough to pass through a projector, and precision engineering for projector design. However, the accumulation of inventions from France, America, Germany and Britain that contributed towards the debut of the film industry cannot be fully appreciated without first looking at wider changes in consciousness towards the visual experience.

By the end of the eighteenth century the modes of perception later to be associated with the cinema were already established within novels and paintings: technology came quickly, but later. Various ways of projecting moving images, such as magic lanterns (which used a candle or lamp and glass slides with pictures to create a moving effect), had existed since the seventeenth century, but it was the industrialized world that became fascinated by motion and the recording of it, for machines had challenged the previous relationship between movement and nature, epitomized by horse and wind.

Themes of multi-dimensions in time, space, perception and memory are illustrated in the new discipline of psychology[4] and appear in the arts, most notably in Marcel Proust's classic novel *À la recherche du temps perdu* (Remembrance of Things Past). Film played a part in this wider change of thinking, which is labelled 'modernism'. In a study of the psychology of film, Munsterberg says: 'It is as if the outer world were woven into our minds and were shaped not through its own laws but by the acts of our attention' (1970: 39). One invention was dependent or built on another. An example is Thomas Edison and W. K. L. Dickson's kinetoscope: its construction in 1888 depended on the film-roll pioneered by the inventor of Kodak, George Eastman, but he had benefited from the discovery by Hannibal Goodwin that celluloid was the best base for a film-strip (Musser 1990: 3). Motives for research were diverse, the resulting applications often unanticipated and the logic sometimes unpredictable. For instance, Edison modelled his kinetoscope on the phonograph, based on the misplaced but understandable logic that a system which recorded and replayed images might be arrived at by imitating one which recorded and replayed sounds.

After 1890 the race was on in the United States, Great Britain, France and Germany to achieve working motion-picture cameras and projectors. Competition only increased the pressure to launch something

Inadvertent precursors of film: Marey and Muybridge

The French scientist Etienne Jules Marey wanted to find a way to make visible those movements that could not normally be seen with the human eye with the aim of proving Charles Darwin's theory of evolution by natural selection. He studied the visual reproduction of human and animal movements, but he needed a camera that could take rapid photographs through a single lens at precise intervals. This was something that the British-born American photographer Eadweard Muybridge achieved courtesy of the sponsorship of the former Californian governor and railway tycoon Leland Stanford. Stanford needed proof to win a bet which was based on his hunch that a horse lifted all four legs off the ground when trotting. After seeing Muybridge's experiment, Marey advanced it in 1882 with chronophotography. This involved the construction of a portable photographic gun with a revolving disc that notched up photographs at regular intervals, which would capture the movement of birds in flight. His 'revolver photography' represented the crucial stage in the development of the film camera. He increased the speed to a hundred photographs a second with the use of paper roll-film, producing sets of haunting images. Marey proudly claimed that chronophotography had helped to clarify the diagnosis of cardiac and vascular diseases. Meanwhile, in the same year – 1887 – 20,000 of Muybridge's photographic sequences were published in eleven volumes, revealing a world that the eye had formerly been unable to see.

quickly rather than going for perfection, so compromise was inevitable. In 1892 Edison, who had already brought the world the telephone transmitter, the phonograph and the electric light, introduced the first projector to use celluloid film on an endless belt, but it lacked a reliable mechanism for the film to move evenly past the lens. During a trip abroad that same year Edison met Marey and saw his transparent film-strips, which prompted the former to use film-strips also and to position the perforations equidistantly so that the film ran smoothly past the lens. This was his one major contribution to moving-picture technology, and it allowed him to be first in the market with a commercial motion-picture machine – but it wasn't a large screen projector. Edison's 'peep show' kinetoscope was limited: it was an individual viewer which displayed unenlarged 35 mm black and white pictures with a maximum running time of about a minute and a half.

Edison was a formidable entrepreneur, so these contraptions were distributed throughout the United States, but the public soon tired of this penny in the slot arcade novelty, as it showed mainly vaudeville acts that were better experienced in the flesh. Another company brought out a 'mutoscope' viewing machine with postcard-sized flip cards rather than strip-film. Meanwhile Edison, one of his former employees, Dickson, and a number of European inventors were working on large-scale projection. It was Louis Lumière who first successfully invented a very smart piece of precision engineering: a small, portable machine that was both camera and projector and had a novel claw drive for moving the film-strip. As he said, 'other machines may have preceded mine, but they didn't work' (Sadoul 1966: 24).

In fact the French invention had come about because Auguste Lumière, a successful cameraman, was dismayed by the prohibitive charges that Edison was making on the sale of film for the kinetoscope, and asked his brother to come up with something better. Louis had previously invented a photographic plate that was in such demand that the family factory in Lyons had expanded to employ over 300 people and was second only to George Eastman's at Rochester, New York. Louis said later in an interview with Georges Sadoul, 'My work has been directed towards scientific research' (Gedult 1967: 39), so the first public showing of the 'cinematographe', on 28 December 1895 at the Grand Café on the boulevard des Capucines in Paris, at which spectators were charged 1 franc, had only an accidental relationship to the concept of film as an entertainment industry.

While celebrities and royalty flocked to the screenings and Lumières cameramen travelled to Egypt, India, Japan and Australia, the distributor of Edison's kinetoscope faced heavy losses. The Lumières' cinematographe's technical specifications gave it an edge over competitors for both production and exhibition. It was fairly light (16 lb, compared to a weight of several hundred pounds in the case of Edison's kinetoscope) and it functioned as a camera, a projector and a film developer; and the fact that it was not dependent on electric current made it portable and adaptable (Nowell-Smith 1996: 14).

Edison backed another projector called the Vitascope; Dickson's Biograph followed the next year. The entrepreneurial, empire-building inclinations of Edison made him different to the numerous other inventors of the period: he wanted to have a stake in every territory, but he often had to secure it by using patent litigation as a commercial weapon. His main target was the American Mutoscope & Biograph Company, the most commercially successful American film enterprise during the late 1890s and again in 1904–5 (Musser 1990: 8; Brown and Anthony 1999). Scholarship has revealed that neither the idea of motion pictures nor most of the practical inventions were his.

Edison had a long-term interest in synchronized sound, but the tests had failed. He regularly made public announcements about

The international launch of cinema: Lumières brothers' films

The Lumières brothers had already trained a squad of cameramen and projectionists and built up a stock of machines and films, soon to total 1200 single shot movies on many subjects, shot all over the world. Although a fee-paying public exhibition had taken place in Berlin two months earlier, the Lumières' business and marketing skill ensured that they created a sensation worldwide. Within a month or two their exhibitions opened in London, then Vienna, Geneva, Madrid, Belgrade and New York, where their team of twenty-one operators proved insufficient for demand. In July 1896 these were followed by Bucharest and St Petersburg. The first Lumières film had been of employees leaving the works, followed by other 'documentary' subjects; the firm also produced fiction and biblical subjects.

breakthroughs for a more ambitious 'total cinema', but these were mainly untruths, proffered to discourage his competitors – false information in private letters, to the press, and even to the government Patent Office. According to Robert Sklar, 'Edison maintained his remarkable half century reign as an American hero by a judicious combination of real accomplishment and the tantalizing promise of even more amazing inventions just around the corner. A credulous press and public came to believe that Edison's fantasies were more real than any other man's working invention' (1994: 10).

Whereas the appeal of works of art relies on uniqueness, film challenged this concept. 'The importance in the history of communication cannot be overrated. Transcending differences of language and national custom, Lumière's "cinematographe" suddenly made the world a smaller and more ordinary place. . . . In shrinking the world, the cinematographe encouraged fashions and trends to spread with lightning speed, obliterating the idiosyncracies of folk art' (Rhode 1976: 16–19). When *Bronco Billy* became fashionable in the United States in 1909, for instance, the French were making Westerns in which the cowboys sported moustaches, and imitations were also manufactured in Germany, Italy and Japan. Such was the potential of film to speak a universal visual language while overcoming distance and difference.

The international appeal of the film industry

According to the French film critic André Bazin, cinema's goal was 'to create a medium that could capture and record human lives and events for posterity as realistically as possible – a subconscious attempt to overcome the fact of death, in the same way that Egyptians embalmed their dead' (1967: 17). Life and death encounters could be viewed from the safety of a cinema seat, and reality could be simulated. There was a novelty to moving images, although the content of films was simple at first. Early cinema audiences liked themes that had never been shown before inside a theatre, such as the wonders of nature and remote places, rare sights, even machines and fast locomotives.

In one of his films, *The Arrival of a Train at La Ciotat*, Louis Lumière had caught the audience unawares and shocked them to such an extent with a single shot of an approaching train that spectators moved from their seats to escape the imminent 'crash'. His artistic approach broke the proscenium theatrical convention of distance between player and audience, but in this case the film appeared to echo an actual crash that had taken place at a Paris station only a few months before. Film has the effect of 'deterritorialization', a concept examined by theorists of globalization as the weakening of the connection between everyday lived culture and territorial location. John Tomlinson argues that this is a mundane experience, taken by ordinary people in their stride, but that it is also 'a complex and ambiguous blend: of familiarity and difference, expansion of cultural horizons and increased perceptions of vulnerability, access to the "world out there" accompanied by penetration of our own private worlds, new opportunities and new risks' (1999: 128). The above audience experience illustrates this point.

In the United States, early cinema became known as a working-class entertainment, and it grew from the bottom up at a time of urbanization. Areas of cities had become segregated by class, with the result that the richer classes could avoid contact with workers' ghettos – the very places where the nickelodeon movie first took hold. This nascent industry would not have taken off without small businessmen who saw the opportunity for a quick buck, taking over from the inventors, scientists and instrument-makers. The showmen associated with cinema were often not very respectable. The big attraction to any aspiring businessman was that the start-up costs were so low. 'All you needed was fifty dollars, a broad and a camera', so it was said – a far cry from today's multi-million-dollar outfits (Puttnam 1997: 35). In New York, movies were shown initially in a curtained-off corner of a store, then empty stores were converted into 'nickelodeons': very soon, according to *Harper's Weekly*, it became 'nickel madness' (51, 1907, p. 1246).

By 1909 there were 8000 nickelodeons throughout America, and the number soon doubled. Movies were also presented as part of the vaudeville show in theatres before venues were built specifically for films. Indeed, the influence of the theatre on early film extended beyond the shared venues. In Japan, even from 1910 onwards, films remained closely tied to theatrical conventions, such as filmed plays where actors delivered the dialogue live from behind a screen. With this particularly popular technique, '*benshi*' narrated the silent films as they unfolded. This method of accompanying live performance was provided in America by, among others, a company called Humanova Talking Pictures (Sklar 2002: 55).

In contrast to the case in the United States where, for the American working classes, entertainment had to be cheap, brief and accessible, cinema in Japan became respectable immediately and was accepted by both intellectuals and the masses, with the result that films displayed an early artistic excellence. The Japanese made a clear distinction between their own approach to film, integrating and leaning heavily on traditional theatre, and Western imports. By comparison, early cinema in Britain and the United States had close creative links to music hall and vaudeville, which had a less respectable, lower-class image. The influence of traditional theatre, particularly strong in Japan, is an example of the process of 'mediazation of tradition' examined by John Thompson (1995: 180) as a feature of modernity. As new media forms emerge, the process of self-formation by audiences becomes more reflexive and open ended: after all, in most places film represented a distinctly new experience.

For the first time, with silent movies an audience did not need English or literacy to gain access to urban popular culture. The fact that the performance lasted only fifteen or twenty minutes was convenient, although it amounted to little more than a flickering and jumpy projection of a series of unevenly moving two-dimensional still photographs. Meanwhile movie-going was of itself fostering new modes of behaviour, leisure, desire and consciousness, to the extent that cultural observers 'were beginning to recognize that the cinema was threatening if not transforming many of American society's most cherished and long standing values' (Musser 1990: 11).

The genre of bawdy, suggestive films started to become popular in America around 1900. When the 'guardians of public morality' – the churches, reform groups, some members of the press and the police – discovered their popularity, movie theatres became tarred with the same brush in their eyes as brothels, gambling dens and the meeting places of criminal gangs. Campaigns were instigated against theatres that showed non-respectable films, and there were seizures in some places and police censorship in others. Then in 1908 a climax of suppression took place in New York, the centre of the movie industry and its largest market. Every cinema was ordered to close for Christmas week.

In America, unlike Japan where it happened naturally, from about 1908 an effort had to be made to attract the middle classes to the cinema. Venues became more sumptuous, sometimes with full orchestras. In fact, the use of elaborate musical accompaniment is sometimes overlooked in the history of silent movies. By 1912, the American production company Kalem was selling piano sheet music scores of its original compositions, and the orchestral score for *The Birth of a Nation* by D. W. Griffith was a strong feature in its success.

The world's leading producer of early fiction films is pirated

Another very popular style of film was the 'trick' movie. Visual special effects were presented as a kind of superhuman surreal magic in the creative hands of the French director Georges Meliès, who had previously been a conjurer and an illusionist. He became the world's leading producer of fiction films during the early cinema period. The illusions that he created of magical appearance, change and disappearance were fashionable for almost ten years, for Meliès made over 500 narrative films between 1896 and 1906. His films were seriously pirated by American producers, for instance by the Edison company, which began making direct or very close copies of Meliès films as early as 1898. As a copyright law was not introduced for film in the United States until 1912, it was perfectly legal to buy a print of one of his films and put somebody else's name on it. English and French films were the most vulnerable, and bootlegging also extended to equipment and stock. 'A cold war, which on occasions became a very hot one, entangled all producers and exhibitors of motion pictures' (Mast 1981: 39). Despite the fact that Meliès had studios at Montreuil outside Paris and distribution offices in Berlin, Barcelona, London and New York, and that his company played an influential role in the American industry, competitors eventually forced him into bankruptcy in 1913. He ended up selling toys from a kiosk at the Gare Montparnasse in Paris (Puttnam 1997: 40).

The initiative in original scores had first been taken in 1908, when the French company Film d'Art commissioned the composer Saint-Saëns. By holding the first commercial screenings of projected motion pictures and producing the first commercial movies, the French made a huge contribution to the founding of the global cinema industry. Charles Pathé turned movie-making into a mass-market industry as the world's largest motion-picture producer. In the Third World his name was almost synonymous with cinema; his company dominated the American market and all others, becoming the single largest producer of films shown in nickelodeons and distributing twice as many films within the United States as all the indigenous companies combined (Nowell-Smith 1996: 14).

Pathé pioneered many techniques that were later adopted else-where. For instance, in 1901, one of his directors, Ferdinand Zecca, made a longer narrative film in six parts entitled *L'Histoire d'un crime*, and his longer films had the effect of creating sufficient confidence in the genre to encourage the first permanent theatres to compete with the existing shared billing at music halls, magic theatres, wax museums and tents at travelling fairs. Pathé was the best producer of comedy until the First World War, and his French company also played an influential role in the American industry, outlasting both the Lumières and Meliès. Its films felt expansive because they exploited the great outdoors, and its fairytale and fantasy productions were also excellent. This was a genre that appealed to audiences, along with the dangerous, the impossible, the grotesque. It was beyond their more limited every-day experiences.

Pathé created subsidiary production companies in many other European countries. According to David Puttnam, Pathé adopted the regimented techniques of mass production for film-making that a few years later Henry Ford was famously to apply to the car industry. He also operated an 'almost seamless vertical integration' which has since become a feature of the global industry, combining distribution, production and exhibition under one ownership. The result of these forward-looking business practices was that, unknowingly, and ten years in advance, Charles Pathé 'laid the foundations of the system which would enable the Hollywood moguls to reign over the movie industry for decades to come' (Puttnam 1997: 41).

The emergence of Hollywood was a slow process, and a painful one for film industries in other countries that were operating internation-ally. The existence of craft features that had characterized the early film industry became threatened by the skyrocketing costs of production and the emergence of a powerful studio system, but in 1910 two-thirds of the movies shown in the world were still made in France. In 1909 France supplied 40 per cent of the new releases in Great Britain (Sklar 1994: 29). French productions were acknowledged as the best in the world. Gaumont, who had acquired a cinema chain, became number two in France. The founder, Léon Gaumont, viewed production as

Fig. 8 Poster of the Pathé brothers: the French were the first to make film a global industry

a sideline, so he gave the work to Europe's first female director, Alice Guy, who made 400 films before moving to America and starting a production company in New Jersey with her husband, Herbert Blaché, and directing many more films.[5]

Pathé's big jump in profits happened between 1905 and 1907. In that latter year the first theatre opened in London that was exclusively for movies, and its programme consisted entirely of Pathé productions. Similarly, Edward Wagenknecht remembers in his reminiscences that his local nickelodeon in Chicago showed only Pathé films (Sklar 1994: 29).

> It was above all the French, followed by the Americans, who were the most ardent exporters of the new invention, helping to implant the cinema in China, Japan, and Latin America as well as in Russia. In terms of artistic development it was again the French and the Americans who took the lead, though in the years preceding the First World War Italy, Denmark, and Russia also played a part. (Nowell-Smith 1996: 3)

The second biggest film company in the world was the Danish Nordisk, which exploited the international market even more effectively than the world's largest film company, Pathé. Both companies engaged in the practice of 'block booking', for which Hollywood has since been heavily criticized – that is, making cinema owners take a batch of unwanted films along with the movies that they did want. Like Pathé, Nordisk was vertically integrated long before Hollywood firms, with cinema chains in Denmark, the Netherlands, Switzerland and Germany and offices in St Petersburg, Budapest and other European cities, as well as production and distribution arms. Denmark's success encouraged the growth of an industry in neighbouring Sweden, and after the formation of Svenska Bio in 1907 Swedish cameramen created a series of outstanding innovations in cinematography.

The growth of American dominance

By 1908 daily cinema attendance was estimated at between 300,000 and 400,000 in greater New York's 600-plus theatres, with a gross annual receipt of over $6 million for that city alone (Sklar 1994: 16). By 1915, the estimated box office in the whole of the country was about 10 million tickets a day: clearly cinema was now reaching beyond its original working-class appeal (Ross 1998: 10).[6] Indeed, the sheer size of its movie-going market, which dwarfed all others, was to help American cultural dominance. At first, artistic appeal rested on better constructed narratives and more grandiose effects. The first director to achieve worldwide appeal by combining the capacity of motion picture for spectacle with myths and stories about America was Edwin S. Porter. He was the country's greatest film-maker from 1899 to 1909 and famous for *The Great Train Robbery*, moving beyond the constraints of Meliès's fixed camera approach with the use of twenty shots from different locations and tight editing.

In this period of rapid growth, distribution or 'exchanges' proliferated, but all control seemed lost. By 1909 legal battles over patents had intensified and Edison had established an organized cartel of producers or trust, called the Motion Picture Patents Company (MPPC), with a separate distribution arm called the General Film Company. This monopoly enabled him to consolidate his control over the personnel and products involved. The aim was to force competitors to use his cameras under licence, and to sell or rent films only to the exchanges and exhibitors who agreed to use licensed products exclusively. Enforcement was exercised via the US Patent Office or the law courts, supported by a spy network (Bowser 1990: 150). All the main producers, including Meliès and Pathé, participated, but Edison retained the lion's share of the royalties that accrued from the system: his net profits soared to over $1 million a year (Sklar 1994: 36).[7]

Despite anti-trust laws such as the Sherman Act of 1890, big business had been forming trusts for over twenty years, prompting Theodore Roosevelt to say that such legislation was about as effective as a papal bull against a comet. The effect, and indeed the intention, of the trust according to Europeans was to keep them out of the market. They contrasted their own free-trade policies with American protectionism. The British film-maker Cecil Hepworth recalled, 'So far as we were concerned, [the object of the trust] was to put a stop to the import of English and other European films.' The statistics bear this out: just before the MPPC started formally, overseas imports of short films accounted for 70 per cent of all those shown. In just under a year, the European share had been halved (Puttnam 1997: 47–9). The only foreign challenge came from Ole Olsen's Nordisk company, whose New York office in charge of distribution, entitled Great Northern, stayed open in defiance. Richard Abel has demonstrated how Pathé's Red Rooster films became the victim of a 'scare', defined as 'foreign' and 'alien' and even 'feminine', especially in relation to 'American subjects' such as Westerns. They were excluded from the market (Abel 1999, 1994).

During the American 'progressive' period, the Democrats selected Woodrow Wilson as presidential candidate, and he accused the Republicans of favouring big business. The political debate that ensued resulted by 1915 in the trust being declared illegal. By that time it had already lost the battle, as its segment of control diminished in favour of the new independents. These producers, who were largely from the Southern European and Eastern European Jewish immigrant groups that had first provided the audiences, had been obliged to hide their cameras and engage bodyguards to protect their cameramen against the trust. Anticipating the gangsterism of prohibition days, thugs had smashed cameras and raided illicit laboratories and machine shops. The independent producers dispersed to locations such as Cuba, Florida and California to avoid prosecution. Carl Laemmle, who had the biggest distribution outfit in the country and went on to found Universal City, was the target of 289 separate legal actions, and in 1912 William Fox had won a lawsuit against the Edison company (Koszarski 1994).

Another independent, William Selig, discovered when he sent his company to Los Angeles that Californian locations were ideal for Westerns, and his enthusiasm encouraged others from New York, Chicago and Philadelphia to move (Bowser 1990: 151). During the second decade of the twentieth century the Los Angeles area became the main centre of supply of films worldwide, and many of the developments that took place after 1907 can be construed as laying the foundations for the Hollywood system within the industry. Hollywood offered more than just locations for Westerns, but at first it was just one of several favoured production locales.

There were other advantages that gave it an edge, and these are discussed by scholars as part of the considerable debate about the combination of motives for relocation: they include distance from trust litigation, a Mediterranean climate for outdoor filming, plenty of space to build studios, an anti-trades union political culture, and lower labour rates. In 1915 Carl Laemmle transformed a former chicken ranch into Universal City, the largest and most modern studio complex in the world. Los Angeles studios already employed over 15,000 people, producing between 60 and 75 per cent of all films made in the United States (Ross 1998: 121). By the time of the First World War, when Hollywood producers were on the point of taking over a large proportion of the world market, four out of the original ten companies that made up General Films – Edison, Biograph (associated with the D. W. Griffith years, 1908–13), Kalem and Meliès – had been taken over, closed down or gone bankrupt.

Very soon the independents had their own structure and, despite splits and company reorganizations, were on the way up. They had pioneered longer 'feature'-length films and extended runs in the face of trust opposition. They also encouraged the star system of billing from the theatre, and, as programmes changed every day, this was the only form of advance publicity for films. The star system gave added value and a new dimension to screen acting. Players such as Florence Lawrence, Theda Bara, Charlie Chaplin, and the golden couple, Mary Pickford and Douglas Fairbanks, became celebrities. One historian describes how the lifestyle of the latter, with their palatial 'Pickfair' residence, symbolized the use of consumption as a means of achieving freedom through leisure, which came to epitomize the new Hollywood dream: 'The movie industry had synthesized consumption to Progressive ends, which perfectly suited the needs of the emerging corporate era. Thus the Hollywood frontier set the stage for the culmination of the consumer culture in the twenties' (May 1980: 146).

Where it lacked talent, the American industry imported it (from Germany and Sweden, for example), as well as technical innovations from Europe to maintain dominance, using these as an insurance for the future. Just as newspapers had their press barons, so films had their moguls (Sklar 1994: 46),[8] such as Carl Laemmle, William Fox and Adolph Zukor. For the first time, they were financed by securities issued by prominent Wall Street investment companies rather than, as previously, exclusively by individual financiers.

Fox made the first breakthrough into middle-class audiences and also championed vertical integration. In addition, Fox acquired many patents, including what was to become Cinemascope. Zukor bought up the French film *Queen Elizabeth*, which featured the only cinema appearance of Sarah Bernhardt, the most celebrated pre-First World War actress. Through the Famous Players Film Company, then, after the merger with Lasky, via the quintessential Hollywood corporation Paramount, he fully exploited the use of movie stars, the studio system and the European practice of longer films as a tactic to attract the middle classes. But, for the achievement of making American movies respectable, powerful and successful, credit should also go to the director D. W. Griffith, whose many films, especially the non-politically correct *The Birth of a Nation*, which was nearly three hours long, are still silent-movie classics (Slide 1970: 135).[9]

The switch from buying movies to renting them for exhibition (called 'film exchange') transformed the American industry, enabling the beginnings of a distribution business to emerge, and consolidating the establishment of new, specifically built permanent venues. These 'cathedrals of motion pictures' set a new standard in service, but had less architectural flair and lavishness than the Berlin venues, for instance. Very soon there were 60,000 theatres worldwide (Bowser 1990: 6). The viewing experience, even in 1915, was still very different to that of today. The feature motion picture was only one part of an evening's entertainment, and people tended to go to the cinema irrespective of the quality of the main feature; in fact a contemporary American survey revealed that this made no difference to the box office. As Marcus Loew was quoted as saying, 'We sell tickets to theaters, not movies' (Koszarski 1994). In 1917 the twenty-seven biggest exhibitors formed the First National Exhibitors Circuit. Some of the most powerful ventured into production as well, while some of the production and distribution giants also started their own chains of theatres.

The American film industry had come a long way from Edison's shack of a studio, resembling a police van, which had been called the Black Maria. The large number of geographically scattered small businesses that had mushroomed in the early days was gradually being replaced by a vertically integrated studio system combining production, distribution and exhibition, based in Los Angeles (with New York as its financial centre) and backed by big finance (de Mille 1959: 288–9).[10] Hollywood was becoming not simply a place in which to relocate, but primarily a way of doing business. Spiralling star salaries meant that other methods of cost cutting and rationalization of production needed to be devised, and by 1916 everything was carefully costed and planned; now only the most powerful individuals, such as Cecil B. de Mille, D. W. Griffith and Eric von Stroheim, could assert their creative independence. The rest of the film industry became subject to the American business practices of scientific management, division of labour and consumer advertising, which were features of the inter-war years (Gomery 1986; Schatz 1988).

By the end of the First World War, 85 per cent of films throughout the world were made in America and 98 per cent of all films shown inside the United States were American – a cultural dominance that was by no means inevitable and did not happen overnight. On many occasions observers were 'perpetually poised to read the last rites for Hollywood and for national industries around the world' (Puttnam 1997: 28). In the case of much of Europe, the predictions carried some truth. The First World War decimated Europe's film industry production while simultaneously offering unprecedented opportunities for an American takeover.

'Universalism' versus cultural specificity

The narrative style of D. W. Griffith and others created a universalism of technique that was to become the Hollywood norm in film production.

This offered the potential simultaneously to break down cultural barriers and to encroach upon indigenous film expression. The problem was that universalism implied that there was only one way to make and watch films, whereas, in different parts of the world, people had already come up with varying stylistic approaches that were eventually extinguished by the Hollywood narrative model and its European counterparts.

For instance, in Sweden, when Charles Magnusson built the most advanced studio in Europe and established a distinctive native style – as opposed to that of the foreign films flooding in – he turned to distinguished men of the theatre – Sjöström and Stiller. They used film to express visually certain subtleties such as motivations and ideas of humanity that were hitherto unknown to the medium. Sjöström's *The Phantom Carriage* was the first film ever seen by Ingmar Bergman, influencing his later classic *The Seventh Seal*. In Woody Allen's film *Manhattan*, one of the characters lists his love of Swedish films as one factor that, for him, makes life worth living. Yet by the advent of the talkies the achievements of Scandinavian cinema were generally forgotten. Film historians are constantly working to rehabilitate, rediscover and reconstruct the evidence of these early days (Allen and Gomery 1985). As David Shipman says, 'Sjöström is the only film maker of the first three decades whose work can be considered as seriously as the major novelists and dramatists of the time' (Shipman 1982: 64).

In Japan, film production also took a very culturally specific route, and a clear distinction was made between Western-style imports and indigenous style, which included a technique of inter-dispersing filmed location sequences or special effects with scenes of live theatre as links in a chain, or 'chain drama'. For years Japanese cinema was dependent on the kabuki theatre until a debate arose as to whether American-style narrative should be introduced. A particular dilemma arose over the traditional use of male actors for female parts (called *oyama*). This example typifies a process studied by social and cultural theorists: according to Anthony Giddens (1991), modern societies become 'detraditionalized'. Cultural traditions are questioned. 'As traditions are called on to defend themselves, they lose their status as unquestionable truths. But they may survive in various forms' (Thompson 1995: 183). Certainly, in the case of Japan, cultural specificity does not preclude artistic flair, for the Japanese have produced some of the greatest directors ever to work in film (Shipman 1982: 222).

In India, the 'father of Indian film', the director Dadasaheb Phalke, was faced with exactly the same problem when he advertised for females to act in his first project and received no answers; so he adhered to tradition and used men for female parts. Phalke had felt inspired to make a movie himself, despite no knowledge or experience of production, when he saw a Western film on the life of Christ and decided that an equivalent approach could be used for the life of the Hindu Lord Krishna. He visited England, bought equipment and stock, and took advice from the film-maker Cecil Hepworth. The result was *Raja Harishchandra*, nearly an hour long, released in 1913. Phalke went on to make many films that reached audiences who could not see Western movies in the big cities. These latter products were likely to reflect the cultural values of the colonial power, Great Britain. This meant that it was up to local producers such as Phalke to fill the gap by providing a film content that reflected indigenous culture. Here lay the origins of India's film industry, which today leads the world in total film production (Sklar 2002: 78).

In Brazil a trend emerged that set the example for other countries. Between 1908 and 1911 there was a 'golden age' of indigenous film production. Documentary films were by far the most numerous, followed by '*fitas cantatas*'. These were a unique genre of musical films – movies of operettas and stage musicals, shown with real performers behind a screen singing in time to the shots. However, after 1911 Brazilian distributors and exhibitors increasingly opted to buy cheaper imported products rather than make their own, more expensive, domestic films. Pathé as the main distributor pioneered a move from purchase of films to (cheaper) rental. The lower price from abroad was possible because European and American movies, on account of their larger home markets, had already been able to recoup their production costs in their own countries. By 1913 Italian and French films jointly dominated sales in Brazil. By 1915 French production had stopped because of the First World War, and Italian films took over the lead; when Italy also entered the war, the United States was able to take over with a two-thirds lead, previously attributed to Italy.

The United States was forced to become self-sufficient during 1914–18. In addition, the star system crystallized during this period, and distribution became the key to power. A system was established abroad whereby local subsidiaries of the home firm had exclusive handling arrangements with the same special marketing that films received at home (Nowell-Smith and Ricci 1998: 35). The size of the American home market still means that cheap foreign sales are considered as 'icing on the cake', whereas smaller countries cannot reach a similar profit situation within their own territory.

Already film had provoked political sensitivities. The first film in Britain to have a major influence on mass audiences, encouraging patriotic fervour, was *The Battle of the Somme*, screened in 1916. Germany demonstrated the potential of intervention by politicians to influence the survival and the future direction of national film industries during the Great War, when the government and the military played a stronger role than elsewhere by launching a production company called UFA (Universum Film Aktiengesellschaft) (Sklar 2002: 72).[11] The American government immediately recognized the importance of film as a weapon of persuasion once war had been declared in 1917. President Wilson established the Committee on Public Information to use the media to 'sell the war to the American public'. Government efforts to monitor the ideological focus of American cinema continued after the war with the creation of the Joint Committee of Motion Picture Activities of the United States Government and Allied Organizations (Ross 1998: 126).

During the war, ideological influence was complemented by censorship and considerable restrictions on media freedom, as well as a government role to boost business. The latter proved both critical and the object of criticism elsewhere: 'The European movie business was twice wrecked by war, and Hollywood, with the energetic aid and encouragement of the American government, was quick to take advantage both times. Hollywood did not acquire its empire by accident: it had competitors, and it colonized or destroyed them all' (Menand 2003).

Stages of globalization: a summary

The introduction to this study outlines three possible stages in the process of media globalization: origins, take-off and acceleration of intensity. These become evident at varying times and speed in the different media industries and countries involved. Although patterns vary, it is still possible to analyse them within the framework of more general theories – indeed, an attempt to do so helps our understanding of why the various components of the media developed into global entities and what this meant for national polities. This theme is ongoing in a comparative context, re-emerging in chapters 5, 7 and 8. This section is a summary of its progress in part I.

There are two aspects to a definition of globalization: firstly within the general sense, applicable to the present, and secondly with reference to media, and to culture in a wider sense. Globalization influences the condition of the world by linking a range of experiences and practices in everyday life and society with a 'rapidly developing and ever-densening [*sic*] network of interconnections and interdependences' (Tomlinson 1999: 2). The range of areas that are affected by these linkages is extensive: 'Nowadays, goods, capital, people, knowledge, images, crime, pollutants, drugs, fashions, beliefs all readily flow across territorial boundaries. Transnational networks, social movements and relationships are extensive in virtually all areas' (Hall et al. 1992: 65, 67). But how much of this 'connectivity' applies to media history in our period? Giddens offers us a conceptual framework. He analyses the social institutions of modernity, arguing that globalization is the global extension of modernity. In particular he draws our attention to the distinctive features of the social and cultural forms of modernity, especially the distancing of time and space in addition to disembedding (already discussed in chapters 2 and 3 in relation to the telegraph and music recording). He refers to these as the 'facilitating conditions' of modernity (1990: 63). However, this meta-analysis is criticized for neglecting the ways that mediated experience touches and transforms day-to-day existence at a local level (Silverstone 1994: 7).

Thompson selects three main aspects to the historical development of media modernity (1995: 76–80):

- the transformation of media institutions into large-scale commercial organizations
- the globalization of media communication and information systems
- the use of electric energy for the purposes of communication.

All of these three trends have their origins in the nineteenth century: the first in the early part (*The Times* of London, the influence of Girardin in France and of the penny press in America); the second in mid-century (the international news agencies and the telegraph); and the last towards the end (the experiments of Marconi and others with transmission signals with electromagnetic waves that eliminated the need for conductive wires).

Progress towards the second stage outlined above – take-off – varied from country to country and between industries, and, as we have seen, was linked to political as well as economic and social considerations. Bismarck used the Wolff news agency as a political tool; the British saw the economic benefits of large-scale investment in transcontinental cable-laying as a means of furthering imperialism and the economic benefits of empire.

Acceleration of intensity, our third stage, was certainly present before 1918 in the case of transcontinental information systems, film and newspaper businesses. The first two were clearly international; so too was the music business and early wireless experiments. But were they truly global? While in terms of acceleration of usage they were, in terms of their reach and flexibility they had not yet reached that stage. Part III deals with the ability of an increasing variety of media to influence and be used by an increasing number of people in an increasingly complex range of ways. Part IV ends with digitalization and convergence, but also with the same principles with which we started, even if they present themselves in different ways. For instance, by the end of chapter 8, pluralism and freedom of expression are still an issue, but contingent on a different set of circumstances as a result of the ever evolving nature of media globalization.

Conclusions

A political press survived into the twentieth century, despite the advent of commercialism. Yet the challenges were many: the mass appeal of entertainment, changing methods of political coverage, powerful newspaper owners with their own agendas, and depoliticization influenced by muckraking, trivialization and marginalization of class conflict. Under the impact of advertising, newspapers were already tending to encourage consumerism rather than citizenship.

The 'objectivity' of mass dailies proved to be a fallacy. During the heyday of imperialism, national chauvinism in more than one country was exploited by both newspapers and film. The strategic importance of propaganda communications became obvious during the First World War.

The full implications of the First World War as both a milestone and a turning point for media development became evident later in the twentieth century, but its impact on wireless and film was immediate.

The sensitive nature of the media's political potential, in both peacetime and war, became apparent with propaganda and communications usage for wireless and film as well as newspapers.

Study questions

From the historical standpoint presented in part I (and elsewhere), how are modernity and media globalization characterized and what is the connection between them?

Looking at various countries in this and the previous chapter, are there more similarities than differences in the way that the content and style of newspapers were influenced by technology and business?

How do you account for the continuing survival of a political press?

Trace the ways in which the media audience was developing and emerging throughout the nineteenth and early twentieth centuries in different countries and the accompanying attitudes of the people in power (in both media and politics) to that public.

PART III

DISCOVERY AND EXPLOITATION OF THE MASSES FORMULA, 1918–1947

> I wrote about what people wanted to hear. I packaged their feelings and sold them back. They wanted to laugh, they wanted to cry, they wanted to dance. I serviced them. I met the market.
>
> Irving Berlin

5 The Business and Ideology of Mass Culture, 1918–1939

The rabble vomit their bile and call it a newspaper.

Friedrich Nietzsche

In all the history of inventing, nothing has approached the rise of radio from obscurity to power.

'Radio – the New Social Force', Outlook, 19 March 1924

We should not have captured Germany without . . . the loudspeaker.

Adolf Hitler

Summary

The *objective* of this chapter is to examine how technologically enhanced media communication was used for propaganda and entertainment purposes to manipulate the hearts and minds of the masses. In the process the media both reflected developing nationalism and contributed to it. From 1918 patterns were set for the rest of the twentieth century, although, crucially, the twentieth century inherited from the previous century new and enlarged channels of communication.

As Eric Hobsbawm has said, the twentieth century was 'the century of the common people and dominated by the arts produced by and for them' (1994b: 192). This period was characterized by:

- the simultaneous institutional growth of film and broadcasting and tensions between new branches of media and older ones, aggravated by commercial competition. Hollywood's global reach, mentioned in the previous chapter, was now consolidated.
- the disastrous economic impact of the Depression, despite the expansion of advertising designed to combat the consequential slump in consumption. Both politicians and advertisers used the media for psychological manipulation, demonstrating a patronizing conception of the 'masses' as a body to be moulded. In Britain, advertising stressed that low-paid workers could buy only a limited range of goods; in the United States, black people also tended to be excluded from advertisers' categorizations.
- a dual potential: both for uniformity and control on the one hand, and for democratization of opportunity on the other, as radio, records and film extended consumer choice. The way that various countries experienced these processes differed according to political and ideological imperatives as much as economic ones.

Introduction

The human toll of the First World War was estimated at 20 million.

This first 'total war' in modern history officially ended on Armistice Day, and in London's Westminster Abbey the ceremony for the burial of the Unknown Warrior was recorded electronically – the original public demonstration of such a technique (Chanan 1995: 56). The war period had seen a spate of technical experiments which were to challenge further ideas about time and space, a process that had already been accelerated by the early history of film and wireless communication. In 1924, at the British Empire Exhibition, King George V sent himself a telegram that circled the globe on all-British lines in 80 seconds (Thompson 1995: 154). Rapid communication was clearly possible, and it was to be further enhanced in this earlier period by exploitation of electromagnetic waves, which had also started as a nineteenth-century phenomenon. As far as electromagnetic transmission with radio was concerned, it tended to be national, regional or urban, or, as Marconi had pioneered, between land and sea. It was not until the first communications satellites were launched in the 1960s that it became really global. Notwithstanding, the take-off in popularity of radio during this period was astounding.

Music, film and radio have all experienced successive waves of technological innovation and, although it was not obvious initially in the case of radio and music, all three catered for a mass market – a feature of twentieth-century media. The power of broadcasting became clear as radio began to provide competition, and hence a commercial threat, to existing media, leading to disputes over operational relationships. Radio was bound to interact with existing cultural competition, whether it was newspapers, live performing arts, cinema, sports organizations, political organizations or music. Early relationships were often tense and influenced the development of both sides, not just radio.

The pattern of the music industry's development was characteristic of the era and shared by the other media industries: 'The main types of development taking place in the 1930s, and extended much further since, are both an immense strengthening of the possibilities of uniformity and control, and a broadening and democratising of opportunities' (Middleton 1990: 67). Advertisers and network radio were to bring this trend to radio content; examples of this dual process had already emerged in newspapers, with the growth of news agencies and chains, and were now consolidated. In film the strengthening of Hollywood's formulas for creative success on the one hand, counterbalanced by the opportunities that 16 mm film introduced on the other hand, presented yet another illustration of this trend.

The First World War had demonstrated how channels of communication could be used for the aims of propaganda: this sort of usage was to become commonplace throughout various parts of the world in peacetime from the 1920s onwards. The growth in support for a variety of totalitarian movements in countries during the 1930s was an extreme extension of nationalism that differed from the nineteenth-century constitutional and colonial expression of national chauvinism. The most obvious, but not exclusive, examples were Soviet Russia and Nazi Germany, but democratic countries also used the media for propaganda: what differed was extent, method and attitude. In totalitarian states, where politics was seen as a holistic expression of everyday life which extended to every corner of society, use of the media to influence hearts and minds was considered natural, necessary and desirable. Hence the Nazis took pride in controlling its application as a weapon of power. Western democracies were more coy about communication that involved persuasion: propaganda was dressed up as 'information', 'psychological warfare' and 'education'.

The larger problem for political culture and society, first discussed by Jacques Ellul (1965), who directed scholarship towards propaganda's sociological role in technological societies, is whether people can also have access to a variety of sources of information and be encouraged to think critically if propaganda becomes prominent. Propaganda was given ideological respectability by the Soviet leadership, became manifest under the Nazis, reached maturity during the Second World War and was consolidated and enhanced by the Cold War, remaining as a sophisticated and widely used option today.

The influence of the Russian Revolution on media

The impact of the Russian Revolution on subsequent international history is virtually immeasurable, for the event released the floodgates for ideology as a motivating force for political, economic and social action – a feature everywhere of the twentieth century. Although the circumstances and context of the 'ten days that shook the world' (Reed 1961) carry their own cultural specificity, the ideological impact defied national boundaries. The overthrow of an autocratic regime and the attempts at the establishment of an alternative 'workers' state' acted as an inspiration elsewhere in the way that the French Revolution had done previously. In media history, the 1917 Russian Revolution set the precedent and the pace for the concept of communication as a form of manipulative persuasion of the masses, a process that necessitated political control – in peacetime as well as during war.

When the Bolsheviks took power in October 1917 the media became an important tool for explaining ideas and gaining public support. Media usage was relatively 'low tech', in that posters and leaflets proved to be the most efficacious means of reaching the linguistically, culturally and geographically disparate population of what was later to become the Union of Soviet Socialist Republics (USSR). As much of the population was still illiterate, the Bolsheviks developed visual symbols and other new imagery, much as the French revolutionaries before them. Mass meetings and outdoor 'agit-prop' such as campaigning trains and ships became important. Film also provided the potential for mass communication, but in practice the industry remained a largely underdeveloped urban phenomenon because of the cost of production, reproduction and exhibition. Nevertheless, Eisenstein and other Russian directors of the 1920s, who were ideologically committed to the revolutionary order, broke new ground artistically with film classics such as *The Battleship Potemkin* and *October*.

During 1921–9, the New Economic Policy (initiated by Lenin) and its support propaganda were constructed as the means of winning over opposition to the new regime, which still had to consolidate after the traumas of the civil war that followed the Bolshevik seizure of power. The Bolsheviks had successfully fought for survival against the combined forces of pro-tsarist 'Whites', armies of the Western powers opposed to the revolution and nationalist groups struggling for independence. The message of the 1920s was that sacrifices would be necessary for an improved future, but that the revolution was justified and its consequences worthwhile.

The new government was quick to appropriate the press, which became the main player in Soviet propaganda: agencies and the principal papers *Pravda* and *Izvestia* were taken over, censorship was introduced and publishing was nationalized. However, a distinction should be made within Russian history between the 1920s and the 1930s. During the earlier period foreign film, especially American, was imported and there was still considerable creative freedom for expression through this medium and also painting; but, by the end of the 1920s, much of this artistically important work was considered to be too advanced and beyond the understanding of Soviet workers.

Nevertheless, elsewhere many people's ideology was influenced by events in Russia. Historically, the appeal of an alternative value system to Western-style industrial capitalism dates back to the nineteenth century, but poverty and hardship during the Depression, the rise of fascism, and the failure of the Western powers to deal with Hitler's expansion all contributed to many people looking at Russia with rose-tinted spectacles. Hence during the 1930s, before the worst excesses of Stalinism had become evident, a considerable number of progressive people believed the Soviet system, despite its difficulties and faults, to be the best choice in opposition to Western capitalism.

Yet, under Stalin, the ground had been laid for the media to grow as a natural extension of the state's culture and an essential part of the political armoury for persuasion, communication and popular support. As such, 'bourgeois' values were to be avoided, and film became more centralized and controlled. Film imports dried up in the 1930s as 'social realism' became the only officially permissible style for writers and artists, with the result that both literature and film production became propagandist. Poster production was also centralized, with the dominant image being either Stalin or the overachieving worker (inspired by the Stakhanovite campaign named after a coal miner who became a national hero by exceeding his production quota). Faced with the dual demands of defending the communist system against external opposition – especially the threat of Nazism and fascism – and making Russia into a foremost modern industrial power, centralized bureaucracy, the cult of the individual leader and merciless purges implemented through fear and terror took over.

Although neither Lenin nor Stalin saw themselves as broadcast communicators, nevertheless the spoken word via the loudspeaker, used in public squares and buildings, became important. In the Soviet Union radio developed locally rather than nationally, with sixty-four stations and almost as many languages. There was little radio listening on a mass scale until the late 1920s, although the first public broadcast was made in 1919 (Briggs and Burke 2002: 163), but by the late 1930s wireless sets were being produced; wired radio was also favoured because it could be controlled, excluding output from other countries. Meanwhile, Soviet programming addressed party activists with dry statistics (ibid.: 217), while the press maintained its lead: by 1940 there were 7 million radio sets, but newspapers could boast a circulation of about 38 million (Brooks 2000: 5).

The growth of broadcasting

Urbanization and greater mobility, combined with the impact of the First World War on both technology and changing attitudes, had led to a new social environment with demand for improved communication systems. Now that experimentation had produced valve receivers and loudspeakers, and electricity was being extended throughout the Western world, continuous wave radio found a mass market. Wireless sets could be produced and marketed on a large scale. Early radio had been a solitary activity requiring a crystal set with headphones, but between the wars people enjoyed radio in groups, at work or as a family sitting round a smart, large piece of furniture called a 'wireless'; social life was now increasingly centred on family and home.

The spread of radio was accompanied by a rapid institutional growth in a new form of media organization: broadcasters, who were communicating the radio transmissions. Radio's take-off was swift, and public enthusiasm for it peaked during the 'golden age' of the 1930s and 1940s. Collective amnesia concerning radio's heritage has not been helped by the fact that most radio history books until recently have tended to concentrate either on technological breakthroughs or on nostalgic accounts of 'classic' programmes, to the exclusion of political, economic and social factors.

Scholars now argue not only that radio can be seen as 'the most important electronic invention of the century', rivalling cinema in its influence, but also that it helped to support community and cultural identity. 'In speaking to us as a nation during a crucial period of time it helped to shape our cultural consciousness and to define us as people in ways that were certainly not unitary but cut deeply across individual, class, racial, and ethnic experience' (Douglas 1999: 11). This relationship between national consciousness and radio was shared by every country studied here.

It is also argued that, in the United States, the dominant ideology of big business influenced radio's history, for power to dominate an important medium also brings with it the power to shape historical perception. 'Close analysis of radio begins to unravel the mask that US commercial media have created for themselves: as a naturally arising, consensus-shaped, and unproblematic reflection of a pluralistic society, rather than the conflicting, tension-ridden site of the ruthless exercise of cultural hegemony, often demonstrating in its very effort to exert control the power and diversity of the alternative popular constructions that oppose and resist it' (Hilmes 1997: xvii).

According to one historian, three factors influenced the form and content of American radio: the desire for national broadcasting; the choice of a specific technology – wired networks – to provide the

Radio take-off American style: influences and patterns for the future

US federal (i.e., government) control had been considered just after the Great War, but 'the strong position of the radio companies, the government's disposition to influence rather than directly regulate, and the geography of the United States all worked against the form of centralised broadcasting so widespread in other parts of the world' (Smulyan 1994: 61). Americans had experienced the private operation of telegraphs, railroads, electric light and telephones, all of which had set an organizational precedent. Here cost determined the nature of development: not only receivers but also broadcasting wired networks had to make a profit because network radio entailed the expense of renting wires. Programming became centralized in order to attract advertisers and for cost efficiency, therefore radio emerged as a means of selling products so that 'most programs merely filled the time between commercials' (ibid.: 8–9). The American public were hugely enthusiastic for the magic of broadcasting and desired a national network system that would unite and connect the country and give them programmes from far away. Farmers, for instance, saw radio as a means of breaking their isolation. This concept appeared earlier than the idea of radio as a commercial system, which was not inevitable: at first local stations were widespread, and during the 1920s the advertising industry itself doubted that advertisements over radio would work.

Furthermore, there was not agreement: broadcasting was a product of resistance as well as of a few large companies, most notably AT&T. The technology of wired networks that AT&T supported was easily understandable to the public and favoured by President Hoover, who saw his role as being to facilitate the speedy growth of a new industry – which benefited AT&T and its technical monopoly.

National audiences were collectively supplied with a range of programmes. Evangelists used radio extensively and were among the first to own stations, with radio preachers setting the scene for the later rise of the electronic church on television (Schultze 1988). Programming diversity was impressive: comedy, variety and quiz shows, Westerns and detective dramas, as well as soap operas. In addition, Presidents Harding and Coolidge in the 1920s and President Roosevelt in the 1930s all used radio for political broadcasts.

service; and dislike and mistrust of radio advertising on the part of both listeners and businesses (Hilmes 1997: xvi). The continuing protests over this last, and the programming forms and organizational structure that responded to them, influenced television. The same relevance for television can also be argued in the case of Great Britain, particularly as the BBC had a monopoly on both media for a long time, and for Japan and France.

In Britain and continental Europe, populations had experienced a high level of government intervention in their lives during the war, and the ideal of public service was strong, so attitudes favoured a proactive role for the state to create 'a land fit for heros to live in' after the hardship of the 1914–18 period. This provided the context for the broadcasting model, whereas in America conditions for commercial expansion prevailed.

Broadcasting structures and impact

Although countries all used the same technology, each evolved its own structures for dealing with broadcasting at local, regional and national level. What emerged reflected social, cultural and economic influences as well as political pragmatism, but what they all shared in common was the realization that there was a scarcity of wavelengths, which necessitated some form of regulation. The way that radio became established institutionally and the style of programming that this entailed in the United States and Britain provided role models for other countries, which opted for their own combination of structural elements.

While political broadcasts became a feature everywhere, political structures for broadcasting varied. Systems do not simply have to be either privatized or state-sponsored – there were, and still are, many different variables and combinations within cultural, geographical and technological contexts. In Australia a mixed system of government and private stations evolved, but fewer stations were needed there than in America, because so much of the population was concentrated around six cities. Despite the fact that, in North America, the United States took eighty-nine out of the ninety-five wavelengths, Canadian broadcasting still blossomed, apparently undeterred by fewer stations and no major manufacturing companies to encourage privatization. The Canadian National Railroad started a national service using government tele-graph lines, and Canadian Radio Broadcasting was established in 1930 as a forerunner to the Canadian Broadcasting Commission, controlled by central government.

In Britain and France it appeared that, given the scarcity of wave-lengths, a state-influenced institution was more appropriate. *The Times* described the British system as 'an independent monopoly with public service as the motive'. The BBC aimed to reach wide audiences in order to sell wireless sets, whereas in America stations sought to attract the largest possible audiences for specific programmes financed by commercial sponsorship.

As broadcasting was still virgin territory, few people had a vision for the future at this stage. One person who did, although he has since been much criticized for it, was the first director-general of the BBC, John Reith. By his own admission, he ran a 'brute' regime, but his architectural

Japan: censored radio for national policy with institutionalization

In Japan the institutionalization of public communication was enhanced by the structures of broadcasting and the close militaristic influence on government which formed part of an integrated and nationalistic authority. The arrival of broadcasting formed a major contribution to Japan's move towards a form of modernity, which embraced the new Western influences and elements of Eastern tradition.

Experimental radio transmissions had started in 1905, but during the 1920s the mass media in the country put down roots easily, possibly due to several culturally specific features. The concentration of new industrialization and urbanization within limited geographic confines because of the existence of mountainous areas, for instance, has produced a sharp contrast in Japan between sparsely and densely populated areas. Before the Second World War new city life coexisted with traditional rural agricultural areas, yet the two shared an ethnic and linguistic homogeneity from Japan's Mongol roots, which in turn helped produce social, economic and cultural standardization as rural traditions disappeared in the face of the onslaught from industrialized, urban modernity. Rapid media growth, despite censorship of the press and the lack of freedom of speech, was facilitated by the pre-war emphasis on education, based on traditional Japanese thought and with a strong emphasis on supervision (Ito 1978: 2).

In 1923 the country was suddenly shattered by trauma, devastation and confusion caused by the great Kanto earthquake, highlighting the need for immediate information to be broadcast to the public. The government acted promptly and legislation stimulated the demand for radio. The ordinance dealing with the authorization and supervision of radio broadcasting, together with the 1915 Wireless Telegraphy Law which regulated the use of radio waves, remained the only definitive broadcasting regulations until 1950. The first radio stations started broadcasting in 1925 in Tokyo, Nagoya and Osaka. A public utility corporation, the Tokyo Broadcasting Station, was established, and similar 'corporate juridical bodies for public service' were established in Nagoya and Osaka. Finance was raised by receiver fees which the broadcasters collected from listeners on the basis of a licence.

Government control was heavier than elsewhere: broadcasters were unable to carry any items banned from the press or publication and programmes had to be approved in advance by the censors of the Ministry of Communications. In 1926 it was decided that national broadcasting should be established, called NHK (Nippon Hoso Kyokai), with its leading management appointed by the Ministry of Communications as a half-private, half-public body with a monopoly of all radio broadcasting. The goal for the new national network was to be ready in time to cover the coronation of Emperor Hirohito in November 1928 for the 500,000 receivers that then existed. Regional and national stations were under the control of the Ministry of Communications. Growing government involvement in communication was formalized in 1936 when an information committee within the cabinet was set up, for the purpose of unifying information and publicity liaison across the various government ministries.

conviction was one of a broadcasting system independent of both government and business with the social responsibility to 'educate, inform and entertain'. His refusal to accept 'the lowest common denominator in taste' now seems out of date and elitist, but broadcasting has always been influenced by the social and cultural environment. Reith was a product of his age, if a somewhat dominating, totalitarian and idiosyncratic one, nicknamed by Churchill 'Wuthering Heights' (Curran and Seaton 2003: 110).

At first public events such as lectures, concerts and theatre shows were broadcast, then radio developed its own formats to exploit the advantages of the medium; for example, sports coverage became popular everywhere. While in the United States entertainment dominated, the BBC's emphasis was more on education and information. Range of content was also important, although attitudes towards audiences and listening habits were different from those of today. According to John Reith, listeners should all appreciate the same variety of programming, irrespective of their social background. He opposed audience research on the grounds that it could expose diversity. Broadcasting was a serious business which necessitated gaps, or interludes, between slots so that the public could adjust to the diversity. The radio experience involved a personal relationship between broadcaster and listener which should be educative and 'character'-forming. The belief that the BBC should communicate accepted values in a unitary way was not dissimilar to the advertising agencies' perception of 'mass audiences', who constituted an amorphous body of people – a concept of 'mass' that was also shared by politicians during the inter-war period in both totalitarian and democratic regimes.

During the 1920s access to radio was limited to more heavily populated urban areas, but by 1938 in the United States more than 90 per cent of urban households and 70 per cent of rural households had at least one wireless set. In Britain by the mid-1920s 85 per cent of the population could receive national or regional programmes, and by the end of the 1930s there were approximately 9 million licensed sets. The mass unemployment of the Depression created plenty of involuntary leisure

Radio's ethnic role in the United States

American radio's promotion of series explicitly designed to back ethnic unity and interracial support, such as *Amos 'n Andy*, which came to dominate the schedules, also drew attention to 'radio's complicity in the conditions that made such appeals necessary in the face of the Nazi threat' (Hilmes 1997: xvi). The complex functions of racial and ethnic 'difference', together with the issues of assimilation and 'Americanism', which another popular series, *The Rise of the Goldbergs*, dealt with, all contributed in the United States of this period to the building of 'imagined communities' (along the lines originally defined by Benedict Anderson), culminating in the ultimate identity-defining process of the Second World War (ibid.: xx).

time and a desire for escapism which radio satisfied to such an extent that polls in America established a significant social and cultural role for it in preference to reading and movies as the favourite inexpensive leisure activity (Gorman and McLean 2003: 56). Therefore radio also had an impact in terms of changing perceptions: the creation of imagined communities and a sense of nationhood, the legitimizing of subcultures and catering for specific audiences such as women.

1930 was an eventful year for radio: the first successful international broadcast exchange took place between Japan, Britain and the USA, occasioned by the London Disarmament Conference; NHK also started to launch local stations in major cities countrywide and set up its technical research laboratories for the study of electronic technology, including television (Ito 1978: 13). The following year NHK established a second broadcasting network in Tokyo and started educational broadcasting, which was eventually recognized by the school system in 1935. Meanwhile in 1933 Osaka and Nagoya also set up a second network.

Although Japan's NHK, with its board of governors and licence fee, appeared to be similar in structure and organization to the BBC, it was more vulnerable to government control – a feature that became increasingly evident during this militaristic phase. In 1935 NHK had started Radio Tokyo as a regular overseas service, initially for one hour a day in Japanese and English, directed towards the western side of the United States. The length of transmissions and the geographic reach of broadcasts were subsequently extended, increasing the importance of the overseas service.

Radio's significance as a vehicle for communicating national policy was emphasized once more during the hostilities between Japanese and Chinese forces that broke out in 1937. Government pressure on the media had increased, with the carrying of patriotic songs, the playing of the national anthem and calls for the population to bow in the direction of the emperor's palace (Briggs and Burke 2002: 224) all intended to enhance the spirit of militaristic nationalism. The further clash

The 'news story of the century': a radio hoax

In 1938 in America Orson Welles dramatized a much altered version of H. G. Wells's *War of the Worlds* for radio, and played an announcer. The sound effects and other radio techniques were so cleverly produced that audiences believed it was real-life reporting, provoking a nationwide panic – evidence of radio's unique power to encourage the imagination, and of the increasing blurring of production style between fact, fiction and promotion that sponsored radio and advertising had first pioneered. Nevertheless, Dorothy Thompson described it as 'the news story of the century . . . [making] a greater contribution to an understanding of Hitlerism, Mussolinism, Stalinism and all the other terrorisms of our time than all the words about them that have been written by reasonable men' (Briggs and Burke 2002: 216).

with China was swiftly followed by a government upgrading of the Cabinet Information Committee into a Cabinet Information 'Division', comprising intelligence, information and propaganda publicity about government policies. In 1940 a further upgrade made the division into a 'bureau' in control of mass media, with NHK accountable to both the minister of communications and the prime minister.

The Nazi takeover of media for propaganda

According to the Nazi minister of propaganda, Joseph Goebbels, radio was to be to the twentieth century what the press had been to the nineteenth. Hitler's use of radio was certainly very different to Roosevelt's experiment with 'fireside chats'. The American president came across as a considered, democratic leader who talked to individuals in the intimacy of their homes, encouraging the positive attitude that people 'had nothing to fear but fear itself'. Hitler's use of radio was as a complement to mass rallies, where he asserted himself above the people: there was never a dialogue. In Japan, too, radio as a form of social dialogue was impossible.

Furthermore, according to Goebbels, newspapers should be 'monoform in will but polyform in the trappings of that will'. The monoform aspect was eventually achieved, but the polyform – another word for pluralism – never materialized – due, he claimed, to the fact that the German press, unlike their British counterpart, had not yet reached a sufficient level of 'maturity' (Zeman 1973: 43–4; Balfour 1979: 34). Thus Goebbels set out to destroy the independence of newspapers and press freedom. But ownership and regulation of the more diffuse, regional newspaper industry proved to be a fairly slow process. A takeover of the film industry proved easier.

Most films were dependent on funding from the state finance bank and, to this form of influence, the Nazis added two more controls: the Reichsfilmkammer, which was set up in July 1933 with ten branches covering every aspect of production, and a Reichsfilmsdramaturg, which was established the following year for censorship of scripts, with the organization of a ratings system that applied to film distribution. The system was enthusiastically implemented by Goebbels who, as a frustrated film-maker, was acutely aware of the propaganda value of movies as mass culture. Therefore no film could be exhibited without rigorous scrutiny by the censors, and there were no movies critical of the regime. It seems that many film industry personnel internalized the values and beliefs that accompanied this powerful all-embracing institutional structure (Weinberg 1984).

Control over newspapers was a more complex challenge for the Nazis, as the press was decentralized and Germany published more newspapers than any other industrially advanced country, with 4703 daily and weekly newspapers, including local editions of parent papers. Large urban conglomerations such as Berlin had twenty and Hamburg

Japan's radio and militarism

In 1931 the Mukden incident, provoked by the Japanese army as a reaction to perceived growing Chinese nationalism in order to give a pretext for Japanese forces to take over Manchuria, demonstrated the government of Japan's lack of control over militarism and led to the country's eventual withdrawal from the League of Nations (Olbas 2003). This internationally significant episode had the effect of leading to extra demand for radio sets. By the following year the number of registered listeners had risen to a million, but the government started to tighten its control over NHK. Increasing overt militarism was sparked by an attempted coup d'état among some young army officers, referred to as the 26 February rising. They called for a Showa restoration (that is, less modern democracy and more traditional imperial power). Although martial law was declared, initially the authorities made no move to quash the rebellion. That day, the government banned radio reporting within Japan and most of NHK's other broadcasts were also suspended. An appeal was made to the rebels to surrender three days later, over the NHK airwaves. The use of radio to solve this problem demonstrated the effectiveness of wireless. Eventually the leaders were imprisoned, and some were either executed or committed suicide, but the cabinet fell (Shillony 1973).

had ten, while small towns had '*Heimatpresse*' newspapers where ownership was local and therefore dispersed, with 81 per cent in family ownership in 1928. In fact the German industry excelled as an educational and cultural medium: 'in the amount of printed material offered to subscribers, the German journals outdid all others' (Hale 1964: 2–3). Yet the Nazis were able to take over because the institutional weakness of the industry during the Weimar Republic – despite a well-developed party political press – was exacerbated by the Depression. Socialist and communist journals were confiscated, a local Nazi press was developed, special ordinances attached privately owned papers to the party publishing combine, and the industry publishers' association was converted into a party institution. The outbreak of the Second World War provided the impetus for further steps which, according to one contemporary, 80 per cent of journalists found unacceptable: 'because of the regimentation and pressure most journalists became hypocrites without any initiative' (Hale 1964: 323).

Comparative press opposition to radio in the United States and Britain

The arrival of a new means of disseminating information and entertainment tends to destabilize the existing media system, so, for instance, radio posed a challenge to the historic relationship between wire services and newspapers. The press–radio war was the first of several twentieth-century industry conflicts, each with a recurring pattern. Already the telephone was replacing the telegraph; soon television would threaten radio and later in the century there would be other media wars. 'They are battles to control the channels of communication, . . . [which] brings not only profits . . . but power to shape the cultural agenda, public opinion, and the nature of social discourse. It is power, to some degree, to determine the way millions of people define and experience reality, and for many, that is a power worth fighting for' (Jackaway 1995).

Whereas in Britain the press saw radio as a threat, and therefore did not generally favour cross-ownership and involvement, in America cross-ownership was widespread, but press opposition was even stronger from those newspapers who did not participate in broadcasting. The result was that in Britain the members of the press were united in their belief that news should remain the premise of the print industry, whereas in America opposition was split between those who had a foot in the door and those who were outside the new system. In both countries the subsequent development of radio was influenced by this background, which has made a significant contribution to the respective media histories. There were attempts on both sides of the Atlantic to undermine radio's inherent advantage of immediacy by trying to handicap the broadcasters from supplying breaking news. Thus, although the structure and ownership of the new radio industries were different, the response against radio, and the tactics for self-defence by the press, were similar.

In both cases the newspapers lost out. In the case of the BBC, the tactics backfired so badly that they actually served to provide an identity for the new broadcaster, as the BBC turned a threat into an opportunity. Restrictions on its bulletins and constraints on types of broadcasting had the effect of making the BBC appear somewhat limited and distant, but, as Sian Nicholson points out, these restraints 'served to mark out its position in an already crowded market-place': its rationed bulletins, its impersonal and unsensational tone, its discriminating approach to 'important' and 'accurate' news, and its close structural ties with, yet semi-independence from, government, all served to give the medium of broadcasting in Britain a unique air of authority and integrity which distanced it from the irresponsible, partisan and increasingly entertainment-led popular press. As growth in the circulation of popular newspapers had been mainly at the expense of news content, people turned to radio for information (Catterall et al. 2000: 142).

Theoretically, news could reach the public without any need for newspapers, or radio could steal the news from the press and simply read it over the wavelengths, but the latter would challenge intellectual property rights. Live radio broadcasts were a solution to the previous dilemma of news being inherently old as soon as it was printed. Despite this fact, or maybe because of the threat it posed, print journalists in America employed what Jackaway calls a 'sacred rhetoric' (1995: 7–8), using cultural ideals as a form of self-defence, claiming that the values of the nation were being challenged, and arguing that print journalists were the only ones suited to the gathering and dissemination of news. Thus they connected the requirements of the established medium to national interest, even saying that radio involved an attack on democracy. At stake was control of the nature, form and content of news.

Steps in press opposition to radio

The United States

At first the members of the American press were not against broadcasting; in fact they were active in promoting it to the public, as it provided them with a popular new topic with which to attract readers. As *Editor and Publisher* noted: 'Newspapers helped build the new plaything of the nation' (Jackaway 1995: 14). Some of the larger city papers, such as those in the Hearst chain, also the *Los Angeles Times*, the *Boston Post*, the *Brooklyn Eagle* and the *Chicago Tribune*, bought up stations or took a financial interest in them; then, with short news bulletins, they could urge listeners to purchase the paper for the full story. At this stage there was no competition over the gathering or distribution of news, because radio lacked the money, staff and equipment to do their own news-gathering; nevertheless, by the mid-1920s, journalists whose papers did not have a financial interest in radio were expressing concern over the threat of radio.

Wire services themselves differed over the issue: Associated Press (AP) operated as a cooperative whereby each member paper contributed a story and was entitled to all the other stories from members, so news was considered the property of all the participants. United Press (UP) and International News Service (INS) did their own news-gathering, selling the bulletins to client newspapers, and saw this as a good opportunity to compete with the bigger AP and to pick up new customers among the newspaper-owned stations. They gave away their bulletins free in exchange for an on-air credit to promote business. This division only harmed the efforts of the anti-radio group to combat the increasing competition of broadcasting, helping the pro-radio side to win through – for instance, with the supply of election results in 1924.

The Depression served temporarily to unite the two sides within print. Although

Britain

Within a year of the broadcast of the BBC's first news bulletin, the British press was launching a campaign against the corporation, and the key battleground was news, which raised issues about definitions of journalism, together with its role and impact on society. Radio always had the advantage of immediacy, which could be used to great effect. For instance, the BBC had the right to interrupt schedules for stop-press announcements such as the successful solo flight across the Atlantic of Lindbergh, the birth of Princess Margaret, and the results of the Americas Cup and Anglo-American polo in 1929–30. At a time of ever increasing demand for authoritative and immediate news there was fierce competition within the newspaper industry between provincial and national newspapers. The press continually complained that radio was killing sports coverage, especially special results editions, and even the news vendors appealed to the BBC to withdraw its results service on Saturdays at 6.15, complaining that it threatened the ability of the vendor to afford a Sunday dinner with his family (Catterall et al. 2000: 133).

Everywhere the Depression was hitting sales and advertising, but once advertising was eliminated as an option in Britain, the press was less hostile. Now it argued that the new BBC public broadcasting system was a very sensible, 'British' way of avoiding the 'chaos' of America. This rhetoric suited the BBC's defence of its mandatory licence fee, which could be burdensome for poor working people. While newspapers focused on the competition from broadcasting, the music and theatre industries also saw radio's threat as commercial, although it was difficult to gauge as the audience was unknown. In a bid to safeguard their monopoly on news-gathering and intellectual property, newspapers argued for schedule restrictions.

the industry had done quite well in the 1920s, between 1929 and 1933 advertising revenue was cut by half, so competition with radio for advertising became more obvious. Friction was increased by radio's victory in scooping two major stories on its own: the kidnap of Charles Lindbergh's baby in 1932 and an attempted assassination of President Roosevelt the following year. Soon after this event, Roosevelt initiated the first of his 'fireside chats' to the nation on radio, proving that the president's news could be communicated to the public without the intermediary of newspapers. During the elections of 1928 and 1932 the wire service eventually decided to provide the returns to radio, after much dispute and hesitation, but a subsequent poll of AP members revealed that 70 per cent were opposed to supplying broadcasters with bulletins. In 1933 UP and INS both joined AP in stopping the sale of news to radio stations, which forced the networks to develop their own service. This led CBS to apply for membership to the National Press Club in Washington for admission to the press galleries; after over 100 letters and telegrams of protest from print journalists they were turned down, and were not finally admitted until the eve of the outbreak of the war, in August 1939.

Towards the end of 1933 newspapers and radio reached the Biltmore agreement, named after the hotel where their conference was held in New York City. It was also known as the Press–Radio Plan, since it set up a Press–Radio Bureau that was to supply two five-minute bulletins a day, with no sponsorship, from news provided by the press associations. The bureau already had competition in the form of wire services that had been established by independent stations specifically for radio. If the stations used one of these services, there was no restriction on the time of day the newscast could be aired or on the broadcasting of commercials with the news. The Transradio Press Service, for instance, had reporters in

Although Reith challenged this prohibitive definition of news, others in the BBC reacted with measured caution, afraid to offend because theirs was a new medium. They thought that people received it differently – as they did.

Once the BBC's charter was established and the opportunity for cross-media ownership therefore passed, press criticism ridiculed the BBC for its dull style, yet blocked Reith's requests for more latitude that would have remedied the complaint. The *Daily Mail* radio correspondent Collie Knox, for example, made a name for himself by constantly condemning the BBC. Newspapers argued that the BBC owed its success to favourable press coverage and therefore had a moral obligation not to interfere in their business – newspapers had a public duty to police the BBC's monopoly (Catterall et al. 2000: 131).

The BBC's elevated standards were seen as a defining virtue that distinguished broadcast news from popular newspapers. Broadcasters were able to argue that the BBC news was transforming listeners' general knowledge of public affairs and also that the existence of the corporation acted as a check against the worst excesses of the tabloid press. Nevertheless, broadcasters gradually took on board more popularist methods of presentation and commercial news values such as human-interest stories, while still encouraging listeners to read further. The British reporter Richard Dimbleby waged a one-person war for more lively news coverage. His account of the Crystal Palace fire and in 1939 his live reports of the fighting on the Franco-Spanish border demonstrated the power of broadcast news. The belated adoption by Britain's popular press of visually arresting techniques such as bolder headlines, plus a trend towards greater conciseness, clarity and brevity, often involving shorter sentences, has been attributed to the influence of radio bulletins.

Broadcasters and the quality press used the success of the BBC and its 'responsible all the main cities and stringers in over 700 smaller towns, correspondents in much of Europe and in Central American capitals, and over 150 station subscribers within nine months. As it became obvious that there was more advantage in working with radio than opposing it, UP and INS withdrew from the Biltmore agreement, so that AP was the only one providing bulletins; AP also lifted its ban on the sale of news for sponsored broadcasts in 1939.

The Biltmore agreement had actually been unworkable in that it was never a signed agreement. Moreover, the independent stations never cooperated; despite outnumbering the network-affiliated stations by three to one, they were responsible for the collapse of the plan. The Depression and economic factors had also weighed heavy, and the ban on selling the bureau's news service for sponsorship did not help the need for money. The re-emergence of the division between the newspaper supporters of radio and the newspaper opponents was crucial; so too was the collapse of unity. 'There was just too much money to be made in radio . . . Those with the means to make the investment in broadcasting were no longer willing to stand aside and let someone else enjoy the profits' (Jackaway 1995: 34).

US news agencies: agents for nationalism or for international understanding?

In the 1920s, American news agencies were challenging the European agencies internationally. In most countries of the world, the growth of radio provided a new source of income for news agencies as the state became an important purchaser of agency services for ministries and state-owned broadcast institutions. Reuters did a complete about-turn from their earlier position, stating there should be no territorial monopoly either internally or in the form of

journalism' to attack the popular press and the power of the press barons. Indeed, one critic called the BBC's influence one of the most 'wholesome' possible, one that may help in the long run 'to save the press itself from some of the evils and dangers which now beset honest journalism' (Steed 1938: 209, 220, 223). Reith worked hard to cultivate its coverage of royal matters by close contact with Buckingham Palace: in 1932 he persuaded the king to give his first Christmas broadcast.

As Nicholson points out, Britain's media consisted of 'a monopoly wireless organisation too fearful of controversy, an elite press too closely associated with the establishment and a popular press too mindful of its profit margins to offer serious domestic and foreign news coverage' (Catterall et al. 2000: 138). During the Appeasement Crisis in 1938–9 there was initial criticism within the BBC that it did not give adequate foreign news coverage prior to the event, but it was credited (and credited itself) with keeping the nation calm.

After Munich the press tried to tighten its embargo procedure, but the 9 p.m. news became the cornerstone of the broadcast day nevertheless. Hence, although the early BBC had failings, it was still revered. It was also the subject of much discussion, encouraged by the popular press, which saw the BBC as news. It developed radio pages for gossip and news and features connected with the new medium, and these helped to boost newspaper sales. When war broke out, British newspapers were up against the concept of public service in the national interest.

Britain's 1926 General Strike: a partisan BBC?

During the inter-war years, controversy abounded: during Britain's General Strike in 1926 the public received their news mainly exclusive 'empires', such as those in operation for the forty years or so before the First World War. They now considered that the greatest safeguard against information distortion was free access to news and competition not only between newspapers but between the agencies themselves (Storey 1951: vii).[1]

Scholars also acknowledge that agencies operating at national level have been an essential tool for emerging nation-states, helping to enhance a country's sense of nationalism. For example, the press historian Michael Emery and his colleagues argue that the rise of the American press associations was 'an epochal development in the history of [American] journalism' and that the 'right of the people to know' was greatly advanced by news agencies, especially because only a few American daily newspapers ever attempted to maintain staff correspondents in the leading news centres of the world (Emery et al. 2000: 242, 246). Connections between news agencies, national identity and globalization are more complex and profound than previously recognized, with a substantial history; but 'what may appear at one level to be "globalization" in the sense of "homogenization", may appear at another level as fragmentation and competition' – exemplified by American agency splits over radio (Boyd-Barrett and Rantanen 1998).

from radio for the first time ever. The BBC broadcast five strike bulletins a day as well as Baldwin's speeches to the nation, of which Reith drafted some of the famous parts. Indeed Reith put the BBC at the service of the government, not only because of his own beliefs but also as a tactical means of ensuring BBC independence in the future. He refused to broadcast advocates of conciliation such as the Labour leader Ramsay MacDonald and the Archbishop of Canterbury, even though the corporation's director-general saw his role as trying to avoid revolution. Nevertheless, the measured style of delivery of broadcasts and the regularity of the service both had the effect of encouraging public confidence in the broadcaster.

The press: popularism, politics, business and advertising ▮

The inter-war years witnessed a continuation of earlier trends in newspaper development: further commercialization involving dependency on advertising and concentration of ownership accompanied by a reduction in the number of titles. The initiatives of the Northcliffe revolution in linking circulation to advertising rates were consolidated during this period. Large circulation sales based on low prices was a general trend, and in Britain 'circulation wars' broke out between major papers, which resorted to gimmicks and door-to-door salesmen. However, 'quality' newspapers could still exist on lower circulations than the new tabloids because their more prosperous readership allowed them to charge higher advertising rates. Meanwhile in the United States total newspaper revenue from advertising nearly tripled between 1915 and 1929, from $275 million to $800 million.

Britain developed a stronger national press at the expense of the provincial press, which became a market mainly for evening papers, with national morning papers, supplied by London-dominated chains, as the norm. In contrast, French regional dailies made such headway that, by the Second World War, their circulation was equal to that of Parisian dailies, each with 5.5 million. In Paris, the number of dailies dropped from eighty in 1914 to thirty-one by 1939 (Kuhn 1995: 18). France's continuous long-term trend in favour of a local press with the profession of journalism still in its ascendancy can be explained by various factors: politicians who held office at a number of different levels, lobbying for their locality in order to develop its resources and backed by people's loyalty to local roots and cultural traditions, and the importance of regional newspapers as a source for a whole range of essential information.

In the United States, journalism as a profession was marginalized during this period (Brennen 1995). The United States experienced two big waves of newspaper mergers: around 1900 and during the 1920s. Research has revealed that these were paralleled by mergers and acquisitions across all business and industry, suggesting that such newspaper developments were a product of larger economic trends rather than specific to the press itself (Adams 1995; Baldasty 1999; Bird 1992). The 1930s allowed little respite for newspapers, which were faced with the 'golden age' of radio and had the growing film industry to contend with.

The inter-war era of the 'press barons' saw the growth of tabloids, which were able to achieve and exploit increased circulations during the 1920s. Early tabloids (the word came from a chemist's pill) were published by Hearst and Northcliffe at the end of the nineteenth century. Both men believed they had a talent for keeping a finger on the popular pulse: as Northcliffe said, 'most of the ordinary man's prejudices are my prejudices.' One prejudice was nationalism. After the war, at a lunch for 7000 staff to commemorate twenty-five years of the *Daily Mail*, Northcliffe permitted a priest to give thanks for him 'guiding aright the destinies of this great Empire' (Catterall et al. 2000: 9). By 1919 he already owned a chain of thirty-one newspapers, including Sunday titles, as well as six magazines, various film interests and two wire services (Smith 1979: 165). By 1929 more than a third of America's total circulation was controlled by seventy chains.

By the end of the 1930s, three-quarters of the income of Britain's national dailies came from advertising, although France's dependency on advertising income has traditionally been not as great. Newspapers now became more overtly depoliticized, demonstrated by a move towards entertainment. The tabloid developed into a daily magazine with content not tied to news topicality, a form of popular journalism that has been described as 'a discourse of seduction' (Chalaby 1998: 184). In the 1920s and 1930s, when the tabloid picked up new readers and became popular, a gap emerged between the 'quality' and the 'popular' press, defined by a difference in content, style, readership patterns and circulation size. Although this distinction has not been so marked in France and Germany, where, mainly as a result of the strength of the regional and local markets, no national daily tabloid emerged, in America the differentiated market for small-format tabloids became apparent at city level: three New York papers – the *Daily News, Daily Mirror* and *Daily Graphic* – which were established in the 1920s proceeded to draw 1.5 million readers without significantly denting the existing newspaper market. Here the style of 'sin, scandal and gossip' became known as jazz journalism, characterized also by bold usage of photos as photo-journalism developed (Gorman and McLean 2003: 22; Douglas 1999: 229).

During this era a concentration of ownership prevailed and chains, often owned by a single proprietor, became the norm. In Britain, from Northcliffe's death in 1922 through to the 1930s, the five predominant companies were Associated Press, Amalgamated Press, Westminster Press and the Beaverbrook and Cadbury groups. The power that was derived from concentration of ownership by ruthless, opinionated, aggressive and politically independent entrepreneurs such as Lords Beaverbrook, Rothermere, Camrose and Kemsley raised a number of fundamental issues relating to the power of the media within society, particularly in influencing policy-making and public opinion. In 1937, nearly one in every two national dailies, the same ratio of locals, and one in three Sunday papers were owned by the above. Such multi-owner-ship was not new – Britain had experienced it during the eighteenth century – but three trends during this period stand out: chain ownership, an expanding market, and a tendency for a few newspapers to become dominant. Rothermere's (previously Northcliffe's) Associated Press was the largest press group in the Western world at the time, with total sales of over 6 million.

In France, although the number of newspapers read per capita by the population was not as high as in Japan and Britain, the phenomenon of the press baron was the same. The best example is that of the textile manufacturer turned newspaper tycoon Jean Prouvost, who rose to power spectacularly during this same period. Before he became the owner of *Le Figaro*, he dramatically reversed the fortunes of *Paris Soir* with a judicious mixture of sensational reporting, pictures, serious writing and sport – to the extent that by 1939 the circulation was over 1.5 million. This victory was followed in 1937 by the launch of *Marie Claire* as a successful weekly women's periodical. Then, just before war started, Prouvost crowned his reputation by turning the former sports magazine *Match* into a weekly illustrated news magazine entitled *Paris Match*, which is still the pièce de résistance of popular French period-ical journalism. However, this huge success was not representative of general trends during the economically and politically challenging epoch of the 1930s.

In Japan as well as in the West, large companies strengthened their hold over ownership and control in a bid for mass circulation, often taking over smaller newspapers (Hunter 1984: 145). Advertising and circulation were equally important to newspapers, but the system of press clubs had already created an institutionalization of the media which prevented the sort of alternative independent power base to political authority that developed among conglomerates headed by power-hungry individuals in America and Europe. Japanese journalists perceived themselves as part of the machinery rather than an alternative to it.

Publishing empires offered newspapers a new scope for independence from political parties and established leaderships and, in the case of Britain, this actually had a destabilizing effect on the public sphere. It was not just a question of the dailies no longer supporting mass-based parties; newspapers still expressed opinions via editorials, news values and the choice of what not to cover as well as the style of what they selected. Colin Seymour-Ure points out, 'The fact that press barons might be winning people's minds without people realising what was happening, simply made the barons' unaccountability worse' (Seymour-Ure 1974: 17–18). In America, Hearst's journalists were given two lists of public figures – those to favour and those to condemn; Orson Welles was on the latter list after the movie *Citizen Kane*. Meanwhile Walter Lippmann articulated an ethic for journalism that involved a greater role for objectivity backed by expertise: his *Public Opinion* (1922) became a founding book of American media studies (Carey 1989: 75).

The most destructive and least subtle example of contemporary journalistic malaise was the attempt by media moguls to use their organizations as alternatives to political parties, or as embryo parties in their own right. During an era of mass circulation in early 1930s Britain, the newspapers of both Beaverbrook and Rothermere went beyond the traditional function of political reporting as a link between electorate and politicians: Rothermere's *Daily Mail* is said to have brought about the Labour Party's failure in 1923. Equally papers became vehicles for propaganda campaigns against the Conservative Party leadership on the issue of empire free trade. They presented candidates (unsuccessfully) in by-elections: Beaverbrook for the 'Empire Crusade' and Rothermere for his United Empire Party. The prime minister, Stanley Baldwin, had his career destroyed by a personal vendetta conducted by Beaverbrook against him, which prompted these words written by his cousin Rudyard Kipling about the press barons: 'They are engines of propaganda for the constantly changing policies, desires, personal wishes, personal likes and dislikes of the two men. . . . These are methods hated alike by the public and the whole of the Press. . . . What the proprietorships of these papers are aiming at is power, and power without responsibility – the prerogative of the harlot throughout the ages' (Cudlipp 1980: 274; see also Curran and Seaton 1997: 49).

Fig. 9 Ernest Hemingway in a trench during the Spanish Civil War, c.1937; other volunteers such as George Orwell also wrote about the fight against fascism

The era of the press barons has inspired much scholarly debate on the significance of their contribution: was it innovative – a maverick interlude within press history – or did it manifest continuity with earlier trends? Some say that the political influence of the press barons was limited because they were not very good at initiating new campaigns; Rothermere's support for Hitler's Nazism and for Mussolini's fascism, for instance, had to be withdrawn as it was not popular with readers. But, as one commentator suggests, less important than their direct impact on events was 'their indirect influence in helping shape the whole environment in which politics was conducted' (Williams 1998: 67).

In the late 1920s and early 1930s politics was conducted in a highly charged manner: ideology and polarization of left and right were fuelled by the hardship of the Depression. In France, the Popular Front government alliance of socialists, communists and radicals faced the dilemma of how to remain united against the common threat of fascism and how to react to the Spanish Civil War: a world conflict was being acted out on their doorstep. In this atmosphere the open press freedom won in 1881 gave licence to vicious personal attacks by the extreme right-wing Action Française: 'The French press of the 1930s certainly tolerated a degree of scurrility, violence, and financial corruption which were abuses of the freedoms laboriously won in the course of the previous century' (Thompson 1968: 108).

In Britain, however, where media tycoons were supposedly independent from the mass political parties, they took office nevertheless. Northcliffe refused a ministerial post but was appointed director of propaganda in enemy countries in 1918, and Beaverbrook became minister of information briefly in that year, helping both Andrew Bonar Law and David Lloyd George to become prime minister. During the

Second World War he was Churchill's advisor, assisting in the organization of Conservative Party campaigns. He and Churchill were the only
two people to have seats in the British cabinet during both world wars.
When Beaverbrook purchased the *Daily Express* he was categorical: 'My
purpose originally was to set up a propaganda paper, and I have never
departed from that purpose all through the years. But in order to make
the propaganda effective the paper had to be successful. No paper is
any good at all for propaganda unless it has a thoroughly good financial
position' (Boyce et al. 1978: 142). By 1936 the *Daily Express* was selling
2.25 million – the largest circulation in the world. As Beaverbrook said,
'In an engine of propaganda the engine matters more than the propaganda' (Brendon 1982: 161). As with Hearst, circulation and profit came
first. Pulitzer had summed up the essence of the approach: 'circulation
means advertising, and advertising means money, and money means
independence.'

Connections between radio, advertising, Hollywood and music

Radio eventually provided a sharp focus for the question of the connection between entertainment and commercialism. Although it was not
clear at first who would pay for radio in the United States, it eventually
became a powerful weapon for corporate business. In the process
public perceptions also evolved, with identity increasingly centring on
consumer taste and preferences, to the extent that Frank Arnold, NBC's
director of development, was eventually able to call broadcasting 'the
Fourth Dimension of Advertising' (Douglas 1999: 5). It was only with the
advent of the networks, which had the power and money to promote
the idea of advertising sponsorship heavily, that the latter became more
acceptable.

At first advertisers viewed radio with great reverence for its potential
to stimulate culture, because initially it had broadcast classical music,
and listener surveys had showed a big increase in the popularity of classical music as a result of such exposure. This advertiser respect for radio
as a cultural 'uplifter' was in sharp contrast to the disdain they showed
for movies, tabloids and confessional magazines: 'Movies played to a
crowd in a garish public setting; they seemed to reflect the indiscri-
minate tastelessness and sensuality of people in the mass. Tabloids
and confession magazines conveyed the aura of subways, screaming
newsboys, and crowded newsstands. Radio, by contrast, reached its
audience as individuals, or in small family groups, insulated by the
home setting from any of the base passions of the mob' (Marchand
1985: 89).

Yet the advertising industry feared that radio was a fad and that
promotions wouldn't work. In 1925, the publication *Radio Age* articulated the opposition of many: 'the broadcasters who succumbed to the
commercial influence are building up a monster who, like Frankenstein,

will slay his creator' (Smulyan 1994: 68). Radio catered for a new sort of audience, not self-selecting and easily defined as in the case of newspapers, but disparate, wide and potentially huge. At first agencies had reassured the newspapers that radio could never be more than a goodwill supplement to press adverts, but, as they began to integrate advertising into the entertainment, they ended up with direct advertising as well as sponsorship.

One of the arguments for radio advertising as opposed to other promotional mediums was that it reached the consumer with messages for home and family at a time when they were enjoying both. Advertising philosophy at the time identified women as the main consumers, so radio followed suit with schedules catering specifically for women, such as daytime drama serials and soap operas (so called because the first sponsors were washing powder manufacturers). Even President Hoover opposed broadcast advertising at first, but he was persuaded by the concept of indirect advertising, which allowed for the sponsor's name, but no direct selling. The 'sponsorship only' approach to advertising relied on the ideal of business paternalism as a form of welfare capitalism, which was popular at the time, so that NBC was considered to be involved in a 'semi-philanthropic' activity when it was first established as a subsidiary of RCA (Marchand 1985: 90). However, the public was not persuaded until the industry itself had waged a long campaign for acceptance, a factor which is often overlooked by historians (Smulyan 1994: 71).

In the United States, radio manufacturers had originally made the programmes in order to boost the sale of receivers, but their reluctance meant that nobody was prepared to provide the entertainment to attract audiences for the advertisers, so the advertisers had to do it themselves; this meant that they had to become entertainers as well as salesmen. Advertising agencies, which controlled the corporate budgets for promotion, did not enter the field of programme-making in a big way until the time of the Depression, when competition and the need for cost efficiencies dictated a tougher focus on programmes that were more effective at selling. Calvin Kuhl, who worked with John U. Reber, director of J. Walter Thompson, describes the change:

> At the beginning NBC naturally turned to Broadway and Vaudeville for writing and directing experience. . . .These people were hidebound in their thinking and techniques. . . .They thought of an audience as so many tuxedo clad and evening gowned bodies in rows of seats before a stage. . . . In the late 20s and early 30s an advertising agency on behalf of a client might approach NBC with a tentative interest in 'buying' a show, and NBC would then dream up a show via its culls from Broadway and Vaudeville. . . . Well, almost immediately after persuading a J. W. Thompson client to buy half an hour of such NBC produced twaddle, John, complaining to NBC of the mediocrity and unimaginativeness of their fare, said 'Hell, if that's the best you can do,

we can do better, with our own writers and directors', which he then
proceeded to do. (Hilmes 1997: 116)

Also, agencies now had another power: the ability to move programming product from one network to another in order to procure the best
deal, which challenged the supremacy of the latter.

Brand names spread like a cancer: after J. Walter Thompson's famous
Lux Hollywood star endorsement campaign, the agency claimed that
'it was impossible to wash your hands in Hollywood unless you used
Lux Toilet Soap', and numerous endorsements – but never paid –
started to appear in mass-circulation magazines (Hilmes 1997: 117;
1990). Sponsored radio shows featured musical groups with names
such as the Ipana Troubadours (toothpaste), while Palmolive soap gave
its soloists Frank Munn and Virginia Rea the new names Paul Oliver and
Olive Palmer. In 1926 the first radio singing commercial was broadcast
by General Mills for Wheaties.

Hollywood also had an important influence on radio: Hilmes has
referred to Hollywood as radio's 'alter ego', its rival but also its contributor (1990: 1). At first studios which owned radio stations tried to start
networks in the United States, but this was unsuccessful as a result of a
combination of factors, including an inability to procure land lines,
regulatory problems, and opposition from both exhibitors and broadcasting interests. In the 1930s the studios therefore became involved
in radio programming, and after 1936 a federal government investigation into AT&T's telephone rate structures for the West Coast made
Hollywood radio production easier (Hilmes 1990: 2).

By the 1930s radio's potential for political communication, hence also
propaganda usage, became more obvious. The scope for consumers to
hear music, information and entertainment was now also greater. In
the United States, advertising agency pressure ensured that 'dialect'
comedy, popular singers and bands gradually replaced the previous
respectable, restrained classical repertoire aimed at more discerning
audiences. Even Lord Reith, with his sense of mission and moral high
ground, moved the BBC gradually towards a greater flexibility in music
provision, faced with a change by record companies from what one
historian had called a role of educating the masses to 'servicing' them
(Curran et al. 1987: 287).

Recorded music production, which had challenged the structure of
the nineteenth-century entertainment business, was itself challenged,
first by the new film industry, then by the rise of radio. In both Britain
and the United States, the industry was specifically shaped by the recession and radio's popularity, which had jointly caused sales of records
and sheet music to slump; this was also accompanied by a decline in
performance.

Music was important to radio right from the beginning, partly
because a wider range of provision had not yet been devised and partly
because the playing of music enabled the deadly sin of silence to be

avoided. For three decades, broadcasters relied on live music rather than phonograph records to fill the schedules in America (Smethers and Jolliffee 2000). Dance music such as the swing and jitterbug was popular in the USA; in Britain classical music, such as the Proms (promenade concerts), was used by the BBC to broaden listeners' horizons. The corporation established its own music department in 1927 and its own symphony orchestra in 1930.

Despite the monopoly of the BBC, even British listeners were able to receive alternative channels, such as Radio Normandie and Radio Luxembourg, which broadcast (in the case of the latter illegally) American-style music. In America, a desire for regional distinctiveness was evidenced by the popularity of barn dance programmes, and country music brought a rural working-class flavour. 'A relationship between radio and music seemed natural. In the 1920s, radio station managers, afraid of alienating racist whites, banned music that they considered "black" and favoured music from certain areas over others, yet because country music became intertwined with blues, they were aware that Afro-Americans would still listen' (Smulyan 1994: 24).

Although recording was to change music culture totally, it was only in the mid-1920s that the disc was linked to amplification and loudspeakers. The principles of amplification had been developed through radio, and it was now radio technicians who took the lead in electrified recording. Nevertheless, radio also caused disorder within the American music recording industry. The American Society of Composers, Artists and Publishers (ASCAP), an organization for the collection of royalties and dominated by theatres, publishing and movie interests, found that radio stations refused to pay up. In 1939 an alternative body entitled Broadcast Music Incorporated (BMI) was established to publish non-ASCAP music. Friction came to a head in 1941 when radio stations refused a doubling of ASCAP royalties, with the result that only non-copyright and BMI music was broadcast. This in turn affected the sort of music that was made available to the public, and, although ASCAP accepted that it had lost, clearly a change in the power structure of the music business was on the agenda once more. Tin Pan Alley's dominant white popular music had been challenged: 'the way for rock and roll was undoubtedly prepared through broadcasts of country music and "cover versions" of rhythm and blues' (Shepherd 1982: 134–5).

The music industry and the Depression

The music industry's history has always featured uneven growth, setbacks and corporate failures as well as technical advances. During the 1920s there was overproduction and falling sales in the face of competition with radio, which forced companies to face restructuring. In 1923 Columbia went into receivership and was subsequently bought up by its British subsidiary. The following year industry sales fell dramatically as a technical struggle for viable electrical recording accelerated. By the 1920s and early 1930s the huge increase in 'wireless' sets had a catastrophic effect on the music industry, and this was immediately exacerbated by the economic disaster of the Depression.

Record companies responded by developing more efforts towards market control. Hence they followed what they perceived as popular demand, and also tried to anticipate it. Yet commercial realities necessitated a reduction of risks in any attempts to appeal to the widest possible group of people (Martin 1995: 240). This in turn led to the creation of musical formulas within genres such as jazz and blues that amounted to a dilution of their origins. Jazz as a musical form had become popular worldwide, even in Russia, where revolutionaries considered it to be a symbol of Western decadence. Jazz musicians provided backing for the classic blues recordings of the 1920s as a market emerged in the United States for 'race records' – that is, discs by singers such as Bessie Smith, Ma Rainey, Mamie Smith and Sophie Tucker that circulated chiefly among the black population (Chanan 1995: 51).

After the repeal of prohibition in America in 1933, enormous numbers of jukeboxes were installed in bars. By 1938 some half a million of these accounted for almost 40 per cent of record production in the United States (Sanjek 1988: 133; Gronow 1983; Martin 1995: 239–41; Curran et al. 1987: 288).

The debut of cinema sound had an important effect on the industry as Hollywood came to rival New York as the primary source of music production in the United States. After the Depression musicals became popular and helped record sales to regain ground. Hence the industry that emerged from near collapse was characterized by recording companies with connections to radio and film that marketed big-name celebrities. As had happened in the film industry, a profusion of small companies was reduced to a number of very large ones. Today's giants, such as EMI, CBS and RCA, evolved into huge multinational entertainment empires.

Over the longer term, mechanical reproduction was to create a demand for an increased amount of music which was beyond the capacity of any national industry to supply (Chanan 1995: 44, 55). In the 1930s the needs of guitarists in popular American bands led to the introduction of the electric guitar, the most successful electric instrument before the keyboard synthesizer of the 1960s (Chanan 1994: 256). New instruments now emerged based on electromagnetic and electronic principles, such as the Hammond organ, which took off after the Second World War. The technological development of amplifiers, loudspeakers, oscillators and new electronic pitched instruments opened up fresh opportunities for amateur usage.

New developments in consumption and advertising method: US initiatives

During the 1920s and 1930s the advertising industry came to power at the centre of the economy, and advertising became respectable – a process likened by Raymond Williams to the dismissal of Falstaff with contempt by the newly crowned Henry V in Shakespeare's play (Williams 1980: 181). These developments can only be fully appreciated in the context of changes that took place in the 1880s and 1890s, when the seeds of the modern system were sown, prompting one historian to comment, 'There is no single point in history before which we were all nature's children, after which we became the sons and daughters of commerce' (Schudson 1993: 179). Yet it is generally agreed that, despite the fact that many people were too poor between the wars to afford the range of products that were advertised, the advertising industry reached its present-day form and came of age.

By the mid-1920s, the boom in tabloid newspapers led advertisers, as keen observers of developments in popular culture, to study the format of sex and crime which had overtaken the standard news story. They reacted with a mixture of fascination and distaste, taking note that three times as many New Yorkers read the tabloids as read the *New York Times*. This led them to focus more on the rising economic power of ordinary people and an assessment of the formulas that attracted them. Equally there were lessons to be learned from the power of pictures, especially close-ups and the movie entertainment mix of 'Luxury, Lackeys and Love' (Marchand 1985: 62). Audience mentality was labelled the 'tabloid mind'; in particular the popularity of the confessional true story offered aspects to be emulated.

Before the war, adverts had concentrated on information about the product itself; after the war, they focused on the benefits of ownership

The influence of *True Story* on the commodity confessional

The American magazine *True Story* presented real-life first-person accounts from 'heroines' who seemed regularly to fall victim to the dangers of an increasingly confusing and difficult modern world. These 'commodity confessional' narratives were aimed at working-class female readers, and one scholar has argued that the formula, which is popular today, had the double-edged effect of providing pleasure and the possibilities of liberation while also representing a form of hegemonic cultural control over the audience (Mandziuk 2001). For advertisers it was simpler: they played on these perceived vulnerabilities in their campaigns.

'Be the Leading Lady in this Little Modern Drama', a 1928 headline announced (Marchand 1985: 11–12). The personalization helped to soften people's fears about the speed and complexity of modern life, and of becoming 'lost in the crowd' or swallowed up by large bureaucratic organizations. Working on these insecurities, the advertiser portrayed a situation where the individual faced an external task or goal that was an impersonal test for business success, popularity, beauty or love. With the benevolent expert advice of advertisers, the product in question would help them jump the hurdle.

that accrued from the product. *Printers' Ink*, America's advertising trade paper, described the shift from product to people as a move from the 'factory viewpoint' to concern with 'the mental processes of the consumer', which now involved the participation of the customer. Advertisers adopted the language and methodological approach of the newly fashionable discipline of psychology, whether behaviourist, Freudian or a mixture of theories.

Bit by bit, the web spun by advertisements became more complex: changes in manufacturing processes and the capacity to increase output without major increases in production costs encouraged a new business emphasis on marketing and distribution. Ironically, while acting as an apostle of modernity, advertising also provided a protection against the worst effects of modern, impersonal large-scale production. Thus the influence on business of the media and advertising agencies further stimulated the development of advertising, which in turn helped people to adjust to additional complexities in modern life, such as the social impact of the automobile and electricity.

As mass-produced and advertised products became more important to people, so the criteria for consumption and the nature of what was deemed desirable in goods also changed, bringing about a qualitative as well as a quantitative shift in consumption. Just one small example was the relatively new habit of self-shaving (instead of paying a barber to do it for you), which was boosted during the First World War when, for instance, the Gillette company had sold the United States War Department 3.5 million razors and 32 million blades (Schudson 1993: 187).

In the United States, more than in Europe or Japan, there was a huge increase from 1919 to 1929 in ownership of goods such as radios, vacuum cleaners, silk stockings, refrigerators, cars and washing machines. Products that were previously available only seasonally or in certain regions could now be obtained year round nationwide, thanks to tin canning and refrigerated railway freight carriages. Although mass production meant more standardization of products, it also led to more choice, as newspapers, radio and movies introduced increasing numbers of people to other worlds and possibilities, creating common national tastes. With the mass-produced automobile, the pace of life now seemed faster, and time was more scarce, so labour-saving devices such as the new washing machine had obvious attractions, and the expansion of consumer credit via instalment payments made purchase easier.

In the brave new world of scientific industrial management, with 'Fordism' (conveyor-belt-style quantifiable production methods) in support of consumption,[2] advertising agencies adopted the methods of science to improve the efficiency of advertising as a marketing tool. It may have had the public relations effect of increasing the status of advertising from a trade to a profession (Kreshel 1990), but traditional Christian values of thrift were also heavily challenged. Consumer convenience, considered a desirable attribute that is usually present only in relatively affluent societies, also became a watchword for what scholars have called 'the democratization of goods'. The fact that a vacuum cleaner or washing machine had the potential to replace the services of a maid was promoted by advertisers as a great equalizer. Certain products that everyone could afford, they maintained, brought satisfaction that no millionaire could compete with. Hence the American Pencil Company claimed: 'Here – write like a millionaire. A millionaire may ride in a sportier car, live in a richer home, and work at a bigger desk . . . but he can't write with a better pencil than you can . . . And the price is ten cents, to everyone' (Marchand 1985: 291).

Women, not men, were considered the primary consumers within American culture: 'The proper study of mankind is MAN . . . but the proper study of markets is WOMEN', opined the trade paper *Printer's Ink* (Schudson 1993: 173). Changes in employment, mobility brought about by the automobile, and the media – especially women's magazines – as tutors of lifestyle all meant that patterns of consumption tended to become public rather than private, centring on women. With their newly enfranchised status, women were now finally part of the public sphere. Women were viewed as purchasing agents for, and efficient managers of, their family with less obligation to wider civic society, but with a duty to nurture husband and children in family harmony by promoting their smooth integration into that society: father at work and children at school and play (Lears 1994: 183–209).

To achieve these ends, managerial professionalism had to be applied to the female sphere with 'scientific cookery' (methodical male values of rationality and objectivity), which turned the kitchen into a sterile laboratory of domestic perfection in which standardization was considered a desirable moral advance, forming part of consumer education. So, for instance, 'the best surprise is no surprise', and processed cheese was therefore superior to farm cheese because of its uniformity. The advocates of 'scientific cookery' 'hoped to regulate the messy sprawl of American society and to filter out the most unsettling aspects of its diversity' (Shapiro 1986: 37).

The advertisers' thinking that females were ignorant, emotional and lacking in taste 'drew upon a long tradition, British and French as well as American, for viewing women as fickle and debased consumers' (Marchand 1985: 66). Men were also patronized as hapless bumblers. So, for instance, women should purchase the shaving cream and safety razors: 'What does a man know about complexion, the skin? He rips and hacks away at his face and then washes it with strong soap, sprinkles on a little powder, and believes he is a beauty parlor wizard. You, the woman of the family, understand what the care of the skin means. . . . They know no better: help them!' (Schudson 1993: 174).

The assumption of public lethargy was compounded by the newly fashionable science of psychology, which was beginning to perfect the intelligence test. Before the war American IQ tests had discovered that a disturbing number of inductees did not possess the minimum level

Women and tobacco advertisements

The historian Michael Schudson has looked at the relationship between the rise in cigarette smoking among women and the role of advertising, equating the concept of convenience with that of the democratization of goods: the more convenient a product, the more it is equally available to both men and women. The spread of smoking among women was one of the most visible signs of changes in consumption during the 1920s. While not quite acting as an apologist for the industry, Schudson demonstrates that, despite the criticism of contemporaries, advertising followed the trend rather than causing it, because many women were smoking before the first advert appeared, although advertising and news coverage helped legitimize the practice. This change in consumption patterns found its roots in cultural change and political conflict. Many people first tried cigarettes during the First World War, when cigarettes seemed more convenient than pipes, tobacco chewing or cigars. The cigarette became connected emotionally with relief and comradeship under horrendous pressure. The taste of cigarettes became milder when, just before the war, blended tobaccos had come to replace the stronger Turkish variety. Large-scale production after the war and the changing

social role of women were both factors in the increase in their smoking, which provoked controversy and as such constituted an ongoing news story. The reaction of various institutions, such as women-only colleges in America (which gradually relaxed the no-smoking rules), provoked public debate. A contemporary account related that some women working in the Wall Street area used to pay to take a taxi at lunchtime as a safe haven for smoking because it was the only place they could smoke with a sense of freedom. The cigarette 'served as a symbol of women's renewed demand for equality' (Schudson 1993: 203).

The first notable cigarette advertisement directed towards women was for Chesterfield in 1926. It depicted a romantic couple at night, the man smoking, the woman sitting next to him, saying (as the caption), 'Blow Some my Way'. A 1927 advert in the *New York Times* showed a famous female opera singer recommending Lucky Strike as being soothing for the throat. The image conjured up sexual openness, a risqué, young and stylish attitude, whereas for men cigarettes implied refinement and a feminine sensibility: the US navy before the war had banned cigarettes for being 'unmanly' in comparison with cigars and pipes.

of intelligence to qualify for military service (Marchand 1985: 67). Now advertisers jumped on the bandwagon, reinforcing the image of an unintelligent public by announcing estimates of average mental age that ranged from nine to sixteen – ammunition for the patronizing tone adopted by advertisers.

Raymond Williams (1980) interprets advertising as an illusory but well-organized system of 'magical' inducements and satisfactions, which rather strangely coexist with a highly developed scientific technology, but in fact blot out the fundamental choice between people as consumers and people as users. Jackson Lears also observes that 'in the 1920s the promise was not merely personal control but magical power' (1994: 229). In the twentieth century, the nineteenth-century 'puff' took on a more ambitious scale as an all-embracing expression of corporate decisions, dressed up by copywriters as the 'consumer's' – that is, 'your' – choice of priorities, methods and style. 'The new psychology

Advertising, politics and the Depression in America

The Depression provided a prime example of the economic trends of capitalism that Marx had predicted – a revival of the economy through expansion of secondary production – that is, a stimulation of demand for consumer goods in order to boost primary, or heavy, industry (Chanan 1994: 250). The growth of advertising intended to promote a desire for consumption in turn led to promotions via the mass-circulation press and radio. During the 1920s and 1930s, advertising took on what we now recognize as a 'modern' style and influence. The way that this happened was intrinsically linked to corporate economic growth and mass production, giving business, aided by advertising, a new respectable relationship with the power structure of individual countries. There was also a more focused attitude towards the masses, who were seen as fodder by politicians and as consumers by business. As Lenin once said, 'politics begins with the masses: not in their thousands, but in their millions.'

Although the initial business strategy for dealing with recession was denial, it is still possible to detect a growing sense of desperation among advertising agencies as the Depression set in. Orders were cancelled, agencies laid off staff and, in America, it seemed that the only work available for copywriters was in radio. The advertisements themselves sounded more desperate in what was now a frantic competition for a shrinking pot of gold. Advertisers appealed to job insecurity with scare campaigns, carrying captions such as 'Fired – and for a reason he never suspected'. The advert was for mouthwash.

The effects of advertising on working people have been the subject of academic dispute. Research has revealed that most workers probably could not afford many of the goods that were advertised, despite the increasing prosperity of the 1920s. Agencies studied the issue of economic threshold very carefully, differentiating between 'buyers' and those who simply did not qualify as 'consumer citizens' (i.e., buyers). According to various different trade definitions in the United States, the latter included families with incomes of less than $1000 a year, tenant farmers, blacks and those without an easy command of English; estimates of the extent of disenfranchisement range from 30 per cent to nearly two-thirds of the population. Therefore in the American context, as elsewhere, the term 'mass audience' actually referred to those with higher than average incomes (Marchand 1985: 64).

However, just because a family did not pass the advertisers' income threshold did not mean that they were not subjected to sales ideology, particularly with street displays and a widespread medium such as radio. Scientific management at the workplace and advertising in the cultural realm were both forms of social control on workers. Consumption distracted people from politics.

Conversely, it was from this period that advertising became closely connected to a whole system of persuasion towards nation-building in politics, with people from the industry involved in propaganda, competition between parties and the formulation of public opinion. In the United States, advertising methods were hijacked by government. Roosevelt became a keen advertiser of government, using blue eagles to symbolize the national recovery administration during his fireside chats to gain support for his political programmes. He shared the advertisers' belief that the people constituted a huge mass audience open to persuasion, or 'democratic communication', as he called it. It worked: although there were only eight chats representing a mere 8 per cent of his radio addresses between 1933 and 1936, 64 per cent of American radios were tuned in to one of them (Briggs and Burke 2002: 219).

The manipulation of mass populations using media devices now redefined the influencing of public opinion as the 'manufacture of consent' – a phrase first coined by Walter Lippmann in 1920. In the United States this was compounded by the methods of the advertising industry, which still privately held the masses in disdain. 'The dominant discourse of consumer culture required the systematic denial of diversity. Advertisers collaborated unwittingly with their critics in creating rhetorical constructions that construed the vast majority of the population as passive, manipulative objects' (Lears 1994: 236).

Hence managerial thought extended to the management of public opinion as it was represented in mass society. So it was that:

'Boundaries became blurred between the discourses of the public and private sectors. Methods for measuring consumer demand migrated from corporate boardrooms to government offices; market research became opinion polling, and public opinion was depoliticized.' What has happened thereafter follows the prediction of de Tocqueville almost a hundred years earlier: the more responsive huge organizations seemed to be, the more they were able to set the boundaries of public discourse. In the process, 'they redefined the essence of the American Way of Life from a vague populism to an equally murky notion of free enterprise' (Lears 1994: 235).

encouraged a more flexible and pragmatic outlook on everything from sexual conduct to government policy' (Lears 1994: 207). But it acted as a smokescreen: 'The magic obscures the real sources of general satisfaction because their discovery would involve radical change in the whole common way of life' (Williams 1980: 189). Therefore, according to Raymond Williams, advertising's power is the result of a failure of social meanings, values and ideals, a failure to create real public participation in everyday economic life, and it has happened because control of the means of production has been allowed to remain with a minority, often taken outside of the country that it affects.

The film business: Hollywood and beyond

Film history's three most important technological transitions have been cinema's 'invention' in 1895, sound standardization in the 1920s and the contemporary integration of computer-generated images. Scholars have seen an institutional pattern of technological assimilation connected to these events (Faden 1999; Custen 1986). For instance, the first company to bring out a major film with sound – *The Jazz Singer* (1927), starring Al Jolson – was Warner Bros., a business that had been around since the days of nickelodeons. The box-office income turned out to be five times the original cost, with the result that this Hollywood giant was valued at $16 million the following year. Even after the Depression had intervened, Warner Bros. was still worth £230 million in 1930 (Briggs and Burke 2002: 169–73). By now the film business was firmly characterized by sophisticated corporate enterprises with a multinational flavour, enhanced by mergers and buy-ins. The year 1919 saw the first large-scale financing of a film from the stock market – $10 million – by Adolph Zukor, who controlled over 300 cinemas by 1921. In Britain the (French) Gaumont–British Picture Corporation was formed in 1927, owning 300 cinemas and connected to the American Fox Films, while Associated British Cinemas was formed in 1928, with connections to (American) First National and (French) Pathé. Within a year its cinema ownership rose from twenty-eight to eighty-eight. In 1933 the Odeon circuit was also launched, but was not involved in production.

While European countries faced international instability, the onset of the Depression with the Wall Street Crash in 1929 had the effect of creating a national mood of introspection in the United States. Newspaper circulations and revenue and cinema audiences were down in a climate where the latter was temporarily blamed for the moral decline of society. Yet by 1934 confidence was recovering, as studio productions became more cost effective in an increasingly focused factory-style environment. The financial institutions as providers of risk capital installed managers to protect their investments and production costs. Film content was also changing, based more on popular novels or plays and conveying a more positive image of American society and human values, although one writer comments: 'films offered a view of American society which was progressive, unified, and free from the traumas which were affecting other areas of the world. They were an element in the reinforcement of isolationism which permeated American society in the inter-war period' (Ward 1989: 130). Another scholar has argued that Hollywood's domination of the overseas market 'depended at least in part on its ability to convince its foreign customers that its output was inoffensive and ideologically neutral.' Therefore there were already issues of censorship, as the State Department took an active interest in the nature of representation for export well before the Second World War (Vasey 1997: 8).

The United States was still the largest domestic market for films in the world, and the size of audiences led to the economies of scale that other national industries could not hope to achieve. This factor underscored the annual output of more than 400 movies a year during the 1930s. Collective distinctiveness of the genre was reinforced by considerable overseas marketing and well-organized distribution. In addition, 'the global reach of the movies helped to reinforce Hollywood's identity as an emissary of consumer culture. . . . "Product placement" in more or less overt forms was well established by the 1930s' (Vasey 1997: 4).

While the commercial side of movies flourished, so also did the star system. The first woman to become a huge celebrity was Mary Pickford, and in 1919 Charlie Chaplin formed his own studio and company – United Artists – with her, Douglas Fairbanks and D. W. Griffith. Very soon, 'Chaplinitis' overtook the world, with merchandising, such as dolls, music, dances and even cocktails, to go with the films. The extent of the craze is familiar today, but this was the first of its kind. Chaplin's films of the 1920s, such as *The Gold Rush*, became legendary, prompting Mack Sennett, for whom he had worked previously, to call him 'the greatest artist who ever lived'. Although other stars also emerged, such as the screen 'lover' Rudolph Valentino, Chaplin's stature continued. His film *Modern Times*, featuring a Henry Ford-style assembly-line factory, has become a classic of social observation.

The Depression prompted some films with a social conscience, such as those of Frank Capra, which promoted community awareness with respect for freedom and principled authority. What is often overlooked in the rush to document Hollywood's power is that the advent of film sound presented an opportunity to express national culture and creative art via moving pictures. It represented a potential threat to Hollywood's hegemony.

There were certainly important movies of the period made outside of Hollywood, such as Fritz Lang's evocative urban classic *Metropolis*, made in Germany, the classic epics of Russia's Sergei Eisenstein and the films of Japan's great Akira Kurosawa. Sometimes European films were influenced by documentary-makers and by radio, yet there was also a perceived divide, according to film-makers, between art movies and commercial ones. But the main reason that Hollywood still continued to dominate lay in the secret of lavish and well-organized distribution. Investment in publicity sold a mix that local producers could not match: stars, formulas, production values and company image as 'guarantees of satisfying entertainment. Only in rare circumstances did investing in the selling of a foreign film, or in its extensive distribution, offer advantages' (Nowell-Smith and Ricci 1998: 36).

Meanwhile the manufacturers of cameras and film stock for the film industry decided to expand technical invention in order to enlarge their market to non-commercial users, at a time when the Depression had taken hold. When 16 mm film was introduced, it led to a new popularity for documentary and the advent of amateur movie-makers, but was kept away from cinema screens by distributors and disdainfully described in the trade press as substandard. Despite this hostility, the move marked the beginnings of a new tertiary consumer industry, widening participation, whereby 'capital proceeds to market not just cultural products but the technical means of cultural production itself' (Chanan 1994: 251–2). In the case of the amateur industry, it was to spawn magazines, competitions and prizes, and was later extended to 8 mm, super 8 and video, followed by hi-fi and computers.

With the introduction of 'talkies' came the 'golden age' of Hollywood, but on the eve of this consolidation there was talk of protectionism in Britain, where only 5 per cent of the films shown were made nationally. Already by the 1920s the Germans and French had established schemes to promote and subsidize their own films and had introduced levies against American imports (Nowell-Smith and Ricci 1998: 35). Although the British government was not prepared to give financial help to the indigenous film industry, it did pass legislation in 1927 introducing a quota system (continued by further legislation in 1937) and controls on advance- and block-booking of films, together with an advisory board on trade. Thus the British Cinematographic Films

Act of 1927 represented a move from outright free trade in cultural products to a recognition of the importance of the medium to national interests, an approach that was to be strengthened by the war situation. The year 1939 saw not only the outbreak of the Second World War but also the release for wartime audiences of two of the most popular Hollywood movies of all time: *The Wizard of Oz* and *Gone with the Wind* (Tracey 2001).

Technical developments in early television

During this period experiments in early television were well advanced, but before the war economies worldwide were not healthy enough for television to move from an experimental medium to a form of mass consumption. The Nazis claimed to have launched the first regular public television service in 1935, preceding the BBC's service by eighteen months, but there were no television sets, so people grouped in special auditoria in Berlin. Television in its experimental stages has a pre-history dating back to 1839 – also a landmark year in the development of the camera and photographic image (Briggs and Burke 2002: 173). Sets had been on sale during the 1920s, although they were very expensive, and in 1929 the BBC, for instance, reluctantly allowed John Logie Baird to develop an experimental service. In the United States, the Russian Vladimir Zworykin also faced difficulties: on the first occasion after the Russian Revolution that he tried to emigrate, he could not obtain work. Yet he successfully patented an entire electrical TV system in 1923 and was employed secretly by Sarnoff at RCA to run a laboratory (Briggs and Burke 2002: 174).

A system was demonstrated at the 1931 Berlin Radio Exhibition amid the jockeying for technical and business influence. The 'father' of Japanese television, Kenjiro Takayanagi, had been conducting ongoing research with innovative usage of the Braun tube combined with the Yagi antenna, the prototype for standard television antennas worldwide. In 1937 NHK set up an experimental station transmitting limited television signals from Tokyo, while Toshiba and NEC simultaneously constructed the first private television receivers. On 13 April 1940, NHK broadcast the first television drama (Smith 1995: 287). The following year the Pacific War started.

Research was taking place in other parts of the world simultaneously, including 'experimental' broadcasts, for example, by the BBC. As with film, television invention was an international affair, and the technical and visual constraints of early efforts are a salutary reminder of the sheer effort of invention (Barker 1991). The first pictures were static head and shoulders close-ups, but, as with early film, there was a novelty value. Big corporations emerged as dominant players early on. Key players included a subsidiary of Zeiss Ikon, Bosch, Telefunken, and the Marconi Wireless Company, plus a newly merged company – Electrical and Musical Industries Ltd (EMI). Baird and RCA also held patents. By the outbreak of war, the Philips company was selling sets that could be used in the Netherlands and Britain. Experimental broadcasts were taking place from Sweden to Japan and France, where the Eiffel Tower housed the most powerful television station in the world, with a capacity of 45,000 watts.

The United States and Japan adopted 525 lines, whereas in Europe the system was mainly 625. However, television had no amateur technical lobby similar to that in the radio industry, which responded to pressure for expansion exerted by 'hams'. In the meantime, on the eve of world conflict, radio still blossomed.

Conclusions

In this age of ideology and politics aimed at manipulating the masses, the role of the media became multi-faceted, illustrated by the following features and trends.

> In the inter-war period radio transformed entertainment and added a whole new dimension to the way in which people received information. The BBC, although a monopoly, emerged as an impressive example of the public service model. A combination of factors in America led to commercialism, despite reactions against it.
>
> To democratic countries in peacetime, 'propaganda' was a dirty word, but to the Nazi and Russian regimes the management of public opinion was central to the functioning of the authoritarian state as a weapon for 'revolutionary consolidation' (Taylor 1998).
>
> Patterns were set from 1922 to 1952 for the basic definitions and uses of broadcasting, but this heritage has often been viewed as a precursor to television studies, rather than having a discrete significance. Nevertheless, radio broadcasters influenced the contribution of television to the political, social and cultural life of countries such as France and Britain, where they later took on the new development of television. Yet this created one of media history's ironies, with 'production and control of the pictures on the television screen in the hands of broadcasting bodies which had dealt with sound before pictures at a time when cinema was showing pictures without sound' (Briggs and Burke 2002: 164).
>
> Radio's cultural influence was also a reflection of longer term social trends, such as increased mass consumption, a breakdown of boundaries between public and private spheres, and a new recognition of the importance of gender and, in the United States, of race as issues.
>
> Whereas the cost of advertising was originally limited and manageable, its importance became grossly inflated. The implications of mass consumption underwritten by advertising and the convergence of corporate and government interests have emerged in contemporary society.

In 1939, the countries that participated in the Second World War were very different politically, constitutionally and socially, as well as in terms of their advances towards 'consumerism'. Their approaches to media also varied. Whereas one of the causes of war in 1914–18 had been competition over the territorial products of imperialism, during the Second World War ideology's role within militarism was central.

Technologically enhanced media communication was used more than ever before to win hearts and minds. During the 1930s the media reflected a growing worldwide nationalism but also contributed to it. Governments had developed important relationships with media organizations that were to come into sharper focus under the spotlight of war.

Study questions

Compare and contrast conceptions of the masses during this period across industries and countries. In your opinion, how did these differ from attitudes today?

How did the role of media in the articulation and encouragement of nationalism differ between countries?

What evidence is there of a simultaneous trend in various media industry developments towards both uniformity and control on the one hand and democratization of opportunity on the other?

6 War and Beyond, 1939–1947

In total war, nations in their entirety confront each other, and all expressions of national life become weapons of war.

Fritz Hippler, cited in Rentschler 1996: 202

In propaganda as in love, anything is permissible which is successful.

Joseph Goebbels, cited in Welch 1993: 17

No permanent propaganda policy can in the modern world be based on untruthfulness.

BBC Handbook, 1941

Summary

The *objective* of this chapter is to demonstrate that the precedent set by the First World War for government to control the media for propaganda purposes was continued and extended during this traumatic period. As the media assumed a changed significance, and the importance of various branches in relation to each other differed, a new attitude and repositioning for the future also started to emerge. Things would never be the same again, despite certain continuities.

Everywhere, total war brought more government intrusion into the media and new institutions for the purposes of propaganda control in the interests of victory. In this situation, the means as well as the end were important: these differed considerably between countries. The control that every government aimed for was achieved either voluntarily or by legislation and compulsory, sometimes brutal, enforcement.

The fact that media transmissions were geared 100 per cent to war led to a different ethics in the use of content: the emotion of film was harnessed to ideological imperatives such as the extermination of the Jews; news analysis could no longer be independently critical. The power to influence minds was all.

During these war years, the relative balance of power between media altered: radio overtook the struggling newspaper industry in importance, while cinema fiction manipulated emotions and feelings as part of the war effort. Cinema newsreels assumed a new significance in the United States, Britain and Germany; music and advertising could no longer operate as industries with an independent creative force.

Despite the total change in priorities and approach, both communication and 'purposeful' entertainment became central to people's lives. Precedents and structures were established that were to be used in years to come.

Introduction

The twentieth-century's two world wars were global, involving not only more countries and more people than ever before but also more intrusion into civilian life than previously. New weapons of mass destruction such as torpedoes, shells and eventually atomic bombs formed a major part of that intrusion, while media communication formed another. For all countries, total war necessitated the government management of information, and this impacted on the institutional relationship between the media industries and the state. Everywhere communication, especially film, was used to define aims in war and in the process to strengthen people's sense of national identity.

Total war involved a war of words by all available means, including the microphone. While fulfilling a national need, both film and radio increased in importance and scale. Within two years of the outbreak of war most European broadcasting stations were under Nazi control. However, radio was used for entertainment, information and propaganda by all sides. Equally, as the biggest mass-entertainment medium, feature films appealed to propagandists for their hidden potential, and Hollywood was the master of movies for democratic propaganda. Democratic countries aimed at an inclusiveness in film (which included documentaries and cinema newsreels), especially for women, whose contribution to the war effort on the home front was praised. In America, Germany and Britain feature films carried propaganda value, illustrated by the fact that in all these countries they could only be exhibited after some form of official approval, although the level of state control of the film industry varied. In contrast, France's industry was decimated.

In the United States and Britain, despite the fact that media were not state owned, patriotism and belief in the common cause meant that both citizens and media personnel were willing to accept that some censorship should exist in the interest of victory. America's declaration of war against militaristic Japan after the attack on Pearl Harbor also meant a commitment to war in Europe against fascist Germany and Italy, who formed an axis with imperial Japan. Just as every country participating in the conflict was required to restructure its economy to war production, so every country's media transmissions were geared 100 per cent to the war effort.

Entertainment was used to boost public and troop morale, and news was used not just as a means of relaying information to the people, but also as propaganda. In America government controls over the industry were the least strong; although Hollywood producers were somewhat disdainful of unrealistic guidelines, they complied with government needs. The more 'total war' threatened national survival, the more governments could appeal to the patriotism of those involved in media communication in order to exercise a greater restraint than normally required by more limited wars. Yet while the media appeared to be open, the question for Britain and America was how to achieve effective communication and simultaneously retain media credibility and public support via an almost voluntary system. As Goebbels said, 'propaganda becomes ineffective the moment we are aware of it' (Carruthers 2000: 82, 91). Throughout the Second World War, propagandists were torn between communication that encouraged hatred of the enemy and depiction of atrocities that could weaken morale because it was too graphic.

Both contemporaries and subsequent historians recognized that Britain's propaganda 'strategy of truth' (exemplified by the approach of the BBC) was a model for integrity. In contrast, the strongest control of the media took place in Japan, where radio became crucial to propaganda, and in Nazi Germany, where increasing state ownership and legislative compulsion led to a uniformity of output. The Nazis made anti-Semitism a means of defining the self and the nation. The crucial nature of communication's role in their regime was such that 'the emotions factory of Nazi propaganda was essential for the technological factory of death' – a unique use of the film medium for the aim of genocide (Bartov 1996: 186). In Russia, Germany and imperial Japan, state control of the means of communication ensured compliance by those within media industries and uncritical support. In these states, propaganda intruded into all corners of society.

One result of this organic connection between government and communication in countries outside of Western democracy was that media content was vulnerable to changes in direction. An individual example in Soviet Russia serves to illustrate the influence of the regime on expression. The classic film *Alexander Nevsky*, which, like the products of the other Russian media in 1938, dealt with themes of national unity, patriotism and how dreadful the enemy was, had been made at a time when Russia felt increasingly threatened by Nazi German expansion. The following year, when Stalin signed a non-aggression pact with Germany, the film was banned, but when the Nazis broke that agreement by invading the Soviet Union in 1941 the film was re-released. Now that Russia was in the war against Germany, public communications made a bid for unity by stressing the clash of the rival ideologies of communism and fascism. The message was a no-compromise victory, in order to demonstrate that Germany was not invincible.

During the war, television was put on hold: in Britain, for instance, it was feared that the transmission aerial at Alexandra Palace would act as a beacon for German radar. Plans for Japan to host the 1945 Olympics with television coverage were abandoned, while pioneers such as Takayanagi and Yagi were drafted into the imperial army and navy to conduct research into military applications of technology such as radar. This was at the very time when television engineering was progressing and people had begun to hear about this next media innovation.

Pressure on newspapers

Everywhere the position of newspapers in relation to radio became less strong, typified by the situation in the United States: there the wartime relationship between radio and newspapers in the field of news was redefined, as radio came into its own with authoritative round-the-clock coverage. Although Britain, like Japan, had one of the highest newspaper readership levels in the world at this time, during the Second World War, with its shortage of newsprint, radio became the dominant news medium. The reputation of British papers immediately before the war had not been helped by allegations such as that of the *Daily Express* – 'There will be no European war' – so industry morale was low. During the war there were the additional handicaps of censorship and disruption of supplies, yet circulation rose to all-time highs, especially among the popular London dailies. British radio audiences throughout the day also continued to rise during the war: 54 per cent of the population listened to the 9 p.m. bulletin in 1944 – a total of 16 million listeners, compared to a combined 10 million reading *The Mirror*, *Express*, *Mail* and *Herald* (Catterall et al. 2000: 140; Briggs 1995: 43).

Within the Japanese newspaper industry a government policy of promoting mergers in the interests of economy and control had the effect of accelerating the pre-war trend towards large corporate ownership of mass-circulation papers. Now there was firm control over the content and length of those publications that were allowed to continue. In 1938 the number of daily papers was 739; in 1941 it was fifty-four (Lee 1985: 83).

Similarly in Germany, where the fascist leadership had also shown a keen appreciation of the power of the media, press freedom had virtually been eliminated before 1939. The war gave the opportunity for total government control. Increasingly non-Nazi newspapers such as the *Frankfurter Zeitung* were closed down or deprived of the ability to survive until, by 1943, the party was totally in charge of the press. By the last year of the war newspapers hardly existed – what survived were uniform publications that amounted to not much more than single sheets with military announcements and hopeless calls for support from Nazi leaders – while Hitler himself deliberately kept out of the limelight. As the minister for propaganda, Goebbels, readily admitted, 'No decent journalist with any feeling of honour in his bones can stand the way he is handled by the press department of the Reich government' (cited in Welch 1993: 39).

Hitler also intervened in the editing of news to avoid the publication of information about failures. He presumably would have agreed with Goebbels, who wrote in his diary in May 1942: 'News policy is a weapon of war. Its purpose is to wage war and not to give out information.' Accordingly, on one occasion when Hitler read that the army had taken 3000 prisoners of war, he instructed that an additional zero be added to the report, insisting, 'Don't put 30,000 but 30,723 and every-one will believe an exact count has been made' (Balfour 1979: 122). After Stalingrad (which Hitler predicted would be a victory), the Führer strengthened his hold over the press and even censored Goebbels's own column in *Das Reich*.

On 14 June 1940, when Hitler's troops entered Paris, through to the liberation of the French by the Allies (25 August 1944), the occupied country was divided into two 'zones' – the north, directly under German control, and the south, with a collaborationist puppet regime – Vichy – under the autocratic rule of General Pétain. The Germans effectively took over newspapers for propaganda purposes and censorship, which was also introduced in Vichy. Newspapers lost their freedom; the regime took over the main source of information, Havas, and renamed it OFI (Office français d'information). The new organization proceeded to issue compulsory propaganda in terms of orders concerning govern-ment information and response to General Pétain. The combination of pressures in France meant that the choice for newspapers was either to become a government promotional sheet, as in Germany, or to close down altogether.

After the occupation of France by the Nazis, the markets abroad that had been built up by the French news agency Havas were temporarily transferred to Reuters, but the European presence in South America, which had been a Havas territory, was generally reduced. The influence of American agencies had been growing on this continent since the 1920s and 1930s, and later the international news agency business was also considerably disrupted by the war. AP and UPI emerged as the most important news agencies servicing South America.

The drama of radio news

Although the use of radio was integral to the conflict worldwide, at first, in 1939, its performance was far from confident. During the early period of the 'phoney war', audiences in Britain became bored by the BBC's interminable diet of organ music, broadcast because of censor-ship restrictions on news. However, by the end of August that year, as both the public and the authorities readjusted, three-quarters of those surveyed in a poll found the BBC more reliable than newspaper news (University of Sussex, Mass-Observation Archive, file report 375). Although wartime radio became identified with news, in the United States news was a relatively late starter. Nevertheless, influen-tial and talented commentators such as H. V. Kalternborn and William Shirer, backed by the CBS director of European operations Edward R. Murrow, had already made Europe's conflict and the real-life drama of Munich 'the greatest show yet heard on American radio'. When war broke out in the Pacific, Japan's NHK immediately carried news flashes on the start of hostilities, while its domestic service was limited to national network broadcasts from Tokyo; most other programmes were suspended, including weather reports. The authorities took control immediately.

As total war progressed, radio came into its own, well illustrated by the BBC's rise to pre-eminence. The extraordinary conflict situation allowed the BBC to argue that, if their radio broadcasting was restricted, national prestige and public morale would be jeopardized and people would turn to German stations. Nevertheless, there was a wartime embargo system, permitting the morning and evening papers to break news. The tone of the BBC was always less overoptimistic and more circumspect than that of the press (in 1941, two-thirds of those questioned in a poll found the BBC 100 per cent reliable), and it continued complete national wavelength coverage throughout, increasingly ignoring embargos. For instance, because the BBC sought out a second opinion for agency feeds, such stories were no longer considered agency 'property'. In addition the corporation broadcast anything that had already been broadcast on foreign stations, without any embargo restrictions.

The BBC was also improving its range of presentational styles – proof in itself of considerable press freedom (Carruthers 2000: 81). There were more eye-witness reports and American-style drama-documentary techniques in topical war features, and increased emphasis on commentary and explanation. Reporters broadcast with the latest technology from as near to the front lines as possible, and the BBC's war reporting unit of sixty-two was given priority access for D-Day coverage. More than 50 per cent of the population continued to switch on to *War Report*, the nightly news programme. In July 1945 the BBC unilaterally ended its scheduling agreement with the press that dated back to pre-war years, and confidently planned eleven daily bulletins across two networks, starting at 7 a.m. The press and broadcasting were now both independent news providers for the first time.

In Japan, by government direction, the same frequencies were to be used throughout the country with the aim of boosting air defence via a radio-wave control headquarters, run by government and representatives of the armed forces as part of an operating programme entitled 'Essentials of Emergency Structure for Domestic Broadcasting'. Further control reduced radio's role to one of raising national morale. Although wireless was the only way of receiving information during the intensification of air raids over the country, both production and supply of receivers fell during the war, declining to 7.5 million by 1945. Meanwhile, the directional antenna technology developed by Yagi for television before the outbreak of war was used by the British army in Singapore in 1940 against the Japanese forces. US navy forces in the Pacific used radar called 'YAGI array' to detect and attack Japanese warships, but were unaware of its significance (Kato in Smith 1995: 288).

In addition to news broadcasts to back up American intervention, short-wave propaganda from the United States was aimed at Nazi

Europe, and the American Forces Radio Service (AFRS) broadcasts were used to boost morale. Wartime AFRS also influenced trends in radio: it used pre-recorded items, reinforcing the technical feasibility of editing and discs, whereas previously the networks had prided themselves on live items only. AFRS also deleted commercial references and advertising, retitling programmes that carried a sponsor's name (Smulyan 1994: 158). Goebbels had no such integrity: in 1942 he spearheaded a decree forcing radio stations to allocate 70 per cent of their broadcasting to light music – which he hoped would then deliver a large number of listeners for the political broadcasts (Welch 1993: 34).

The role of radio was at its most dramatic in France, also carrying significance for the future. During the occupation, the Nazis seized people's radio sets. From 1940, as many of the population fled their homes in the north, through to liberation in 1944, the radio airways in France were the scene of a verbal war between Nazi, Vichy and resistance propaganda. The roles of the French resistance, of General de Gaulle's exile in London and of the Free French 'Ici Londres' broadcasts from the BBC, which were so vital for passing information to the active resistance movement, have all been well aired. De Gaulle was unique among the military in his early appreciation and exploitation of the medium:

> the political personality of de Gaulle, which was decades later to be the foundation stone of the broadcasting structure, was created at that moment by the transmitters of the BBC. It was at that time that he first realised, more powerfully and more skilfully than any other world leader, the political potential of broadcasting and its particular applicability to the chaotic conditions of the French nation. (Smith 1973: 157; see also Fondation Charles de Gaulle 1994: 109, 196)

Churchill was also superbly adept at radio performance: despite his unease about the BBC's quasi-autonomy, as prime minister, Churchill more than any other British politician successfully exploited the medium of radio with classic broadcasts. The most moving and famous was his uplifting talk over the airways on 18 June 1940: 'if the British Empire and its Commonwealth last for a thousand years, men will still say: "This was their finest hour" ' (Taylor 1992: 491). That same day General de Gaulle's first Free French broadcast was also transmitted by the BBC from London, going down in the annals of French broadcasting history to such an extent that streets in France are named in commemoration of the date.

Fact, fiction, truth and propaganda

It was only at the outbreak of war that the democracies realized the need for propaganda, but British attitudes this time round were coloured by the experience of the First World War, when exaggeration and lies about

German atrocities had been heavily criticized. This previous experience caused an initial reluctance to exploit Nazi barbarism for propaganda purposes, so, for instance, the full extent of concentration camps and the genocide of Jews in the Holocaust was not fully appreciated until the end of the war (Seaton 1987). At first officials adopted a policy of 'no news is good news', maintaining military secrecy over the arrival of British troops in France; newspapers were seized for reporting the event and newsreel coverage was banned. There was also an initial ban on all photography of military subjects, but later this was lifted. Although the popularity of newsreels slumped temporarily because of lack of news, for the rest of the war period they were very popular indeed. Cinemas were closed temporarily in anticipation of a short airborne conflict with clusters of population as bombing targets.

By 1940 the British government recognized the need to integrate censorship with propaganda functions by merging the Press and Censorship Bureau with the Ministry of Information (MOI). News was given top priority in the encouragement of the war effort by press, broadcasting services and film, to the extent that the BBC's Sir John Reith, who was influential in developing the idea of 'propaganda with truth', called news 'the shocktroops of propaganda'. The MOI's news division aimed to 'tell the truth, nothing but the truth and, as near as possible, the whole truth' (Taylor 1995: 213). Bad news was issued only gradually, like a drip feed, and the worst casualty statistics from the Battle of the Atlantic were never released (Nicholson 1996: 199).

Nevertheless, the BBC succeeded in maintaining the delicate balance between avoiding giving information to the enemy on the one hand, and maintaining an image of free honesty on the other. Officials set a high priority not only on pre-censorship but also on public trust, avoiding disbelief and feelings of manipulation by a more subtle approach that still provided people with facts. This achievement enhanced the BBC's reputation for accuracy and reliability both at home and abroad. As George Orwell commented, from about 1940 the corporation's prestige was such that the saying 'I heard it on the radio' was almost equivalent to 'I know it must be true' (cited in Lashmar and Oliver 1998: 19).

In Nazi Germany, however, the integrity of fact was not on the agenda. The distinction between factual films, that is, cinema newsreels, and fictional movies, also for the cinema, became increasingly blurred. Both were made under Hitler's strict supervision in order to boost morale and the will to fight. The aim was to inspire 'mass intoxication' with the cause. Newsreels were also screened in countries about to be attacked by Germany in order to convince people that resistance was pointless in the face of the might and invincibility of the Nazis. By 1940 all other news production companies were closed down in favour of centralized production by Deutsche Wochenschau with special military film units. German news cameramen were trained soldiers

The contribution of Goebbels to propaganda

Admittedly in the earlier days Goebbels managed to create an enthusiasm for struggle and endurance among Germans, and this, according to historians, accounts for the strength of the home front during the first half of the war period and the survival of the regime until 1945. But his power in the control of news was challenged by the importance of the military propaganda divisions such as the OKW/Wpr (Wehrmacht).

Goebbels considered news films, which were popular initially with cinema-goers, to be a priority, but, with Germany's fortunes on the wane after the defeat of Stalingrad and losses in North Africa and then in Europe, newsreels became less and less credible. Audiences began to turn off, despite the fact that cinema attendances themselves actually doubled. The problem was that, like Hitler, Goebbels wanted to report victories and was not prepared to cover failures. As the newsreels were shown in cinemas before the feature film, crowds would wait outside for the newsreel to finish before entering, until Goebbels ordered that the box offices had to close during the screening so that customers were obliged to buy their tickets and see the news first (Gorman and McLean 2003: 90).

Goebbels was said to have admired Britain's restrained approach of 'propaganda with facts', despite his own strategy of fictionalizing of news. As war progressed, the OKW gained more influence over the media at the expense of Goebbels, who increasingly made public appearances instead of the Führer. Henceforth, Goebbels turned his attention more and more to film propaganda. Subjects included film propaganda in favour of 'euthanasia action' (Reeves 1999: 119ff.). Under his active control, German wartime feature films turned into huge extravaganzas, historical dramas simultaneously offering a way of illustrating the heritage of German greatness and of reminding audiences of Hitler's power, comparable to that of Frederick the Great and Bismarck. The film *Kolberg*, on the theme of German opposition to Napoleon's armies, required the loan of 187,000 soldiers and 4000 sailors from the forces during a period of active duty (Welch 1993: 234).

who carried cameras into battle. Their close-up footage was carefully edited to remove deaths and bloodshed – still considered more of a priority than the cameramen's lives. By October 1943 over 1000 of them were reported either killed or missing in action (Carruthers 2000: 79; Hoffman 1996: 95).

The more the Nazi regime disintegrated as war took its toll, the more it was terrorist repression rather than powerful propaganda that became the norm, leading to debate among historians as to exactly how successful the Nazi form of media management and control actually was (Kershaw 1987: 167–225). The use of fictional situations for factual propaganda purposes rather than balanced coverage of events meant that the public did not believe the messages. According to one historian, people laughed and jeered at the newsreels they had once applauded (Taylor 1998: 148–9). Indeed, in Germany and its occupied territories people enthusiastically tuned in to BBC broadcasts, despite facing harsh penalties for listening (Balfour 1979: 96).

In the United States initial mass support for the war was less than in Europe, for a number of reasons. The country had a history of isolationism from world affairs and was geographically separated from the arenas of conflict, so the threat of German invasion did not appear immediate, even after the Japanese bombing of Pearl Harbor, followed by Germany's subsequent declaration of war on the United States, in December 1941. Nevertheless these two events shattered the appeal of the America First movement, which campaigned for non-intervention in the war. Yet, because there was still apprehension about American intervention in what was still seen by many as prima-rily a European conflict, the public relations task was to give a clear explanation to both the public and the armed forces about the need for involvement.

The government had to sell the Allies as reliable partners, 'their Bolshevism and imperialism notwithstanding' (Carruthers 2000: 96, 106), and also persuade the 13 million-strong black population that the Allies' cause was the just one. Black people tended to be alienated from the white majority by institutionalized segregation in the south-ern states and by a history of discrimination and prejudice. The African-American press proclaimed that there would be no 'close ranks', and many blacks identified with the Japanese as non-whites. A survey in 1942 revealed that if, hypothetically, they were under Japanese rule, 18 per cent of those interviewed felt that they would be treated better than by American whites, 31 per cent considered that their treatment would be the same and only 28 per cent thought they would be worse off (Gorman and McLean 2003: 95; Perry 2002). The public relations imperative was reinforced by a poll in summer 1942 that revealed a third of respondents were willing to sign a separate peace treaty with Germany.

Among the concerted public relations efforts in America, some classics emerged, such as 'The Kid in Upper 4', an advert which heralded the beginning of advocacy advertising and which has been dubbed one of the twenty adverts that 'shook the world' (Pinzon and Swain 2002). A famous series of seven orientation films (in which the director Frank Capra participated), entitled *Why We Fight*, was designed to give recruits, who stood to lose their lives in battle, a rationale. Its archive sources included Leni Riefenstahl's *Triumph of the Will*. Other big-name directors, such as John Huston and John Ford, enlisted in the armed forces and went on to make propaganda films. An example of the power of the medium was provided by John Huston's famous documentary trilogy made while he was in the army – *Report from the Aleutians* (1943), *The Battle of San Pietro* (1945) and *Let There Be Light* (1946), although the last film was so graphic that the War Department would not release it to be shown to the general public.

Not all propaganda was conducted by the American government, as media ownership was in private hands; there was less regulation than in Britain. On the one hand, the level of media penetration in the United States was the greatest of anywhere in the world, so the potential for reaching people was considerable. On the other hand, the tradition of open government, exemplified by press freedom and congressional influence over the executive, meant that censorship could not be imposed. It was established by free will, along with regulation. A comparison between the British and American approaches to government influence over media communications and propaganda reveals that, although public attitudes towards war differed initially, administrative systems were not dissimilar.

By and large the machinery and institutions of communication that evolved in both Britain and America during the Second World

Britain's Ministry of Information

Whereas the BBC had planned its wartime adaptations before the conflict broke out, the British government was less well prepared for the new propaganda role, mainly because Chamberlain had hoped all along for appeasement with Hitler in a bid to avoid war. There was often friction between the MOI and programme-makers, despite the fact that the MOI argued that it defended the corporation's independence – a line that was at variance with the views of Churchill, who always favoured an outright government takeover of the BBC ('an enemy within the gates, doing more harm than good').

The BBC was actually quite security conscious: communists were banned from the airways, and it agreed to a studio 'switch sensor' as live programmes were transmitted, as a safeguard against the event of on-air speakers saying something that was unscripted and dangerous (Carruthers 2000: 83).[1] Newsreels at all stages of production were submitted to the heaviest scrutiny of any media, because this was considered the most important form of propaganda. The MOI viewed footage and read proposed scripts, as well as approving final versions. Film production teams supported the war effort despite the fact that the instructions with which they had to comply were often explicit and detailed: for instance, pan shots of bomb damage were obliged to start and finish on parts of the building that were still intact. However, there were occasions when the MOI actively supported the filming of bomb damage, particularly if commentary could indicate that there was strong British resolve in dealing with it, for this demonstrated a positive outlook to the American audience (Cull 1995: 107).

The system that the MOI evolved was similar to that in Britain during the First World War: facts could be censored if there was a danger that the information would help the enemy, and 'D-notices' were issued to advise editors 'voluntarily' not to publish a whole range of items, but opinion and comment were free from regulation. A principled decision was taken not to jam enemy broadcasts – even those of the one-man-band 'enemy from within', the eccentric Lord Haw Haw, who broadcast pro-Nazi messages.

The MOI also set up an 'Ideas Committee', which was strongly supported by the voluntary efforts of many feature-film producers and documentary-makers – a fruitful collaboration between state and media industries. Although the British Board of Film Censors continued to check films for decency and morality, the MOI also took on a supervisory role over wartime film, considering wider issues of how to use the medium to promote 'the positive virtues of British national characteristics and the democratic way of life' (Aldgate and Richards 1995: 11–12). It never actually banned an entire film, although it had the powers to do so.

Fig. 10 Churchill inspecting air-raid damage

The American Office of War Information

The American OWI (Office of War Information), and in particular its Hollywood branch, entitled the Bureau of Motion Pictures, promoted the defence of American democracy and the need to show the Allies in a positive light. Attempts by the OWI (which was established as a government agency in 1942) to gear the media up to the war effort were often met by hostility from producers and company executives in the film industry because they resented outsiders telling them how to make movies. Nevertheless, as the feature film offered a powerful vehicle for persuasion, the OWI tried to influence Hollywood producers to offer positive material on the issue of race relations, for instance, in order to gain black support for the war.

The OWI introduced guidelines on how to present the war in addition to its review of film scripts. Eventually the OWI and the film industry reached an agreement that a compulsory pre-production review was required only for feature films with a military theme – for the rest, it was voluntary. Nevertheless, the Hollywood tradition of avoiding controversial political and social subjects, which was underlined by Hays's 1930 censorial Production Code, provided ammunition for those who resented further interference. Hollywood suspicions were made worse by an anti-trust suit which the Roosevelt administration had filed in 1938 against the eight major companies for violation of laws on restraint of trade. Although it was suspended in 1940, it was revived again in 1944. In addition, the OWI controlled exhibition in liberated areas and, although it did not have the power of direct censorship, it had close relations with the Office of Censorship, which controlled export licences for films – and export formed an important part of the business.

The OWI was not totally successful in promoting Hollywood films that criticized militarism as a system, and as such the essence of enemy ideology, rather than hatred of individual German or Japanese people. The latter was very much a reaction to Japan's aggression and hostilities in China, its attack on Pearl Harbor in 1941 and the cruelty towards Allied prisoners of war and civilian internees that followed. In general the media supported the armed forces and government agencies in moves to restrict information and pictures of casualties, racial conflict and disagreement between American servicemen and other Allied forces, but in 1943 the restrictions were eased because politicians feared public complacency about the war. The result was that, between 1943 and 1945, media news coverage of the horrors of the conflict, such as Japanese atrocities, was more detailed and explicit than it had been during the earlier period of the war.

There were voluntary guidelines for domestic self-censorship: to encourage compliance, the Office of Censorship enlisted print editors and publishers who were well known and respected in their home states to liaise on an informal basis between the censorship headquarters and the press, especially thousands of weekly papers. The volunteers, who were called 'missionaries', exercised a strong voluntary influence, using calm reason and appeals to both egalitarianism and patriotism (Sweeney 2001).

War worked well because of a compatibility of interest between state and people. As Daniel Hallin concludes: 'a wartime relation between the state and civil society developed which involved not primarily the suppression of civil society by the state, but co-operation, co-optation [sic] and blurring of the lines, in which state functions were often taken on by institutions like the press, and vice versa' (Corner et al. 1997: 209).

The fortunes of wartime film

The Nazis used the feature film as a vehicle for propaganda messages that would provide the ideological groundwork for Hitler's attacks on the 'enemy within', such as the final solution, underpinned by erroneous theories of biological determinism, promoted in such films as *Ich klage an* (1941). Similarly, when the anti-Jewish film *Jud Süss* was released, Himmler ordered everybody for whom he was responsible, including concentration camp guards, to view it. Hence, 'mass culture also became a crucial precondition for mass murder . . . audiovisual instruments that ensured uplifting fictions no matter how bitter the realities' (Rentschler 1996: 222). In Nazi Germany, the 'non-political' film did not exist, although only an estimated 15 per cent of movies had openly political messages – the rest were more subtle. Thus movies helped condition the average German psychologically to support the Nazi ethos to such an extent that most people, sometimes unwittingly, became what the historian Daniel Goldhagen has called Hitler's 'willing executioners'.

In Britain, the emotional impact of indigenous films was more innocuous: film content demonstrated the national and regional idiosyncracies of the country that were being fought for, with examples of the various social classes all pulling together for the war effort. Britain's small film industry experienced a 'golden age' for domestic films, with a wartime boost to both cinema box office and critical reputation. Despite a reduction in the number of studios, from twenty-two to nine, rationing of film stock, a tax on ticket prices and a loss of two-thirds of all technical personnel to conscription, average weekly attendance at cinemas still increased from 19 million in 1939 to over 30 million in 1945 (Aldgate and Richards 1995: 3).

On the other side of the English Channel, France's film industry had collapsed with the fall of the country to the Nazis, creating an opening for America once more in French overseas markets. The combination of damage and disruption to Europe's struggling film production, plus consumer demand, meant new exports for American movies. Almost as many films were produced as in peacetime. The government, which was owed a considerable amount of money by Hollywood, declared the business an 'essential war industry'. This meant that studios were guaranteed supplies of film stock at a time when shortages were generally a problem almost worldwide; it also meant that the stars considered most indispensable were exempted from conscription to the armed forces. Film exports were consequently strong during wartime because of the shortage of celluloid among the Allies. Washington recognized the importance of film as a morale booster abroad, and by this policy 'effectively perpetuated the monopoly status of the big studios' (Carruthers 2000: 94). By 1945 the war had enabled the number of cinemas in the United States to reach an all-time high.

The American motion-picture industry was persuasive in arguing its case in relation to the war effort: it was said that movies could provide both distraction from the horrors of total conflict and education for the cinema-going public. Cinema could also strengthen the morale of troops abroad. The longer the war lasted, the more the public appreciated a trip to the cinema as a distraction from harsh realities. Soldiers really desired what was called 'the three Ls' – laughs, lookers and letters – and movies provided two out of the three. The industry recognized the need to cooperate because it was in its interest to retain public support (for box office), support from banks (for funding) and the tradition of help from the armed forces for filming, facilities and equipment.

Many writers and some directors who believed in the potential of film as a vehicle for social change were supportive of the war effort. Although blacks, in alliance with white liberals, saw film as an ideological weapon to achieve change in real life, the American armed forces were racially segregated until 1948. Even blood plasma was stored separately. Initially there had been an army recommendation that blacks should not have access to arms, so they tended to be recruited in logistical organizational support. Yet in some combat movies Americans were presented as fighting together in ethnically integrated units in defence of their country's ideals against fascism and totalitarianism. Ethnic inclusiveness became a feature of Hollywood movies such as *Casablanca*, *Lifeboat*, by Hitchcock, and *Saunders of the River*, with Paul Robeson.

Issues of race and prejudice were not confined to the United States. In Australia during 1942 there was a strong public backlash against a propaganda campaign of the Department of Information called 'Know your Enemy'. One radio script, for instance, referred to Japanese people as 'a despicable, ape-like race' and 'the little monkey-men of the north'.

Within Japan, the government-controlled broadcasting service was, as elsewhere, an important weapon for propaganda. The Japanese people's own sense of superiority led them to depict Westerners as foreign demons: arrogant, barbaric, decadent and impure. Scholarship has traced the existence of long-standing racial prejudice and stereotypes that lay behind these images. In particular, the internment camps within the United States that were introduced for more than 70,000 Japanese-Americans living in the Pacific coast area have been the subject of research (Dower 1996: 39; Dower 1986; Nornes and Yukio 1994: 104–8).

Media and post-war social change

The impact of six years of total war on those countries which suffered bombing and, in the case of Japan, nuclear destruction almost belies description: human loss, suffering and devastation that remains indelible in the memories of those who lived through it. For both Europe and Japan it was a tabula rasa, recorded for posterity in films, books and pictures:

> so many writers have tried to grasp its horror. So many charts and numbers have analyzed the drama, so many studies have endeavored to rationalize the end; none of those has numbed human perception; the pain one feels at the sight of bombed out Dresden and Coventry has never vanished. Europe in the fall of 1945 lay in ruins. The War had leveled centuries of civilization, ancient cities and cathedrals, hallowed beliefs and ideas. Holocaust survivors roaming the streets bore witness to one of the most gruesome crimes against humanity. Somber groups of policy makers, military officials, and civilians from different countries discussed how to relieve shortages of food, coal, housing and other basic necessities. (Gienow-Hecht 1999: 1)

When in 1946 the British Broadcasting Corporation restarted television transmission, the interrupted 1939 Mickey Mouse film was played at the point where it had left off and described as a resurrection (Briggs and Burke 2002: 171, 236). In fact, things would never be the same again, and there was no going back. Now people wanted a better, fairer, more equal world for the future: what one writer has called 'the great hunger on the European continent for spiritual rebirth after the ravages of fascism' found its expression in culture and great art – for instance, Schoenberg's concert piece *A Survivor from Warsaw*, which commemorated the Warsaw ghetto. Ordinary people looked to governments for change. It is within this context that communism gained support in Europe, Asia and elsewhere, and that democracies elected left-wing parties. For many countries the Second World War radically changed attitudes towards the purpose of the press and broadcasting and towards their audiences, creating a desire for and expectations of post-war reform that reflected the genuine desire for social change.

Fig. 11 American newspapermen inspecting bodies at Dachau

Popular influences in France and Britain

Within France, the communications industry was experiencing its biggest trauma since the 1789 revolution: indeed, the changes that were to emerge in the country's media policy and institutions after the war have themselves been labelled a revolution – a reflection of attitudes in the aftermath of war and occupation. The task of reconstructing the film industry was huge. The shortage of indigenous product, coupled with popular demand to see American films as a sign of freedom regained (audiences had been deprived of this during the Nazi occupation), led to the Blum–Byrnes Agreement in 1946 which established quotas for US product. It was heavily criticized at the time and afterwards. Meanwhile, French film-makers worked under economic and technical constraints that influenced the production and consumption of films (UNESCO 1950), but they showed remarkable ingenuity in their craft (Crisp 1997). The industry was rebuilt and survived precariously with government support. In 1946 the relationship between Hollywood and French cinema was called 'the fight between the clay pot and iron pot': this has remained the case (Nowell-Smith and Ricci 1998: 54).

The nationalization of broadcasting was supported by all of the political parties, faced with the challenge of moving forward, and can only be fully appreciated within the proper historical context. When the Nazi regime collapsed, so too did Vichy, opening the floodgates to intense reactions against collaborationists and Pétainist-style right-wing policies. The pre-war Third Republic was also discredited for its apparent failure to prevent occupation and defeat; accordingly, in a 1945 referendum, 96 per cent of the population voted against the reintroduction of France's pre-war constitutional system. A new constitution and new political institutions were clearly the order of the day – and, in their wake, a fresh media system.

Not only newspaper owners who had collaborated but also newspaper titles from the occupation period were now prevented from operating. Prouvost, who had collaborated with the Nazis and become a 'minister' in Pétain's Vichy regime, was now forced to go into hiding and was banned from participating in the new post-war press. He has been referred to since then as a traitor (Faucher and Jacquemart 1968). Collaborators' assets such as publishing equipment were sequestrated, then handed to newspapers who had supported the resistance.

What has not been discussed so much until recently is the extent and nature of the French people's collaboration with the Nazis. The details of local participation in this process of 'colonization' have only gradually been exposed by a continual process of investigative research, which, as in post-war Germany (Goldhagen 1996), later provoked fundamental historical, political and moral debate within these two countries. Amid the confusion, disorder and depleted media resources within France, one man had had a clear run. Gerhard Hibbelen stepped in to build a press empire in the form of a trust which embraced more than fifty different sorts of journals and almost half of the Parisian press (Dioudonnat 1981). The post-Vichy reaction against this was hardly surprising.

Legislation in 1944 provided for pluralism by preventing concentration of ownership and monopoly; financial openness was required of the press in return for protection from economic pressures that could limit independence. For example, it now became illegal for a 'patron' to control more than one daily newspaper: the pre-war era of the 'press barons' was not to be repeated. Once more, the collectivist ideals of the resistance were visible, but the ideological intention of this revolution in media policy was to remove the economic threats to press freedom. In 1881, when press freedom had been introduced, the concern had been to preserve political liberty in content.

The point of this massive increase in state participation in media communications was not to curb editorial expression, as authoritarian regimes had done, but to enhance it. The British and the new German systems were less interventionist. State intervention in France was advocated 'as a pre-requisite for the effective functioning of the market by improving the conditions of competition. The state, it was argued, could help the market work more fairly and effectively' (Kuhn 1995: 55). State aid for newspapers was introduced and a new national press agency, Agence France Presse (AFP), was established (Institut Charles de Gaulle 1994: 55–60). Immediately after the liberation the provincial press achieved permanent market dominance over national newspapers. Local papers played a crucial role, for instance, in supplying essential information about the availability of food supplies in their areas during rationing, but, according to one historian, the 'golden age' of France's press was now over (ibid.: 67–75).

The Fourth Republic was declared in 1946, with a tripartite political system inherited from the resistance: the socialists, the Christian democrats and the communists (until the last were expelled from government in 1947) were presided over by de Gaulle as prime minister without a parliamentary party base. The new government, influenced by the collectivist ideals of the resistance charter and also by Vichy's use of wartime planning, rapidly launched a number of important social and economic reforms as well as passing legislation to nationalize radio and television. As in Britain, there were also measures for social welfare and the nationalization of coal, gas and electricity; in addition the French interventionist model included major banks and the Renault car company as part of a new role for indicative planning.

The government's new media system gave opportunities to a whole new spectrum of entrants to the industry, encouraging diversity and mitigating the worst economic excesses of the market. According to one writer, 'The Liberation gave a new impetus to the ideas of "popular culture" and "shared culture" which had been prized and fought for in the 1930s' (Rigby and Hewitt 1991: 129–46).

Nevertheless, the inexperience of many owners was no match for subsequent market conditions as the influence of the resistance's idealism gradually paled in the face of the economic and business reality of post-war retrenchment. Advertising, although never as big a contributor to newspaper business as elsewhere, was inevitably attracted to the more successful media ventures, and even the participation of politicians – sometimes as newspaper proprietors themselves, following a long French tradition – could not prevent a relentless trend towards longer term economic concentration.

In Britain in 1945, Churchill was defeated in the polls. Conservative critics of the BBC accused the corporation of being a Trojan horse for the socialist landslide election victory. The reality was that 'Aunty Beeb' had become more accessible during wartime. Furthermore, the BBC's political coverage had matured: it was less deferential than it had been in the cautious, early years. While retaining the charter obligation to remain impartial, it was now more experienced at dealing with hard political issues head on. The overwhelming feeling that social justice was now needed was articulated in Britain by the Beveridge Report, which reviewed welfare and social security, proposing a new 'cradle to grave' system of state-supported benefits that has survived, if somewhat precariously, through to the present. Lord Beveridge's broadcast explaining the revolutionary changes was transmitted in twenty-two different languages worldwide, an example of how the now greatly respected MOI could use public-service broadcasting: 'the purpose of victory is to live in a better world than the old world', the broadcast stated.

Beveridge was not the only social reformer to use the BBC to communicate ideas: Orwell, Shaw, Huxley, the Webbs, Wells and Keynes also set the tone; indeed, Keynes shared the Reithian belief that public affairs should be managed by an elite of smart, independent civil servants. Yet the war had ensured that broadcasting 'professionalism' was also accompanied by a new perception of leisure by programme providers. More light entertainment had been introduced, such as ITMA (*It's That Man Again* – taken from a *Daily Express* headline about Hitler), a comedy for ideological purposes with an audience of 15 million – 40 per cent of the population. A new listener research department was introduced to monitor response to output, resulting in a greater range of political opinions and regional accents. The weight now attached to public opinion led the BBC to recognize differences in people's taste, interests and abilities.

Organizational reforms within the corporation created a variety of 'services', or channels, to cater for the new perceptions of diverse taste that were now identified. The Light Programme was for popular entertainment, the Home Service for the encouragement of citizenship, family and home, with more talk programmes, and the Third Programme for a range of cultural excellence, with Reithian-style mixed programming. As the director-general explained in 1948: 'Before the war the system was to confront [the listener] with pendulum-like leaps. The devotees of [Irving] Berlin were suddenly confronted with Bach. . . . Since the war we have been feeling our way along a more indirect approach. It rests on the conception of the community as a broadly based cultural pyramid, slowly aspiring upwards.' At the same time internal competition within the corporation was established for the first time.

Although these progressive changes were aimed at the whole of society, old hierarchical assumptions underlined class divisions. Nevertheless, this package of internal reforms carried as much symbolic importance for the future development of the BBC in terms of its departure from Reithian assumptions of cultural homogeneity as changes on the other side of the channel brought to the French system. The goal for reformers in both countries was the furtherance of democratic pluralism through public-service broadcasting, even if their respective starting points reflected national, social and political influences.

Re-education or cultural imperialism in Japan and Germany?

In April 1945 Harry Truman took over from Franklin Roosevelt as president of the United States. Over sixty Japanese cities had already been subject to low-level saturation bombing when three months later Truman received news of the nuclear test at Alamogordo. He immediately thought of biblical prophesies of the apocalypse and approved the use of the atomic bomb against Japan. A few days after the cataclysmic annihilation of Hiroshima and Nagasaki he wrote, 'when you have to deal with a beast, you have to treat him like a beast.' In mid-August that year, Japan capitulated.

Fig. 12 Mushroom cloud over Nagasaki, 1945

On 15 August, after the government had decided to accept the terms of unconditional surrender laid down in the Potsdam Declaration of the Allied Powers, the emperor made his first ever broadcast in the form of a pre-recorded imperial proclamation announcing that the war was over. Unfortunately few listeners could understand his very formal court language (Briggs and Burke 2002: 224). As in Britain, the initial use of radio by the royal incumbent was an important event for the medium, and for listeners. Radio-wave control and normal services were resumed on 1 September, with stations using the same frequencies and output power as they had before the war.

Japan was in a state of misery during 1945: as in most of bomb-devastated Europe and the other theatres of war, many people were homeless and often jobless. In all the centres of conflict, including Britain, food was rationed, and in Japan it was so scarce that govern-ment expenditure was directed towards the avoidance of starvation. As inflation took hold and poverty loomed, the media novelty of tele-vision now seemed a low priority. After the end of the war the Allies occupied the country to carry out a thorough process of 'demilitariza-tion and democratization', with the United States as the predominant force (Dower 1996: 366). In only six years the United States initiated Japanese sovereignty, with the introduction of a new democratic system, put the economy on the road to recovery and sowed the seeds for Japan's future superpower status.

A defeated country was reinvented using America's own self-image, but the process involved secret mechanisms of censorship under the direction of General Douglas MacArthur, Supreme Commander for the Allied Powers (as the sole executive for the occupation), at precisely the same time that the apparatus of censorship and repression of the old imperial state was being dismantled. As Mark Selden says: 'U.S. censors set out to mold Japanese public opinion, to shield the United States from public criticism, and to preserve a U.S. monopoly on information pertaining to the effects of the atomic bomb on its victims' (Braw 1991: ix). Research involving interviews with the public and declassified documents reveals that this had the effect of silencing atomic bomb victims and concealed basic information about the consequences of atomic warfare, such as radiation. The post-war global nuclear debate was therefore distorted.

America was also to influence the shape and direction of broad-casting, which resulted in Japanese broadcasters being subjected to rigorous control and censorship, although the brief was for the USA to give guidance only. In this heavily interventionist political context, MacArthur approved all important policy proposals by the Japanese government (Hunter 1984: 28, 192), drafting a new constitution which removed the emperor's power and prevented militarism. Some scholars have suggested that these conditions resulted later in a broadcasting system that was vulnerable to government control (Luther and Boyd 1997). For example, one of the administrative commissions set up according to the American model during the Allied occupation was the Radio Regulatory Commission. It was responsible for a number of important decisions that set the framework for future broadcasting policy, such as the licensing in 1952 of commercial radio broadcasting, the standard system for television broadcasting, and a policy for licensing TV broadcasters (Ito 1978: 41).

The system of intensive control over Japanese cinema was wide-ranging and comprehensive. Prohibited subjects included period films, religion, certain attitudes towards women and children, criticism of the occupation, the atomic bomb, militarism, wartime activities, war crimes, and xenophobia (Hirano 1992).

Several hundred newspapers sprang up after Japan's defeat, but most of them disappeared within a few years as a result of competition; by 1953 numbers were down to 135. After the occupation the press was not subject to any official or wide-ranging censorship, and press freedom was claimed to be one of the safeguards against a revival of former militarism.

After Germany's defeat, the Allies initiated a comparable system of 'de-Nazification and democratization' which impinged on the media. The American and British military participated in the encouragement

Hibakusha cinema: 'lest we ever forget'

Censors prevented Japanese film-makers from realizing projects centred on the atomic bomb: in particular, the visual effect of the bomb and any depiction of civilian victims were prohibited. Although Hibakusha cinema has addressed the experience since the occupation, nevertheless, as with the Holocaust, every generation needs to search for its own truth: 'Nostalgia and apocalyptic visions, even appeals to prior incarnations – these are the means by which today's Japanese barely maintain their tenuous psychological equilibrium . . . Japan as a nation is well on its way to losing, to eradicating, history' (Broderick 1996).

of a broad process of cultural transformation that was deemed necessary in the aftermath of Nazi rule. The new press and broadcasting industries were supposed to reflect Germany's new democratic, pluralistic political and social institutions. The newspaper industry, for instance, was re-created during the 1940s and 1950s, with press freedom integrated into the constitution of the new federal West German state in 1949. But implementation of these principles was complicated by the economic realities of the post-war situation and by the precarious nature of the state.

The newspaper industry was dominated by powerful financial interests such as the Axel Springer group, which published the only newspaper approaching a national daily – the *Bild Zeitung*, which sold 4 million copies a day (Briggs and Burke 2002: 225). However, at its highest point there were 225 other 'editorial unities' and even more actual titles. In practice, newspapers were local and regional, and the differences between some papers amounted only to their advertising and front pages (Smith 1979: 166; Ward 1989: 189). At national level, in 1946 Rudolf Augstein established *Der Spiegel*, which was modelled on *Time* magazine. Many small-circulation papers followed the pattern of the 1920s and 1930s by once more becoming part of larger groups in order to gain security. America also funded some organs. Munich's *Neue Zeitung*, for example, was staffed by German emigrants in order to help Americanize the outlook of post-war Germany. Nevertheless, research into the details of acculturation on the ground has revealed the limitations of US influence (Gienow-Hecht 1999).

Largely due to British persuasion, a very decentralized radio system was introduced, with nine regional public broadcasting stations, each with three different radio programmes. The concept reflected the Allied intention to avoid the homogeneous, manipulative mass audience on which Nazi propaganda had fed. Unfortunately for broadcasting, innovations were limited, partly because in Germany the press still harboured suspicions of radio (and TV) similar to those that existed in the United States and Great Britain up to and, to a certain extent, during the war. For the moment the mass market remained with the press.

In a historical context it could be said that attempts by some countries to inflict culture, way of life, ideology and goods on other peoples of the world was a feature of nineteenth-century European colonialism, led by the British empire. Critics of twentieth-century 'cultural imperialism' argue that, though a feature of Cold War politics, it started in the immediate post-war years of 1945–8 as part of the 're-education' of Germany and Japan towards Western-style democracy, with the export of American culture used as a means for US consumer products to reach new markets. Scholarship has focused on the extent of control exercised as American political influence expanded, and the success or otherwise of cultural transmission. Herbert Schiller, for instance, has drawn attention to a connection between business, military and government circles within the United States and 'mind managers' – communications specialists who influenced both domestic and overseas consumers (Schiller 1989, 1973, 1976). Ralph Willett and Emily Rosenberg argue that those involved in twentieth-century foreign policy deliberately propagated the idea of American 'free trade', culture and information in order to expand the national market (Willett 1989; Rosenberg 1982).

The issue of whether or not 're-education' was successful depends on how success is measured: on the one hand, West Germany became a parliamentary democracy and Japan was no longer militaristic, but, on the other hand, both countries accepted financial help for reconstruction ('Marshall Aid') without making a strict obligation to defer to the American approach. Indeed, how to make the approach presented a dilemma in itself for the US government: it could not use the already discredited totalitarian methods. Anti-communism must not appear similar to the Nazi 'Jewish–Bolshevik' conspiracy theory. Although re-education was therefore presented as anti-fascist, individual case studies of the way in which messages percolated down to local level, such as the example of the US-organized Munich newspaper *Neue Zeitung*, reveal that locals selected and changed the cultural transfer in order to suit their own requirements.

In Germany, middle-class perceptions of 'high culture' meant that American offerings of baseball, jazz and Hollywood were not seen as in any way comparable to a Teutonic cultural heritage of Beethoven or Schiller, for instance. Those involved in selling the US alternatives had to work hard to convince Germans, who believed that '*Kultur*' was simply in a different league (Gienow-Hecht 1999: 4–11).

Similarly, a quantitative analysis of change and the persistence of tradition in the Japanese consciousness over a thirty-year period from 1944, using data from some 1500 persons nationwide, found that nationalism and traditional social norms persisted, although they were undergoing changes. However, there had been a strengthening of tendencies towards democracy and to put 'private life' first (Kojima 1977). Therefore the picture is unclear, as is academic debate on how to measure effects: traditionally this has been examined in an ideological light, rather than from a scientific perspective, but even this has been challenged (Salwen 1991).

Advertising, corporations and government in post-war America

The war provided the opportunity for a new relationship between business and government, and in this situation the advertising agencies prospered. During both world wars advertisers influenced national thinking in a way that had the effect of connecting commerce with civic morality. According to Jackson Lears, by 1940 'The American Way of Life' (which was now being fought for) had become a 'transcendent communal belief'. Advertising helped corporate industry appropriate that identity 'and redirect its chief connotation from populism to free enterprise' (Lears 1994: 246).

The institutional and social base for affluence was now wider. For instance, by 1945 record sales had recovered to their 1921 level and the basic structure of the modern music industry was now in place (Gronow 1983; Curran et al. 1987: 19). Unions no longer demanded reduced working hours, as production and consumption rose together. The government commitment to prosperity and the managerial model of a mixed economy were exemplified by the Full Employment Act of 1946. Ideas of military Keynesianism to construct a permanent war economy had influenced this measure, which stimulated whole sectors of the economy and of the country. After the Second World War American corporations surfaced with a new positive face in the coalition of business, government, agriculture and labour which set the policy agenda for consumer culture – a phrase which carried a fresh resonance with the new prosperity that war had brought.

Conclusions

In the film industry, the United States won, Europe and Japan lost. In the broadcasting industry, the picture was more complex because of restructuring in France, Germany and Japan, but the most noticeable victor was Britain's BBC, now the biggest news organization in the world, with a reputation as strong abroad as it was popular at home. There had also been a growth in staff numbers, from 4800 when the war started in September 1939 to 11,663 employees by 1944. The BBC's output in hours had trebled and its transmitter power had been multiplied by five. Foreign-language broadcasting had increased from ten languages in 1939 to forty-five in 1943 (Briggs 1995: 18) – more than the Voice of America, the new international network of the United States, during the Cold War. VOA was intended as a wartime expedient but became a permanent feature of 'cultural diplomacy' during post-war years.

Some of the precedents that were set had originally been influenced by the First World War – for instance, for the peacetime Cold War cooperation between governments and media regarding public communication as propaganda. As an example: the BBC made a wartime decision that 'black' and 'white' radio propaganda activity should be organizationally separate, with the 'black' variety kept well away from the corporation's airways (Briggs 1995: 60; Jowett and O'Donnell 1999). 'White' meant accurate propaganda, 'black' meant a false source involving lies, and 'grey' meant that accuracy was uncertain, with the source not always identified. This wise decision served to increase the BBC's reputation for fairness and objectivity. Wartime propaganda had taught the media all about the delicacies and dilemmas of public communication, skills that were sorely needed during the Cold War.

Whereas the new order was imposed on Japan and Germany, in Britain and continental Europe the desire for social justice and an increased role for the state in its achievement formed part of the democratic process and was to provide a major thread in the new world order. In terms of the idealistic application of social principles within media system reform, the Resistance model was significant, if short-lived. As one historian has commented: 'Either neoclassical economists have ignored (or misused) an essential ingredient of every society; or if they are correct, the enormous investment that every society makes in legitimacy is an unnecessary expenditure' (cited in Krauss 2000: 1).

Immediately after the Second World War television's future institutional importance for the public sphere was not yet obvious. Television lay posed precariously between the stages of experiment and take-off in many countries, especially in the United States, where NBC and CBS had launched some limited schedules in New York during 1941. Despite patent disputes and reluctance by RCA and the networks to rush into a new development which initially had no clear commercial potential, the 'small screen' was still destined to emerge into the biggest picture ever within media history – or at least the one that has generated the most discussion.

Study questions

Using the examples of media in Britain and the United States, what was the difference between persuasion and propaganda in the Second World War?

Compare and contrast the vulnerabilities during the war of newspapers and newsreel on both sides.

What were the issues of ethnicity and race raised by the films on both sides during the war?

In the light of the Goldhagen thesis of 'Hitler's willing executioners', what responsibility should the Nazi media carry?

Are criticisms of cultural imperialism justified in the case of Allied policy towards Germany and Japan in the aftermath of war?

PART IV

THE GLOBAL AGE, 1948–2002

> After all, history is not like a bus-line on which the vehicle
> changes all its passengers and crew whenever it gets to the
> point marking its terminus.
>
> Eric Hobsbawm, *The Age of Empire*

7 Cold War and the Victory of Commercialism, 1948–1980

If you let a television set through the door, life can never be the same again.
Daily Mirror, 1950

Chewing gum for the eyes

Frank Lloyd Wright, architect, on television

The most vicious thing about this blacklist was that anyone – even the most ignorant crank – could point the finger at someone and the charge could hold. . . . If our sponsor had cancelled our contract, it was entirely likely that no other sponsor or network would have been willing to carry us; and with the fall of the Lucy show, Desilu Productions would have collapsed too, affecting thousands of people and costing us millions of dollars . . . if news of my registration [as a communist in 1936] had been revealed during the worst witch hunt days – between 1945 and 1950 – my career probably would have been finished. . . . I was one of the lucky ones. Lucille Ball, *Love, Lucy*

Summary

The *objective* of this chapter is to present the argument that the dominance of ideology in the twentieth century continued via Cold War propaganda, providing the backdrop and a peacetime framework worldwide for American media hegemony and gradual international acceptance of the 'American way of life'. The trading path that had been trailed by Hollywood's business empire was reinforced by television sales and made easier by new technologies such as cable, satellite and computers. Debate in many parts of the world about public versus private in media institutions highlighted once more the role of sponsorship and advertising as facilitators of mass consumption.

The dialectics of continuity versus change meant that the earlier postwar years were fraught with new developments yet still beholden to the legacy of the Second World War. Cold War politics ensured a continuing role for propaganda, or 'psychological warfare', within media operations and usage – with economic and employment implications. The emergence of media globalization was facilitated by Cold War politics, which created frameworks of international support for the 'American Way of Life' as expressed by media products with business dominance.

The rise of television internationally challenged the positions of other media industries, while the ascendancy of advertising and mass consumption prompted further discourse on public versus private within the media. Technological developments influenced the ways in which individual media were used: newspapers declined, radio survived. While the media's reach, with its new devices and instruments, was extended, this was accompanied by convergence of ownership.

Introduction

When the prime minister Harold Macmillan told the British people that they had 'never had it so good', he expressed the mood of political acquiescence that economic expansion had brought to late 1950s Britain and America. By the 1960s the mood had changed. The growth of the consumer market eventually gave advertisers even greater muscle. Ironically, the BBC's popularity may have been at an all-time high, but within ten years its monopoly was destroyed as a new debate about the role of commercialism arose in most of the world where governments had a stake in broadcasting. The discourse was similar to the one that had been conducted in America's early days of radio; it was to have a long-term influence on both the structure and the content of post-war twentieth-century broadcasting.

Mass consumption was becoming more flexible and varied as it achieved total assimilation within society's Zeitgeist. The concept was discussed by Marshall McLuhan in 1960 in terms of a 'global village' with a range of media. At the same time, content showed signs of greater homogeneity, largely due to commercialism. In the music industry, commercial growth meant increased consolidation of ownership by the large record companies, which did not necessarily satisfy demand for diversity, with the result that each phase of concentration was succeeded by unplanned competition from independents. Thus stylistic change, such as rock and roll, weakened the industry's ability to control the market, but introduced greater freedom for both artists and consumers (Peterson and Berger 1975). Young people were cultivated as a consumer group by the music industry throughout the 1960s. The music industry has always had to contend with instability and an uncertain and unpredictable market as a result of changing taste and regular technological innovation, but this period more than any other supports Michael Chanan's conclusion on music's resilience: 'Through a century of transformation by electronic technology, it responded with enormous and often anarchic energy, and in the process has only renewed its utopian dreams' (Chanan 1995: 286).

Creativity always occurs within a political context, and in this period, especially, international affairs were pivotal. The post-war era saw the division of Germany into communist East and democratic West and the creation of a Soviet Eastern bloc which survived until the collapse of communism in 1989. The world was ideologically torn by a battle of global politics at a time when countries such as Britain, France and Belgium were still obliged to disengage from colonialism. National liberation struggles and the worldwide potential appeal of communism made this a dramatic epoch for the media. The use of widespread propaganda in peacetime was a new departure in Western democracy which conditioned society's thinking at every level.

In Germany, by 1948 Cold War considerations began to confuse, then to overtake, the impetus to re-educate away from Nazism. Now West Germans, as well as the Japanese, were allies in the common fight against communism. The concomitant political and business pressures to make anti-communism an issue resulted in the USA in the imposition of blacklists in the film, television and radio industries. Moreover, the extent to which tensions permeated all levels of public life and lingered on should not be underestimated. For instance, Spassky and Karpov's 1972 world chess final turned into a publicity-fuelled battle between America and Russia – a microcosm of Cold War conflict, with FBI involvement over allegations concerning the use of computers for cheating. More positively, there were important results in the fields of technology and communications at both a day-to-day and a research level: the satellite was first developed by Russia, for instance.

Less than five years after America dropped the atom bomb on Hiroshima and Nagasaki, the Truman government now viewed Japan as the key to Asia's balance of power. Asia as a continent was crucial in terms of its ability to tip the global scales towards the Soviet Union. American policy towards Japan changed from reform to economic reconstruction, and very soon the United States was urging Japan to rearm. The occupation came to an end in April 1952, when Japan re-entered world politics as an essential ally of the country that had used atomic weapons against her so effectively. As John W. Dower says, 'This transformation from "savage" enemy to "freedom-loving" ally was breathtaking' (1989: 368).

Now the communists, especially the Chinese, were portrayed as savages. To the wartime racist 'Yellow Peril' was now added the 'Red Peril'. Faced with a communist revolution in China and the Union of Soviet Socialist Republics as the new communist empire in post-war Eastern Europe, 'gung-ho' media overenthusiasm emerged during 1948–9. This was exemplified in the USA by calls for intervention in the Chinese Civil War on behalf of the nationalist forces led by Chiang Kai-shek, followed by extreme opposition to the new communist regime that triumphed, and demands for the use of nuclear arms in the Korean War (Nagai and Iriye 1977: 55–6).

In the United States in particular, the influence of foreign policy on media content, working conditions, and attitudes towards the industry within the public sphere all had crucial implications on the kind of culture that was disseminated worldwide. Both America and Russia attached a top priority to winning over opinion at home and internationally by using the media to influence content. The Soviet interpretation of events and negative image of American 'imperialism' found wide support in Asia, Africa and Latin America, where a history of colonial exploitation seemed to lend credibility to the communist world-view.

Yet, for many countries, economic and military aid proved to be a higher priority than anti-American political propaganda. Third World governments were often wary of open allegiance, so they played off the Soviet Union against the United States, and later the Soviet Union against China, in an effort to gain the best deal for assistance.

The electronic media of radio and television, in addition to the established appeal of cinema and newspapers, gave politicians and their supporters a more potent and far-reaching platform for propaganda than had ever existed throughout media history. This meant that ways of using – and abusing – communication were crucial. One longer term effect of the media's lack of criticism of government policy during the Cold War was that a climate of acceptance was laid for later failures in foreign affairs which had the effect of delaying protest, epitomized by the Vietnam War. Public anger eventually reached a peak in 1968 as the conflict provided a focus for opposition groups, especially student rebellion in Europe. American political propaganda was often masked as entertainment, but this should not detract from its pivotal role in the collapse of communism. Cold War-inspired fiction abounded on both sides of the Atlantic, as the spy thrillers of writers such as Ian Fleming, Len Deighton and John le Carré became bestsellers, with characters such as James Bond immortalized in celluloid. The success of cultural diplomacy and psychological warfare was demonstrated by the fact that they often went unrecognized.

Cold War thinking and media reactions

Cold War media: the American side of the story

The campaign against 'communist' dissent in the United States was spearheaded internally by Senator Joseph McCarthy. His aim was to root out spies and traitors from government, media and other institutions where they could have influence. The effectiveness of his investigations, conducted by the House Committee on Un-American Activities (HUAC), depended on the publicity that successful exposure by the media implied.

In the United States a large number of victims who had never been communists were hit by blacklisting because they had supported 'radical' causes. Past activities such as opposition to General Franco during the Spanish Civil War or being against the lynching of blacks in the south were scrutinized publicly, as was active support for the idea of America and Russia working together, or for President Roosevelt's New Deal. Very few real Soviet spies were actually detected during the short 'McCarthyist' period, but the film, radio and television industries were torn apart. Those people who were communists were not accused of masterminding a violent uprising or revolution, and membership of the party was not illegal or treasonous. Yet many careers were ruined as innocent people were caught up in this paranoia. The blacklists remained in existence until the early 1960s.

The fact that media ownership was not public but private did not prevent the industry making a crucial contribution to the global Cold War battle against communism. During this period journalists relied heavily on official sources for coverage of home and foreign affairs, with a staple diet of government press conferences, on- and off-the-record briefings, announcements, statements and speeches – all of which gave a platform for officials and politicians to address the public. Many programmes were actually scripted by the Department of Defense and other agencies (Bernhard 1999; MacDonald 1985; Whitfield 1991).

The main message to the media, vastly oversimplified and hence inaccurate, was that opposition to the United States in other parts of the world was the work of a homogeneous organization masterminded by Moscow, ideologically driven by the motivation for global takeover. This would result in a form of slavery rather than freedom via the rule of law and democracy, so that the future of civilization was at stake. Hence American

intervention anywhere in the world was justified in order to contain the Soviet threat. Oversimplified, extreme views that were given credibility by sections of the media became the tyranny of the intolerant majority that John Stuart Mill had feared (see chapter 2). The result was that radical or liberal beliefs were misconstrued as communist sympathies.

However, the United States took positive economic action on the European continent with the Marshall Plan (1947), which provided finance for the post-war reconstruction of Germany, while the launching of NATO (the North Atlantic Treaty Organization) provided an umbrella defence organization to respond to any further Soviet expansion.

Cold War media: the Soviet side of the story

Russia's successful victory over Nazism in Eastern Europe, at great human cost, was followed after the war by impressive results in some industries and technological expertise such as the launch in 1957 of the Sputnik – the first artificial satellite (Giblett 2001). These were significant achievements which fuelled people's pride, patriotism and expectations of economic growth, and were reflected in publicity along with the strength of the armed forces.

The West was now viewed as the belligerent 'imperialist' enemy. In particular America, with its extremes of wealth and poverty, high unemployment and banal popular culture, was depicted as a racist persecutor of unions, illustrated in cartoons typically by a fat banker and a Ku Klux Klansman (Gorman and McLean 2003: 107). As in the pre-war period, Soviet media served the state via 'Agitprop' – the Department of Agitation and Propaganda of the Central Committee of the Communist Party. This body transmitted government messages to the various media and other organizations, such as 'Cominform' – the Communist

Information Bureau – created in 1947 to encourage international support for policy. From the late 1940s it published a weekly magazine entitled *For a Lasting Peace, for a People's Democracy*. The Soviet news agency TASS and the Ministry of Foreign Affairs also provided information to the exterior, and the KGB (Committee for State Security) worked on deceptions and falsehoods, or 'black propaganda'.

Surprisingly, perhaps, many Soviet people grieved at Stalin's death; but the brutal suppression by the Red Army of Hungarian dissent in 1956, and of Czechoslovakia's reform movement later in 1968, demonstrated that coercion was no substitute for freedom within the Soviet empire. By the 1980s the desire for freedom in the satellite states, symbolized by the anachronism of the Berlin Wall and the fact that the repressive regime had become stagnant, was an outward manifestation of deeper issues (Bruner 1989). Economic crisis, low living standards and official incompetence, compounded by corruption, were too widespread to be tolerated much longer.

Although public discussion of corruption and other social problems, such as alcoholism, the high divorce rate and poor workmanship, were permitted by the authorities, the media also stressed the progressive Soviet desire for peace, disarmament, democracy and liberation for capitalist exploited workers internationally. The Russian government never felt secure enough to allow its people exposure to alternative international points of view and felt particularly vulnerable to criticism of living standards in the satellite states. The result was that very large numbers of the population voted with their feet by listening to Western broadcasts – first radio and eventually, in the 1980s, satellite television. Religion survived decades of persecution, so it is possible to argue that there was never outright acceptance of the regime. However, there is also evidence that most people accepted the critical stance against America, as interviews with émigrés have illustrated, and that acceptance of the regime's values was widespread: propaganda can only be effective when it taps into existing beliefs, values and experiences.

For many in the West, the way that the Russian and Chinese models had evolved in practice demonstrated imperfections and a betrayal of ideological roots: Russia and China were not truly Marxist, so the socialist utopia had yet to be achieved. Believing this to be the case, important writers such as George Orwell, Bertrand Russell and Isaiah Berlin, knowingly or unknowingly, cooperated with Western secret service initiatives. Politically, it was possible to oppose American government policy as a pacifist without being a communist. Opposition to American intervention in Vietnam and support for causes such as peace and nuclear disarmament acquired a fashionable transcontinental appeal.

Apart from miscalculated military activities, the Cold War also provided a political incentive for worldwide 'cultural diplomacy' in order to persuade hearts and minds away from communism. This laid the ground for gradual acceptance internationally of 'Americanization' in the form of music, fashion and media products such as television programmes, books and films. The assault was extravagantly financed by the government's various cultural programmes via the CIA and backed up institutionally by a number of front organizations such as the CCF (Congress for Cultural Freedom, founded in 1950 and based in Paris). As part of its task to win over intellectuals and opinion-formers in Western Europe it organized concerts, art exhibitions and conferences, and financed the publication of hundreds of books and a number of magazines, such as *Encounter* in Britain, *Der Monat* in Germany, *Preuves* in France, *Quadrant* in Australia and *Quest* in India.

Inside the United States, ideological influence on America's films, television and radio came at a time when both political parties agreed on the need to combat the Soviet 'Reds under the beds'. Media outlets were subject to pressure from all directions, not just withdrawal of advertising or Wall Street's financial support for the film industry. America's international film industry was in a weak position to resist political pressure from outside its ranks: firstly because of the debilitating effect that new competition from television was having and secondly because of a

US journalism and 'un-American ideologies'

Journalists in the United States who dissented from the mainstream beliefs were marginalized or moved to non-contentious work. The test of political correctness entailed a nationalistic endorsement of 'Americanism' based on opposition to 'un-American ideologies'. Within journalism there was also an exchange of employees between regular jobs and the propaganda programme, and one scholar has argued that the existing news format and the free press ideology served to 'camouflage' propaganda (Parry-Giles 1996). Although the *New York Times*, the *Washington Post* and some other leading publications, and famous columnists such as Walter Lippmann, opposed McCarthy's tactics and ideology, most journalists retained their 'objectivity' by not questioning the rhetoric of politicians. The Hearst newspapers and Robert McCormick's *Chicago Tribune*, for instance, supported the witch-hunt of communist 'subversives'.

In order to pre-empt any criticism of a soft approach to communists, the media adopted a strident line which was actually more extreme than government policy during 1948–50. This clamour produced the tactical effect of limiting the options that were open to the White House for a compromise agreement with Russia.

Film industry 'un-American activities'

Bitter labour disputes had soured relations within the industry and prompted conservative elements in the form of the Motion Picture Alliance for the Preservation of American Ideals, which pushed for a special investigation. During the subsequent enquiries in 1947, people in the spotlight were divided into 'friendly' (pro McCarthy) and 'unfriendly' witnesses, with the Screen Writers' Guild and the Screen Actors' Guild as particular targets. There were hearings in Washington at which studio heads such as Walt Disney and Jack Warner and celebrities including Ronald Reagan and Gary Cooper testified. One result was that the 'Hollywood Ten' exercised their right to free speech and refused to answer whether they had ever been members of the Communist Party: for this they were indicted for contempt of Congress and sent to prison for up to one year. During 1951–2 further HUAC investigations followed and the 'Hollywood Ten' were fired. A similar fate awaited 300 other Hollywood employees who were also blacklisted and unable to work unless they renounced their beliefs: in fact, former Communist Party members were required to supply names of past colleagues if they wanted to avoid blacklisting.

Careers of writers, directors, producers and actors were ruined, and some, among them Charlie Chaplin, moved abroad, never again to work in Hollywood. CIA agents and representatives of the Joint Chiefs of Staff advised Hollywood on content, while studios also cooperated with the State Department and other federal agencies to ensure that only the correct sort of films were exported.

long-standing anti-trust action by the federal government. The latter, which finally went against the studios in 1948, made them more vulnerable to public criticism and demonstrated the feasibility of political intervention, even though industry leaders protested (in vain) that they would not be dictated to when it came to hiring and film content.

By 1951 the machinery was fully in place for an all-out worldwide offensive, supplemented by documentaries, newsreels, libraries and the supply of American material via its press service to newspapers and magazines. An increase of $80 million over the existing $32 million overseas information budget was accompanied by the equally aggressive tactics (Ivie 1986) of 'psychological warfare' and black propaganda with acts of violence such as sabotage, subversion and assassinations, generously funded by a special secret wing of the new CIA entitled the Office of Policy Coordination.

During this period of heavy investment in cultural diplomacy, information against communism was supplied on a non-attributable basis to Britain's media – including the BBC – by the Information Research Department (IRD) as part of the East–West international superpower diplomacy to influence hearts and minds. The IRD also secretly funded and distributed worldwide the publication of books and articles against communism by approved authors. In addition, CIA money was behind the growth of communication research in American universities between 1945 and 1960: indeed, one writer has revealed that the very decision to use propaganda as an instrument of government created a need to develop a means of assessing that policy's effectiveness and that the communication research paradigm provided the answer (Parry-Giles 1994).

Media production influenced by Cold War politics

McCarthy himself became an astute user of the medium of television to propagandize, and interminable HUAC hearings were broadcast live. However, the television medium was also to be his undoing when it became a platform for investigative exposure against him by journalists Ed Murrow and Fred Friendly, although the role of the former in McCarthy's downfall has been exaggerated (Briggs and Burke 2002: 235). Television entertainment programmes also communicated the anti-communist menace.

A few films from this period, such as *High Noon*, contained faint suggestions of opposition to the prevalent anti-communist line (Whitfield 1991: 146–9),[1] and many were well-crafted Hollywood classics, such as *The Inn of the Sixth Happiness*, with Ingrid Bergman, and *The Third Man*, from the Harry Lime novels, but most depicted the Cold War conflict with heavy-handed portrayals of gangster-like, corrupt Soviet bosses who conspired to overturn American freedom and democracy. Domestic culture was portrayed more subtly: the European tour of George Gershwin's popular musical *Porgy and Bess* with an all-black cast, for instance, was funded by 'psychological warfare' as a means of combating Soviet criticism of American racism at a time when legal cases concerning segregation were hitting the headlines.

The Second World War had illustrated that radio was the most effective weapon in the overseas propaganda arsenal, and this continued to be the

Clandestine radio

Secret radio transmissions have also traditionally formed part of both military psychological operations and civilian activist politics during periods of conflict. CIA, press and wire services still monitor the international airways for clandestine broadcasting that can provide intelligence on revolutionary protest. Clandestine stations differ from pirate and foreign broadcasters in a number of ways: they are non-profit-making, they do not have offices and the location of their transmission is often unclear – which often makes them vulnerable to enemy 'black propaganda' or broadcasting which is deliberately misleading in terms of its source. For example, in 1958 the Cuban rebel army in the Sierra Maestra, under the leadership of Che Guevara, established its own station, Radio Rebelde, which commanded such a large audience that it became the target of a black station claiming the same name, frequency and provenance, but broadcasting anti-Castro messages. Revolutionaries decried the black operation as a 'trick used by Batista to deceive the people'. Similar efforts existed in Asia and the Middle East as well as the Eastern bloc. Surprisingly the number of clandestine stations worldwide increased after the collapse of communism (Craig 1988; Soley 1993, 1982; Carruthers 2000: 6).

case during the post-war period. The West invested heavily in powerful transmitters which enabled Voice of America (VOA) and the BBC to be heard in the communist bloc, despite attempts by the authorities to jam the airways – evidence in itself that broadcasting efforts were taken seriously. VOA devoted almost half of its budget to broadcasting behind the Iron Curtain, and transmitted in forty-six languages worldwide. The CIA secretly funded two German-based stations to supplement the services of West Germany's Deutsche Welle: Radio Free Europe for Eastern Europe and Radio Liberation, which became Radio Liberty, for the Soviet Union. In addition the American Forces Network broadcast news, information, popular music and variety via powerful transmitters to the armed forces still stationed in Germany, so Europeans could tune in. The continent was saturated with radio propaganda, which prompted the European Broadcasting Conference to reallocate medium-wave frequencies in 1948 – a restriction that was ignored by the United States, which continued with some unauthorized broadcasting in Germany (Craig 1990).

The BBC's external service continued its international reputation for objectivity and fair reporting, because propaganda was both subtle and credible, notwithstanding formal and informal links with the British Foreign Office. In contrast, VOA's reputation was less elevated because of a cruder and more strident style of broadcasting and a lack of independence from the American government. Even music by outstanding Russian classical composers such as Rimsky-Korsakov was banned. Music was viewed politically as a means of increasing the popularity of the American way of life, with jazz and rock and roll as trump cards, along with blue jeans, Coca-Cola and McDonald's.

Active anti-communist broadcasting encouraged rebellion and expectations of Western intervention against Russia in 1956. As this never materialized, radio was seen as contributing to suffering during the

Television and the Berlin Wall

In 1961 the Berlin Wall was erected between the Russian and Western sectors of the city. At the time the event seemed to increase tension, but in retrospect it allowed a relationship to develop with Russia, facilitating a debate about the future in which the Federal Republic's television played a crucial part (Ward 1989: 191). However, the German Democratic Republic allowed no such discourse on the role of media within society: pluralism was constrained by a system of state licensing and a monopolistic news agency. The authorities tried to control the flow of programmes from the FRG while also providing technical excellence to compete with the West. Within East Berlin, the most impressive new building was the television tower, a symbolic landmark immortalized by the movie director Wim Wenders. Within the GDR, one television programme, *Der schwarze Kanal* (The Black Channel), replayed parts of West German programmes, selecting elements that were to the credit of the East, and to the discredit of the West, as a form of counter-propaganda (Hesse 1990; Ward 1989: 191).

Hungarian uprising, and such criticism led VOA to emulate the BBC's more measured objectivity. Thereafter, aggressive psychological warfare gave way to the longer term, more gradualist approach of cultural diplomacy. Although radio was increasingly viewed as one of many tools for cultural assault, the Cuban missile crisis of 1962 illustrated that the medium was still crucial to international diplomacy. At a time when the nuclear threat was at its most imminent, both sides used it to communicate with each other as well as for disseminating propaganda.

Henceforth, however, the rise of television was to play a key role worldwide. In East Germany, for instance, political attitudes were influenced by the credible images portrayed by neighbouring West German television.

Later in the 1980s, satellite transmissions defied physical boundaries such as the Berlin Wall, and the materialism that programmes demonstrated had an impact on the way people viewed the communist system.

As the inter-war period had indicated, for a long time the wider social environment had not been receptive to the diffusion of the television medium, although television had been conceived and patented in the nineteenth century (Winston 1998). After the Second World War, the purchase of sets was contingent on rising living standards as countries reconstructed their economies. Meanwhile in Europe and Japan both the concept and structures of public-service broadcasting became institutionalized as a form of national consciousness, a process that had started with radio before the war.

Public-service television in Japan, Britain, France and Germany

Public-service broadcasting played a central role in the development of black and white television in the 1940s. Although the spread of the popularity of viewing was less rapid in France and Germany, the 'age of television' took off in the 1950s, using by and large the same technology worldwide, enhanced by improvements to magnetic tape-recording (first developed in Germany) and outside broadcast facilities. At first special events, such as a royal spectacle, were often viewed in public halls, cinemas and, in the case of Queen Elizabeth's coronation in 1953, which was watched by 20 million people, pubs.

As the radio industry had first discovered, royalty was a big audience puller, and the BBC's television coverage was dubbed the 'apogee of its post-war history' (Ward 1989: 78). However, the British were dismayed to hear that, when the film of their event had been sent to America by aeroplane and then screened on television, there had been a deodorant advert just before the ritual anointing, and that NBC's chimp – J. Fred Muggs – was irreverently touting tea during the commercial interludes (Curran and Seaton 1997: 161). As with radio, this confirmed once again Britain's determination to avoid what was seen as the worst excesses of the American commercial system.

In Japan there was comparable excitement over a royal wedding. Here 'street television' had become an enormous success, for the majority of people could not afford their own sets. As many as 20,000 people crammed into the streets of Tokyo for the first big televised boxing match: trams and taxis were halted, and people even climbed trees and fell off balconies that collapsed under the weight of those trying to get a view. This was the year of the first post-war broadcast, by NHK. But, like the BBC, as a public broadcaster NHK was financed by subscription fees, autonomous from yet accountable to government, therefore the Japanese broadcaster was able to encourage government and popular enthusiasm for the new medium. Japanese and British broadcasting systems displayed many similarities: both were pioneers in the phenomenon of television, only to face competition later from commercial broadcasters which tended also to have newspaper ownership.

By the late 1950s television sets in Japan were selling much more rapidly as, due to the adoption of production-line methods by manufacturers, the price came down by a third: in 1958 the price of a 14 inch black-and-white receiver was 60,000 yen, and average monthly salaries had risen to 25,000 yen (Smith 1995: 292). Now there were six commercial stations and one educational channel, but it was in the 1960s that television came of age. In 1958 gross national product was only $23.5 billion, yet by 1971 it had risen to $208.4 billion: Japan was becoming an important economic world power, although people's standard of living in the 1970s was still below that of other advanced nations (Ito 1978: 4).

Whereas before the war the country was a mixture of traditional and modern, now the industrialized style dominated as the old ways of life disappeared. Television became really popular with farmers, bridging the gap between rural and urban, old and new. An ongoing feature of Japan's modernization was that the social, cultural and economic life of people was becoming standardized and more equal, a contributory factor in the development of the media and also encouraged by it. For example, local and regional dialects disappeared as television's Tokyo dialect dominated, becoming the standard way of speaking (Smith 1995: 296).

Everywhere in the 1960s, public-service broadcasting took a lead in the creation of programming content, and also in the propagation of colour TV, which stimulated consumer demand for the medium – and therefore for TV sets. In Japan, the growth of the electronic industries connected with broadcasting was stimulated by events such as the royal wedding and the Tokyo Olympics. Growth was remarkable, for, as one writer puts it, the country 'has been much quicker in its response to shifting world demands than have other countries . . . foreign technology has been rapidly introduced and assimilated' (Ito 1978: 5).

The intention in France in 1958 was to view television as a positive instrument of culture and creativity (Institut Charles de Gaulle 1994: 87): this philosophy was in tune with early predictions that television would be taken up by a discerning section of the population with up-market expectations. In Germany, Britain and Japan as well, perceptions of culture were linked to the desire to exploit the medium's educational potential in a bid for public-service broadcasting to retain the 'high moral ground', as the BBC called it. However, it was argued at the time (and has been again more recently) that internal competition helped the corporation to improve more than the influence of external competition from the commercial sector. At the same time, one of Japanese television's responses to cultural competition was to develop its own indigenous genre of serial called 'home drama', which dealt with the everyday lives of typical urban middle-class families, an illustration of the medium's ability to reflect national characteristics.

Despite obvious successes in programme-making, by the 1950s it was already clear that the concept of public-service broadcasting and the licence fee as a method of funding would need to be defended. As a public body the BBC has always been obliged to defend its independence, particularly whenever there have been official enquiries such as the Pilkington Report of 1962, which warned that, if the BBC's share of ratings went down, this would lead to a continuing lowering of standards. In fact, the 1960s came to epitomize public-service broadcasting 'at its most provocative, irreverent and challenging' (Kuhn 1985b: 20), as the corporation continued to make successful programmes and to break new ground with creative genres such as satire (*That Was the Week That Was*, for instance). In 1964 it launched a new channel, BBC2, and by the end of the decade Britain had a large number of new local radio stations run either by the BBC or commercially under regulation from the IBA (Independent Broadcasting Authority).

In Japan and in Britain a differential black and white or colour licence was established to fund NHK and the BBC, although neither government owns public broadcasting. Both broadcasters have been at the cutting edge of international technical developments: by 1975 Japan had colour television in 91 per cent of households, and in 1967 the BBC played the key role in a worldwide television satellite experiment, linking NHK and other stations in New York, Sydney and elsewhere. The following year NHK began its own experiments in direct satellite broadcasting. In Japan educational broadcasting had been strong since the early days, with NHK introducing its first educational channel in 1957. However, the BBC took a different route, rejecting the idea of a dedicated channel and opting for the integration of educational programmes in mainstream schedules, although by 1939 it already had an elaborate schools broadcasting service on which television could build. In Japan the channel catered for adult education as well as for schools; in addition, commercial broadcasters offering at least a third of air-time to education were given priority by the government. But in 1970 this latter policy collapsed due to lack of support by commercial sponsors for educational programming. Including the important educational broadcasting by NHK and others, by 1977 Japan had 91 television broadcasting organizations.[2]

The fact that NHK, like the BBC, had paved the way in television history led to what one writer has called a 'strange relationship' between public and private sectors which echoes the British experience: 'At one level, commercial stations exercised restraint in deference to NHK's spirit of public service. Conversely, NHK became acutely conscious of the competition with commercial stations offering programmes of greater popular appeal' (Hunter 1984: 17–18; see also Smith 1995: 300–3).

As mentioned in the previous chapter, German broadcasting was organized regionally under the influence of the Allies, centring on individual Länder. The system that was introduced for television became part of that radio structure, and was financed by a combination of licence fee and commercials in order to avoid too much influence by advertising. In 1950 ARD (Arbeitsgemeinschaft der öffentlich-rectlichen Rundfunkanstalten der Bundesrepublik Deutschland) was set up to coordinate the activities of the nine broadcasting organizations in order to pool resources for their development, then in 1954 ARD started its own network, using programming from individual regions. After some legal disputes between the Länder and the federal government over local versus national broadcasting rights, ZDF (Zweites Deutsches Fernsehen) was set up as a second channel with 'coordinated contrast', to reflect the overall German experience, and was funded in the same way, to complement rather than compete for audiences. While post-war constitutional arrangements excluded the federal government from any role in broadcasting policy, the two main political parties, the Christian Democrats and the Social Democrats, have been overinfluential on the committees running the organizations, with representation according to their electoral strength (Kuhn 1985b: 94).

The political sensitivity of public-service broadcasting as a responsibility of the state is best illustrated in Italy and by the evolution of the system in France, where it had always been subject to fierce political controversy (Kuhn 1985a: 50). In 1964 de Gaulle linked television more closely to the state. French television usage required a boost of a five-year plan and forty-five transmitters before it increased to 5 million sets in that year. A new broadcasting organization, ORTF (Office de Radiofusion Télévision Française), was established, but its independence was challenged by increased politicization of the media, until it was abolished by President Giscard d'Estaing.

This time it was replaced with seven autonomous organizations to run radio, regional television and network TV, and an independent production company as supplier of technical operations, research and archives, together with a council to oversee operations. Although the state corporation had been dismembered, the new structure was still a public monopoly. This 'liberal' move by Giscard followed a number of critical parliamentary reports, scandals and attacks on the organization for bureaucracy and mismanagement, plus a strike by broadcasting unions and a financial deficit. The reform effectively dismantled one of de Gaulle's main public institutions but did not prevent relations between government and broadcast media from continuing to be an issue. Throughout the 1970s, France's television service consisted of three state-influenced channels; when Giscard left office in 1981, there were still no commercial or cable channels operating within the country.

By the 1970s in Britain, broadcasting was also under fire as concerns for pluralism and multiculturalism became more important, reflected in the Annan Report of 1977. Crucially, this recognized not only class divisions and inequalities of representation by and in the media, but also that the 1960s had produced a new climate of opinion in which society was being questioned. France and Germany were not alone in feeling social and political strain. The homogeneity that the Reithian middle-class culture had sought to foster was now replaced by audience segmentation in a divided country. The BBC's task was further complicated by a growth in both professionalism and trade unionism, prompting a new director-general to comment that the prescriptions for broadcasting of ten years previously were of little value in a rapidly changing social and political environment. The public-service broadcasting tenets of balance, objectivity and impartiality were already being questioned when the election of Mrs Thatcher in 1979 provided a watershed for both politics and broadcasting in the United Kingdom. As Ralph Negrine wrote, the challenge now was to create new vehicles for a different era: 'Television was still too scarce a resource – and perhaps too important a political weapon – to be granted the freedom to exploit the richness and diversity of contemporary life' (Kuhn 1985b: 24).

By definition, public-service broadcasting everywhere has been accountable and reactive, even if threatened by the potential of satellite and cable. While the latter freed up broadcasters from the constraints of the shortage of airway space, in operational terms the new multi-channel environment amounted to an extension of commercialism.

The growth of television commercialism and sponsorship ▨

Everywhere developments were made easier by hijacking existing radio industry structures. As with radio's revolution in the 1920s, this next communication revolution, spearheaded by television, was coloured initially by a shortage of programming. The American commercial system was the only one geared to the selling of programmes, so it had a comparative advantage (Noam 1991). This was consolidated by the fact that television ownership took off earlier in the United States, where war devastation and reconstruction on home soil was not an issue. The number of television sets being made rose exponentially – from a mere 178,000 in 1947, for instance, until, five years later, over a third of the population possessed one (Briggs and Burke 2002: 234).

The number of sets owned by a country's population was a crucial factor in calculations about commercial viability: but risks had to be taken, and politicians encouraged a climate for this to happen. Yet there were fears in Britain and Europe over the influence of commercialism on programme content. This issue was raised in 1947 by Lord Beveridge in a report on the BBC. He also recommended decentralization of the corporation and regional services. Although his recommendations were ignored in 1951 by the incoming Conservative government, which opted instead for Selwyn Lloyd's minority report supporting commercial broadcasting, nevertheless the concept of regionalism for television was taken on board for the new commercial franchises.

In 1954 British legislation introduced commercial television – Independent Television (ITV) – after a protracted and intensive campaign by supporters including big players in the entertainment industry, such as Pye Radio, the J. Walter Thompson advertising agency, and London's largest theatre management (Curran and Seaton 1997: 160). The Conservative government, which had defeated Labour in 1951, believed that commercial television would promote industry, commerce and the free market, but many people, including an 'anti' campaign led by prominent establishment figures, feared cultural degradation and tasteless adverts. The Independent Television Authority (ITA) regulator was introduced to control advertising, which was limited to 'spot ads', while 'American-style' sponsorship was rejected, on the grounds that the former would give advertisers less power over content. Commercial broadcasters were subject to the similar public-service provisions to which the BBC had been subject when a monopoly (Kuhn 1985b: 6).

Although a commercial competitor was clearly a threat to the BBC – causing its audience share in the 1950s to drop as low at times as 27 per cent – nevertheless, as the BBC became more market orientated, the differences between the two systems became eroded. Eventually they settled down in a comfortable duopoly, with many groups in society resisting any further newcomers. Of course, there were always differences in funding: the BBC's resources were stretched by the fixed licence fee, whereas advertising revenue had clear potential for expansion. In 1962 the Pilkington Report drew attention, among other things, to the fact that commercial broadcasters were making excessive profits from 'the use of a facility which is part of the public and not the private domain' (Briggs and Burke 2002: 239). As terrestrial broadcasting depended on a limited supply of airwaves, this was considered a finite public resource alongside other utilities such as water, electricity and gas. One of ITV's managers later described his franchise as 'a licence to print money'.

By comparison, commercial television in Japan found sponsorship difficult to achieve because there were so few receivers. The electronics industry was not fully developed and at first the cost of an imported American television was 250,000 yen – equivalent to the total annual salary of an urban middle-class white-collar worker (Smith 1995: 289). Unsurprisingly, there were only 866 sets in circulation in 1953, and most of these were owned by businesses and organizations such as electrical retail shops, hotels, restaurants, government and private firms and business executives. Nevertheless, a commercial station – Nippon Television – started, backed by the president of *Yomiuri* newspaper, Matsutaro Syoriki, who had the vision to support TV as an act of faith.

In contrast, the American approach was thriving. It has been described by one writer as unique in the world: 'Freer than any other, risking all the consequences of mass media shaped by the exigencies of commerce – a system which grew to be so prosperous and powerful that its influence, for better or worse, came to be felt throughout the world' (Smith 1995: 259). In the United States there was no question but that television should develop along the same lines as radio. The system centred on the needs of commerce, illustrated by the corporate growth of advertising, with its powerful weapon of sponsorship.

It followed therefore that business systems for advertising sales and the measurement of ratings were fully developed at an early stage. As the needs of advertisers came first, the acid test for television was programme popularity, and this could best be measured by ratings, which became all-powerful locally and nationally. Indeed, complaints about the reliability of ratings (which could make or break within the business) rose to such a level in the early 1960s that Congress decided to investigate (Head 1982: 382). The system was first applied to the radio industry, pioneered in 1941 by the A. C. Nielson company with the Audimeter. Sponsorship also required the intricate measurement of audiences, which in turn determined the sort of programmes that were offered. The use of opinion polls for marketing purposes was not confined to the United States: in France they were employed regularly by radio and television management within the state-influenced monopoly system by the late 1950s and continued to grow in importance through to the 1970s (Rigby and Hewitt 1991). It was not only the system of broadcasting that differed here, it was also the influence of findings of polls on programme content and style, which varied from country to country according to national histories and culture.

Attitudes towards the potential influence of commerce on programming were clearly distinctive in the United States. The impact of sponsorship in the late 1940s and early 1950s extended beyond content to the image and public behaviour of television stars, who had to conform to the image of the sponsor's product. Careers rested on the stars' projection of 'naturalness', which would encourage audience trust – and sales. As George Burns explained: '[Gracie and I] don't try to kid people, but we never forget we're supposed to sell Carnation milk. We make every effort to do it as honestly as possible. If we don't sell the product, we don't have a show.' This assessment was endorsed by an advertising agent who stated that celebrities who 'refused to deliver commercials won't be around long' (Murray 2001).

For 'popularist' media historians, the 1940s and 1950s were a defining epoch in terms of mass communication. Yet, by the mid-1950s, changes began to take place in the way prime-time American entertainment TV was produced, sponsored and scheduled. For example, from a single sponsor licensing a programme, network advertising shifted to many sponsors purchasing commercial insertions in programming. This reduced individual sponsor power.

Although in 1959–60 a huge public controversy over the rigging of TV quiz programmes prompted cynicism and disenchantment with the medium, thereafter commercial structures and programme formats remained stable until the mid-1970s. By that time the rise of satellite-delivered cable services and a proliferation of independent stations were beginning to challenge network power. The era of network hegemony up to that time resulted from specific economic and political forces and 'structures with complex determinants' (Boddy 1990: 8; Barnouw 1968; Allen 1987; Castleman and Podrazik 1982). With this new 'magazine' format, television's entire flow, from programmes to advertisements to announcements, was framed by the networks. The concept derived from print magazines (Hilmes 1990: 140).

By the late 1950s shows were smartly made and cheap to buy. The sheer size of the American domestic market meant that production costs had already been recuperated. Although US series were useful time-fillers, there were some big hits as audiences worldwide developed a love-hate relationship with the American way of living. In Japan people responded enthusiastically to the ideas of a different lifestyle, and imported television programmes changed popular culture. The first imported series in Japan was *Superman* (1956), followed by the long-running *I Love Lucy* (1957). Japanese broadcasters also watched these avidly – not for the domestic habits, the fashions or the latest home decor – but to pick up production techniques (Smith 1995: 298). By the mid-1950s CBS already had business roots in Cuba, Puerto Rico and Canada. Despite the fact that rapid growth of television sets in the early days was primarily a characteristic of the United States, and to a

Fig. 13 Lucille Ball and Desi Arnaz in *I Love Lucy*

lesser extent also of Britain, the rest of Europe and other parts of the world had all caught up by the mid-1960s, when the global audience topped 750 million (Briggs and Burke 2002: 240). By this time, each of the three American television networks had about 200 affiliated stations, with around 60 per cent of their programming as national. American overseas sales boomed, especially outside of Europe. Transnational initiatives such as the Asian Broadcasters Union (1964) were also launched.

Cross-over media influences and further media wars

A regular feature of the arrival of new media forms is their interaction with existing platforms of communication, referred to earlier in this study as 'media wars'. Predictably, therefore, the rise of television as a new popular medium forced adjustments as the relationship between players became crucial.

Newspaper decline

The survival of radio added to broadcasting's weight as it increasingly challenged the future of Western newspapers. Cross-ownership and business concentration became more common within the industry.

Table 7.1 *Number of copies of daily newspapers per 1000 inhabitants, 1960–1984*

Country	1960	1970	1979	1984
France	252	238	196	185
West Germany	307	326	323	350
Great Britain	514	463	426	414
Japan	396	511	569	562

Sources: Albert 1990: 34; Charon 1991: 396; Kuhn 1995: 28.

Newspapers could hardly compete – except in Japan, where they still prospered. There the first commercial backers of television had been newspaper owners, although the power of TV to report instantly on events caused apprehension. The response was comparable to that of some American newspaper groups to radio before the war. *Asahi* and *Mainichi* followed *Yomiuri's* lead into the medium. After 1960 this resulted in the creation of information conglomerates where national and local news, commentary and staff could be shared at all levels, including that of rotating vice-presidents between affiliate TV stations and newspapers.

Similarly, in the United States local newspaper ownership was increasingly slipping into the hands of local radio and television stations, prompting court decisions in the 1970s to dismantle local 'cross-ownership' of broadcast and print media: in fact, press owners often reacted by swapping their local radio and television stations with those owned by newspapers in other cities (Smith 1979: 165).

By the 1970s Japan had 110 newspapers with a total daily circulation of about 40 million: the 1960s was a decade of consolidation. Nevertheless, almost everywhere except Japan, circulation figures indicate the effect of television on newspaper sales (see table 7.1).

The strength of the print media in Japan during this period was unique, deriving from its huge circulation, reliability and importance in society. The Japanese had proved to be keen readers, treating the printed word with reverence, trusting it, and accepting newspaper content as accurate, which enabled newspapers to consolidate their extraordinary influence. People were also consistent in their trust of television news, which was mainly via NHK, whereas television news in the United States in the late 1960s and early 1970s did not inspire public confidence (Krauss 2000: 4).

Most of the Western world continued to experience industry concentration, illustrated in the United States by the merger of United Press with the International News Service. The newspaper crisis was also shared by European countries such as Sweden and Switzerland which had managed to retain nineteenth-century-style small businesses based on party politics and 'opinion'. At the turn of the century, Vienna had been the artistically prolific, avant-garde creative and journalistic capital of the world: by this period it had only seven newspapers. In the whole of Germany, for instance, the number of titles had fallen by 1976 to 122 – half of its post-war peak (Smith 1979: 166; Murschetz 1998).

In addition, the introduction of computer technology had a dramatic impact on the way the newspaper industry operated from the 1970s onwards, making production easier. The ability of computers to reassemble, store and analyse information meant that for the first time journalists could do page lay-out electronically ready for printing, so that new editions could be turned out more cheaply and editorial offices could be separated from printing works. Production costs were thus reduced, which was good news for small-circulation newspapers, but the overall change from being labour intensive to capital intensive was bad news for print workers, as large numbers of jobs were lost amid a climate of industrial conflict and worker unrest.

Film and television

In France and Italy national cinema was at the apex of its artistic influence with New Wave, a seminal artistic genre which is the subject of varying interpretations. Previously the films of Truffaut, Godard, Antonioni and others were analysed and appreciated as a radical break with tradition, though it has also been argued that such directors were the creative heirs of the classic cinema – a recognition of continuity (Crisp 1997). Hollywood, however, was challenged by the more rapid take-off of television as a mass medium in the United States. Business readjustments were necessary, particularly because technical improvements such as videotape and outside broadcasts meant that television programmes could be broadcast at any time and in any place.

As a real mass audience arose for television, especially in the United States, by 1956 cinema audiences had slumped to almost half the 1947 level and the number of cinemas had dropped by more than 25 per cent. Hollywood was initially forced onto the defensive by the take-off of television, but calls for pay TV faced opposition from the radio networks. Film companies also made attempts to acquire television licences and buy up television companies. In 1948, for instance, Twentieth Century-Fox attempted to purchase ABC (Briggs and Burke 2002: 235). Apart from financial considerations, there was an operational logic: some of the features of the new television systems were akin to those of the film industry, and both required a division of labour between programme-making and transmission (distribution).

In television's very early days, before the national networks became all-powerful, there were regional differences in programme style, and Broadway theatre also influenced the techniques of live TV. By the 1950s the 'golden age' of live drama gave way to a new format – the filmed drama series. Prime-time programming moved from New York to Hollywood as anthology was replaced by the continuing-character filmed genre. According to one scholar, this represented a retreat from 'aesthetic experimentation, program balance and free expression' (Boddy 1990: 2), but the format was to provide a more fruitful relationship between the growing broadcast medium as purchaser and Hollywood as supplier. Television's dependence on the Hollywood filmed series increased with the demise of the game-show craze. Some ongoing formulas, such as *Bonanza* and *Gunsmoke*, were destined to run for twenty years or more as a plentiful source of production work and income, making cross-over of technical staff, creative talent and financing all much easier. In addition, business accrued from the sale of old films to television, all of which enabled the film industry to recover, despite the blows of the McCarthyite period. A greater flexibility within the 'Dream Factory' was emerging, exemplified by 'independent' producers and directors making low-cost but often successful movies (for instance, the 'film noir' genre) and challenging Hollywood traditions in the process.

In contrast to the cross-over between the film and television industries in the area of fictional programming shared by the United States, Britain and France, in Japan television employment was characterized by what one writer has called 'happy amateurism'. Although some employees came from the movies, many tended to be new to the industry, from newspapers, from journalism or straight out of college. 'Their planning, execution and broadcasting were fundamentally amateurish and this characteristic remains in today's Japan' (Smith 1995: 297). With the exception of the films of Kurosawa and a few other directors, most spectacular movies failed to recapture audiences, especially from the 1964 Olympics onwards. Initially, in 1958, film companies decided not to offer their products to television, but, failing to beat TV, had to join it. Traditional motion-picture companies disappeared, to be replaced by video production divisions as subcontractors to broadcasters, who often required commercial breaks and specific shorter time slots.

The market share of domestic movies in Japan continued to decrease as the United States, compared to other countries, became particularly adroit at exploiting the emerging video media of pay television and video cassettes. This provided an economic base for increases in commercial film investment levels that other countries could not sustain. Despite the break-up of the studio system with the advent of television and cross-ownership, Hollywood's institutional model was still admired.

Television and radio

At first the growth of television also led to a decline in radio listening: in Britain the number of radio licences was at a peak in 1950, but fell as the number of combined radio and TV licences rose in 1955 to 4.5 million. In Japan radio listening declined from three hours a day in 1950 to thirty minutes in 1965 (Briggs and Burke 2002: 237; Smith 1995: 301).

Yet watching TV never completely replaced listening to the wireless: indeed, in France the amount of time spent listening stayed more or less the same despite the arrival of television viewing. In that country radio still dominated in the 1940s and 1950s. Even in 1961, 80 per cent of the French population had a radio, whereas less than 20 per cent had a television set. In 1960, there were only thirty staff journalists working in television for the state broadcaster RTF, as opposed to 310 who worked in radio. By 1989, 98 per cent of the French population had at least one radio (Kuhn 1995). Again, although the radio licence in Japan was abolished in 1968, within five years there were still fifty-one radio organizations.

The predominant influence of radio on television in countries such as Britain, France, Japan and most other European countries was an organizational and structural one: the monopoly control of radio was extended to TV, with the same management and regulatory system (Briggs 1993). For instance, in 1950 Japan's radio and broadcasting law revalidated NHK's legal status as well as guaranteeing freedom of expression in broadcasting. Cross-over influence among media industries was evident before the Second World War; yet this period in history was unique in the extent to which a cross-over from radio to television was both possible and likely.

Radio and music

Technology saved radio by enabling it to reinvent itself in a more portable and individualized way that ensured its worldwide survival, to the extent that by the mid-1960s almost every household had a radio set. Breakthroughs that improved the quality of transmission and reception, such as FM, were accompanied by changing radio usage within consumer lifestyles. The latter came to be affected by the profusion of transistor radios, hi-fi stereo tuners, car radios, radio alarms, walkmans and other devices that made listening more flexible and adaptable. Radio's response to the new serious competition from television was to concentrate more on the local and the specialized, resulting in a more diverse range of music being played, which in turn affected the record industry.

By the early 1950s sales of discs had outstripped those of sheet music; then radio stimulated demand for rock and roll, which was emerging as more than a passing fad (Peterson and Berger 1975: 165; Martin 1995: 249), and for black music styles that had been marginalized by the major record companies. The response of the big four record companies, RCA Victor, Decca, Columbia and Capitol, which in 1948 shared 75 per cent of the market (ibid.: 248), was to try and follow the successful example of Decca, which had signed up Bill Haley and the Comets from the independent label Essex: *Rock Around the Clock* was the big hit of 1955. Similarly, RCA signed up Elvis Presley from Sun Records for a mere $33,000 plus a cadillac. Although some of

Presley's early songs were based on black music, his career soon took on a more anodyne commercial flavour after it came under the control of a major label.

In the late 1950s, concentration in the music industry was challenged by increasing numbers of independent record companies supplying the huge range and quantity of music that radio now required. As early as 1951 the American DJ Alan Freed was successfully introducing black 'rhythm and blues' styles to white audiences, but his ability to thrive as an independent operator was later destroyed by litigation, prompted by the majors' attempt via the industry's ASCAP publishing association to eliminate competition (Elliot 1990: 75). In the volatile market of the time, another means to achieve this same end, according to Peter Martin, was for the majors to resort to illegal methods such as 'payola' to radio DJs to play specific discs (Martin 1995: 253).

Music, technology and convergence

The big players now had converged media interests in radio, movies, songwriting and publishing, which meant that control of distribution and marketing tended to centre around actual or rising star names, to the detriment of independent and smaller businesses. The period 1964–9 saw record sales exceeding the gross revenues of all other media (Peterson and Berger 1975: 167), but success sometimes went in waves and could be ephemeral, as the experience of Capitol Records demonstrated. Capitol had initially shown little interest in the Beatles, but through their parent British company, EMI, had acquired the US distribution for the 'Fab Four'. Although this lucky stroke made them a hefty profit, the company was devastated by a combination of the Beatles' break-up, the Beach Boys' move to their rising competitor Warners and a slump in country-music sales. Corporate concentration meant that in the late 1960s the majors were now divisions of large multinational corporations, so that by 1973 only two real independents – Motown and A & M – were in the top eight music companies (Martin 1995: 251). By this time, record sales started to slump again, and this time it was blamed on the ubiquitous cassette player.

In 1963 the audio cassette was launched. The Dutch multinational Philips monopolized the emerging market for a portable tape format, although the company handed out manufacturing rights to anyone who chose to produce the cassettes, provided they used Philips specifications (Chanan 1994: 258). A new wave of independents sprang up, but they were gradually taken over. Cassettes significantly increased the availability of music by enabling people to record from the radio at home, or from their new synthesizers, which arrived in the late 1960s.

The synthesizer broke down professional barriers between engineers, composers, musicians and producers and eventually raised a question mark over the whole business of recording a 'performance', as a studio was no longer required for the making of a high-standard recording (Martin 1995: 257, 260; Lopes 1992: 57). Once more the reaction to change in industry practices was a media war – another expression of the conflict between increased public access to new forms of media and the requirement to defend authors' remuneration. There were calls within the industry for a tax on blank tapes and litigation for the protection of copyright and performers' rights to royalties.

Electro-acoustics and magnetic tape-recording changed musical style: it allowed producers and engineers to manipulate performances and musicians to do the same with sound. Disc-cutting moved from the studio to the record factory, leaving the engineer to become the mixer with the aid of a whole new range of studio equipment, including the multitrack tape-recorder and stereo. Multitrack recording meant that mixes could take place afterwards, during re-recording or remixing, which became one of the main distinguishing features between classical music and popular music. The remix also led to new genres such as reggae. In 1967, the Beatles' *Sergeant Pepper* album became a milestone (although the band was not the first to use such techniques) because it was designed as a studio product and not for live performance (Chanan 1994: 270, 272).

From the late 1970s a further threat to the institutional power of the large record companies appeared in the form of the spread of 'punk' music record labels, with their own alternative production and distribution methods. Punk was not just about rebellious image and style: the movement laid the foundations for future radical music using independent labels with their own, more modest economics. For instance, in 1974–5 EMI needed to sell 20,000 records to break even, whereas a few years later 'DIY' punk labels could break even with sales of as little as 2000 (Martin 1995: 252).

When sales suddenly slumped in 1979, the effect was to strengthen the trend for the big players in the record industry to become part of the globalization of media, electronics and telecommunications: all of the six major companies during the 1970s had diverse interests. MCA (Music Corporation of America), for instance, had already become the biggest independent television company in Hollywood and in 1959 bought up the American Decca company and its Hollywood subsidiary, Universal. In 1967 the Kinney Corporation, with interests in supermarkets, cleaning firms, funeral parlours, car parks and plumbing, had acquired WEA (Warner-Elektra-Atlantic) (Chanan 1995: 152–3).

'A symbolic gadget for the nomads of modernity'

Until the 1960s, studio professionals had been the only people to sport headphones, but now these became available to the general public, presaging the computer industry's 1990s dream of virtual-reality headgear. Previously stereo and high-quality home-recording equipment had taken off when made available to the general public rather than only to specialists. Now in 1979 Sony capitalized on headphones by introducing the 'walkman'.

Just as early wireless technology had been adopted for military use, so satellite technology was also developed for Russian and American military purposes. The technology which facilitated global communication also raised issues of national control – a 'reterritorializing' of 'spaces of identity' in the case of Europe (Wilson 1999). According to Manuel Castells (1997), the network society that ensued operates holistically in economic and political fields as much as in communications, and it is flexible, varied and pervasive. Certainly, by the end of the 1970s cable and satellite had found a domestic market. Television sets could be connected to video recorders, which fundamentally changed the way that people used their leisure time for viewing, and the choice of programming – particularly films – available to them. The next step would be to connect the computer to the television and the telephone, heralding the concept of media convergence.

The influence of radio and television on politics and the public: some comparisons

When it came to communication via broadcasting, politicians cut their teeth on radio then, sometimes apprehensively, transferred the skills that they had developed to television. It was radio that first attracted them to broadcasting, but it was television that displayed the performance 'warts and all', making politics less distant, more accessible. In the process boundaries between public and private were further redrawn, promoting a trend that newspapers had started and to which radio had contributed. There was also a movement of personnel and of successful programme formats from the one broadcast medium to the other. Hence, in the case of both Britain and France, the unified nature of the broadcasting systems had a positive impact.

In America, the growth of advertising, public relations and television as a communications weapon for politicians meant that the medium played a crucial part in elections. Kennedy, for instance, would probably not have been elected without it. But, as both Pierre Bourdieu and Daniel Boorstin have noted, the forms and conventions of production dictated the nature of both the viewing experience and the experience for those appearing on television. Politicians in America accepted the existing genres (Bourdieu 1998; Boorstin 1963).

Conversely, relentless news coverage of civil disturbances at home and of carnage abroad during the Vietnam War offered no respite for president Lyndon B. Johnson. It produced the impression that he was not in control, making it impossible for him to seek another term of office. His successor, Richard Nixon, put pressure on television stations to be more 'loyal' towards government policy at a time during the late 1960s when the foreign policy of the United States in South-East Asia was the key issue in international affairs. Vietnam was called the first 'television war', provoking debate about the effects of global coverage. Some people believed that daily battle news led to public boredom,

Television: is the medium the message? Some early research

As early as 1958 the influential Japanese writer Soichi Ohya produced a series of essays on the effects of television in which he argued that the medium was the new means of 'creating 100 million idiots', the implication being that people would read less and watch more television. By 1975, Japanese children aged ten to fifteen years were watching an average of four hours a day (Smith 1995: 299). Since the 1950s, similar research studies have abounded in Britain, the United States and elsewhere. What was the effect of the messages that viewers were receiving? The wider issue of how the medium constructed meaning in the 'global village' was addressed by Marshall McLuhan in *Understanding Media* (1964), where he argued that 'the medium is the message'. This perspective tends to overstate the role of communications in determining influence, while discounting the impact of other contextual factors on society. Nevertheless, media effects research continues unabated: for instance, in Britain in the 1980s it was found that, while current affairs programming contributed to pluralism, fictional programming encouraged 'mainstreaming', as did heavy television viewing, which was linked to political centrism. Earlier research had already addressed and supported the hypothesis of cultural homogenization in relation to American society (Piepe et al. 1990; Neuman 1982).

Effects vary according to the stage of media development, contexts and geography. Whereas in developed countries economic productivity resulted in media growth and increased press freedom, in less developed countries the media 'tend to be used to facilitate the functioning of the economy and to perpetuate the power of the rulers' (Weaver et al. 1985). News agencies provide an example: domination by America and Europe, which transmitted most of the news between countries within the Third World, was seen by some leaders and intellectuals as a neo-colonialist affront to their national or cultural pride and sovereignty (McNelly 1979). Therefore television's growth as a medium worldwide raises questions of technological nationalism, technological democracy and, overall, the role of technological determinism.

However, specialist media research regularly reveals apparent inconsistencies in these 'macro' trends: for instance, content analysis of magazine advertisements in France, West Germany, Britain and the Netherlands during a period of economic unification between 1953 and 1989 shows an increase in symbols of nationality – when a more international character would be expected. Changes in individual countries conform to differing time-scales: the emergence of private broadcasting and concerns about American television, as one writer has pointed out, became prominent in Europe decades after they were evident in Canada (Snyder et al. 1991; Young 2003). Furthermore, countries that are at the receiving end of 'cultural imperialism' do not always retain the short straw: Japan, for instance, moved after 1965 from an information-importing to an information-exporting country (Ito 1990).

others that it encouraged opposition to American intervention. The effects of news coverage have also been hotly debated, with claims that the civil rights movement in America would not have existed without television. Protests involving civil disorder tend to be newsworthy, but were said by some to be given more prominence by virtue of the media attention to them. A similar argument emerged later in relation to terrorism when Mrs Thatcher referred to the 'oxygen of publicity'.

For libertarian media historians, May 1968 was a defining date, when worker and youth protests erupted in Europe. In France they were centred mainly around barricades erected in Paris's Latin Quarter. Radio became part of events as they unfolded and was therefore criticized by some for provoking the trouble, running 'the risk of creating a media event to serve its own appetite for news and sensation' (Kuhn 1995: 82; Institut Charles de Gaulle 1994: 196).

During the revolt, the use of radio by student leaders to mobilize support among the student body was strategic. The medium helped to gain the sympathy of the public on the issues of university reform and police violence against protesters as young people became politically important in Germany and France. It was also used as a forum for debate and negotiation between the two main players – the authorities and the student protesters. Finally de Gaulle, choosing not to appear on television, reasserted his authority and that of the Fifth Republic via radio, in a move designed to be reminiscent of 18 June 1944. It had the desired effect: a huge demonstration in support of the Gaullist regime meant that law and order was reimposed.

This was the second occasion that radio became integral to politics in post-Second World War France. The first was during the Algerian War for Independence. As the conflict was drawing to a close in 1961, elements of the professional army staged a revolt in opposition to de Gaulle's policy of independence for the country from colonial rule. De Gaulle immediately went on television to condemn the rebellion categorically, and the speech was heard by hundreds of thousands of French conscripts who listened in on their transistor radios at the barracks. They were persuaded that their leader was determined to take a firm stand and therefore backed him against the renegades. It was called a 'transistor victory' against the attempted coup, reminiscent of radio's role in pre-war Japan during a military rebellion.

Newspaper reactions

Campaigning journalism, creativity and newspaper survival

Pessimists predicted the demise of the newspaper but, like radio, it has proved to be resilient and flexible. Things were not all bad: as one writer has pointed out, by comparison with today's poor journalism, the period from the end of the Second World War through to the mid-1980s was one when journalism was at a peak of performance in terms of fairness and the use of its power (Hallin 1998). In the United States, the investigative journalism of the *Washington Post* exposed the White House in the Watergate scandal, bringing about the downfall of President Nixon and vindicating the role of the free press. Campaigning journalism as part of the Fourth Estate, which had gone by the board during the McCarthyite era, was restored to its former glory.

Meanwhile West Germany had its own press scandal, involving the investigative journalism of *Der Spiegel*. In 1962 the West German government arrested the editor and author of a series of articles questioning the defence capability of the Federal Republic: they were accused of treason, a reflection of the increasing criticism of the complacency of leading politicians and the tenuous nature of press freedom in an abnormal political situation. Such challenges not only demonstrated the continuing role of serious journalism in developing political consciousness; they also helped sales of the printed word.

There were also creative forces at work in journalism: in 1972 Tom Wolfe coined the phrase 'New Journalism', defining a movement worthy of critical attention. Writing techniques that emerged in the 1960s were peppered with immediacy and emotional engagement, seeking a larger

Differences in Japan: newspapers and society

In a survey of fifty-eight countries in 1987, Japan above all was found to be less inclined to control the press (Feldman 1993: 14–15). However, self-censorship has become well entrenched: traditionally, the imperial royal family is considered by the press to be above criticism; likewise China, in support of the government's policy of cordial relations, is not to be denigrated. Journalistic restraint was influenced by the inherent instability of Japan's new imposed democracy between 1947 and 1960. Although by the end of the 1980s the country was perceived as having a successful parliamentary system, the success of the US experiment was by no means a foregone conclusion in the early days. Left and right were split over the nature of democracy and the imposed constitution, as well as the past and future collective personality of the nation (Krauss 2000: 6).

The nature of Japan's press contributed to the closing of the cultural gap between differences in gender, age, residential area, dialect and socio-economic status. People were receiving the same information due to the small number of national newspapers with wide circulation and the limited number of television channels collaborating in their news and entertainment programming. One analyst takes the implications even further: 'the result of this media exposure is reflected in the process of dramatic change that Japanese society now experiences, and is expressed in an overall sense of satisfaction with life and the resultant support of conservative movements, a sense of helplessness in politics and society, a growing lack of interest in communicating with other people, and a belief in materialism' (Feldman 1993: 23).

News coverage in Japan carries more emphasis on the civil service, national bureaucracy and allied organizations – unique by comparison to other parts of the world, where politicians and cabinet officials tend to dominate public affairs communication. Although the Japanese press stated a commitment to fairness and neutrality, it regularly criticized the ruling Liberal Democratic Party and the government, acting as public watchdog over the political leadership. However, opposition parties were rarely able to capitalize on this sufficiently to gain power. As one writer concludes, the government–press relationship was characterized by a lack of investigative reporting, for newspapers could not criticize the government from the standpoints advocated by the left-wing parties. One feature of the industry was its traditional heavy dependence on borrowing, hence on the business world as well as on circulation, both of which are limiting factors on editorial policy. Furthermore, the way the press clubs operated and the organizational characteristics of the news-making procedure did not encourage serious investigation of the political leadership (Lee 1985: 86).

truth by a more imaginative approach to reporting. Although the passions of the movement in the United States were short-lived, the wider validity of long-form journalism from a personal perspective has remained.

Subsidy or monopoly?

Despite the launch in Paris of two new morning papers, *Le Quotidien* and *Le Matin*, and in New York of one short-lived paper, most cities were down to only one organ with the same specialism or approach. While France, Scandinavia (except Denmark), Austria and Italy reacted to the loss of titles with subsidies, Germany and Britain continued to hope that the market would eventually improve and rejected financial intervention. The thinking behind the granting of subsidies was that it would guarantee that citizens taking part in the political process were accurately informed. The public-service culture of newspapers had gradually become endangered by increased commercial competition, public austerity programmes from the 1970s onwards, and changing taste among readers.

The pre-First World War and inter-war predominance of the wealthy, capricious and sometimes politically motivated press barons was now giving way to a more contemporary phenomenon of newspaper ownership by tycoons and more anonymous corporations with wider business interests elsewhere. For instance, in Britain the *Daily Express* retained a style of 'personal ownership' under the Canadian immigrant Max Aitken, who became Lord Beaverbrook, but this feature disappeared with changed ownership. Similarly when Lord Thomson died, his huge international empire (including *The Times* and the *Sunday Times*) merged with oil interests, as did that of the Astor family (*The Observer*).

Advertisers and a political press in Britain

In the United Kingdom, with its minimalist approach to press regulation, there was also a further decline of political papers. The issue was much debated during the 1960s and early 1970s with the demise of the *Daily Chronicle* (originally the *Daily News*, with Charles Dickens as its first editor) and the *Daily Herald*. This latter newspaper, on its deathbed, was still read by 4.7 million people, nearly twice as many as the readership of *The Times*, the *Financial Times* and *The Guardian* combined (Curran 2002: 102). But its readers were considered the wrong sort of people for stimulating advertising income, and its share of national advertising revenue was a mere 3.5 per cent. It appeared that, whereas the middle classes spent enough money to warrant newspapers with a variety of political stances, the working-class market could not sustain a minority paper, a problem which Anthony Smith has described as 'buried inside the question of class structure and income distribution' (1979: 181). Within this climate, editors were obliged to continue a trend which had first surfaced during the nineteenth century: the appeal of their papers had to be widened in order to retain advertising.

In West Germany publishing tycoon Axel Springer exercised considerable political influence with the support that his 'yellow' tabloid *Das Bild* (an old-style *Boulevardblatt* established in 1952) gave to the conservatism of the Christian Democrat chancellor Konrad Adenauer. Indeed, there was a uniformity of conservatism across Springer's many titles, emphasizing both the internal and the external dangers to the new state, prompting one writer to reflect that: 'Rather than opening up discussion, he was concerned with closing it down and reiterating the "national" outlook of the FRG. Ever watchful of historical parallels, some Germans remembered the career of magnate Hugenberg, and his eventual support for National Socialism' (Ward 1989: 190; see also Lohmeyer 1992). Conservative influence was also strong elsewhere: in the United Kingdom, one analyst has argued that the enduring influence of newspapers has been to contribute 'significantly to the remarkable stability and underlying conservatism of British society' (Curran 2002: 103).

Continuing trends towards concentration in the newspaper industry have led scholars to debate whether daily newspapers are natural monopolies; it seems that, although it does not demonstrate the normal features, the press does have a tendency towards monopoly. Several scholars have argued that newspaper monopoly has been facilitated by the industry itself, by its own practices and through government intervention, which it called for and achieved. In the case of the UK, Colin Sparks argues that the nature of the daily press market results from the natural workings of the free market (Sparks 1995; Lacy and Picard 1990; Barnett 1980).

During this period the press was concerned that circulation was not rising to the same extent as population, with fewer young people reading newspapers. Yet niche markets became more important: magazines were obliged to change in order to serve discrete interests within the mass population (Smith 1979: 181; Compaine 1980). Indeed, specialist financial newspapers such as the *Wall Street Journal* and London's *Financial Times* were doing well in North America, Britain and the Far East. In Germany the *Frankfurter Allegemeine Zeitung*, essentially a local newspaper, gained an international reputation for quality.

Conclusions

As protest over United States foreign policy escalated, media criticism surfaced and became a potent force once more, but the McCarthyite era delayed that process.

Right up until the 1980s, Russians were depicted negatively within the media. Forty-odd years of anti-USSR imagery took its toll: studies revealed that 25 per cent of American students believed that the atom bomb was invented by Russians and 28 per cent of people who responded to a *New York Times* survey believed that the Soviet Union had fought against the United States during the

Second World War (Dennis et al. 1991: 31; Gorman and McLean 2003: 117).

American mass culture and material abundance had a universal appeal that the Soviets could not match. The US government's exploitation of that appeal was the most successful aspect of the West's Cold War propaganda (Gorman and McLean 2003: 124).

An international machinery was now in place for the continuation of propaganda techniques and future influence. Furthermore, the status of both the BBC and Britain's Information Research Department was enhanced once more by their emphasis on factual balance.

Support for the American way of life and American society proved to be an essential foundation for the inevitable link between global culture, trade and politics.

Study questions

Using the examples of television, radio and other media, discuss the influence of social and economic factors in determining the timing of popularity 'take-off'.

How far were the alternative television systems – American commercial TV and public-sector broadcasting in Britain, France, Germany and Japan – reflections of political, economic and social outlooks?

Using the Vietnam War and previous historical examples featured in this study, examine the role of the media as both reporter and agent of rebellion in various countries.

If a measure of the success of cultural diplomacy and psychological warfare in a media context is that it goes unnoticed, how do we analyse its longer term impact?

Assess the contribution of the Cold War to media globalization.

8 Continuity and Change since 1980

We are here to serve advertisers. That is our raison d'être.

CEO of Westinghouse

It doesn't matter whether it comes in by cable, telephone lines, computer, or satellite. Everyone's going to have to deal with Disney.

Michael Eisner, chairman, Disney/ABC

Summary

The *objective* of this chapter is to argue that although, up to 1980, media history was characterized by a strong preponderance towards continuity of issues and themes, within that overarching context the last two decades have witnessed a reconfiguration of one of these: power relations. The transnational media corporation that only customizes for national cultural considerations if profit dictates has replaced the traditional historical relationship between the state and the media. This has had implications for freedom of cultural expression in a world order that has been moving towards free trade, whatever the national repercussions.

Privatization and deregulation in the 1980s encouraged the growth of multinationals as they replaced the power of national governments over media. Cable, satellite and digital technology all helped this process, contributing to the intensification of media globalization.

The rule of market economics over media development has been accompanied by concentration of ownership. As multinational corporate players traded internationally, using the above technology, this trend was central to the intensification of media globalization. Although the process of globalization has extended the potential reach to more people, this has not been a democratic process: convergence of media forms has been characterized by unaccountable oligopoly. The scale and methods of multinational corporations emerged as more comprehensive and pervasive than ever before, aided by the digital revolution and the acquisition of subsidiaries.

Introduction

Cold War attitudes lingered in the West: research into the coverage by the *New York Times* and *Newsweek* in 1980 and 1989 of student demonstrations in South Korea and China respectively has revealed that ideology was a more important news factor than national interest in influencing the American media's news coverage. Political change in Russia had little impact, yet conversely changes to the media system in the former Soviet Union had a profound influence on *Izvestia*'s coverage of the events (Wang 1995; Malinkina and McLeod 2000). North American television's news coverage of Cuba also continued to be negative, despite the major international political changes that emanated from the end of the Cold War (Soderlund et al. 1998).

Until the 1980s, newspapers and basic broadcasting systems tended to be nationally owned and regulated: international news agencies, exportable films, TV shows, music and books were exceptions to the norm. This changed in the 1980s with privatization of communication systems and deregularization, an approach espoused by President Reagan in the United States, Margaret Thatcher in Britain, the International Monetary Fund and the World Bank, and accelerated by the development of new satellite and digital technologies. Technology, market power, the quality of services and the changing media landscape all served to make life more difficult for public-service broadcasting. The new climate meant not an end to regulations, but rather a rearrangement in their operation which enabled transnational giants to flourish, dictated by market economics instead of by national governments.

Globalization and the rule of the unaccountable 'free market'

In 1990, one scholar highlighted the apparent contradiction that emerged as a trend of the twentieth century in the developing globalization of the world's information and entertainment businesses: while these industries had grown beyond the power of nations to control them, posing a threat to democracy in the process, the technologies that provided the basis for globalization also enabled minority voices to find audiences through greater accessibility (Smith 1990). How did this happen? The process needs to be understood at a macro-level and also as it relates to individual media sectors.

The new form of internationalism, with all its contradictions, was very different to the previous post-Second World War Bretton Woods agreement that it replaced. Whereas this latter international system had controlled cross-border movement of capital and permitted the organization of international finance via national governments, by the 1980s neo-liberal thinking had come to dominate the regulatory bodies of Bretton Woods. By the late 1990s multinationals were responsible for about two-thirds of world trade, and more flexible systems of production caused greater corporate mobility. The gradual collapse of Bretton Woods was accompanied by an increase in the growth of multinationals and in private finance.

All of these factors helped to erode national democracies. Some governments reacted to the new financial climate by introducing market-friendly monetary policies as advocated by the International

Monetary Fund (IMF), such as low taxation, low public expenditure, privatization and deregulation. Often the alternative was to face IMF penalties for currency collapse. Hence largely unregulated global financial markets encouraged conservative management of economies: 'in short, the autonomy and effectiveness of governments as agencies of economic management were cumulatively undermined by globalization' (Curran 2002: 117–18).

The process was never a democratic one – quite the reverse. Although deregulation within broadcasting tended to lead to expansion and competition at first, this provoked a fragmentation of audiences, meaning that certain people were excluded. Those who remained within the frame became subject to a process of market segmentation (according to age, gender and ethnicity, for instance), encouraging content producers to focus on formats, which also became concentrated (Katz 1996).

Deregulation did not lead automatically to corporate expansion: for example, American firms were initially cautious about the commercial potential of high-definition television. Indeed, the business repercussions tended to involve streamlining – for example, amalgamation or networking. Then the process came full cycle as further concentration of ownership emerged, enabling a new oligopoly to be created (Bennett et al. 1993: 156–86).

Cultural industries now became subject to a variety of free-trade and regional integration agreements, operated largely by non-elected organizations and structures such as NAFTA (North Atlantic Free Trade Association) and GATT (General Agreement on Tariffs and Trade), in addition to the democratically elected EU (European Union). In general, global regulation tended not to be subject to public accountability – one factor behind the protests from 1999 onwards in cities that hosted the meetings of international regulators, such as Prague, Genoa and Seattle. The agreements of the WTO (World Trade Organization), for instance, had three main objectives: to help trade flow as freely as possible, to achieve further liberalization gradually through negotiation, and to set up an impartial means of settling disputes. When applied to cultural and audiovisual services, the disciplines of the GATT brought into question all existing national regulations governing these sectors. For instance, opponents observed that public-service broadcasting and investment obligations on TV channels could be outlawed, just as support by the EU media programmes to encourage indigenous production could be challenged (Tongue 2003).[1]

Regulations that had been introduced to require a certain percentage of national ownership for specific media were now considered to restrict market access by foreign competitors. For example, every OECD country except the United States had established special rules regarding children's TV; 188 states ratified the UN Declaration on the Rights of the Child, which included the right of access to creation and cultural diversity. Accordingly, in Australia all pre-school TV had to be Australian – an approach that laid it open to challenge from the WTO.

Similarly the 'TV Without Frontiers' Directive of the EU, which provided for 51 per cent of screen time to be made up of indigenous drama/film/documentary, was threatened.

Nation-states were now left with the dilemma of how to defend cultural creativity and the freedom to shape their own cultural policies in the context of a drive by the WTO to extend free-trade rules to film and television. The questions raised by this trend went beyond cultural protectionism versus the free flow of information to the issue of oligopoly within the increasingly concentrated and converged corporate sector. Although the proportion of total output traded internationally was not much higher in the early 1990s than it was just before the First World War (Hirst and Thompson 1996), concentration of ownership had become an issue internationally.

By the 1990s, in revenue terms, the overwhelming majority of the world's film and TV production, cable and satellite channel and system ownership, magazine and book publishing and music production was now provided by about fifty companies, and the first nine of these, Time Warner, Disney, Bertelsmann, Viacom, News Corporation, Sony, TCI, Universal and NBC, dominated many of these media sectors. The larger of these media firms formed part of wider industrial conglomerates, such as General Electric, owner of NBC, with sales in 1997 of $80 billion.

Although some of the bigger players, such as Bertelsmann and Sony, originated from outside the United States, even within the second tier of top media firms about a half were American. Writers such as Edward Herman, Robert McChesney and Ben Bagdikian, who track media monopoly, argue that, within the United States, a communications cartel came to operate at every step in the mass-communications process, from the creation of content to its delivery into the home and helped by the digital revolution: 'an influence whose scope and power would have been considered scandalous or illegal twenty years ago' (Bagdikian 1997: ix; see also McChesney and Herman 1997). Working on the premise that corporate growth via the acquisition of subsidiaries allows market domination and wards off competitors (particularly if there are joint ventures), the cartel system advanced the cause of the global market, promoting commercial values and influencing the political agenda on account of its huge sway over government agencies and national legislators.

Faced with this awesome presence, the ability of countries to use television to frame their own social perceptions depended on money as well as policy (Tongue 2003: 4). In general, a larger percentage of programme hours have been domestically produced in wealthier countries or those that invest a large proportion of their gross domestic product in broadcast media, such as some Far Eastern countries. Nevertheless, the numbers seem to indicate loss of economic muscle to the nation-state. For instance, in 1985 the United Kingdom had an audiovisual trade surplus with the USA of £151 million. Since the advent of cable and satellite channels, this has become a deficit of £403 million, meaning fewer jobs and less indigenous audiovisual creation. By 2002, the EU–US audiovisual trade deficit was $8 billion.

Despite experiences of deregulation, privatization and liberalization of markets, in the Asia-Pacific region national priorities, both political and social, have dictated the approach to telecommunications. A study of Taiwan points out that nation-states also try to be 'active agents' to curb the globalizing tendency territorially (Thomas 2003; Waterman and Rogers 1994; Nien-Hsuan and Sun 1999). Within Latin America, the development of a popular 'telenovela' entertainment format, which has been imported by Europe, provides an example of cultural pluralism and contraflow, although this interpretation of what Anthony Giddens has called 'reverse colonization' is questioned by some scholars (Meers 1998; Giddens 1999).[2] Attempts to universalize from the American and British experience should be resisted, because other countries assimilate cultural influences in complex ways, so there may well be some evidence of positive cultural globalization. However, this revisionist perspective is criticized by James Curran for its reluctance to engage critically with economic power and its political consequences, which has also involved a shift of power from national electorates and organized labour to global capital (Curran 2002: 174). He points out that cultural globalization theory, which arose from the late 1960s onwards as a challenge to modernization theory, seeks to present an optimistic picture that everything is for the best, with globalization as a means of correcting the earlier pessimistic 'dogmas' of cultural imperialism.

As cultural globalization supporters point out, there is evidence that the process is encouraging subnational identities and movements, such as Basque nationalism, as part of a decline in the importance of the national. The global seems to promote the local at the expense of the national. However, the flow generated by cultural globalization is not equal because it is structured by the dynamics of media ownership, particularly in film, news wholesaling and computer operating systems.

Home video, satellite and cable

Satellite-delivered cable channels first became a reality in the 1970s, when there was also limited experimentation with interactive television. Cable television introduced a multichannel, narrow casting capability to broadcast television. Some people hoped that cable would mean a more progressive future for television with greater access, while others were more concerned with the business potential.

One study has addressed public reaction to cable television over a five-year period, noting a change from initial naïve enthusiasm to disappointment, then on to modified appreciation. Researchers have also tracked the effect of cable on broadcast television, noting that, while the power of the cable industry in programming and advertising increased, this was having a negative impact on broadcast television, although the latter remained competitive.

US cable growth accompanied by deregulation disputes

In the United States, cable licences were issued at local authority level, but deregulation of cable systems by a decade-long string of federal actions challenged municipal monopoly as an abuse of the First Amendment. While the idea was to create greater programme diversity, the business effect of the growth of chains in America between 1977 and 1989 (which also happened with newspapers and movie-theatre operators) provided owners with an economic base that increased their bargaining power with product suppliers.

Satellite transmission also provoked new competition among the providers of videos and debate on the usage of this new medium, its effects and potential market. In Third World countries the home video cassette recorder had become particularly popular: as early as 1985, a study revealed that this was the case even among lower socio-economic groups in Asia, the Middle East and Africa. The phenomenon led to calls for a policy initiative, particularly by the nations of Africa, to promote their own cultures through the use of video systems (Shija 1988; Boyd and Straubhaar 1985).

When international satellite television broadcasting took off, various countries expressed concern about national sovereignty, but dishes and cable systems flourished despite their attempts to control reception. The new technology acted as a catalyst for both expectations and fears, often exaggerated, about Western versus national interests. Research into the potential of integrating regional markets via satellite broadcasting across borders has found that service providers in Asia, for instance, have to take into account linguistic and cultural differences when establishing their markets. If such factors were powerful enough to make or break either world or regional markets, this demonstrated the effectiveness of resistance and appeared to challenge the rhetoric of 'cultural imperialism'. Revisionist scholarship has also examined the political strategies employed by US policy-makers to establish an 'imagined community' using satellite technology and television programming. More recently research interest has widened to address the challenge of piracy of programmes and feature films by satellite, although the topic lacks the glitter of the original swashbucklers in the days of the British empire (Boyd 1988; Ferguson 2003; Curtin 1993; Sinclair 1997).

Within the satellite world, one empire stands out: that of the digital operator Rupert Murdoch, with his News Corporation and channels such as Sky. His fiefdom was built from a single newspaper in Adelaide, South Australia. He proved masterful at cross-promotion of its various properties, at influencing politicians and at propagating the sort of tabloid values displayed on Fox Television in the United States. The global expansion of News Corporation has spread across Japan, India, China and Latin America and into continental Europe. According to Sumner Redstone, the CEO of Viacom, Murdoch 'basically wants to conquer the world' (Bagdikian 1997). Although News Corporation was late in using music for expansion, the approach changed once the DVD revolution started.

Cable TV may not have been destined to replace the broadcast industries, but a new phase of development emerged for the television medium when the broadband environment arrived. The Internet and the broadband infrastructure offered the consumer enhanced functions such as interactivity and personalization via cable TV. Business experts now discussed new concepts such as the 'value chain' and 'complementary convergence'. Yet, despite the apparent simplicity of the concept of convergence, because of the importance of preserving the unique characteristics of each product, suppliers continued to offer telecommunications and video programming products under two separate interfacing devices with different distribution infrastructures (Chan-Olmsted and Kang 2003; Waterman 1991; Dimmick et al. 1992; Wirth 1990; Sparkes and Kang 1986).

Globalizing influences in news, television, and press reaction

Multinationals tended to expand using both vertical and horizontal integration, so a film, for instance, was expected to spawn a soundtrack, a book and merchandising such as dolls and toys, with the potential also for CD-ROMs, video games, amusement-park rides and even a spin-off television show. Obviously certain genres of content such as action movies, light entertainment and sport lend themselves more easily to such exploitation. Conversely journalism and public affairs are less attractive, unless they serve business interests. As one journalist observed, 'We have experienced an expansion of technology but the agenda of the media has shrunk' (Pilger 2001).

The conglomerate Time Warner became a major force in virtually every medium and on every continent when in 1989 it was formed through the merger of Time Inc. and Warner Communications. Although in 1992 the corporation split off its entertainment group, selling 25 per cent to US West and 5.6 per cent to each of the Japanese corporations Itochu and Toshiba, in 1996 it regained from Disney its position as the world's largest media firm with the acquisition of Turner Broadcasting. Challenges to national cultural practice seemed to emanate almost automatically from the nature of multinational operation.

In 1995, for example, the Canadian government tried to assert the primacy of home-produced content in major magazines. Foreign investment guidelines required a 'net benefit to Canada' test by specifying the production of a majority of national content. When Time Warner's magazine *Sports Illustrated* announced its intention to publish a 'split-run' edition by inserting Canadian advertisements into editorial matter from its US edition, the Canadian government imposed an 80 per cent tax on advertising value, with the result that the US government called in the WTO. The WTO found not only that the measures were inconsistent with GATT, but also that the magazine's split-run edition in Canada was 'directly competitive and substitutable' for the Canadian news magazine *Maclean's*, although the content of the two magazines was completely distinct. In other words, one nation's cultural output was deemed to be substitutable for another.

Time Warner's strategy in television was to merge the former Turner global channel CNN with their HBO International (the leading subscription TV channel in the world) and new Warner channels in order to make a frontal assault on the global market. The focus on global television as the most lucrative area of growth, using programme production and channels, contrasted with News Corporation's development of entire satellite systems. CNN became the premier global television news channel, beamed via ten satellites to over 200 nations and 100 million subscribers. In 1997 a Spanish-language service was launched for Latin America, based in Atlanta. Faced with a challenge from News Corporation and NBC-Microsoft, CNN International nevertheless announced that its long-term goal was to operate or participate in joint ventures to establish CNN channels in French, Japanese, Hindi, Arabic and perhaps one or two regional languages. The news division provided just 20 per cent of Time Warner's revenue; music contributed another 20 per cent, with nearly 60 per cent of the Warner Music Group revenues coming from outside the United States. Similarly, the corporation could count about 1000 cinema screens abroad and boasted the second largest book publishing empire in the world, in addition to theme parks, retail stores, comics and extensive film, video and television holdings.

The nature of news in an international environment continues to fascinate scholars. Despite the trend towards greater homogeneity as media influence continues to grow, a comparative study of the CCTV network in China and ABC in the United States concluded that it is a nation's social structure that influences the selection and presentation of news the most: each network's choice of topics and presentation style was influenced more by this than by circumstances of the events themselves, supporting the 'social construction of reality' perspective (Chang et al. 1998). Furthermore, TV news clearly influences the public agenda for issues: a prime example of this was in Germany in 1986, when coverage of the Chernobyl nuclear accident affected public concern about the energy supply. For some time scholarship has suggested that, in the case of coverage of terrorism and of missing children, the style of television treatment actually becomes part of the social policy process (Fan et al. 1994; Altheide 1991). This was the case with 11 September 2001 for civil rights policy as well.

During the 1980s the main news agencies (AP, UPI, AFP, Reuters and TASS) were obliged for financial reasons to diversify their information services, and some were forced to seek government support to survive. They faced competition not just because of deregulation but also due to the television multichannel news arena. The result in terms of the quality of news was a mixed bag. Although local media continue to provide an important role for audiences in terms of the sense of identity, time and place that they provide, the role of multinational wire services as facilitators of such processes is debatable. Within the United States it seemed that local sources tended to air more unique stories and that individual initiative mattered: for example, editors who included ethnic minorities within their list of news sources were more likely to cover stories about ethnic minorities (Alleyn and Wagner 1993; Davie and Jung-Sook 1993; Hiundman et al. 1999; Cho and Lacy 2000).

In Japan, the involvement of news agencies appeared more positive: researchers found that the extent to which local daily newspapers offered international news coverage was connected not to circulation issues, but rather to whether or not the papers subscribed to wire services: those who did favoured international copy. Yet, globally, that international copy contained inequalities in attitude: one study examined how AP, Reuters and Inter Press Service covered six major United Nations summit meetings, half hosted by Western countries and half by the developing world. The Western hosts received overtly more positive coverage. Countries that are central to the world system are more likely to be in the news than peripheral or 'semi-peripheral' countries, who have to jump the hurdle of many filters before becoming news (Giffard and Riverburgh 2000; Chang 1998).

At first it was thought that 24-hour global news could be transmitted from a central point and occasionally be augmented by local bolt-ons, but the interest that audiences clearly have in what affects them most closely, and reflects values that they understand, has added to the complexity of news. The bulk of news worldwide is still communicated by local and national organizations, and these outlets tend to promote the national and local agenda, which retards the development of global politics. Although the international news agencies are dominant suppliers, coverage is often selected for its national or local relevance, or else it is given such an angle in presentation.

In 2001, a survey found that 75 per cent of news broadcast by America's CBS network dealt with events within the United States; earlier surveys have revealed a similar pattern in Britain (Curran 2002: 180). It is argued that one reason for the apparent neglect of international affairs is the trend towards 'dumbing down' and the move towards entertainment at the expense of serious public affairs that deregulation, competitive market forces and concentration of ownership have accelerated. A comparative study of news in Britain, Germany and the United States demonstrated that journalistic values, media cultures and economic and legal conditions were responsible for the degree of 'tabloidization' in a given country (Esser 1999). In Britain, for instance, the tabloid press became more intrusive, more shrill and frequently more unethical in approach. Critics believed that the popular press was losing its sense of essential function and becoming too obsessed with the cult of celebrity. At the same time, the more recent dominance of the 'war against terror' as the driving force of the George W. Bush presidency clearly demonstrated the need for public under-standing and discourse on Islam and related economic, political and religious factors in world affairs.

Sins of distortion and prejudice were not confined to tabloids, or to any one country. At the same time, the printed word also showed potential for redemption. In the local versus global debate, regional and alternative newspapers were seen by some as the last hope for public-sphere communication. Newspapers were obliged to develop flexible and creative ways to survive under the weight of market forces, the rise of the Internet, multichannel television and an increase in the choice of radio stations. In Canada in the 1990s, for example, street newspapers emerged as a growing form of communicative democracy (Howley 2003). The worldwide rise of free daily newspapers, first introduced in Sweden in 1995, represented another fresh departure. By 2002, eighty free daily newspapers had been established in twenty-six countries, although only sixty of them survived the year. An efficient cost structure and an appeal to a new and younger readership seem to be the key to success, although some existing local and national newspaper firms launched 'freebies' mainly to prevent other companies from entering the market. In other cases, entrepreneurs launched into the new grow-ing market (Bakker 2002).

Another press strategy has been the online edition. Although the nature of this business is still evolving, early studies seem to indicate that electronic editions have not revolutionized usage. For instance, the potential for a newspaper to reach long distances is still outweighed by local usage, although, as newspapers transformed themselves into 24-hour news machines, electronic newspaper readers began to use the medium in new ways, following Roger Silverstone's theory (1994) that non-professional users of the Internet 'domesticate' it to fit into the relevant activities and structures of their own lives (Tumber 2001).

The direct access provided by the medium and the lack of editorial filter means that the traditional journalistic role of providing informa-tion and interpretation for the citizen as a normative function of the profession became threatened. Journalists evolved into 'information architects' because the arrival of online journalism offered greater fluidity, challenging the primacy of news as well as the sort of skills required for the profession. In the process the press appeared to be losing authority and credibility, but whether this was due to news-papers' own inadequacies or to the rapidly changing media scene was open to debate.

Technology, convergence and the Internet

Gradually sector-specific definitions – for instance, between audiovisual and e-commerce industries – which historically had guided understanding of mass communication, became eroded by technology and cross-media ownership. This process is referred to as 'convergence', now a somewhat ubiquitous and overused word. As distribution channels expanded, audio-visual markets became more like telecommunications markets, exemplified by multimedia technology involving the provision of several hundred voice, data and video channels via an interactive coaxial cable system. As with previous new developments, changes provoked a reaction from the existing players. Although the participation of telephone companies, for instance, in home video distribution was economically and technologically motivated, it produced a rethink on media channels and their content. However, history has regularly demonstrated that the speed of take-off for new technologies is always contingent on consumer response. Initial sales estimates for DVD and its impact on the home video market in the late 1990s, for instance, were overoptimistic, although by 2002 32 per cent of the British population, for example, owned a DVD machine, and take-off since then has been rapid.

The DVD was only part of the technology representing the 'digital age': by the 1990s equipment changes were par for the course for most media industries, and, as with previous inventions, this one also brought greater speed, convenience and accessibility. Yet historians take a longer view, enabling them to debunk the hype attached to language. 'Revealing and useful as it may be to affix labels like "Digital Age" to past and present phenomena, at best they tell us more about perceptions than they do about facts. Their chief characteristic is complexity' (Briggs and Burke 2002: 320).

Complexity and speed of technological change during this period facilitated the emergence of 'technobabble' at a speed matched only by that of channel 'zapping' in the new multichannel environment. 'Television, video cassettes, video tape recorder/players, video games and personal computers . . . all form an encompassing electronic system whose various forms "interface" to constitute an alternative and absolute world that uniquely incorporates the spectator/user in a spatially de-centered, weakly temporalized and quasi-disembodied state' (Briggs and Burke 2002: 321). This summary acts as a salutary reminder that cyber-space is but a construct, reminiscent of Baudrillard's assessment of the effect that the media has had on reality. By the 1980s public exposure to the media was so phenomenal that the great French scholar was prompted to argue that the public were saturated by mediated images to the extent that the virtual became the 'real', producing 'hyper reality' (Baudrillard 1983). Nevertheless, cyberspace, like any other media space, has been subject to the vagaries of business, stock-market fluctuations and the boom or bust economics of e-commerce that loomed large by the turn of the twenty-first century.

The telecommunications and computer operators that are linked to the world of media giants certainly made a lot of progress in colonizing the Internet. Microsoft's Bill Gates became the world's richest man, while his empire expanded from its 80 per cent hold on the operating systems of personal computers into other areas such as photo libraries, with the acquisition of the world's most important historic collection, the Bettmann Archives. The presence of commercial advertising and sales on the Internet very soon came to dwarf all other content provision: 'concerted corporate efforts are turning the Internet into the most direct mass merchandising vehicle ever invented with much of the sales promotion directed at children' (Bagdikian 1997: xi). During this time Microsoft battled with politicians, legal authorities and competitor companies on the fundamental issue of monopoly introduced by the 'Windows' technological system. The global dimension clearly raised not just legal but also ethical issues, provoking a variety of suggestions on the regulation of the Internet and information and communication technologies industries in the brave new converged world.

The impact of the Internet on media history and consumption is still being assessed and is subject to a range of both utopian and dystopian interpretations. The literature that this debate has spawned is extensive, giving rise to 'cyberstudies' and other new areas of study (Castells 2001; Gauntlett 2000). For a while it seemed that the rise of the Internet might challenge the monopoly power of the global media giants: there has been much debate on whether the medium is reshaping communication behaviour, discourse, communities and people's perceptions. Within the public sphere, the Internet has enabled people on the far sides of the globe to communicate, and the anti-capitalist campaign has used this to its advantage, but there is also a danger of fragmentation of political discourse. In Canada, for example, the Internet has already had a considerable influence on policy development and on new legislation in areas such as child pornography, broadcasting and privacy (Bol 2002).

However, there are inequalities of access to information and of new media literacy that compromise the ability of this new public space to become truly representative. In general the Internet remains concentrated in the highly developed nations, although it is growing in all regions. The blind, the poor and people in continents such as Africa are still disadvantaged.

Despite the hopes of democracy and internationalization via the Internet, a survey of 4000 websites discovered that sites are more likely to be linked to other sites in the same country; when they do cross borders, they are more likely to lead to pages hosted in the United States than to pages anywhere else in the world. Similarly, as early as 1997 it was argued that in many respects cyberspace is an extension of the colonial logic and European expansionism of the past (Gunkel and Gunkel 1997; Halavais 2000). The dominant ethos 'is wanting to recognize and absorb those differences within the larger, overarching framework of what is essentially an American conception of the world.'

Despite the overwhelming influence of commercialism, online publishing fundamentally changed the nature of information storage,

The challenge of the Zapatistas

The most studied example of Internet usage in the public sphere is that of the Zapatistas. The movement has attracted interest from many political activists, journalists and scholars because of its challenge to corporate power and the forces of globalization – a case study that defies the dominant rhetoric and economic ideologies of consumerism and capitalism that tend to dominate the web.

Chiapas Indians are not the most predictable of users. As Castells has pointed out, their use of the Internet influenced the Mexican government to take the movement seriously through negotiation, transforming their protest from militarily weak insurgency into the 'first informational guerrilla movement' with international backing (Castells 1997: 79).

Fig. 14 Zapatista group saluting: their use of the Internet represents a new form of popular protest

retrieval and dissemination, offering the possibility of a more dynamic relationship between publisher and reader and a blurring of the traditional distinction between them. Interestingly, one of the early pioneers, Vannevar Bush, first had such a vision in the year that the Second World War ended: 'Consider a future device for individual use, which is a sort of mechanized private file and library. It . . . is a device in which an individual stores all his books, records, and communications, and which is mechanized so that it may be consulted with exceeding speed and flexibility. It is an enlarged intimate supplement to his memory' (Bush 1945).

A former editor of Britain's *Sunday Times*, Harold Evans, explained how the 1970s pre-digital campaigning journalism of his newspaper on issues such as the Thalidomide drug compensation story would have been different if the Internet had existed as a tool: 'If we'd had the web back then and could flash forward to a time when most of the population have computers, we could go on the web and say, "Anyone who took the drug Thalidomide between these dates, please get in touch with us". Or instead we'd have an interactive chat line . . . we could [also] have saved a lot of time by researching the scientific data electronically' (Ward 2002: 20).

Music industry convergence

By the 1990s the entertainment business was dominated by huge multinational, multimedia communications empires of which the big-name record companies such as CBS, RCA and EMI were now part – an intensification of a process that started much earlier and which was explored in previous chapters. Bouts of concentration, when they were able to control the market more effectively, tended to be followed by phases of competition from small, specialist new entrants in an uneasy coexistence that amounted to a form of unequal dual economy (Peterson and Berger 1975).

The pace of change that had gained momentum with radio's reaction to the arrival of television, then by the advent of the cassette player, was now accelerated once more by the rise in popularity of the CD, which brought to an end the forty-year reign of the 12 inch vinyl LP (although it has risen from the dead with the rise in popularity once again of the DJ, using mixing and electronic sampling). In the late 1980s a new wave of independents also opened up to cater for a range of specialist tastes within classical music on CD.

The way that music has become available to the public is ever changing. Just as, in the 1970s and 1980s, video enabled experimental and political usage by community groups and individuals, so more recently the techniques of reproduction have amplified the attack on old interests. This has enabled a parallel process with its own creativity to develop as the means of circulating music beyond the control of the major industry players. The market encouraged consumption and favoured improved technology as innovation, but, as the costs of innovation increased, so the trend emerged for the creators of hardware rather than software, such as Sony, to take the lead. This led to casualties en route.

In 1980 Decca, after a decline in the 1970s, was sold off to Polygram, a joint subsidiary of Siemens and Philips (Chanan 1995: 153). During that decade, mergers signalled further concentration of ownership, fuelling criticism of cultural homogeneity. First RCA was bought up by Bertelsmann and CBS by Sony; then Warner merged with Time and MCA (including Universal Studios) went to Matsushita for $6.9 billion. This meant that three of America's four majors were owned by other countries. In 1989 the Sony purchase of CBS was consolidated by its acquisition of Columbia Pictures and Tristar Pictures for $3.4 billion (Thompson 1995: 168). The corporations themselves were subject to change: a study of Sony defined its business values as decidedly Japanese in origin, but as transnational in scope; as operations increased, so too did the challenge of complex change within the corporation (Gershon and Kanayama 2002).

Video also brought a new branch of creative production: music videos, with their own channels on television. In Canada, where cultural policy strategy was orientated towards improving the marketing and distribution of indigenous Canadian cultural products, it was decided that the country needed a national music video broadcaster. In Europe, too, state and community interests supported musical activity, but there was often a tension between the transnational practices of the major record companies and local interests. Indeed, the cultural imperialism debate has even included the effects of global corporate influences such as popular music on local culture.

In 2000, CD sales fell by 36 per cent, illustrating the apparent decline in physical music sales – that is, CDs, cassettes and vinyl – due to the availability of free online music systems such as Napster. This opened the floodgates for greater access to music, symbolizing an increasingly different role for the record companies. Their primary interest is no longer in making music; rather they are now concerned with the creation of rights, secured via complex multimedia packaging: 'servicing programme-greedy satellite and cable companies, providing Hollywood soundtracks, seeking sponsorship deals, coming to terms with advertising agencies' (Frith 1987b). The stakes are high: with a global market volume exceeding $40 billion, music is a prime mover among entertainment products.

By 2001, an estimated 30 million American adults – 29 per cent of all adults – had downloaded music files over the Internet, while 53 per cent of young Americans had done the same. The future of music as a product among the young people's market appeared to be under threat of survival (Kretscher et al. 2001). Litigation has traditionally involved national music copyright societies which act as collection services for payment to rights holders, but the rise of the global media corporation, combined with new digital production and distribution technologies, challenges the principles under which copyright collection operates. If the present structure of music copyright continues to collapse, big corporate players and global music products will be the beneficiaries.

Deregulation and public-service broadcasting

A public-service orientation has always had to struggle in the face of commercial competition. In this period the threat not only increased in scale, but was worsened because the state's regulatory responsibility had been reduced in most countries. Undeniably a tension arose between different types of policy objectives in this climate: on the one hand there are social, political and cultural considerations; on the other hand economic constraints have dominated.

The introduction of further commercial television in West European countries during the 1980s heralded an enormous increase in the number of channels and also provoked a passionate debate about the consequences of ending the monopoly of public broadcasting. The increasing importance of technology and markets now had to be balanced against historical obligations to provide a universal non-profit service that contributed to a democratic and pluralistic society by supporting national culture and language with high journalistic and programming standards.

Although by 2002 the European Commission had estimated that there were some 1500 channels available within their geographic area (Betzel and Ward 2003: 16), public-service audiovisual policies were still seen as important tools for building political pluralism and cultural diversity. Institutionally, this role was supported by national legislative regulatory frameworks providing content obligations to ensure that diversity and a range of different interests in society were catered for and that public policy objectives were met. Varying regulatory models reflected national traditions and the integration of television into social, political and economic structures within the confines of the nation-state. In the case of the United Kingdom and Germany, self-regulation was intro-duced, although, as chapter 7 indicates, in Germany the remit of public-service broadcasting derived from Article 5 of the German constitution as interpreted by the German Federal Constitutional Court, rather than from broadcasting legislation as elsewhere.

Structures form an important part of the comparative political eco-nomy approach to analysis of public-service broadcasting, but their importance should not be exaggerated. The same structure can gener-ate different outputs at different times, just as very similar structures can be associated with very different outputs. As Asa Briggs points out, there are both conscious and unconscious broadcasting policies, so that not all of media history is reflected in legislation (Ito 1978: vii, viii). In Germany, for instance, the change from a public monopoly to a dual broadcasting system began before the move towards unification of West and East, accelerated by the collapse of the Berlin Wall in 1989.

Supporters of the 'liberal' market maintained that deregulation would bring greater diversity of content and audience. At the same time, the prevailing ethos of professional independence for broadcasters was increasingly challenged by ideas of financial managerialism. The effi-cient pursuit of the profit motive seemed to necessitate a widening of consumer appeal that was often accompanied by banality. Opponents predicted 'dumbing down' and a decline in political awareness and participation in public citizenship, as well as a marginalization or disap-pearance of programming catering for minorities and less predictable artistic taste. Curran and Seaton articulate the practical results of the debate in terms of programming as it related to the United Kingdom:

> If financial pressures were the only influence, the programme-makers' aim would always be simply to reach the largest possible audience for the smallest amount of money. In practice this would have meant a diet of American soap opera, variety shows, filmed series, quizzes, and chat shows, based on proven formulae, endlessly repeated. . . . Current affairs would have been confined to news

NHK as a success story

By the early 1990s Japan's public broadcaster NHK provided more television news than any other (non-all-news) organization in the world – nearly half of its general channel air-time, dominating the domestic commercial competition in this area. The proportion of news and information increased from a third of its programming in the early 1980s. Confidence in NHK was at an all-time high at the end of the 1990s, with people trusting it twice as much as the government and also more than the courts, newspapers and commercial broadcasting. Although the number of people employed by the organization fell from 16,000 to 13,000 between the mid-1980s and the late 1990s, it is still one of the two largest broadcasting agencies (along with the BBC), and in 1996, 35 million Japanese households had contracts with NHK to pay receivers' fees (Krauss 2000: 3).

bulletins, and advertising spots would have been longer, more frequent and more intrusive. . . . commercial broadcasting did not develop all these features in Britain, because of the framework of public regulations within which it was obliged to operate. (Curran and Seaton 1997: 182)

Elsewhere the issues were similar: a study of data from EU member states to assess the relationship between preference for either commercial or public television and political knowledge found that in most countries preference for public TV is accompanied by greater knowledge of EU political matters (Holtz-Bacha and Norris 2001).

Despite the increasing competition between channels, public broadcasters were still subject to political pressure to maintain audience share. Although a 100 per cent licence fee existed in only a few countries, such as Britain and Japan, funding still became an issue. In countries that adopted a mixed formula there were marked differences in the balance between public and commercial sources of revenue. Where there was no licence fee or positive direct state funding, such as in Portugal and Spain, the public-service model was much weaker, becoming dependent on the state or the market, or on both, as 'state commercial broadcasters'. Conversely, the BBC and Germany's ZDF and ARD are still seen as the strongest public-service broadcasters in Europe, and these organizations also enjoy the greatest level of funding.

In addition, Britain's Channel 4 was often cited as an effective model that combined commercial funding with a public-service ethic. Similarly, the example of ARTE, the Franco-German cultural television channel (established originally as 'La Sept' in the 1980s), demonstrated that deregulation does not have to equate to bland commercialism (Emanuel 1993). In 1982, when Channel 4 was launched, it was given a public-service remit for content – in particular, a mission to cater for minorities who were perceived as being underrepresented and underserviced up to that point. Its production was – and still is – carried out mainly out of house with a publishing commission model, from which independent production companies in the private sector benefited. ITV companies each contributed financially, but the channel used advertising. Critical and innovative programming emerged, frequently from independent producers, in a move to foster cultural diversity.

This has worked at national level by the creation of a regulated space beyond the state for cultivating pluralism, but by the end of this period the need for transnational institutional space was becoming clear, one which extended beyond the domestic policies of individual states (Thompson 1995: 242). UNESCO had tried this in the 1970s and early 1980s with NWICO (New World Information and Communication Order) in order to help less developed countries in the field of communication. The United States withdrew in 1984, followed by the United Kingdom in 1985, depriving the initiative of 30 per cent of its budget and limiting the effectiveness of policy recommendations, but the debate had been launched (ibid.: 156–7).

Broadcasting policy in France exemplifies, on the one hand, the dichotomy between the forces of commercialization and centralization and, on the other, cultural protection with quotas which are used to compensate for the results of this process (Machill 1996). The intention was to establish general requirements to broadcast programmes aimed at culture, education or science. Elsewhere systems of cultural protection, which varied from country to country, did not necessarily involve quotas. The Netherlands, for instance, was unique in setting a maximum limit for entertainment of no more than 25 per cent on public channels. At EU level, the Television without Frontiers Directive established a European works and independent production quota.

The response of public-service broadcasters to the questioning of their role has been to take on a broader range of commercial and expansionary approaches, but such strategies, in Germany and Britain, for example, have led to conflict with policy-makers and commercial players who wanted a more restricted role for publicly funded provision. Hence problems in defining the remit of public-service broadcasting have been accompanied by difficulties in procuring adequate sources of finance (Steemers 2001). The dilemmas were highlighted by the need to respond to a digital future, and by the 1990s there was a huge growth in the number of channels and new platforms for delivery. Although the development of services exploiting new technology was seen as a legitimate function for the public sector, these broadcasters were slow to assume a leading role, with the result that the multichannel environment was usually driven by commercial operators.

However, the advent of digital terrestrial TV allowed the public services in Europe to champion a technological development that promised to free up the previously limited analogue spectrum. Therefore some public broadcasters started to move into this area, sometimes in strategic partnerships with governments, regulators and, occasionally, commercial broadcasters. German, British and Italian public broadcasters offered the widest range of additional digital services, and the

BBC launched a range of niche channels for children, the arts, youth and news, although audiences were initially small. In Spain the platform collapsed when the leading operator suffered huge losses, and in the UK the original operator withdrew, to be replaced by a partnership that included the BBC. Public-service niche digital channels were generally limited and of a modest scale, with the exception of those provided by the BBC, whose budget extended to €395 million out of an overall total of €3.55 billion (Betzel and Ward 2003: 22). Such activities are still subject to restrictions on advertising and cross-promotion, although there are no legal provisions governing Internet activity by the public sector in most countries.

In Europe the fortunes of public-sector television have become multi-layered on account of the European Union's interest in securing fair trade and competition, faced with assertive pressure from the corporate sector for liberalization of regulatory regimes. Such pressures have posed the greatest threat to public-service broadcasting. Within the EU, the protocol on public-service broadcasting annexed to the Amsterdam Treaty (Treaty of European Union, 1997) acknowledged the right of member states to support it. The Commission of the European Communities set out a framework for state funding of public broadcasters within the competition rules of the EU with a communication in 2001, requiring accountability and monitoring in order to ensure compliance.

In essence, the roots of the democratic accountability of this regulatory culture, which have their origins in radio and were inherited by television, were still strong despite neo-liberal deregulation and funding problems that were exacerbated by the need to consider other platforms for delivery. Yet it had become clear that public-service broadcasting could not operate in isolation. On every continent competition existed between public and commercial – in Asia, for instance, between CNN and BBC World (Shrihande 2001). Nevertheless, public-service broadcasting demonstrated an instinct for survival by remaining part of the new environment, despite regular forecasts of its imminent demise. One study, analysing the performance of public-service broadcasters in the EU using market shares, found that they had been more resilient than expected and generally maintained their market position (Picard 2002). Another study of American public television found that the popularity of comparable cable networks did not dilute the brand perception of public television and the audience's viewing behaviour (Chan-Olmsted and Yungwook 2002).

In a global age characterized by ever increasing homogeneity, public-service broadcasting as a reflection of national culture and diversity has been a remarkable survivor. However, many analysts believe that its survival in the future will increasingly mean cooperation, and protection, at transnational level as trade and media become more global. European television and film, for instance, were both perceived to be in crisis in 1992: this was not a new feeling, but its intensity, backed by empirical evidence, was greater (European Institute for the Media 1993).

The relationship between deregulation and endangered species of programming

In the United States, the Federal Communications Commission spent much of the 1980s and 1990s abandoning what are called 'behavioural controls' in radio, that is, definitions of acceptable content in terms of public-service elements. These included requirements on stations to offer 'community service' items, controls on the amount of air-time permitted for advertising, and obligations to deal with controversial issues in a fair and balanced way. The Telecommunications Act of 1996 permitted market-driven growth among group owners by changing station ownership restrictions. The subsequent increased concentration did not lead to more listener choice, but did influence higher advertising rates (Fairchild 1999; Drushel 1998). A study of radio news in 1995 found that newscasts were not serving the public interest by offering political voices to the audience and were not providing relevant information for listeners to evaluate the government (Wasburn 1995).

Radio

Deregulation has not been confined to Western Europe, or simply to the television industry. Radio has been subject to deregulation world-wide, yet it continues to be a vital broadcast medium. In Germany there was a dramatic increase in the number of radio stations following reunification, and more recently web radio has become popular. In Britain large numbers of regular listeners to the BBC's up-market talk channel, Radio 4, protested over proposed changes to the schedules, demonstrating the importance of the station's broadcasting to daily life in the country (Levy 1993).

In Europe, three types of radio – national, independent and commu-nity – developed to meet the diverse needs of listeners. At the beginning of radio, there was a shortage of programmes, then once more with the introduction of digital radio the number of channels exceeded the amount of programming available to fill them. By the 1990s there was also more competition for existing audiences because of a fragmenta-tion of the previous mass audience, threatening the traditions of public-service broadcasting. Segmentation of audience and market was just one clear trend that accorded with the pattern of deregulation and corporate concentration mentioned above. Another, according to one study, was for a small number of industrial groupings to reflect the concentration of digital activity. These operators showed a propensity to exploit the potential of multimedia and interactivity in order to create new sources of revenue, again highlighting the tendency towards convergence (Hendy 2000: 52–3).

Advertising

One of the consequences of giving complete freedom to market forces has been the continuous growth of advertising. In addition, public-relations companies have expanded rapidly as new opportunities for persuasion and promotion have opened up (Miller and Dinan 2000). Simultaneously advertising was able to extend the approach, begun during the inter-war years, of manipulating the irrational. The result was an unprecedented ascendancy. Advertising culture continued to encroach upon public space through the relentless expansion of sponsorship into new areas such as opera and almost every branch of sport. 'Like it or not, commoditized cultural space has become so pervasive that it becomes impossible to continue thinking of any part of the cultural domain as a reserved and uncontaminated territory' (Chanan 1994: 283).

Meanwhile the ubiquitous television commercial became like a simulation of a communication that seemed more real than reality (Baudrillard 1983). This process has not happened without protest. Naomi Klein (2000) draws attention to the process whereby advertisers and the big corporations appropriated previously non-commercial causes and minority styles as part of an all-pervasive marketing ethos. A good example of this is the 'greening' of adverts to reflect public concern over environmental issues, which emerged as an important political factor during the late 1980s and early 1990s (Hansen 2002). The roots of this process, which every branch of the media is continuing to experience, date back to the nineteenth century. Only the intensity, reach and speed have increased. An endless cycle of consumption and reproduction for the mass-media industries is a postmodernist condition in which 'the echoing imitation, instead of dying away, gets louder' (Chanan 1995: 151).

Film

From the 1980s the economics of film that had been evident from the early days of Hollywood came more into focus. Films and programmes needed to cover their costs in the home market and then be sold on at a tenth of the price. For smaller countries the numbers didn't add up. By around 2003, production of filmed television costume drama, for example, could cost $2 million an hour, but an off-the-peg US programme could range from just $5000 to $100,000 an hour. Clearly the home market needed to be big enough for the original production costs to be covered. Indigenous media production was good for job creation: for every one job on a TV or film set, 1.7 jobs are supported in the local economy, but success was also gauged by effective distribution and exhibition.

The issues involved in media product purchase are not simply economic: a feature film tended to carry more cultural weight, more prestige and a longer shelf life than a TV programme, all reasons, for example, why EU countries collectively and separately developed special measures of support to ensure the survival of their indigenous film industries. These ranged from programmes supporting all facets of film development, production and exhibition to national film funds, and in France a tax on cinema tickets that was ploughed back into further film production. Indeed, as early as 1982, a French government report argued: 'The lesson of these last 20 years in Europe is clear: there can be no national cinema without a policy of aid to the national cinema. This is true for France, Italy, Germany. . . . The example of Great Britain [which made the opposite choice] is very instructive in this respect: a film industry survives, but British cinema has practically disappeared' (Hill and Gibson 2000).

British cinema has revived somewhat, but is dependent on American distribution and financing for survival (Wickham 2003), while French companies during the 1990s continued to produce some 100 to 120 films a year in a sector with about 70,000 employees, many of them new to the industry. In the 1980s audiences declined, but in the following decade they increased again (Nowell-Smith and Ricci 1998: 57).

Although cinema retained its creative energy, even in France it still became increasingly difficult to get audiences into cinemas for domestically made films. With the possible exception of the Polish-French films of Kieslowski in the early 1990s, no predominant figures have emerged to define the recent era in the way that Godard and Truffaut did in the 1960s (Sklar 2002: 507). In contrast, film studies over the last twenty years or more have shown fascination for the creativity of four Japanese directors, Ozu, Kurosawa, Mizogushi and Oshima, and with the 'postmodern' nature of popular culture. A number of Japanese corporations have taken over Hollywood studios, but their power has not been used as a window for Japanese national culture.

French philosophy has always remained constant: films as 'Creations of the spirit are not just commodities', as President Mitterrand said in 1993, defining his country's position in a battle with GATT (General Agreement on Tariffs and Trade) when the latter sought to remove tariffs on cultural products, thereby challenging a range of measures for special cultural protection in different European countries and via the EU. By 2003, it was estimated that, if WTO rules were applied to film, affecting screen quotas such as those in Korea, or the various EU support systems, then the USA would dominate the world market in a monopolistic sense in five years. Already, US film made up 80 per cent of all television film. In the UK, 85 per cent of all films shown in cinemas were American, and elsewhere in Europe box office was 80 per cent American, while Europe accounted for less than 1 per cent of American box office (Puttnam 1997: 7; Tongue 2003: 7). Some 40 per cent of American TV and film income was earned overseas, with more than half coming from Europe. One writer concluded in 1998 that the main task for Europe was to organize its distribution (Nowell-Smith and Ricci 1998: 60). As Puttnam comments, the position of the two sides has changed very little over 100 years: 'the struggles over GATT were part of a long-running war of attrition over the very concept of culture' (1997: 8).

Organized opposition began to emerge within the international film community. In July 2002, the International Forum of Directors' Organizations in Montreal reaffirmed the fundamental principles of a cultural ecology based on the need for diversity and asserted the right of all individuals and all peoples to choose their own modes of expression. 'Coalitions for Cultural Diversity across the Globe' produced a declaration in Paris in 2003 calling for a treaty to be established that would provide a legal foundation for the fundamental right of states and governments freely to establish their own cultural policies (Tongue 2003: 9). The campaign for special treatment of creative products as a means of national and local self-expression continues. As the British film-maker John McGrath once said: 'If we imported 90% of our rice from another culture we would not be overly concerned, but to import that level of audiovisual culture would be of the gravest concern' (Tongue 2003: 9).

Conclusions

Within the media globalization debate the emphasis in this study has been on the way that economic globalization changed the world during the decisive epochs of the nineteenth and the early twentieth centuries. More recently this has led to media saturation, which has been accompanied by forms of hegemony derived from extensive cross-platform ownership. Analysis of this process within scholarship has focused around theories of cultural imperialism and, more recently, cultural globalization. The problem with both of these perspectives is that they underestimate continuity because of their emphasis on the profound changes that globalization has effected.

For that reason, this study has broken down the process historically into three stages: origins, 'take-off' and intensification. This chapter analysed the last of the three. In the stages dealt with previously, there has been no uniformity across national boundaries or media sectors, although there has been a common thread of continuity in some sectors dating back to nineteenth-century origins.

Throughout the ages, people have always clamoured for information from faraway places: in the early days of Australian settlement crowds in Perth would await the arrival of the ship from London carrying *The Times*, just as crowds waited in New York for the ship carrying the latest Dickens instalment. But modern forms of communication have added a new dimension of 'interconnectedness and indeterminacy' as well as a greater sense of responsibility for distant people and events (Thompson 1995: 118). New tools for communication over the last 150 years have permitted easier and greater international links. But did the telegraph, telephone, telex, cable, satellite and Internet help bridge the gaps in global inequality, as 'modernization' theorists argue, or did they enhance the control and exploitation of Western powers, as cultural imperialists maintain?

The two interpretations are not mutually exclusive. There are instances of both processes taking place, sometimes simultaneously, sometimes separately, and with differing examples. The two largest media firms in the world, Time Warner and Disney, now generate around one-third of their income outside the United States, and what sells abroad influences what is consumed at home, which may lead to more hybridized forms of culture (McQuail 1994). But is this two-way flow an equal one? Or are the alternative world influences on the conglomerates more akin to tributaries that lead to and from a main river? This can only be answered by examining the power of the dominant media owners and historical analogies of nineteenth-century media monopoly and imperialism – so the argument then comes back full circle to a political economy approach.

The comparative approach between epochs as well as countries and media branches raises many questions. For instance, what differentiates Reuters as an instrument of nineteenth-century British imperialism and the pre-First World War Wolff–Havas–Reuter news agency cartel from today's global cartel of conglomerates? There are three new features.

Firstly, there is more extensive cross-ownership, both within media industries, which are now wider and more extensive, and with other trading areas. Reuter's other business was financial information, not construction, garages, electricity or consumer retail. Herein lies a major difference between past and present: for the first time in media history, news is produced by companies outside of journalism, which throws up the possibility that independent news could be replaced by self-interested commercialism posing as news (Kovach and Rosenstiel 2003: 13).

Secondly, faster, easier and more instant geographic reach exists today – satellite and the Internet ensure this – although nineteenth-century journalists were pretty enterprising in their intrepid efforts to bring news speedily to the remoter parts of the globe, often facing danger in the process. The *Gold Coast Independent* concentrated on news brought to it from all over West Africa by canoe or by hazardous jungle journeys.

Thirdly, the scale is now different: access to consumers has been enhanced to the point of saturation and to the extent that the degree of media exposure has the effect of obscuring reality. In 1856 W. H. Russell, war correspondent of *The Times*, travelled through the Crimea on horseback, writing his dispatches alone, by hand and by candlelight. He had few competitors. In 2003 the Pentagon opened the battlefields in Iraq to about 600 US and 100 British and other international journalists and embedded them with military units for the duration of this most recent Gulf War. Russell's lone pen caused the downfall of a British prime minister and rocked the empire, while also raising issues of journalistic dilemma and independence. In 2003 the depth of access granted to correspondents, the routine use of videophone and satellite technology, and the resulting speed of contact and exposure of operations were all unprecedented (Toledano 2003). But the same problems of ethics emerged, and it could be argued that Russell's influence on politics was more instant.

Such differences of scale, speed and reach, in addition to changing patterns of business ownership, do not happen overnight and their development is never an even one; nor is it necessarily a fair one when linked inextricably to the advance and survival of modern capitalism. The starting point for modernity can be clearly linked to the victory of the liberal system of economic organization, which began with the first industrial revolution in Britain, was supported by the ideologies of the Franco-American political revolutions, and was underpinned theoretically by nineteenth-century British political economy and utilitarian philosophy (Hobsbawm 1994a: 9). The first was important because it established the production capacity and system for economic penetration globally; the second was significant because it inspired the leading institutions for bourgeois society.

How do the media slot into this development? Existing structures of authority have sometimes been challenged by the growth of modern communications as the latter have created new centres of power themselves – such as the corporate influence of the media multinational. Sometimes the media have offered channels for communication that bypass existing institutions, but on other occasions technological proximity has meant that new forms of information and expression have been assimilated into the system. The institutionalization of broadcasting illustrates this point, and the Internet looks set to follow as the technologies that use it adapt themselves to the current political culture rather than creating a new one.

In the meantime, the nature of the power has also changed. In 1995 the editor of *Vanity Fair* summed it up: 'The power center of America . . . has moved from its role as military-industrial giant to a new supremacy as the world's entertainment-information superpower.' The present trajectory of almost unrestricted international capital has provoked a strong reaction:

> In the last five years, a small number of the country's largest industrial corporations has acquired more public communications power – including ownership of the news – than any private businesses have ever before possessed in world history. Nothing in earlier history matches this corporate group's power to penetrate the social landscape. Using both old and new technology, by owning each other's shares, engaging in joint ventures as partners, and other forms of cooperation, this handful of giants has created what is, in effect, a new communications cartel within the United States. (Bagdikian 1997: x)

The global media cartel appears to be evolving into a global communications cartel, and sadly this process has taken place with very little public debate within the United States.

The never-ending story of unequal global economics continues to run. Although Time Warner experienced a catastrophic loss in 2002 from a write-down of its AOL online arm, net profits were up again by 2003/4 as New Line cinema benefited from the *Lord of the Rings* franchise and Warner Bros. continued to earn from *Harry Potter* and *The Matrix*. Warner Music was sold for €2 billion and the CD and DVD manufacturing operations were sold for €0.88 billion. Nevertheless, this one example of the scale of numbers should not mask our appreciation of the historical dimension to current trends in order to appraise economic power critically.

'Globalization may make it easier for peoples to encounter new cultures, but it makes the journey less worthwhile as individual cultures become more like each other' (Briggs and Burke 2002: 332). For this, media products must take some responsibility. 'The world is encouraged to covet and then buy US products. We are also encouraged thereby to adopt their cultural and political values' (Tongue 2003: 4). The inescapable fact is that national industries and products are promoted on the screen.

Over the years, regulation of media industries has emerged as a tool of policy influence that can help to correct media inequalities, while also enhancing social and cultural influence in the face of gratuitous commercialism. Historically, regulation has always shaped the nature of public-service broadcasting, a factor that justifies its continuing existence. The arguments for its support have always gone beyond pure numbers to philosophical assumptions about the role of media in society and the perceived importance of broadcasting for a range of different areas in social and political life. In the past this approach has been based on the nation-state, and national considerations are still important, including language, political systems, power structures and cultural traditions. Now, because the transnational is more important, the efforts of the EU to improve its democratic procedures and to link the issue of cultural identity to the screen are also significant. It amounts to a recognition that every region and nation has its own unique culture and the right to participate creatively in the most influential cultural medium.

Equally the issue of media democracy at every level of consumption has a rich heritage. The ways in which the public participate in TV, in radio and via the Internet require further research: at face value, such participation may appear to be very different to that of the crowd, for instance, in the French Revolution, but the principles are the same (Chapman 2005). A study, for instance, of the ways in which community-based networks could play a role in the strategic planning, implementation and application of broadband infrastructure in Canada is not dissimilar in principle to community use of newspapers in Lyons in the 1830s: media usage could once more facilitate 'imagined communities' (Matear 2002; Hibberd 2003).

The growing sense of interconnection and interdependence that global communications and technological proximity can generate, first

Fig. 15 Silvio Berlusconi making a speech, February 2004; Berlusconi owns three (private) national television stations

identified by McLuhan, calls for universal values and ethical behaviour by the media more today than ever before. However, the trend towards convergence should be measured against a longer historical view: 'There are times when the historian of the media feels that the best metaphor to use in relation to the recent past is that of "the thicket". The technology changes so fast and becomes so obtrusive that broader history is forgotten, and in examining that, not everything converges' (Briggs and Burke 2002: 319).

By way of summary on continuity in media history, the following points from this chapter link back to previous chapters.

> Control of media expression is the key to power; how this relates to pluralism is still an issue for most societies. The phenomenon of a media organization as a substitute for a political party arose in the 1930s in Britain and has lived on with Silvio Berlusconi's 'Forza Italia' movement, which made a successful impact in the 1994 general election (Statham 1996).

> Even the relentless growth of selling wasn't new. 'Contemporary merchandising [thus] seeks ways of colonizing for commerce the information space created by the new technologies. But this is old news. The 19th century may not have had the circuit boards we have, but they had selling wired already; they had naturalized merchandising' (de la Motte and Przyblyski 1999: 353–4).

> Although the proportion of total output traded internationally was not much higher in the early 1990s than it was shortly before the

First World War (Hirst and Thompson 1996), undoubtedly in the twentieth century growth in forms and volume of communications and entertainment was continuous. However, within that general pattern, 'The trajectory is uneven and erratic, with openings and closures, ebb and flow' (Curran 2002: 51).

Global popular culture, including the Internet, is dominated by the English language and is centred in the West. However, this study does not support the findings of Starr (2004) that media history is the story of gradual and sometimes rapid American ascendancy. The questioning and uncertainties that emerged during the period of this chapter about the 'triumph of the West' (Latouche 1996), amid apprehensions, for instance, concerning the sustainability of high-consumption lifestyles, present a challenge for the future. The last 200 years provide a rich legacy of cultural diversity as well as shared beliefs across national boundaries, continents and time-spans. That is the nature of pluralism worldwide – past and present.

To preserve that value in the future, international regulatory plural-ism rather than unrestrained transcontinental commercial mono-poly will be necessary. Furthermore, there is a need more than ever before for international human rights law that protects freedom of expression in the media in the context of greater diversity of ownership and of culture, plus respect for, rather than marginal-ization of, the traditions of social and community control of the media.

Study questions

How far is convergence connected to increasing concentration of ownership?

How far have the threats to democracy in relation to the media changed over the last 200 years?

Examine the changing nature and fortunes of public-service broad-casting since 1980, using comparisons between continents, coun-tries and decades.

Selecting either two different industry sectors transnationally, or media in two different countries, analyse the role of past heritage in influencing our understanding of current issues.

Notes

CHAPTER 1   NEWSPAPERS: RADICALISM, REPRESSION AND ECONOMIC CHANGE, 1789–1847

1   The 1870s in Japan saw the growth of privately sponsored reading projects such as newspaper tea rooms where women read to customers during the taking of tea. However, participants were not the working class as in Britain, but a small number of the intellectual elite.

2   Marat's *L'Ami du peuple* also had many imitators, and there were even two royalist papers entitled *L'Ami du roi*.

3   During the mid-1820s, more newspapers were sold in Paris than in London. Parisian figures are staggering: 235,000 dailies by 1858, 1 million by 1870 and 2 million by 1880.

4   Copies of these first ever newspapers are still available in the British Museum. Although the first prototypes of a newspaper, one-page flyers entitled *kawaraban*, produced irregularly on woodblocks and reporting sensational events such as lovers' suicides and disasters, appeared in Japan during the Edo period in 1615, the origins of modern newspapers have their roots in Britain. The *Oxford Gazette* soon moved to the capital to become the *London Gazette*, appearing with government approval in 1665. The first daily was the *Daily Courant* at the very beginning of the eighteenth century.

5   This scurrilous, immoral world, where commercialism had hijacked literary probity, was immortalized by Balzac in *Les Illusions perdues* (Lost Illusions). See also de Maupassant's *Bel Ami* (1885).

6   Daniel Defoe's *Robinson Crusoe* (1719) was the first serialized novel and Dickens's *Pickwick Papers* also appeared in Britain in 1836.

7   Among the dissident labour newspapers in the United States were the *Mechanics Free Press* (1828–31) in Philadelphia and the *Free Enquirer* (1828–35) and the *Working Man's Advocate* (1829–49) in New York City.

8   Political satire was important during the repressive period 1835–48 and again in late nineteenth-century France.

CHAPTER 2   THE FOCUSING OF POLITICAL COMMUNICATIONS AND THE NEWSPAPER BUSINESS, 1848–1881

1   Unlike that of his American contemporary Bennett (editor of the *New York Herald*), who used his front page to announce that he had fallen in love, and then that he was marrying, Barnes's name only ever appeared in the pages of his paper as part of a two-line obituary after he died. It did not even mention he had edited the newspaper for just on a quarter of a century.

2   Although they were under siege from the Prussians at the end of the Franco-Prussian War, the Parisians continued to fight after their government had declared an ignominious armistice. In defiance, they elected their own government and introduced a form of democratic self-government which has created a legend in working-class history, but was ultimately doomed to failure as they suffered attack from their own government troops.

3   In the years 1869–74 social unrest was prevalent: there were around thirty riots a

year, led mainly by farmers who were against the introduction of military duty (de Lange 1998: 38).

4　His partner in the business later accused him of stealing the takings of their book-shop, which was never proved.

CHAPTER 3　COMMERCIALIZATION, CONSUMERISM AND TECHNOLOGY

1　Although Britain's *The Guardian* has remained in the same family ownership, it did not count as a 'national' until at least 1945.

CHAPTER 4　POLITICS, NEW FORMS OF COMMUNICATION AND THE GLOBALIZING PROCESS

1　The 'Dreyfus Affair' was rocking the public internationally, simultaneously exposing the inherent anti-Semitism and difficult position of both militarism and religion within French politics, while also increasing newspaper circulation. Captain Dreyfus had been wrongly accused of forgery.

2　The one token man was the night janitor. Circulation hit 50,000 and content was as far-ranging as that of its competitors. The idea was to create a new public identity for women as being as knowledgeable as men, especially in politics, high finance and the law. In 1903 Northcliffe launched the *Daily Mirror* as a paper produced by and for women, but the experiment was a failure. It was relaunched as a tabloid.

3　Once the Japanese neared the Russians at sea, they were able to hear their messages and locate their ships, thus preventing fifty-six out of a fleet of fifty-nine ships from reaching their destination of the Russian port of Vladivostok. The Japanese became the first Asian nation to win an international war.

4　Freud discovered the key to psychoanalysis, as expressed in *The Interpretation of Dreams*, during the same year, 1896, that the Lumière brothers created and screened their most famous films.

5　Unfortunately none of Alice Guy's films have survived.

6　As the base of support for cinema in the United States widened out from just the working class, so also ideas about class consciousness and radical movements portrayed in films became more conservative. According to Steven J. Ross, this change was directly linked to the rise of Hollywood.

7　Sklar (1994) suggests that this may have been his aim in establishing the organization.

8　The term came into use in 1915, 'nicely describing the immigrant producers in the eyes of the public – part splendid emperors, part barbarian invaders', according to Sklar (1994).

9　*The Birth of a Nation* depicted the Ku Klux Klan in a favourable light as champi-ons of the Anglo-Saxon ideal during the Civil War. Between 1908 and 1913, D. W. Griffith directed over 400 films for the Biograph company.

10　According to Cecil B. de Mille, there was a price to pay: 'When we operated on picture money there was a joy in the industry, when we operated on Wall Street money, there was grief in the industry.'

11　UFA went private under banking control after the war.

CHAPTER 5　THE BUSINESS AND IDEOLOGY OF MASS CULTURE, 1918–1939

1　They also stated that there should be no government subsidies, for fear that the piper could call the tune, and that the best form of ownership is a cooperative one, controlled by the press itself.

2　Henry Ford, with his standardization of product and factory assembly lines, spearheaded the fashionable concept of time and motion studies as 'scientific management'. He was a hero in the Soviet Union (Briggs and Burke 2002: 190).

CHAPTER 6   WAR AND BEYOND, 1939–1947

1 In France, the communist newspaper *L'Humanité* had been banned since just before the war started.

CHAPTER 7   COLD WAR AND THE VICTORY OF COMMERCIALISM, 1948–1980

1 It has been suggested that the star of *High Noon*, Gary Cooper, who spoke to HUAC as a supporter of McCarthyism in 1947, was oblivious to the subtle criticism of the dominant conformity.
2 The first experimental use of satellite linked to regular broadcasters was between Japan and the USA on 23 November 1963: the Japanese were expecting a live broadcast message from President Kennedy, but he had been assassinated the previous day in Texas.

CHAPTER 8   CONTINUITY AND CHANGE SINCE 1980

1 The communication by the United States to the WTO concerning audiovisual services dated 18 December 2000 refers to subsidies carefully restricted to specific purposes, with parallel precautions to ensure that the potential effects of distortion on trading are effectively limited or significantly neutralized.
2 The 1999 BBC Reith lectures by Giddens, published as *Runaway World*, sparked huge intellectual controversy, especially in France.

References and Bibliography

Abel, Richard (1994) *The Cine Goes to Town: French Cinema 1896–1914*. Berkeley: University of California Press.

Abel, Richard (1999) *The Red Rooster Scare: Making Cinema American, 1900–1910*. Berkeley: University of California Press.

Adams, Edward E. (1995) Chain growth and merger waves: a macroeconomic historical perspective on press consolidation. *Journalism & Mass Communication Quarterly*, 72, pp. 376–89.

Adams, Edward E. (1996) Secret combinations and collusive agreements: the Scripps newspaper empire and the early roots of joint operating agreements. *Journalism & Mass Communication Quarterly*, 73, pp. 195–205.

Adams, Edward E. (2001) How corporate ownership facilitated a split in the Scripps newspaper empire. *Journalism History*, 27 (2), pp. 56–63.

Adams, Edward E., and Baldasty, Gerald J. (2001) Syndicated service dependence and a lack of commitment to localism: Scripps newspapers and market subordination. *Journalism & Mass Communication Quarterly*, 78, pp. 519–32.

Aikat, Debashis (2001) Pioneers of the early digital era: innovative ideas that shaped computing in 1833–1945. *Convergence*, 7 (4), pp. 52–81.

Aitken, Hugh G. J. (1976) *Syntony and Spark: The Origins of Radio*. Princeton, NJ: Princeton University Press.

Aitken, Hugh G. J. (1985) *The Continuous Wave: Technology and American Radio, 1900–1932*. Princeton, NJ: Princeton University Press.

Albert, P. (1990) *La Presse française*. Paris: Documentation française.

Aldgate, A., and Richards, J. (1995) *Britain Can Take It: The British Cinema in the Second World War*. Edinburgh: Edinburgh University Press.

Allen, Robert C. (1987) *Channels of Discourse: Television and Contemporary Criticism*. Chapel Hill: University of North Carolina Press.

Allen, Robert C., and Gomery, Douglas (1985) *Film History: Theory and Practice*. New York: McGraw-Hill.

Alleyne, Mark D., and Wagner, Janet (1993) Stability and change at the 'big five' news agencies. *Journalism Quarterly*, 70 (1), pp. 40–50.

Altheide, David L. (1991) The impact of television formats on social policy. *Journal of Electronic Media*, 35 (1), pp. 3–21.

Anderson, Benedict (1991) *Imagined Communities*. 2nd edn, London: Verso.

Angenot, Marc (1989) *1889: un état du discours social*. Montreal: Editions du Préambule.

Armes, Roy (1987) *Third World Film Making and the West*. Berkeley: University of California Press.

Bagdikian, Ben (1979) More mergers means less news. *Journalism Studies Review*, July.

Bagdikian, Ben (1997) *Media Monopoly*. 5th edn, Boston: Beacon Press.

Bagehot, Walter (1915) *The Works and Life of Walter Bagehot*, 9 vols. London: Longman.

Bakker, Piet (2002) Free daily newspapers: business models and strategies. *International Journal of Media Management*, 4, pp. 180–7.

Baldasty, Gerald J. (1999) *E. W. Scripps and the Business of Newspapers*. Urbana and Chicago: University of Illinois Press.

Balfour, M. (1979) *Propaganda in War*. London: Routledge & Kegan Paul.

Ball, Lucille (1996) *Love, Lucy*. New York: Boulevard Books.

Barker, David (1991) The emergence of television's repertoire of representation, 1920–1935. *Journal of Broadcasting and Electronic Media*, 35, pp. 305–18.

Barker, Hannah (2000) *Newspapers, Politics and English Society, 1695–1855*. Harlow: Longman.

Barnard, Stephen (2000) *Studying Radio*. London: Arnold.

Barnett, Stephen R. (1980) Newspaper monopoly and the law. *Journal of Communication*, 30 (2), pp. 72–80.

Barnhurst, Kevin G., and Nerone, John (2001) *The Form of News: A History*. London and New York: Guilford Press.

Barnouw, Erik (1966) *A History of Broadcasting in the United States*, vol. 1: *A Tower in Babel*. New York: Oxford University Press.

Barnouw, Erik (1968) *A History of Broadcasting in the United States*, vol. 2: *The Golden Web*. New York: Oxford University Press.

Barnouw, Erik (1970) *A History of Broadcasting in the United States*, vol. 3: *The Image Empire*. New York: Oxford University Press.

Bartov, Omer (1966) *Murder in our Midst: The Holocaust, Industrial Killing and Representation*. Oxford and New York: Oxford University Press.

Baudrillard, Jean (1983) *Simulations*. New York: Semiotexte.

Bazin, André (1967) *What is Cinema?*, trans. Hugh Gray, 2 vols. Berkeley and Los Angeles: University of California Press.

BBC Radio Collections (1997) *A Celebration of BBC Radio: 75 years of the BBC*. London: BBC Worldwide.

Beck, Ulrich (1992) *Risk Society: Towards a New Modernity*. London and Newbury Park, CA: Sage.

Bellanger, Claude, Godechot, Jacques, Guiral, Pierre, and Terrou, Fernand (1969) *Histoire générale de la presse française*. Paris: Presses Universitaires de France.

Benjamin, Louise M. (1993) In search of the Sarnoff 'radio music box' memo. *Journal of Broadcasting and Electronic Media*, 37, pp. 325–35.

Benjamin, Walter (1969) *Illuminations: Essays and Reflections*, ed. Hannah Arendt. New York: Schocken.

Bennett, T., Frith, S., Grossberg, L., Shephard, J., and Turner, G., eds (1993) *Rock and Popular Music: Politics, Policies, Institutions*. London: Routledge.

Bernhard, Nancy E. (1999) *US Television News and Cold War Propaganda, 1947–1960*. Cambridge: Cambridge University Press.

Betzel, Marcel, and Ward, David (2003) *The Regulation of Public Service Broadcasters in Western Europe*. Düsseldorf: European Institute for the Media.

Bird, S. Elizabeth (1992) *For Enquiring Minds: A Cultural Study of Supermarket Tabloids*. Knoxville: University of Tennessee Press.

Black, Jeremy (2001) *The English Press 1621–1861*. London: Sutton.

Boddy, William (1990) *Fifties Television: The Industry and its Critics*. Urbana and Chicago: University of Illinois Press.

Bol, Jennifer (2002) Spinning a legal web: the impact of the Internet on Canadian law. *Canadian Journal of Communication*, 27, pp. 439–46.

Boorstin, Daniel (1963) *The Image*. Harmondsworth: Penguin.

Boorstin, Daniel (1973) *The Americans: The Democratic Experience*. New York: Random House.

Bourdieu, Pierre (1998) *On Television*. London: Pluto Press.

Bowser, Eileen (1990) *The Transformation of Cinema 1907–1915*. New York: Charles Scribner.

Boyce, George, Curran, James, and Wingate, Pauline, eds (1978) *Newspaper History from the 17th Century to the Present Day*. London: Acton Society Trust Press Group.

Boyd, Douglas A. (1988) Third World pirating of US films and television programs from satellites. *Journal of Broadcasting and Electronic Media*, 32, pp. 149–61.

Boyd, Douglas A., and Straubhaar, Joseph (1985) Developmental impact of the home video cassette recorder on Third World countries. *Journal of Broadcasting and Electronic Media*, 29 (1), pp. 5–21.

Boyd-Barrett, Oliver, and Rantanen, Terhi (1998) *The Globalization of News*. London: Sage.

Branham, Robert James (1994) Debate and dissent in late Tokugawa and Meiji Japan. *Argumentation and Advocacy*, 30, pp. 131–49.

Braw, Monica (1991) *The Atomic Bomb Suppressed: American Censorship in Occupied Japan*. New York: M. E. Sharpe.

Brendon, P. (1982) *The Life and Death of the Press Barons*. London: Secker & Warburg.

Brennen, Bonnie (1995) Newsworkers during the interwar years: a critique of traditional media history. *Communication Quarterly*, 43, pp. 197–209.

Briggs, Asa (1961) *The History of Broadcasting in the United Kingdom*, vol.1: *The Birth of Broadcasting*. Oxford: Oxford University Press.

Briggs, Asa (1993) From maiden aunt to sexy upstart. *Media Studies Journal*, 7, pp. 113–21.

Briggs, Asa (1995) *The BBC: The First Fifty Years*. Oxford: Oxford University Press.

Briggs, Asa, and Burke, Peter (2002) *A Social History of the Media*. Cambridge: Polity.

Broderick, Mick, ed. (1996) *Hibakusha Cinema: Hiroshima, Nagasaki and the Nuclear Image in Japanese Film*. London: Kegan Paul.

Bromley, Michael, and O'Malley, Tom (1997) *A Journalism Reader*. London and New York: Routledge.

Brooks, Jeffrey (2000) *Thank You Comrade Stalin! Soviet Public Culture from Revolution to Cold War*. Princeton, NJ: Princeton University Press.

Brown, Richard, and Anthony, Barry (1999) *A Victorian Film Enterprise: The History of the British Mutoscope and Biograph Company, 1897–1915*. Trowbridge: Flick Books.

Brown, Stephen H. (1992) Contesting political oratory in nineteenth-century England. *Communication Studies*, 43 (3).

Bruner, Michael S. (1989) Symbolic uses of the Berlin Wall, 1961–1989. *Communication Quarterly*, 37, pp. 319–28.

Burke, Edmund (1968) *Reflections on the Revolution in France*. Harmondsworth: Penguin.

Bush, Vannevar (1945) As we may think. *Atlantic Monthly*, July.

Butler, Marilyn, ed. (1984) *Burke, Paine, Godwin and the Revolution Controversy*. Cambridge: Cambridge University Press.

Campbell, W. Joseph (2000) Not likely sent: the Remington–Hearst 'telegrams'. *Journalism & Mass Communication Quarterly*, 77, pp. 405–22.

Carey, James W. (1989) *Communication as Culture: Essays on Media & Society*. Winchester, MA: Unwin Hyman.

Carruthers, Susan L. (2000) *Media at War*. London: Macmillan.

Castells, Manuel (1997) *The Power of Identity*. Oxford: Blackwell.

Castells, Manuel (2001) *The Internet Galaxy: Reflections on the Internet, Business and Society*. Oxford: Oxford University Press.

Castleman, Harry, and Podrazik, Walter (1982) *Watching TV: Four Decades of American Television*. New York: McGraw-Hill.

Catterall, Peter, Seymour-Ure, Colin, and Smith, Adrian, eds (2000) *Northcliffe's Legacy: Aspects of the British Popular Press, 1896–1996*. Basingstoke: Macmillan.

Censer, Jack R. (1994) *The French Press in the Age of Enlightenment*. London and New York: Routledge.

Chalaby, Jean K. (1998) *The Invention of Journalism*. Basingstoke: Macmillan.

Chanan, Michael (1994) *Musica Practica: The Social Practice of Western Music from Gregorian Chant to Postmodernism*. London: Verso.

Chanan, Michael (1995) *Repeated Takes*. London: Verso.

Chang, Tsan-Kuo (1998) All countries not created equal to be news: world system and international communication. *Communication Research*, 25, pp. 528–63.

Chang, Tsan-Kuo, Wang, Jian, and Chen, Chin-Hsien (1998) The social construction of international imagery in the post-Cold War era: a comparative analysis of US and Chinese national TV news. *Journal of Broadcasting and Electronic Media*, 42, pp. 277–96.

Chan-Olmsted, Sylvia M., and Kang, Jae-Wong (2003) Theorizing the strategic architecture of a broadband television industry. *Journal of Media Economics*, 16 (1), pp. 3–21.

Chan-Olmsted, Sylvia M., and Yungwook, Kim (2002) The PBS brand versus cable brands: assessing the brand image of public television in a multichannel environment. *Journal of Broadcasting and Electronic Media*, 46, pp. 300–20.

Chapman, Jane (2005) Republican citizenship ethics and the French revolutionary press 1789–1792. *Ethical Space*, spring.

Charon, J.-M. (1991) *La Presse en France de 1945 à nos jours*. Paris: Seuil.

Cho, Hiromi, and Lacy, Stephen (2000) International conflict coverage in Japanese local daily newspapers. *Journalism & Mass Communication Quarterly*, 77, pp. 830–45.

Cole, G. D. H., and Postgate, Raymond (1946) *The Common People 1746–1946*. 2nd edn, London: Methuen.

Collins, Irene (1959) *Government and Newspaper Press in France, 1814–1881*. Oxford: Oxford University Press.

Collins, Ross F. (2001) The business of journalism in provincial France during World War I. *Journalism History*, 27(3).

Compaine, Benjamin M. (1980) The magazine industry: developing the special interest audience. *Journal of Communication*, 30, pp. 98–103.

Conboy, Martin (2002) *The Press and Popular Culture*. London: Sage.

Conboy, Martin (2004) *Journalism: A Critical History*. London: Sage.

Corner, John, Schlesinger, Philip, and Silverstone, Roger, eds (1997) *International Media Research: A Critical Survey*. London: Routledge.

Craig, Stephen R. (1988) American Forces Network in the Cold War: military broadcasting in post-war Germany. *Journal of Broadcasting and Electronic Media*, 32, pp. 307–21.

Craig, Stephen R. (1990) Medium-wave frequency allocations in post-war Europe: US foreign policy and the Copenhagen conference of 1948. *Journal of Broadcasting and Electronic Media*, 34, pp. 119–35.

Cranfield, G. A. (1978) *The Press and Society from Caxton to Northcliffe*. London: Longman.

Crisp, Colin (1997) *The Classic French Cinema, 1930–1960*. Bloomington: Indiana University Press.

Crouthamel, J. L. (1989) *Bennett's New York Herald and the Rise of the Popular Press*. Syracuse, NY: Syracuse University Press.

Cudlipp, Hugh (1980) *The Prerogative of the Harlot: Press Barons and Power*. London: Bodley Head.

Cull, N. (1995) *Propaganda for War: The British Propaganda Campaign against American 'Neutrality' in World War II*. Oxford: Oxford University Press.

Curran, James (2002) *Media and Power*. London and New York: Routledge.

Curran, James, and Seaton, Jean (1997) *Power without Responsibility*. 5th edn, London: Routledge.

Curran, James, and Seaton, Jean (2003) *Power without Responsibility*. 6th edn, London: Routledge.

Curran, J., Smith, J., and Wingate, P., eds (1987) *Impacts and Influences*. London: Methuen.

Curtin, Michael (1993) Beyond the vast wasteland: the policy discourse of global television and the politics of American empire. *Journal of Broadcasting and Electronic Media*, 37, pp. 127–45.

Curtis, L. Perry (2001) *Jack the Ripper and the London Press*. New Haven, CT, and London: Yale University Press.

Custen, George F. (1986) Hollywood history and the production of culture. *Journal of Communication*, 36, pp. 123–32.

Davie, William R., and Jung-Sook, Lee (1993) Television news technology: do more sources mean less diversity? *Journal of Broadcasting and Electronic Media*, 37, pp. 453–64.

Delporte, Christian (1999) *Les Journalistes en France, 1880–1950: naissance et construction d'une profession*. Paris: Seuil.

Dennis, Everette E., Gerbner, George, and Zassoursky, Yassen N. (1991) *Beyond the Cold War: Soviet and American Media Images*. Newbury Park, CA: Sage.

Dimmick, John W., Patterson, Scott, and Albarran, Alan B. (1992) Competition between the cable and broadcast industries: a niche analysis. *Journal of Media Economics*, 5 (1), pp. 13–30.

Dioudonnat, Pierre-Marie (1981) *L'Argent nazi à la conquête de la presse française, 1940–1944*. Paris: Editions Jean Picollec.

Douglas, George H. (1999) *The Golden Age of the Newspaper*. Westport, CT: Greenwood Press.

Douglas, Susan J. (1987) *Inventing American Broadcasting 1899–1922*. Baltimore: Johns Hopkins University Press.

Douglas, Susan J. (1999) *Listening In: Radio and the American Imagination*. New York: Random House.

Dower, J. (1986) *War Without Mercy: Race and Power in the Pacific War*. New York: Pantheon.

Dower, J. (1989) Occupied Japan and the Cold War in Asia. In Michael J. Lacey, ed., *The Truman Presidency*. Cambridge: Cambridge University Press; Washington, DC: Woodrow Wilson International Center for Scholars.

Dower, J. (1996) *Japan in War and Peace: Essays on History, Culture and Race*. London: Fontana.

Drushel, Bruce E. (1998) The Telecommunications Act of 1996 and radio market structure. *Journal of Media Economics*, 11 (3), pp. 3–20.

Du Boff, Richard B. (1984) The rise of communications regulation: the telegraph industry, 1844–1880. *Journal of Communication*, 34 (3), pp. 52–66.

Dunnett, Peter J. S. (1988) *The World Newspaper Industry*. London: Croom Helm.

Elliot, M. (1990) *Rockonomics: The Money behind the Music*. London: Omnibus Press.

Ellul, Jacques (1965) *Propaganda: The Formation of Men's Attitudes*. New York: Knopf.

Emanuel, Susan (1993) Cultural television: Western Europe and the United States. *European Journal of Communication*, 8, pp. 131–47.

Emery, Michael, Emery, Edwin, and Roberts, Nancy L. (2000) *The Press and America: An Interpretative History of the Mass Media*. 9th edn, Boston and London: Allyn & Bacon.

Engel, Matthew (1996) *Tickle the Public: A Hundred Years of the Popular Press*. London: Gollancz.

Esser, Frank (1999) 'Tabloidization' of news: a comparative analysis of Anglo-American and German press journalism. *European Journal of Communication*, 14, pp. 291–324.

European Institute for the Media (1993) *Growth or Decline? The European Television and Film Industries in Crisis*. Proceedings of the 4th Plenary Meeting of the European Television & Film Forum, Seville, 24–6 Sept 1992. Düsseldorf: European Institute for the Media.

Faden, Eric S. (1999) Assimilating new technologies: early cinema, sound, and computer imagery. *Convergence*, 5 (2), pp. 51–79.

Fairchild, C. (1999) Deterritorializing radio: deregulation and the continuing triumph of the corporatist perspective in the USA. *Media, Culture and Society*, 21, pp. 549–61.

Fan, David P., Brosius, Hans-Bernd, and Kepplinger, Hans Mathias (1994) Predictions of the public agenda from television coverage. *Journal of Broadcasting and Electronic Media*, 38, pp. 163–77.

Faucher, Jean-André, and Jacquemart, Noël (1968) *Le Quatrième pouvoir: la presse en France, 1830–1960*. Paris: Imprimerie de l'Auxerrois.

Featherstone, Mike (1995) *Undoing Culture*. London: Sage.

Feldman, Ofer (1993) *Politics and the News Media in Japan*. Ann Arbor: University of Michigan Press.

Ferenczi, Thomas (1993) *L'Invention du journalisme en France: naissance de la presse moderne à la fin du XIXème siècle*. Paris: Plon.

Ferguson, Niall (2003) *Empire: How Britain Made the Modern World*. London: Allen Lane.

Foner, P. S. (1947) *History of the Labor Movement in the United States*. New York: International Publishers.

de Forest, L. (1950) *Father of Radio: The Autobiography of Lee de Forest*. Chicago: Wilcox & Follett.

Freud, Sigmund (1969) *Civilization and its Discontents*. London: Hogarth Press.

Frith, S. (1987a) Copyright and the music business. *Popular Music*, 7 (1).

Frith, S. (1987b) The making of the British recording industry, 1920–64. In J. Curran, J. Smith and P. Wingate, eds, *Impacts and Influences*. London: Methuen.

Furet, François (1981) *Interpreting the French Revolution*. Cambridge: Cambridge University Press.

Gauntlett, David, ed. (2000) *Web Studies: Rewiring Media Studies for the Digital Age*. London: Arnold.

Geduld, Harry M., ed. (1967) *Film Makers on Film Making*. Bloomington and London: Indiana University Press.

Gershon, Richard A., and Kanayama, Tsutomu (2002) The Sony Corporation: a case study in transnational media management. *International Journal on Media Management*, 4, pp. 105–17.

Giblett, Rod (2001) Sublime satellites: from Cold War to Gulf War. *Australian Journal of Communication*, 28, pp. 137–50.

Giddens, Anthony (1984) *The Constitution of Society*. Cambridge: Polity.

Giddens, Anthony (1990) *The Consequences of Modernity*. Cambridge: Polity.

Giddens, Anthony (1991) *Modernity and Self-Identity: Self and Society in the Late Modern Age*. Cambridge: Polity.

Giddens, Anthony (1999) *Runaway World: How Globalization is Reshaping our Lives*. London: Profile.

Gienow-Hecht, Jessica C. E. (1999) *Transmission Impossible: American Journalism as Cultural Diplomacy in Post War Germany, 1945–1955*. Baton Rouge: Louisiana State University Press.

Giffard, Anthony C., and Riverburgh, Nancy K. (2000) News agencies, national images, and global media events. *Journalism & Mass Communication Quarterly*, 77, pp. 8–21.

Gilchrist, J., and Murray, W. J. (1971) *The Press and the French Revolution: A Selection of Documents Taken from the Press of the Revolution for the Years 1789–1794*. London: Ginn.

Girardin, Saint-Marc (1859) *Souvenirs et reflexions politiques d'un journaliste.* Paris: M. Levy Librairie nouvelle.

Goldhagen, Daniel (1996) *Hitler's Willing Executioners: Ordinary Germans and the Holocaust.* London: Little, Brown.

Gomery, Douglas (1986) *The Hollywood Studio System.* New York: St Martin's Press.

Gorman, Lyn, and McLean, David (2003) *Media and Society in the 20th Century.* Oxford: Blackwell.

Gorn, Elliot J. (1992) The wicked world: the 'National Police Gazette' and gilded-age America. *American Media Studies Journal,* 6 (1), pp. 1–15.

Gough, H. (1998) *The Newspaper Press in the French Revolution.* London: Routledge.

Gough-Yates, Anna (2003) *Understanding Women's Magazines: Publishing Markets and Readerships.* London and New York: Routledge.

Gronow, P. (1983) The record industry: the growth of a mass medium. *Popular Music,* 3.

Gunkel, David J., and Gunkel, Ann Hetzel (1997) Virtual geographies: the new worlds of cyberspace. *Critical Studies in Mass Communication,* 14, pp. 123–37.

Halavais, Alexander (2000) National borders on the world wide web. *New Media & Society,* 2 (1), pp. 7–28.

Hale, Oron J. (1964) *The Captive Press in the Third Reich.* Princeton, NJ: Princeton University Press.

Hall, Stuart, Held, David, and McGrew, Anthony (1992) *Modernity and its Futures.* Cambridge: Polity.

Hallin, Daniel (1998) A fall from grace. *Media Studies Journal,* 12 (2), pp. 42–7.

Halloran, Richard (1970) *Japan: Images and Realities.* Tokyo: Charles E. Tuttle.

Hansen, Anders (2002) Discourses of nature in advertising. *European Journal of Communication Research,* 27, pp. 499–511.

Hardman, T. H. (1909) *A Parliament of the Press.* London: Horace Marshall.

Hardt, H., and Brennen, B., eds (1995) *Newsworkers: Toward a History of the Rank and File.* Minneapolis and London: University of Minnesota Press.

Harrison, Stanley (1974) *Poor Men's Guardians.* London: Lawrence & Wishart.

Hatin, E. (1866) *Bibliographie de la presse périodique française,* vols 4–6. Paris: Librairie de Firmin Didot Frères.

Hattersley, Roy (2003) *Victorians Uncovered: William Stead: Unscrupulous Journalist or Moral Crusader?* <www.channel4.com/h...icrosites/V/victorians/hattersley.html> (accessed 24 July 2003).

Head, Sydney W. (1982) *Broadcasting in America: A Survey of Television, Radio and New Technologies.* 4th edn, Boston: Houghton Mifflin.

Headrick, D. R. (1981) *The Tools of Empire.* Oxford: Oxford University Press.

Hendy, David (2000) *Radio in the Global Age.* Cambridge: Polity.

Herbert, John (2001) *Practising Global Journalism: Exploring Reporting Issues Worldwide.* Oxford: Focal Press.

Hesse, Kurt R. (1990) Cross-border mass communicating from West to East Germany. *Journal of Communication,* 5, pp. 355–71.

Hibberd, Matthew (2003) E-participation, broadcasting and democracy in the UK. *Convergence,* 9 (1), pp. 47–65.

Hijiya, James A. (1992) *Lee de Forest and the Fatherhood of Radio.* Bethlehem, PA: Lehigh University Press; London: Associated University Presses.

Hill, John, and Gibson, Pamela Church, eds (2000) *World Cinema: Critical Approaches.* Oxford: Oxford University Press.

Hilmes, Michele (1990) *Hollywood and Broadcasting: From Radio to Cable.* Urbana and Chicago: University of Illinois Press.

Hilmes, Michele (1997) *Radio Voices: American Broadcasting, 1922–1952.* Minneapolis and London: University of Minnesota Press.

Hilmes, Michele (2002) *Only Connect: A Cultural History of Broadcasting in the United States.* Belmont, CA: Wadsworth.

Hirano, Kyoko (1992) *Mr. Smith Goes to Tokyo under the American Occupation, 1945–52.* Washington, DC, and London: Smithsonian Institution Press.

Hirst, P., and Thompson, G. (1996) *Globalization in Question.* Cambridge: Polity.

Hiundman, Douglas Blanks, Littlefield, Robert, Preston, Ann, and Neumann, Dennis (1999) Structural pluralism, ethnic pluralism, and community newspapers. *Journalism & Mass Communication Quarterly,* 76, pp. 250–63.

Hobsbawm, Eric (1994a) *The Age of Empire.* London: Abacus.

Hobsbawm, Eric (1994b) *Age of Extremes: The Short Twentieth Century, 1914–1991.* Harmondsworth: Penguin.

Hoffert, Sylvia D. (1993) New York City's penny press and the issue of women's rights, 1848–1860. *Journalism Quarterly,* 70, pp. 656–65.

Hoffman, H. (1996) *The Triumph of Propaganda: Film and National Socialism, 1933–45.* Providence, RI: Berghahn Books.

Hogan, J. Michael, and Williams, Glen (2000) Republican charisma and the American Revolution: the textual persona of Thomas Paine's *Common Sense. Quarterly Journal of Speech,* 86 (1), pp. 1–18.

Holt, H. (1909) *Commercialism and Journalism.* Boston: Houghton Mifflin.

Holtz-Bacha, Christina, and Norris, Pippa (2001) 'To entertain, inform and educate': still the role of public television. *Political Communication,* 18, pp. 123–40.

Howley, Kevin (2003) A poverty of voices: street papers as communicative democracy. *Journalism,* 4, pp. 273–92.

Huffman, James (1997) *Creating a Public: People and Press in Meiji Japan.* Honolulu: University of Hawaii Press.

Hume, Janice (2003) Lincoln was a 'Red' and Washington a Bolshevik: public memory as persuader in the appeal to reason. *Journalism History,* 28, pp. 172–81.

Hunter, Janet E. (1984) *Concise Dictionary of Modern Japanese History.* Berkeley: University of California Press.

Innis, H. A. (1972) *Empire and Communications.* Toronto: University of Toronto Press.

Institut Charles de Gaulle (1994) *De Gaulle et les médias.* Paris: Plon.

Ito, Masami (1978) *Broadcasting in Japan.* London: Routledge & Kegan Paul for the International Institute of Communications.

Ito, Youichi (1990) The trade winds change: Japan's shift from an information importer to an information exporter, 1965–1985. *Communication Yearbook,* 13, pp. 430–65.

Ivie, Robert L. (1986) Literalizing the metaphor for Soviet savagery: President Truman's plain style. *Southern Speech Communication Journal,* 51, pp. 91–105.

Jackaway, Gwenyth (1995) *Media at War: Radio's Challenge to the Newspapers, 1924–1939.* Westport, CT: Praeger.

James, C. L. R. (1980) *The Black Jacobins: Toussaint L'Ouverture and the San Domingo Revolution.* London: Allison & Busby.

Jowett, G. S., and O'Donnell, V. (1999) *Propaganda and Persuasion.* Newbury Park, CA: Sage.

Jussawalla, Meheroo (1991) Privatization and national priorities in the Asia-Pacific region. *Asian Journal of Communication,* 1 (2), pp. 41–51.

Kanesada, Hanazono (1924) *The Development of Japanese Journalism.* Osaka: Osaka Mainichi Shimbunsha.

Katz, Elias (1996) And deliver us from segmentation. *Annals of the American Academy of Political and Social Science,* 546, pp. 22–33.

Kaul, Arthur J. (1986) The proletarian journalist: a critique of professionalism. *Journal of Mass Media Ethics,* 1 (2), pp. 47–55.

Kellner, D. (1989) *Critical Theory, Marxism and Modernity.* Baltimore: Johns Hopkins University Press.

Kennedy, Paul (1987) *The Rise and Fall of the Great Powers.* New York: Random House.

Kershaw, Ian (1987) *The 'Hitler Myth': Image and Reality in the Third Reich.* Oxford: Clarendon Press.

King, A., ed. (1997) *Culture, Globalization and the World System.* London: Macmillan.

King, H. (1895) The rank and pay of journalists. *Forum,* 18, pp. 587–96.

Klein, Naomi (2000) *No Logo.* London: Flamingo.

Knightley, Philip (1989) *The First Casualty: From the Crimea to Vietnam: The War Correspondent as Hero, Propagandist and Myth Maker.* London: Pan.

Koenigsberg, Allen (1990) *The Birth of the Recording Industry.* <http://members.aol.com/allenamet/BirthRec.htm>.

Kojima, Kazuto (1977) Public opinion trends in Japan. *Public Opinion Quarterly,* 41, pp. 206–16.

Koss, Stephen (1984) *The Rise and Fall of the Political Press in Britain,* 2 vols. London: Hamish Hamilton.

Koszarski, Richard (1994) *An Evening's Entertainment: The Age of the Silent Feature Picture, 1915–1928.* Berkeley and Los Angeles: University of California Press.

Kovach, Bill, and Rosenstiel, Tom (2003) *The Elements of Journalism.* London: Guardian Books.

Krauss, Ellis S. (2000) *Broadcasting Politics in Japan: NHK and Television News.* Ithaca, NY, and London: Cornell University Press.

Kreshel, Peggy J. (1990) The 'culture' of J. Walter Thompson, 1915–1925. *Public Relations Review,* 16 (3), pp. 80–93.

Kretscher, Martin, Klimis, George Michael, and Wallis, Roger (2001) Music in electronic markets: an empirical study. *New Media and Society,* 3, pp. 417–41.

Kristeva, Julia (1974) *La Révolution du langage poétique.* Paris: Seuil.

Kuhn, Raymond, ed. (1985a) *Broadcasting and Politics in Western Europe.* London: Frank Cass.

Kuhn, Raymond, ed. (1985b) *The Politics of Broadcasting.* London: Croom Helm.

Kuhn, Raymond (1995) *The Media in France.* London: Routledge.

Labrosse, Claude, and Rétat, Pierre (1989) *Naissance du journal révolutionnaire, 1789.* Lyons: Presses Universitaires de Lyon.

Lacy, Stephen, and Picard, Robert (1990) Interactive monopoly power in the daily newspaper industry. *Journal of Media Economics,* 3 (2), pp. 27–38.

Lambrichs, Nathalie (1976) *Les Libertés de la presse en l'an IV.* Paris: Presses Universitaires de France.

Lancaster, Bill (1995) *The Department Store: A Social History.* Leicester: Leicester University Press.

de Lange, William (1998) *A History of Japanese Journalism: Japan's Press Club as the Last Obstacle to a Mature Press.* Richmond, Surrey: Japan Library.

Lashmar, Paul, and Oliver, James (1998) *Britain's Secret Propaganda War.* Stroud: Sutton.

Latouche, S. (1996) *The Westernization of the World.* Cambridge: Polity.

Lears, Jackson (1994) *Fables of Abundance: A Cultural History of Advertising in America.* New York: Basic Books.

Lee, Jung Bock (1985) *The Political Character of the Japanese Press.* Seoul: Seoul University Press.

Lerner, Daniel (1958) *The Passing of Traditional Society: Modernizing the Middle East.* Glencoe, IL: Free Press.

Levy, Suzanne (1993) Devoted to 'Auntie Beeb'. *Media Studies Journal,* 7, pp. 123–7.

Lippmann, Walter (1922) *Public Opinion.* New York: Harcourt Brace.

Livingston, Kevin T. (1993) Australia's 19th-century communication revolution. *Australian Journal of Communication,* 20, pp. 154–64.

Lloyd, C. (1999) *Attacking the Devil: 130 Years of the Northern Echo.* Darlington: Northern Echo.

Lohmeyer, Henno (1992) *Springer: ein deutsches Imperium: Geschichte und Geschichten.* Berlin: Edition Q.

Lopes, P. D. (1992) Innovation and diversity in the popular music industry, 1969–1990. *American Sociological Review,* 57 (1), pp. 56–71.

Lull, J., ed. (1987) *Popular Music and Communication.* London: Sage.

Luther, Catherine A., and Boyd, Douglas A. (1997) American occupation control over broadcasting in Japan, 1945–1952. *Journal of Communication,* 47 (2), pp. 39–59.

McChesney, Robert (1997) *Corporate Media and the Threat to Democracy.* New York: Seven Stories Press.

McChesney, Robert, and Herman, Edward (1997) *The Global Media: The New Missionaries of Corporate Capitalism.* London: Cassell.

Macdonald, B. (1988) *Broadcasting in the United Kingdom.* London: Mansell.

MacDonald, J. Fred (1985) *Television and the Red Menace: The Video Road to Vietnam.* New York: Praeger.

Machill, Marcel (1996) The French radio landscape: the impact of radio policy in an area defined by antagonistic forces of commercialization and cultural protection. *European Journal of Communication,* 11, pp. 393–415.

McKendrick, Neil, Brewer, John, and Plumb, J. H. (1982) *The Birth of a Consumer Society: The Commercialization of Eighteenth Century England.* Bloomington: Indiana University Press.

McNelly, John T. (1979) International news for Latin America. *Journal of Communication,* 29, pp. 156–63.

McQuail, Dennis (1994) *Mass Communication Theory.* 3rd edn, London: Sage.

Malinkina, Olga V., and McLeod, Douglas M. (2000) From Afghanistan to Chechnya: news coverage by Izvestia and the New York Times. *Journalism & Mass Communication Quarterly,* 77, pp. 37–49.

Mandziuk, Roseann M. (2001) Confessional discourse and modern desires: power and pleasure in True Story magazine. *Critical Studies in Media Communication,* 18, pp. 174–93.

Marchand, Roland (1985) *Advertising the American Dream: Making Way for Modernity, 1920–1940.* Berkeley: University of California Press.

Martin, Marc (1993) *Trois siècles du publicité en France.* Paris: Odile Jacob.

Martin, Peter J. (1995) *Sounds and Society: Themes in the Sociology of Music.* Manchester: Manchester University Press.

Marz, William (1977) Patent medicine advertising: mass persuasion techniques and reform, 1905–1976. MA thesis, California State University at Northridge.

Masaichi, Midoro (1930) *History of the Meiji and Taishi Eras: The Press.* Tokyo: Asahi Shimbunsha.

Mast, Gerald (1981) *A Short History of the Movies.* 3rd edn, Oxford: Oxford University Press.

Matear, Maggie (2002) Canada must make broadband infrastructure a priority. *Canadian Journal of Communication,* 27, pp. 461–7.

Mathiez, A. (1998) Les journées des 5 et 6 octobre 1789. *Revue Historique,* 67.

May, Lary (1980) *Screening Out the Past: The Birth of Mass Culture and the Motion Picture Industry.* New York: Oxford University Press.

Meers, Philippe (1998) Latin American telenovela: between media imperialism and cultural pluralism. *Communicatie,* 27 (3), pp. 2–24.

Menand, Louis (2003) Paris, Texas: how Hollywood brought the cinema back from France. *New Yorker,* 17 and 24 February.

Middleton, Richard (1990) *Studying Popular Music.* Milton Keynes: Open University Press.

Mill, John Stuart (1963) *The Early Letters of John Stuart Mill 1812–1848*, ed. Frenus E. Mineka. Toronto: University of Toronto Press.

Mill, John Stuart (1968–) *On Liberty*, in *The Collected Works of John Stuart Mill*, vol. 12. Toronto: University of Toronto Press.

de Mille, Cecil (1959) *Autobiography*, ed. Donald Hayne. Englewood Cliffs, NJ: Prentice-Hall.

Miller, David, and Dinan, William (2000) The rise of the PR industry in Britain, 1979–1998. *European Journal of Communication*, 15 (1), pp. 5–35.

Morienval, Jean (1934) *Les Créateurs de la grande presse*. Paris: Editions Specs.

Morris, Anthony (1984) *The Scaremongers: The Advocacy of War and Rearmament 1896–1914*. London: Routledge.

de la Motte, Dean, and Przyblyski, Jeannene, eds (1999) *Making the News: Modernity & the Mass Press in Nineteenth-Century France*. Amherst: University of Massachusetts Press.

Münsterberg, Hugo (1970) *Film: A Psychological Study*. New York: Dover.

Murray, Susan (2001) Our man Godfrey: Arthur Godfrey and the selling of stardom in early television. *Television and New Media*, 2, pp. 187–204.

Murray, William James (1986) *The Right-Wing Press in the French Revolution, 1789–92*. Woodbridge: Boydell, for the Royal Historical Society.

Murschetz, Paul (1998) State support for the daily press in Europe: a critical appraisal: Austria, France, Norway and Sweden compared. *European Journal of Communication*, 13, pp. 291–313.

Musser, Charles (1990) *The Emergence of Cinema: The American Screen to 1907*. New York: Charles Scribner.

Nagai, Yonosuke, and Iriye, Akira (1977) *The Origins of the Cold War in Asia*. New York: Columbia University Press.

Nasaw, David (2000) *The Chief: The Life of William Randolph Hearst*. Boston: Houghton Mifflin.

Negrine, Ralph (1994) *Politics and the Mass Media in Britain*. 2nd edn, London: Routledge.

Nelson, Michael (1997) *War of the Black Heavens: The Battles of Western Broadcasting in the Cold War*. London: Brassey's.

Nerone, Ralph (1987) The mythology of the penny press. *Critical Studies in Mass Communication*, 4, pp. 376–404.

Neuman, Russell W. (1982) Television and American culture: the mass medium and the pluralist audience. *Public Opinion Quarterly*, 46, pp. 471–87.

Neuzil, Mark (1996) Hearst, Roosevelt, and the muckrake speech of 1906: a new perspective. *Journalism & Mass Communication Quarterly*, 73, pp. 29–30.

Nicholson, Sian (1996) *The Echo of War: Home Front Propaganda and Wartime BBC, 1939–45*. Manchester: Manchester University Press.

Nien-Hsuan, Letitia, and Sun, Se-Wen (1999) Globalization and identity politics: reflections on globalization theories from the Taiwanese experience. *Asian Journal of Communication*, 9 (2), pp. 79–98.

Noam, Eli (1991) *Television in Europe*. New York: Oxford University Press.

Nornes, Abé Mark, and Yukio, Fukushima, eds (1994) *The Japan/America Film Wars: World War II Propaganda and its Cultural Contexts*. Langhorne, PA, and Chur, Switzerland: Harwood Academic.

Nowell-Smith, Geoffrey, ed. (1996) *The Oxford History of World Cinema*. Oxford: Oxford University Press.

Nowell-Smith, Geoffrey, and Ricci, Steven, eds (1998) *Hollywood & Europe: Economics, Culture & National Identity, 1945–95*. London: British Film Institute.

O'Boyle, Lenore (1967–8) The image of the journalist in France, Germany and England, 1815–48. *Comparative Studies in Society and History*, 10, pp. 290–302.

Olbas, Peter B. (2003) On Japan and the sovereign ghost-state: Hugh Byas, journalist-expert, and the Manchurian incident. *Journalism History*, 29 (1), pp. 32–42.

Paine, Thomas (1974) *The Rights of Man*. Secaucus, NJ: Citadel.

Parry-Giles, Shawn J. (1994) Propaganda, effect, and the Cold War: gauging the status of America's 'war of words'. *Political Communication*, 11, pp. 203–13.

Parry-Giles, Shawn J. (1996) 'Camouflaged' propaganda: the Truman and Eisenhower administrations' covert manipulation of news. *Western Journal of Communication*, 60, pp. 146–67.

Perry, Earnest L., jun. (2002) It's time to force a change: the Afro-American press campaign for a true democracy during World War II. *Journalism History*, 28 (2), pp. 85–95.

Peterson, R. A., and Berger, D. G. (1975) Cycles in symbol production: the case of popular music. *American Sociological Review*, 40.

Philp, M., ed. (1991) *The French Revolution and British Popular Politics*. Cambridge: Cambridge University Press.

Phipps, C. H. (1857) *A Year of Revolution: From a Journal Kept in Paris in 1848*. 2nd edn, London: Longmans, Brown, Green, Longmans & Roberts.

Picard, Robert G. (1996) The rise and fall of communication empires. *Journal of Media Economics*, 9 (4), pp. 23–40.

Picard, Robert (2002) Research note: assessing audience performance of public service broadcasters. *European Journal of Communication*, 17, pp. 227–35.

Piepe, Anthony, Charlton, Peter, and Morey, Judy (1990) Politics and television viewing in England: hegemony or pluralism? *Journal of Communication*, 40 (1), pp. 24–35.

Pilger, John (2001) Speech to the Department of Journalism, London College of Communication, University of the Arts, London, 15 February.

Pinzon, Charles, and Swain, Bruce (2002) The kid in upper 4: how Nelson Metcalf Jr. sold support of the soldier next door to a disgruntled public during World War II. *Journalism History*, 28, pp. 112–20.

Plowden, Alison (1974) *The Case of Eliza Armstrong*. London: BBC.

Popkin, Jeremy (1990) *Revolutionary News: the Press in France 1789–1799*. Durham, NC: Duke University Press.

Popkin, Jeremy (2002) *Press, Revolution and Social Identities in France, 1830–1835*. University Park: Pennsylvania State University Press.

Postman, Neil (1985) *Amusing Ourselves to Death: Public Discourse in the Age of Show Business*. New York: Viking Press.

Pulitzer, J. (1904) The School of Journalism in Columbia University: the power of public opinion. *North America Review*, pp. 641–80.

Puttnam, David (1997) *The Undeclared War: The Struggle for Control of the World's Film Industry*. London: HarperCollins.

Rader, Daniel L. (1973) *Journalists and the July Revolution in France*. The Hague: Martinus Nijhoff.

Ramachandran, T. M., ed. (1985) *Seventy Years of Indian Cinema, 1913–1983*. Bombay: Cinema India International.

Read, Donald (1999) *The Power of News: The History of Reuters*. 2nd edn, Oxford: Oxford University Press.

Reed, John (1961) *Ten Days that Shook the World*. London: Lawrence & Wishart.

Reeves, Nicholas (1999) *The Power of Film Propaganda*. London: Cassell.

de Rémusat, Charles (1958) *Mémoires de ma vie*, ed. Charles H. Pouthas, 3 vols. Paris: Plon.

Rentschler, E. (1996) *The Ministry of Illusion: Nazi Cinema and its Afterlife*. Cambridge, MA: Harvard University Press.

Reporters sans frontières (2003) *Freedom of the Press throughout the World: 2003 Report*. London: John Libbey.

Rétat, Pierre (1985) Forme et discours d'un journal révolutionnaire. In *L'Instrument périodique*, ed. Claude Labrosse and Pierre Rétat. Lyons: Presses Universitaires de Lyon.

Reynolds, Amy (2001) William Lloyd Garrison, Benjamin Lundy and criminal libel: the abolitionists' plea for press freedom. *Communication Law and Policy*, 6, pp. 577–607.

Reynolds, Beatrice K. (1971) Context of Girondist rhetoric. *Western Speech*, 4, pp. 256–63.

Rhode, Eric (1976) *A History of the Cinema from its Origins to 1970*. New York: Hill & Wang.

Rigby, Brian, and Hewitt, Nicholas (1991) *France and the Mass Media*. London: Macmillan.

Rogers, J. E. (1909) *The American Newspaper*. Chicago: University of Chicago Press.

Rorabaugh, W. J. (1986) *The Craft Apprentice: From Franklin to the Machine Age in America*. New York: Oxford University Press.

Rosenberg, Emily S. (1982) *Spreading the American Dream: American Economic and Cultural Expansion, 1890–1945*. New York: Hill & Wang.

Ross, Stephen J. (1998) *Working Class Hollywood: Silent Film and the Shaping of Class in America*. Princeton, NJ: Princeton University Press.

Rudé, George (1958) *The Crowd in the French Revolution*. Oxford: Clarendon Press.

Sadoul, Georges (1966) *Louis Lumière*. Paris: Seghers.

Salwen, Michael (1991) Cultural imperialism: a media effects approach. *Critical Studies in Mass Communication*, 8 (1), pp. 29–38.

Sand, George (1882–6) *Correspondance, 1812–1876*. 3rd edn, 6 vols., Paris: Calmann Lévy.

Sanjek, R. (1988) *American Popular Music and its Business*, vol. 3. New York: Oxford University Press.

Saxton, Alexander (1984) Problems of class and race in the origins of the mass circulation press. *American Quarterly*, 36, pp. 211–34.

Schatz, Thomas (1988) *The Genius of the System: Hollywood Filmmaking in the Studio Era*. New York: Pantheon.

Schiller, Herbert (1973) *The Mind Managers*. Boston: Beacon Press.

Schiller, Herbert (1976) *Communication and Cultural Domination*. White Plains, NY: International Arts and Sciences Press.

Schiller, Herbert (1989) *Culture Inc.: The Corporate Takeover of Public Expression*. New York: Oxford University Press.

Schramm, Wilbur (1964) *Mass Media and National Development*. Stanford, CA: Stanford University Press.

Schudson, Michael (1978) *Discovering the News: A Social History of American Newspapers*. New York: Harper.

Schudson, Michael (1993) *Advertising: The Uneasy Persuasion: Its Dubious Impact on American Society*. London: Routledge.

Schultze, Quentin J. (1988) Evangelical radio and the rise of the electronic church, 1921–1948. *Journal of Broadcasting and Electronic Media*, 32, pp. 239–306.

Seaton, Jean (1987) The BBC and the Holocaust. *European Journal of Communication*, 2 (1), pp. 53–80.

Seaton, Jean, ed. (1998) *Politics and the Media: Harlots and Prerogatives at the Turn of the Millennium*. Oxford: Blackwell.

Seymour-Ure, Colin (1974) *The Political Impact of Mass Media*. London: Constable.

Shapiro, Laura (1986) *Perfection Salad: Women & Cooking at the Turn of the Century*. New York: Farrar, Straus & Giroux.

Shepherd, J. (1982) *Tin Pan Alley*. London: Routledge.

Shija, William M. F. (1988) The role of video in enhancing intercultural communication: a challenge for culturally high-context countries. *Howard Journal of Communication*, 1 (2), pp. 12–26.

Shillony, B. A. (1973) *Revolt in Japan: The Young Officers and the February 26, 1936 Incident.* Princeton, NJ: Princeton University Press.

Shipman, David (1982) *The Story of Cinema*, vol. 1: *From the Beginnings to 'Gone with the Wind'.* London: Hodder & Stoughton.

Shrihande, Seema (2001) Competitive strategies in the internationalization of television: CNN and BBC World in Asia. *Journal of Media Economics*, 14, pp. 147–68.

Silverstone, Roger (1994) *Television and Everyday Lives.* London: Routledge.

Sinclair, John (1997) The business of international broadcasting: cultural bridges and barriers. *Asian Journal of Communication*, 7, pp. 137–55.

Sklar, Robert (1994) *Movie-Made America: A Cultural History of American Movies.* New York: Vintage.

Sklar, Robert (2002) *A World History of Film.* New York: Harry N. Abrams.

Slide, Anthony (1970) *Early American Cinema.* New York: A. S. Barnes.

Slide, Anthony, ed. (1996) *The Memoirs of Alice Guy Blaché.* Lanham, MD, and London: Scarecrow Press.

Smethers, J. Steven, and Jolliffee, Lee B. (2000) Singing and selling seeds: the live music era on rural midwestern radio stations. *Journalism History*, 26 (2), pp. 61–70.

Smith, Anthony (1973) *The Shadow in the Cave.* London: Allen & Unwin.

Smith, Anthony (1979) *Newspapers: An International History.* London: Thames & Hudson.

Smith, Anthony (1990) Media globalization in the age of consumer sovereignty. *Gannett Center Journal*, 4 (4), pp. 1–16.

Smith, Anthony, ed. (1995) *Television: An International History.* Oxford: Oxford University Press.

Smith, Leslie F. (1994) Quelling radio's quacks: the FCC's first public interest programming campaign. *Journalism Quarterly*, 71, pp. 594–608.

Smulyan, Susan (1994) *Selling Radio: The Commercialization of American Broadcasting, 1920–1934.* Washington, DC: Smithsonian Institution Press.

Snyder, Leslie B., Willenberg, Bartjan, and Watt, James (1991) Advertising and cross-cultural convergence in Europe, 1953–1989. *European Journal of Communication*, 6, pp. 441–68.

Soderlund, Walter C., Wagenberg, Ronald H., and Surlin, Stuart H. (1998) The impact of the end of the Cold War on Canadian and American TV news coverage of Cuba: image consistency or image change? *Canadian Journal of Communication*, 23, pp. 217–31.

Soley, Lawrence (1982) Radio: clandestine broadcasting, 1948–1967. *Journal of Communication*, winter, pp. 165–80.

Soley, Lawrence (1993) Clandestine radio and the end of the Cold War. *Media Studies Journal*, 7, pp. 129–38.

Solomon, William S., and McChesney, Robert (1993) *Ruthless Criticism: New Perspectives in US Communication History.* Minneapolis: University of Minnesota Press.

Sparkes, Vernon M., and Kang, Namjun (1986) Public reactions to cable television: time in the diffusion process. *Journal of Broadcasting & Electronic Media*, 30, pp. 213–29.

Sparks, Colin (1995) Concentration and market entry in the UK national daily press. *European Journal of Communication*, 10, pp. 179–206.

Sreberny-Mohammadi, Annabelle, and Mohammadi, Ali (1994) *Small Media, Big Revolution: Communication, Culture and the Iranian Revolution.* Minneapolis: University of Minnesota Press.

Starr, Paul (2004) *The Creation of the Media: Political Origins of Modern Communications.* New York: Basic Books.

Statham, Paul (1996) Television news and the public sphere in Italy: conflicts at the media/politics interface. *European Journal of Communication*, 11, pp. 511–56.

W. T. Stead Resource Site (2003) <www.attackingthedevil.co.uk> (accessed 17 July 2003).

Steed, Henry Wickham (1938) *The Press*. Harmondsworth: Penguin.

Steele, J. E. (1990) The 19th-century *World* versus the *Sun:* promoting consumption (rather than the working man). *Journalism & Mass Communication Quarterly*, 67, pp. 592–600.

Steemers, Jeanette (2001) In search of a third way: balancing public purpose and commerce in German and British public service broadcasting. *Canadian Journal of Communication*, 26 (1), pp. 69–87.

Stensaas, Harlan S. (1986) The rise of objectivity in US daily newspapers, 1865–1934. PhD dissertation, University of Southern Mississippi.

Stensaas, Harlan S. (1986–7) Development of the objectivity ethic in daily newspapers. *Journal of Mass Media Ethics*, 2 (1), pp. 50–60.

Storey, G. (1951) *Reuter's Century*. London: Max Parrish.

Streitmatter, Rodger (1999) Origins of the American Labor Press. *Journalism History*, 15 (3), pp. 99–106.

Sweeney, Michael S. (2001) Censorship missionaries of World War II. *Journalism History*, 27 (1), pp. 4–15.

Tawney, R. H. (1920) *Life and Struggles of William Lovett*. New York: A. A. Knopf.

Taylor, A. J. P. (1992) *English History 1914–45*. Oxford: Oxford University Press.

Taylor, P. (1995) *Munitions of the Mind: War Propaganda from the Ancient World to the Nuclear Age*. Manchester: Manchester University Press.

Taylor, Richard (1998) *Film Propaganda: Soviet Russia and Nazi Germany*. London: I. B. Tauris.

Thomas, Bella (2003) What the poor watch on TV. *Prospect*, January, pp. 46–51.

Thompson, David (1968) *France: Empire and Republic, 1850–1940*. New York: Walker.

Thompson, Graham M. (1990) Sandford Fleming and the Pacific cable: the institutional politics of 19th-century imperial communications. *Canadian Journal of Communication*, 15 (2), pp. 64–75.

Thompson, John (1995) *The Media and Modernity*. Cambridge: Polity.

Thompson, J. Lee (2000a) *Northcliffe: Press Barons in Politics 1865–1922*. London: John Murray.

Thompson, J. Lee (2000b) *Politicians, the Press and Propaganda: Lord Northcliffe and the Great War, 1914–1919*. Kent, OH, and London: Kent State University Press.

Thompson, Kristin, and Bordwell, David (1994) *Film History: An Introduction*. New York: McGraw-Hill.

Thornton, Brian (2000) The moon hoax: debates about ethics in 1835 New York newspapers. *Journal of Mass Media Ethics*, 15 (2), pp. 89–100.

The Times (1947) *The History of The Times: The Twentieth Century Test 1884–1912*. London: Office of The Times.

de Tocqueville, Alexis (1945) *Democracy in America*. New York: Knopf.

de Tocqueville, Alexis (1970) *Recollections*, ed. J. P. Meyer. Garden City, NY: Doubleday.

Toledano, Margalit (2003) Embedding strategy and trust: post-war implications for sustainable public relations. *Australian Journal of Communication*, 30 (1), pp. 43–51.

Tomlinson, John (1999) *Globalization and Culture*. Cambridge: Polity.

Tongue, Carole (2003) Broadcasting, cinema and globalization: the challenge to cultural diversity. Speech at the Department of Law, Europa Institute, Edinburgh University, 28 February.

Tracey, James F. (2001) Revisiting a polysemic text: the African American press's reception of 'Gone with the Wind'. *Mass Communication and Society*, 4, pp. 419–36.

Tumber, Howard (2001) Democracy in the information age: the role of the fourth estate in cyberspace. *Information, Communication & Society*, 4 (1), pp. 95–112.

UNESCO (1950) *The Film Industry in Six European Countries*. Paris: UNESCO.

Vasey, Ruth (1997) *The World According to Hollywood*. Exeter: University of Exeter Press.

Wadsworth, A. P. (1955) Newspaper circulations, 1800–1954. *Transactions of the Manchester Statistical Society*.

Wang, Shujen (1995) Ideology and foreign news coverage: propaganda model re-examined. *Asian Journal of Communication*, 5 (1), pp. 110–25.

Ward, Ken (1989) *Mass Communication and the Modern World*. London: Macmillan.

Ward, Mike (2002) *Journalism Online*. Oxford: Focal Press.

Warner, C. D. (1881) *The American Newspaper*. Boston: J. R. Osgood.

Wasburn, Philo C. (1995) Top of the hour radio newscasts and the public interest. *Journal of Broadcasting and Electronic Media*, 39 (1), pp. 73–91.

Waterman, David (1991) A new look at media chains and groups, 1977–1989. *Journal of Broadcasting and Electronic Media*, 35, pp. 167–77.

Waterman, David, and Rogers, Everett M. (1994) The economics of television program production and trade in Far East Asia. *Journal of Communication*, 44 (3), pp. 89–111.

Weaver, David (1990) Setting political priorities: what role for the press? *Political Communication*, 7, pp. 201–11.

Weaver, David H., Buddenbaum, Judith M., and Fair, Jo Ellen (1985) Press freedom, media and development, 1950–1979: a study of 134 nations. *Journal of Communication*, 35 (2), pp. 104–17.

Weightman, Gavin (2003) *Signor Marconi's Magic Box: How an Amateur Defied Scientists and Began the Radio Revolution*. London: HarperCollins.

Weinberg, S. (1984) Approaches to the study of film in the Third Reich: a critical appraisal. *Journal of Contemporary History*, 19, pp. 105–26.

Welch, D. (1993) *The Third Reich: Politics and Propaganda*. London: Routledge.

Whedbee, Karen (1998) Authority, freedom and liberal judgement: the presumptions and presumptuousness of Whately, Mill and de Tocqueville. *Quarterly Journal of Speech*, 84, pp. 171–89.

Whitfield, Stephen J. (1991) *The Culture of the Cold War*. Baltimore: Johns Hopkins University Press.

Wickham, Phil (2003) *Producing the Goods? UK Film Production since 1991: An Information Briefing*. London: British Film Institute National Library.

Wilke, Jurgen (1989) History as a communication event: the example of the French Revolution. *European Journal of Communication*, 4, pp. 375–91.

Willett, Ralph (1989) *The Americanization of Germany, 1945–1949*. London: Routledge.

Williams, Francis (1969) *The Right to Know: The Rise of the World Press*. London: Longman.

Williams, Kevin (1998) *Get Me a Murder a Day!: A History of Mass Communication in Britain*. London: Arnold.

Williams, Raymond (1980) Advertising: the magic system. In *Problems in Materialism and Culture: Selected Essays*. London: Verso.

Wilson, Helen (1999) The space of radio in the network society. *Australian Journal of Communication*, 26 (3), pp. 99–110.

Winston, Brian (1998) *Media, Technology and Society: A History: From the Telegraph to the Internet*. London and New York: Routledge.

Wirth, Michael O. (1990) Cable's economic impact on over-the-air broadcasting. *Journal of Media Economics*, 3 (2), pp. 39–53.

Young, David (2003) Discourses on communication technologies in Canadian and European broadcasting policy debates. *European Journal of Communication*, 18, pp. 209–40.

Zeldin, Theodore (1980) *France 1848–1945*, 4 vols. Oxford: Oxford University Press.

Zeman, Z. (1973) *Nazi Propaganda*. London: Oxford University Press.

Zinn, H. (1980) *A People's History of the United States*. New York: Harper & Row.

Index